DRUG POLICY REVOLUTIONS

Trajectories in Argentina, Portugal, and Uruguay

Sebastián A. Cutrona and Nilda M. García

BRISTOL
UNIVERSITY
PRESS

First published in Great Britain in 2025 by

Bristol University Press
University of Bristol
1–9 Old Park Hill
Bristol
BS2 8BB
UK
t: +44 (0)117 374 6645
e: bup-info@bristol.ac.uk

Details of international sales and distribution partners are available at bristoluniversitypress.co.uk

British Library Cataloguing in Publication Data
A catalogue record for this book is available from the British Library

ISBN 978-1-5292-5012-1 hardcover
ISBN 978-1-5292-5014-5 ePub
ISBN 978-1-5292-5015-2 ePdf

Cover design: Lyn Davies Design
Front cover image: Stocksy/Marc Tran
Bristol University Press uses environmentally responsible print partners.
Printed and bound in Great Britain by CPI Group (UK) Ltd, Croydon, CR0 4YY

FSC
www.fsc.org
MIX
Paper | Supporting responsible forestry
FSC® C013604

Contents

List of Graphs and Tables

Graphs

Tables

Introduction: Drug Policy

On 16 December 2017, just 100 miles away from Hong Kong, thousands of residents of Lufeng, a Chinese city in the southern Guangdong province, gathered in an open-air sports stadium to witness ten people be sentenced to death for drug law violations. Handcuffed and surrounded by armed guards, the convicts stood on a podium in front of the crowd to listen to the verdicts read over loudspeakers before they were immediately taken away for execution. The public trial, which included students in their school uniforms among the audience, was organized by the local government in a clear attempt to send a message about the seriousness of committing drug-related crimes in a city known for the production of ketamine and crystal methamphetamine (Allen 2017). Even though China does not publish the number of executions it performs, the Dui Hua Foundation, a nonprofit organization based in San Francisco, California, estimates that in 2017 alone the Asian country carried out around 2,200 death sentences, most of them for crimes associated with the possession and trafficking of illegal drugs (Dui Hua 2020).[1]

More recently, in April 2022, Nagaenthran Dharmalingam, a Malaysian national convicted of drug charges, was hanged in Singapore's Changi prison. The 34-year-old man had spent more than a decade on death row after being caught by security authorities crossing the border with 42.7 grams of heroin (around three tablespoons) strapped to his left thigh. After a medical psychological assessment, experts concluded that Dharmalingam suffered from an intellectual disability, showing an IQ of 69. This case became highly controversial and received international condemnation. The widespread awareness of Dharmalingam's situation and multiple efforts to change his destiny were not enough to stop his execution. In this region, however, the execution for drug offenses is not uncommon. According to Harm Reduction International (2022), approximately 93 per cent of all confirmed death sentences for drug offenses worldwide in 2021 were recorded in Southeast Asia. With the highest number of known sentences documented in Indonesia, 35 countries still retain the death penalty for a range of drug offenses. In 2021, for example, at least 237 death sentences were reported worldwide, representing a 11 per cent increase with respect to the previous year (Harm Reduction International 2022).

Nagaenthran Dharmalingam, one of the four individuals executed for drug offenses in Singapore during the first half of 2022 (Amnesty International 2022), would have faced criminal charges in most countries. In Portugal, however, the possession of small amounts of heroin is considered just an administrative offense. Under the decriminalization policy adopted in 2001, people caught with less than ten daily doses of any psychoactive substance – with no distinction between the so-called 'soft' and 'hard' drugs – are not charged with a criminal offense, but are rather referred to dissuasion commissions, the institutions replacing Portugal's criminal courts in cases of possession for personal consumption. About 144,111 proceedings were registered between 2002 and 2019 (*Serviço de Intervenção nos Comportamentos Aditivos e nas Dependências* 2020), showing the extremely different consequences and experiences for individuals committing similar drug offenses. In Portugal, the goal of the government dealing with people who use drugs is 'to be present', João Goulão, the architect of Portugal's decriminalization policy, admitted in an interview (Ferreira 2017).

Further east from Europe, in the Russian Federation, Brittney Griner, a two-time Olympic gold medallist and champion in the US Women's National Basketball Association (WNBA), was arrested on 17 February 2022, at Moscow's Sheremetyevo airport, after being caught with vape canisters containing cannabis oil in her luggage. Griner, who pleaded guilty to drug charges before a Russian criminal court, was sentenced to nine and a half years in prison and a fine of one million roubles (about US$16,000). The sentence was handed down even when her defence attorney introduced evidence indicating her need for medicinal cannabis to treat chronic pain and injuries. Unlike the laws in Phoenix, Arizona, where Griner started her career as a WNBA player and where recreational use of cannabis has been legal since 2020, in Russia the possession of many psychoactive substances is still a major cause of imprisonment despite the country's 2004 drug policy reform.[2] Recent estimates suggest that approximately 130,000 individuals are currently incarcerated for drug law offenses, accounting for 28 per cent of the country's prison population (Aebi and Tiago 2020). In 2010, for instance, nearly two-thirds (no less than 64.7 per cent) of the people charged with drug offenses were convicted for possession with no intent to supply (Merkinaite 2012).

In the meantime, some 8,000 miles away from the prison facility where Brittney Griner was detained, more than 87,000 users have registered with the Uruguayan government to access cannabis through the three legal options: growing at home, joining a social club, and/or buying the product at licensed pharmacies (*El Instituto de Regulación y Control del Cannabis* 2023). In 2013, Uruguay became the first country in the world to legalize the recreational use of cannabis, regulating every stage of the commodity chain. The South American country also began to export cannabis in 2019, reaching major markets such as Portugal and Switzerland. In 2020, for example, cannabis growers placed around ten tons of flowers in the international market and the revenues are expected to increase to US$94 billion by 2024 (Uruguay XXI 2021). Tabaré Viera, the minister of tourism in the Lacalle Pou administration (2020–2025), also admitted that Uruguay is considering a new reform to allow tourists to have 'the same treatment as a resident to access cannabis' (El Observador 2022).

Domestic cannabis tourism is already a reality in other countries and regions around the world. In the US, 23 states, two territories, and the District of Columbia have already legalized the psychoactive substance for adult nonmedical consumption. The revenues of this emerging industry, often referred as 'canna-cation', are growing fast and steadily as discrepancies between federal- and state-level legislation continue to exist. From 'bud and breakfast' hotels to cannabis farm tours, recent estimates indicate that approximately US$4.5 billion or 18 per cent of the legal cannabis sales are driven by tourism (Yakowicz and Kelleher 2022). Not surprisingly, a national study recently found that 29 per cent of all active leisure travellers or 18 per cent of all US citizens are interested in conducting cannabis-related activities on vacations (MMGY Travel Intelligence 2021).

Yet people who use drugs do not have to necessarily travel to buy cannabis in more flexible and liberalized markets. Neighbouring the US, in Ontario, Canada, cannabis and other smoking accessories can be delivered through Uber Eats. The new official initiative prospered after the Canadian government reformed its drug control policy on 17 October 2018, becoming the second country in the world to legalize the possession and consumption of cannabis for recreational purposes. Since November 2021, people who use cannabis have been able to download the Uber Eats app, verify their legal age, and then place an online order to collect their products at a nearby Tokyo Smoke retailer. According to BDS Analytics (2021), Canada's cannabis market is forecast to expand in the following years with sales expected to reach approximately US$6.7 billion in 2026.

Clearly, countries approach illicit drugs in radically different ways. The stories of Nagaenthran Dharmalingam, Brittney Griner, the residents of Lufeng, or the growing number of individuals and companies residing in countries with less punitive legislation illustrate how drug policies not only affect people's everyday lives, but can also have long-standing consequences for the economy, security, and public health of entire nations. Yet there has been wide disagreement over the presumed benefits or costs of drug policies. While some believe that drug use and its related harms would be higher in the absence of prohibition (Inciardi and McBride 1989; Wilson 1990; Inciardi 1999; United Nations Office on Drugs and Crime [UNODC] 2009), others understand that control policies rather than drugs themselves are responsible for the problems facing many countries around the world (MacCoun and Reuter 2001; Global Commission on Drug Policy 2016). Critics of criminalization maintain that prevalence rates and various drug-related harms in the areas of public health and security have not decelerated despite the great increase in the number of arrests for possession or use of illegal drugs since the 1970s (Andreas and Nadelmann 2006; Babor et al 2010).

Not surprisingly, drug policy debates regained attention after several countries across the world and subnational jurisdictions embarked on different liberalization reform routes (Decorte, Lenton, and Wilkins 2020). The recent experiences of national governments that moved away from strict criminalization, including the decriminalization of illicit drugs in Portugal or cannabis legalization in Uruguay and Canada, as well as state-level liberalization reforms such as the 'expiation' notices in South Australia or cannabis legalization in Colorado or Washington State, have reinvigorated scholarly research in the field. As Kleiman, Caulkins, and Hawken (2011) maintain, however, there is still wide disagreement around the consequences of these drug policy reforms. Furthermore, the available evidence is mostly limited to industrialized countries (Babor et al 2010) and the theories informing research are relatively scarce (Stevens et al 2019). The questions remain: What are the impacts of these reforms? Which drug policy presents more favourable results in the realms of prevalence, health, and security?

Drug Policy Revolutions: Trajectories in Argentina, Portugal, and Uruguay contributes to the effort to inform the debate by providing a multidisciplinary, theoretically informed, and empirically grounded analysis of a fundamental dimension of drug policy: the different ways states define the possession and use of illicit drugs for recreational purposes. Focusing on three relevant alternatives to criminalization, namely depenalization, decriminalization, and legalization/regulation, this book integrates into a single study three aspects to understanding drug policies: (i) an account of the evolution of drug policies in countries that have adopted some level of liberalization, (ii) the institutional architecture implemented to monitor drug-related problems after policy change, and (iii) an evaluation of the likely effects of the reforms across three different realms (that is, drug use, health harms associated with consumption, and drug-related security concerns).

Implementing a controlled before-and-after comparison, this book builds on the drug liberalization experiences of Argentina, Portugal, and Uruguay. Alongside the three case studies, we cover the drug policy spectrum by analyzing the evolution of the classic criminalization approach prevailing in the US at the federal level and its international implications. This work also provides regional-specific analyses of control countries that have not undertaken major liberalization initiatives. The purpose of the control groups is to contemplate relevant contextual factors that could have contributed to the alteration of drug consumption trends and other associated behaviours alongside the three case studies.

The purpose of this book is to evaluate relevant drug policy reforms and their estimated impacts, drawing fundamental lessons about the experiences of countries that have adopted some level of liberalization. We thereby seek to increase the understanding of various drug policy scholarly debates not only of students of various social sciences, but also of policymakers, government officials, or any private citizens interested in or concerned about drug policy reform. This analysis is timely and coincides with a wave of drug policy liberalization initiatives taking place all around the world.

The remaining part of this introductory chapter is structured in four main sections. First, we conceptually define the drug policy alternatives addressed in this book: criminalization, depenalization, decriminalization, and legalization/regulation. Indicating the inclusion criteria for the three case studies, we present a typology of the spectrum of liberalization reforms based on the ways states define the possession and use of small quantities of illicit drugs for recreational purposes. In the second section, we introduce the methodology and theoretical assumptions leading this work. We then discuss the limitations of this research. Finally, we conclude by presenting the content of the chapters.

Drug policy: Terminology and reform typology

Drug policy refers to laws and programs intended to affect both people's decisions to use (or not) psychoactive substances and the consequences of consumption (Kleiman 1992). Its conceptualization commonly encompasses different governmental instruments that fall into three broad categories: prevention, treatment, and enforcement (Heymann 2001; Kleiman 2001).[3] More generally, this drug policy triad is often summarized as a long-standing debate over whether psychoactive substances are framed as a medical or criminal problem (Boyum and Reuter 2001). Some countries treat drugs primarily as a health matter and emphasize prevention and treatment, whereas others focus their efforts and resources primarily on law enforcement initiatives. While the emphasis on prevention and treatment is linked to drug policies designed to reduce the demand, the prevalence of law enforcement, both domestically and overseas, is often intended to reduce the supply of illicit drugs (Moore 2001). As Babor and colleagues (2010) maintain, the variation across countries reflects differences in attitudes towards drug consumption itself, towards individual rights, and towards the role of government officials in controlling substances.

Drug policy is also jurisdictionally multilevel, often involving authorities in the international, national, and subnational spheres (Ritter 2022). At the international level, the United Nations has adopted three major conventions: the Single Convention on Narcotic Drugs of 1961, the Convention on Psychotropic Substances of 1971, and the Convention against Illicit Traffic in Narcotic Drugs and Psychotropic Substances of 1988. This multilateral regulatory framework binds signatory states to restrict the cultivation, production, manufacture, trafficking, possession, and consumption of illicit drugs.[4] The application of and compliance with the three conventions are monitored by the International Narcotics Control Board, an institution introduced in the 1961 Single Convention, which is often referred to as the 'guardian' or 'watchdog' of the multilateral drug control system (Bewley-Taylor and Trace 2006). Two other international bodies also hold responsibility under the drug control conventions: the Commission on Narcotic Drugs, formed by countries elected as members by the Economic and Social Council of the United Nations, and the United Nations Office on Drugs and Crime (UNODC), which serves as the secretariat for the entire system (Room et al 2010).[5]

The multilateral framework created by the conventions and supervised by the United Nations has limited the freedom of signatory members, pulling them towards prohibition and criminalization. Until recently, almost every country in the world prohibited drugs and criminalized personal consumption through police and military enforcement (Levine 2003). Yet states have found some 'room for manoeuvre' (Dorn and Jamieson 2000). In practice, several countries and local jurisdictions have reformed their drug control policies in different ways, suggesting that prohibition has already come to a turning point (Levine 2002). At the national and subnational levels, governments have not only moved away from criminalization, required under the 1988 convention, but have gone beyond and legally permitted the use of psychoactive substances such as cannabis. Starting with the Netherlands and several state legislatures across the US during the 1970s, the liberalization trend among Western democracies prospered in the 1990s, peaking with the arrival of the new millennium (Reinarman, Cohen, and Kaal 2004).

Still, there is no international consensus around alternative drug control policies (Bewley-Taylor 2012). Government officials around the world have disagreed over one particular aspect, which is the primary focus of this book: the extent of criminal sanctions. As illustrated in the opening of this introduction, in some countries the possession and use of substances such as cannabis are prohibited and violations to drug laws are considered a criminal offence, although in practice the law is not enforced. In other countries or subnational jurisdictions, criminal penalties for possession or use have been removed from the statute books. In more drastic liberalization reforms, illegal drugs, both in formal and practical terms, are neither prohibited nor criminalized.

The complex variety of drug policy alternatives makes an analytical examination challenging (Room et al 2010). Scholars, pundits, and society alike often disagree on the ways different drug control policies are labelled. As Kleiman, Caulkins, and Hawken (2011, 26) put it, 'the language of the drug policy debate is illogical and inconsistent; that makes it hard for people who disagree to figure out exactly what it is they disagree about'. As a result, there is no internationally agreed-on framework for the classification of the various drug policy alternatives to criminalization (Stevens et al 2019).

Focusing on the ways states define the possession and consumption of psychoactive substances for recreational purposes (also referred as 'simple possession'), our analytical approach builds on the framework developed by the European Monitoring Centre for Drugs and Drug Addiction (EMCDDA) (2016). In the next paragraphs, we present the definitions and descriptions of each of the drug policy alternatives explored in this book. We also establish the typology under which we base our empirical analysis.

Criminalization

Criminalization refers to legal frameworks where the possession and consumption of small quantities of psychoactive substances for recreational purposes is defined as a criminal offense by a statute enshrined in criminal law. As a result, criminal charges (for example, a felony or a misdemeanour charge) are brought to individuals violating the legislation and a public record (that is, 'criminal record') is kept following a conviction in court (Hall and Pacula 2003). Criminal sanctions, among other things, are intended either to stop the consumption of certain psychoactive substances or to deter individuals from initiating the use of illicit drugs. This first control policy has been also called 'prohibition' or, for rhetorical purposes, the 'war on drugs' (Kleiman, Caulkins, and Hawken 2011).

Criminalization has been the most widely implemented approach to control the possession and use of different psychoactive substances for recreational purposes. Still today, most countries around the world retain full prohibition (Ritter 2022). The Economic and Social Council (2013) estimates that in 2011 approximately 83 per cent of all drug offenses globally were recorded for personal possession of drugs. Even though the nature of the offenses and their respective sanctions are formally established by domestic criminal laws, scholars have pointed out that the international system entered a global drug prohibition regime a long time ago (Nadelmann 1990; Bewley-Taylor 2012).

The US (federal) drug policy is the best-known example of criminalized drug prohibition (Reinarman and Levine 1997). As mentioned in Chapter 3, the US has waged – especially on the international front – a war on drugs since the early twentieth century. Its role in promoting punitivism at the multilateral level, together with its various foreign policy interventions, especially in Latin America, has been fundamental for the prohibition and criminalization of several psychoactive substances around the world. Despite the adoption of different liberalization reforms in the 1970s and the recent legalization of recreational use of cannabis across several states,[6] the US drug control policy at the federal level remains highly punitive. By the late 1990s, when the war on drugs was still at its peak on many fronts, someone was arrested for a drug violation every 20 seconds (Egan 1999). It is estimated that the US has spent more than one trillion dollars in combating illicit drugs since President Richard Nixon securitized drugs cataloguing them as 'public enemy number one' in 1971. Not surprisingly, as one of the consequences of such an approach, in 2018 the US harboured the world's largest prison population (2.3 million people) or an incarceration rate of 716 (Heller and Galea 2020), with around one-fifth of them behind bars for drug violations (Martin et al 2019).

Criminalization includes a myriad of decisions and practices surrounding the prosecution and punishment of certain crimes (Randhawa 2022), which are often the responsibility of different actors (Lacey and Zedner 2017). In this book, we observe the evolution of drug policy in the US, focusing on its legislation, institutions, and actions within the criminal justice system at the federal level. Assessing the US is necessary to understand the full drug policy spectrum and the basis of prohibition and criminalization. It also helps to untangle the likely rationale behind the subsequent international shifts in drug policy paradigms addressed in this book. Since several states across the country have adopted a substantial variety of drug liberalization reforms, we do not intend to compare prohibition versus more flexible local policies. Instead, we seek to call attention to the stringency of the US punitive apparatus prevailing at the federal level, major trends associated with illicit drug consumption, the contexts of policymaking, and the implications of criminalization for global drug policy.

Depenalization

Depenalization represents the second drug control policy addressed in this book. It also illustrates the subtler liberalization reform. Unlike decriminalization and legalization, where the noncriminal nature of the drug-related penalty is clearly stipulated by a law, in depenalization schemes, the punishment is subject to a greater deal of interpretation. As Room and colleagues (2010) note, de facto drug liberalization reforms like depenalization contrast their de jure counterparts because depenalization schemes are realized by the way the legislation is used or applied in the various stages of the criminal justice system. Since this analytical differentiation is not always considered, drug policy scholars and pundits alike often use the terms depenalization and decriminalization interchangeably. Moreover, alternative concepts such as 'prohibition with cautioning' or 'diversion' have been utilized to describe the same or similar drug liberalization policies.

Under depenalization regimes the possession and use of psychoactive substances for recreational purposes is still typified as a criminal offense by law, but the legislation is not necessarily enforced due to policing, a precedent of the case law, or prosecutorial administrative guidelines.[7] Law enforcement officers and courts may still be required to adjudicate cases based on their interpretation of the legal structure under their jurisdiction. The law in the books, in other words, differs from the law in action, meaning that law enforcement authorities often do not bring criminal charges to individuals possessing or using small amounts of illicit drugs despite these offenses falling formally within the criminal justice system.[8] In practice, therefore, a depenalization system often entails a reduction of the use of formal criminal sanctions, implying that offenders are not arrested or prosecuted (Pacula et al 2005; Stevens et al 2019). Yet the lack of uniformity in the application of the law explains the various manifestations of this drug policy.

In this book, we use the case of Argentina to illustrate depenalization. Since limited research exists on the liberalization reforms underway in several Latin American countries (Babor et al 2010; Youngers 2016), this first case study serves to guide our research away from broadly studied high-income countries. Indeed, there is already plenty of work dedicated to other widely known depenalization schemes such as those adopted in the Netherlands (for example, Sylbing and Persoon 1985; Engelsman 1989; MacCoun and Reuter 1997; Abraham 1999; Korf 2002; Reinarman et al 2004; Reinarman 2009). The case of Argentina remains understudied and hence can point us to different lessons.

As mentioned in Chapter 4, illicit drugs were depenalized in Argentina in 2009 after the 'Arriola ruling'. Under this decision, the country's Supreme Court of Justice declared the second paragraph of Article 14 of Law 23.737, which criminalizes the possession and consumption of illicit drugs, unconstitutional. We find that similar to other widely researched cases of depenalization such as the Dutch 'coffee shops' or the declassification of cannabis in the UK, depenalization in Argentina has created major discrepancies between the existing legislation and various law enforcement practices adopted by different police forces and the judiciary power, respectively.

Decriminalization

Decriminalization represents a step forward from depenalization in the drug liberalization spectrum (Table 0.1). In this case, drug policy reform is largely accomplished through de jure models, meaning that decriminalization is achieved either through legislative reform or on the basis of a constitutional

Table 0.1: The possession and use of small quantities of psychoactive substances for recreational purposes across the drug policy liberalization spectrum[9]

	Criminalization	*Depenalization*	*Decriminalization*	*Legalization*
Legal status	Prohibited	Prohibited	Prohibited	Permitted
Type of offense	Criminal	Criminal	Civil or administrative	No offense
Penalty	Prison or even death	None or prison depending on criteria of security officer or judge	Rehabilitation, community service, or fine	Not punished (within the regulatory framework)

court resolution (Eastwood 2020). That is to say, the decision not to criminally penalize the possession and consumption of controlled illicit drugs is no longer left to law enforcement authorities' criteria, but is rather typified in a new normative framework. As Pacula and colleagues point out (2005), decriminalization policy not only reduces the burden on the criminal justice system due to lower incarceration costs, a similar consequence of drug depenalization reforms, but it may also produce larger savings because the resources involved in enforcing and processing civil offenses are less intensive compared to those required to deal with criminal offenses.

For the purpose of this analysis, decriminalization refers to legal schemes where the possession and consumption of small quantities of controlled psychoactive substances for recreational purposes is not considered a criminal offense. Decriminalization regimes maintain prohibition but at the same time establish different civil or administrative penalties as substitutes. Similar to the cases of depenalization, the ban on the sale of psychoactive substances is also preserved under decriminalization policy reforms.

It is estimated that more than 30 countries around the world had adopted some form of cannabis decriminalization by 2016 (Eastwood, Fox, and Rosmarin 2016). In this book, our case study to assess decriminalization is Portugal. Unlike other international experiences, where the possession or consumption of only certain substances such as cannabis are decriminalized, the Portuguese drug reform includes all illicit drugs. This case, therefore, offers a unique opportunity to evaluate the possible impacts of this approach on consumption, health, and security. Furthermore, Portugal's drug policy reform was applied nationwide and has lasted for more than two decades, offering a wider jurisdictional scope and greater span of time compared to subnational decriminalization experiences such as the Australian Capital Territory, the Northern Territory, and Western Australia, or less consistent arrangements like those adopted in countries such as Italy, Spain, or the Czech Republic. Chapter 5 analyzes the historical roots of the Portuguese drug policy reform. It shows how dissuasion commissions became the centrepiece of decriminalization, substituting Portugal's criminal courts for cases of possession of small quantities of illicit drugs intended for personal consumption.

Legalization/regulation

Legalization can take many potential forms (MacCoun and Reuter 2001). Regimes vary substantially in several dimensions, including the degree of government involvement, usage regulations, the kind of organizations allowed to supply the drug, the legal framework under which those organizations operate, the nature of the products distributed, and the price (Caulkins et al 2015). Regardless of the various alternatives, legalization approaches broadly fall into the category of de jure reforms. Since legalization clearly stipulates that the possession and consumption of drugs for recreational purposes – under certain circumstances – is neither a criminal offense nor prohibited, it likely violates international control treaties (Room et al 2010).

Here we refer to legalization as the removal of all criminal, administrative, and monetary penalties for the possession and use of small quantities of controlled substances for recreational purposes – the medical use of drugs is not considered. It also entails a broader flexibilization reform as it eliminates prohibition on the supply through different options, including legal retail dispensaries, social clubs, or home-growing. Since such provisions are commonly limited to certain populations (for example, adults), spaces (for example, home), psychoactive substances (for example, cannabis), and quantities (for example, grams), possession and consumption are regulated rather than completely liberalized. Hence, some drug policy scholars often prefer the term 'regulation' rather than simply 'legalization'.

Legalization is a relatively new phenomenon (Pacula and Smart 2017), which has been restricted mainly to cannabis and not to other psychoactive substances such as cocaine or heroin. Starting with the 2012 ballot initiatives in Colorado and Washington State, the legalization of cannabis possession and use for recreational purposes was first adopted at the subnational level in the US. We address the case of Uruguay to illustrate the most radical and highest step on drug policy liberalization reforms. Contrasting other countries that adopted a commercial version of this drug policy such as Canada, in 2013, Uruguay became the first country in the world to legalize the cultivation, production, acquisition, storage, commercialization, and distribution of cannabis. This case study offers both a larger scope to analyze the likely effects of legalization and the opportunity to assess the role of the state in controlling the drug market.

This parsimonious classification, of course, is neither static nor universal. Several drug policies around the world fall between the four alternatives or can even meet more than one criterion. Furthermore, criminal sanctions are not the only instruments that affect drug-related problems. In addition to the legal status of drugs and its enforcement, the other two main governmental instruments of drug policy (that is, prevention and treatment) can also impact drug use patterns and other areas such as public health and security. Indeed, certain actions and initiatives that are not considered within the simplified spectrum of drug policy can also affect consumption and other drug-related patterns.

The impacts of drug liberalization: Methodological notes

Drug Policy Revolutions: Trajectories in Argentina, Portugal, and Uruguay builds on the notion that drug policies should be evaluated based on empirical evidence instead of ideological principles. In addition to the analysis of the historical roots and current institutional scenarios of the four drug policy alternatives briefly reviewed in this introduction and more extensively addressed throughout the chapters, this book incorporates a third central aspect to this research: an evaluation of the possible impacts of the three drug liberalization reforms on three main realms: consumption patterns, health, and security.

There is no perfect methodological approach to investigate drug policy (Ritter 2022). Nonetheless, MacCoun and Reuter (1997) note that there are at least three general strategies to assess the likely impacts of changes in the legal status of drugs. First, studies can draw upon existing theory and research. Second, researchers can also conduct a demonstration experiment or a quasi-experimental evaluation, although such initiatives are rather unusual due to political, legal, ethical, and logistical impediments. Third, various works have extensively relied on analogies to experiences of other places, historical periods, substances, or behaviours in order to project the effects of drug liberalization reforms. This third strategy, albeit there are some differences, has been labelled in various ways, including 'impact studies' (Room et al 2010), 'reasoning by analogy' (MacCoun and Reuter 1997), and 'before-and-after studies' (Babor et al 2010).

Following the third methodological strategy, in this book we implement a controlled before-and-after research design. Drawing primarily on already available information and constructing our own datasets, in addition to interviews, we conduct this research in three main stages. First, we utilize key indicators to measure before-and-after trends in drug use patterns, harms associated with the consumption of psychoactive substances, and drug-related security matters. To deepen our analysis, in the second stage, we add control groups conformed by countries from the same geographical region of each of our case studies that have not changed the legal status of drugs for recreational purposes and compare the indicators over time. Last, the third stage consists of the validation of the findings against interviews and prior empirical and theoretical studies.

The scope of this multidisciplinary research varies per case study. Each of the countries is analyzed around the timeframe under which it went through policy changes intended to regulate the possession and use of illegal drugs for recreational purposes. Although the analysis starts first for countries that reformed their drug policies earlier (that is, Portugal) relative to the new liberalization initiatives (that is, Argentina and Uruguay), the book contemplates both the years prior and those after the change in the legal status of drugs for each of the cases.[10] The focus on the pre-reform years until the last available evidence allows a better before-and-after assessment of the impacts of drug liberalization. As pointed out before, alongside the three case studies surveyed in this book, we also provide regional country-specific analyses to measure the likely effects of drug policy reforms. The inclusion of sets of countries that did not undertake a liberalization reform as control groups allows us to better estimate variation if there had been no legal changes in the status of drugs (Single 1989; Babor et al 2010; Smart and Pacula 2019). Cross-national comparisons with control groups, to be meaningful, match survey year, measure of prevalence, and age groups (MacCoun and Reuter 2001). Following the guidelines set by Hughes and Stevens (2010) in their analysis of Portugal's decriminalization policy, the comparators, when information is available, belong to the same geographic region, favouring the detection of regional trends.

As stated earlier, we start the analysis of the estimated impacts of drug liberalization policies by conducting a before-and-after assessment in three main realms: (i) drug consumption patterns, (ii) health harms associated with the use of various illegal psychoactive substances, and (iii) drug-related security matters. We discuss the relevance and define each of the selected measures and indicators in the following sections.

Drug use patterns

What are the impacts of depenalization, decriminalization, and legalization on the prevalence and frequency of drug consumption? Do drug liberalization reforms affect the initiation age of drug use? Do they increase the consumption of younger groups? Do drug prices increase or decrease after changes in the legal status of drugs? What are the likely impacts of those reforms on the potency of drugs available?

To explore the latter questions and evaluate the estimated effects of drug liberalization on the use of psychoactive substances, we focus on three prevalence measures: lifetime use (LTP), last-year use (LYP), and last-month use (LMP). Although various studies utilize only LTP rates, this indicator provides a general overview, likely reflecting the sporadic or experimental use of drugs. Under these circumstances, LYP and LMP measures can best illuminate recent and current drug use patterns, respectively (Gabri et al 2022). Consensus exists, indicating that LYP and LMP use rates are the most adequate measures to evaluate the prevalence of illicit drugs (World Health Organization 2000; EMCDDA 2010; UNODC 2010a). As Korf (2002) notes, these two indicators are particularly relevant when assessing the estimated impacts of drug policy reform, as both measures allow scholars to avoid the so-called 'generation effect' – that is, drawing conclusions about the consequences of liberalization initiatives based on the evaluation of people who used drugs in their youth or before the reform but who are no longer users.

The three prevalence measures are assessed at the general population level. Yet this book also focuses, when information is available, on the 15–24 age group. Adolescence is a period of quick brain development, when young people are especially vulnerable to the harms of illicit drug use (Hall et al 2016; Romer, Reyna, and Satterthwaite 2017). In the case of cannabis, for instance, the available evidence shows that consumption is associated with higher risks of developing cannabis use disorder (Stinson et al 2006), cognitive impairment (Meruelo et al 2017), structural brain abnormalities (Batalla et al 2013), and impaired respiratory function and cardiovascular disease (Hall and Degenhardt 2009). The 15–24-year-old population is also more at risk of initiation (Hughes and Stevens 2012). What is more, this age can determine the possibilities of individuals using drugs in the future (Cerda et al 2016; UNODC 2018b).

The analysis in this book focuses solely on illegal drugs; that is, we concentrate on the substances listed in the four schedules of the 1961 Single Convention on Narcotic Drugs and its successor multilateral control mechanisms.[11] Yet the type of psychoactive substances evaluated in each chapter are subject to data availability. Cannabis is the main psychoactive substance for which there is significant evidence (Babor et al 2010).[12] Although it is by far the most widely used illicit drug, cannabis is not considered a major source of social or health harms compared to other psychoactive substances (Degenhardt and Hall 2012). This work also incorporates into the analysis – when data are available – the consumption of other substances such as cocaine, heroin, stimulants, ecstasy, and LSD, among others.[13] The prevalence levels of drugs that carry higher risks of chronic or acute harms are assessed not only in countries that have changed the legal status of those psychoactive substances (that is, Portugal and Argentina), but also among the case studies that have only reformed their cannabis drug policy (that is, Uruguay). Since the impacts of a specific regime for a particular psychoactive substance may depend on the legislation applied to other drugs that are likely substitutes or complements, we also attempt to observe whether cannabis liberalization affects the association between cannabis and the use of other drugs. In effect, prohibition commonly rests on the idea that cannabis is a gateway to more dangerous drugs, implying that its liberalization may affect the use and harms of other substances such as heroin and cocaine (Goode 1997; MacCoun 2011).[14]

Drug liberalization can affect consumption through several mechanisms, including availability, prices, perceived harmfulness, legal risks, the social stigma associated with the legal status of the drug, and others (MacCoun and Reuter 1997; Smart and Pacula 2019). In this book, we mainly assess drugs' seizure, price, and purity. These supply-side factors are crucial to understanding illegal drug markets and their regulation and enforcement (Caulkins and Reuter 1998; Caulkins 2007; Laqueur 2014). On the one hand, the consumption of psychoactive substances is presumed to be affected by changes in price (Félix and Portugal 2017; Hunt and Pacula 2017; Caulkins et al 2018) and law enforcement practices (Pacula et al 2003) following a drug policy reform. If the demand is sensitive to price, different forms of liberalization are expected to decrease the value of drugs. Variations in prices are hence evaluated before and after the changes in the legal status of drugs. The potency, on the other hand, is also assessed to untangle how policy reforms affect the quality of the available psychoactive substances. Since certain illegal drugs are commonly diluted or adulterated, the analysis of potency becomes central in studies addressing the effects of drug policy reforms (Caulkins 2007). As shown in Chapter 1, research indicates – albeit not unanimously – that prohibition and criminalization often favour the production of more potent illicit drugs, as higher potency likely decreases the bulk of the transaction and its associated enforcement risks (McCoy 1991; Thornton 1998; Room et al 2010). Hence, advocates of drug policy reform claim that legalization can lead markets to deliver safer and less-potent substances (Cowan 1986; Buckley 1996).

Health harms

What are the estimated effects of depenalization, decriminalization, and legalization on drug use disorders? How do liberalization reforms affect treatment demand or the number of drug-related patients in treatment? Are overdoses and viruses/infectious diseases such as HIV, AIDS, and hepatitis among people who use drugs more prevalent under drug liberalization? Has consumption become more problematic following these reforms?

This study draws on the notion that drug policy cannot be grasped in isolation from broader health contexts. Under certain circumstances, patterns of drug consumption can lead to adverse health consequences. Harms may accrue to people who use drugs or to society at large (Moore 2001). Such problems can arise from a combination of the routes of administration and the psychopharmacological properties of the substances, together with broader contexts of drug use like poverty (Marmot and Wilkinson 1999), marginalization (Strathdee et al 1997; Galea and Vlahov 2002; Corneil et al 2006), and social deprivation (Wilkinson 1996; Wadsworth et al 2004; Wilkinson and Pickett 2008; Stevens 2011). Nevertheless, certain policy decisions can also have direct and indirect consequences on the health of people who use drugs. Various scholars point out that the levels and stringency of prohibition on the use of psychoactive substances can affect drug-related harms such as death and illness (Fitzgerald 2005; Reuter and Stevens 2007).

Unlike the epidemiological indicators of drug use such as prevalence, frequency, and initiation age rates, there is no clear-cut data on the severity of the health harms linked to the consumption of different psychoactive substances (Hall, Degenhardt, and Lynskey 2001; Korf 2002). The boundaries between relatively benign and malign patterns of drug consumption are not totally clear (Moore 2001; Degenhardt et al 2004). As a result, the magnitude of the adverse health consequences of illicit drug use is often poorly quantified (Degenhardt and Hall 2012). Consequently, in this study the health harms associated with drug consumption are empirically assessed by looking at three specific indicators: (i) the number of people seeking or in treatment for drug-related issues, (ii) notifications of viruses (for example, HIV) or infectious diseases (for example, AIDS), and (iii) overdoses.

Drug treatment data are a valid indicator to assess changes in the burden and morbidity attributable to the use of psychoactive substances (MacCoun 2011; Freeman et al 2018). Infectious diseases and overdoses constitute key complementary measures to evaluate the dangers of illicit drug consumption (EMCDDA 2021).[15] Of course, the relevance of each of the epidemiological indicators varies per case study. Since the available evidence suggests that the health effects associated with cannabis consumption appear less severe, the evaluation of the number of users in treatment, infectious diseases, and overdoses in countries that changed the legal status of only cannabis (for example, Uruguay) is rather limited compared to more comprehensive liberalization reforms that include other drugs such as cocaine and heroin (for example, Portugal).

Security

Does drug liberalization lead to rising crime rates? How do depenalization, decriminalization, and legalization/regulation affect homicides, theft and robberies, and other drug-related crimes? How does liberalization affect prison populations? Have law enforcement practices changed after drug policy reform?

From a policy perspective, untangling the relationship between drug use and crime is important since it affects both criminal justice and drug policy (Seddon 2000). Not surprisingly, government officials have devoted a great deal of time to debating the association between drugs and crime. The empirical relationship between them, and the theories framing the so-called 'drug-crime nexus', however, have not been extensively tested and research is relatively limited (MacCoun, Kilmer, and Reuter 2003; McBride, VanderWaal, and Terry-McElrath 2003; Keene 2005; Stevens 2011; Dragone et al 2019).

In this book, we do not attempt to test the drug-crime nexus, at least in strict methodological terms. Instead, we look at the security landscapes of countries that have adopted different drug liberalization reforms to estimate their impacts on crime. Our analysis primarily focuses on intentional homicide rates. Given the complete liability of the direct perpetrator, intentional homicides constitute a reliable proxy for insecurity (UNODC 2013). We additionally evaluate other types of crimes that are commonly associated with the drug market such as theft and robbery (Hughes and Stevens 2010).[16] Following the criteria set by EMCDDA (2003), certain 'drug-related crimes' are also assessed in this book. Specifically, we estimate the effects of drug liberalization reforms on 'criminal offences in breach of drug legislation' and 'crimes committed under the influence of illicit drugs', respectively.[17] Inmates can provide valuable information about drug markets outside prisons (Bergman and Fondevila 2021). While the analysis of the violation of the drug law and imprisonment rates is especially relevant in depenalization schemes (for example, Argentina), where judiciary and law enforcement authorities may have greater room to interpret the new legal framework, the examination of crimes committed under the influence of different psychoactive substances is subject to data availability.

Limitations

This study, especially when evaluating the estimated impacts of drug liberalization reforms, has its limitations. First, the case studies address counterfactual questions. Although enquiries like 'What would have happened if Argentina, Portugal, and Uruguay had never reformed their drug control policies?' are difficult to answer, we use control groups of countries to estimate the likely impacts of liberalization reforms if there had been no legal changes in the status of drugs for recreational purposes. As already noted, controlled comparisons can mitigate several limitations when projecting the impacts of drug policy reforms (Single 1989; Babor et al 2010; Smart and Pacula 2019).

Second, despite the methodological benefits of including control groups, this study does not rely on more sophisticated statistical techniques such as difference-in-difference or time-series analysis. While the incorporation of tests of statistical significance characteristic of such research designs can certainly facilitate causal inference, the descriptive nature of our analytical approach is intended to be also accessible to an undergraduate and general readership. Nonetheless, the literature review conducted in Chapters 1 and 2 introduce fundamental scholarly debates, pointing out relevant academic works for readers willing to engage with more specialist sources.

Third, most indicators assessed are often measured differently across countries and regions (Newburn and Sparks 2004). Cross-national comparison problems include differences in sampling methods, size, years, and modes of interview. While these variances are less visible among European countries, data of the Latin American case studies suffer from significant inconsistencies. Following MacCoun and Reuter (2001), in this book we attempt to match survey years, prevalence measures, and age groups.

Fourth, two out of the three case studies of this book are countries from the same region. Argentina and Uruguay share a border, have interconnected socio-political histories, common characteristics of European immigration, similar ethnic-national origins, and share common cultural and social practices. Due to their 'lesser importance' within the political economy of illicit drug, both countries have also received less pressure from the Global North – especially the US – to wage the war on drugs. Although Argentina and Uruguay liberalization processes and levels are different, the objective of generalizing the conclusions must be nonetheless tempered with caution.

Fifth, drug policy research has shown that international comparisons are particularly difficult because outcomes are often influenced by non-policy factors, ranging from culture and geography to politics and the economy (Room et al 2010; Félix, Portugal, and Tavares 2017). It is difficult to untangle the effects of psychoactive substances from the contexts in which consumption takes place. As already highlighted, factors such as inequality, poverty, access to housing, or the presence of a welfare system can have equal or greater effects than the levels of prohibition and criminalization, respectively. Moreover, some of the case studies in this book had preexisting (that is, Uruguay)[18] or co-occurring (that is, Argentina)[19] drug liberalization environments that may affect drug consumption patterns and associated harms. For example, as Smart and Pacula (2019) maintain, it is important to consider that jurisdictions that harboured robust cannabis distribution through medical dispensaries may conflate heterogeneity among the countries or states that do not change the legal status of drugs for recreational purposes. Thus, we cannot stress enough the relevance of other forces that affect how societies relate to different illegal drugs, although their analysis is beyond the scope of this book.

Sixth, most of the data assessed, especially related to drug use patterns, are based on self-reports and surveys. The usefulness of polls depends on factors such as the honesty, openness, and memory of the individuals interviewed

(Reinarman, Cohen, and Kaal 2004; Rehm et al 2005). Another related peril lies in the influence of the normative contexts where drug policy reforms are evaluated. In more stringent legal frameworks (for example, Argentina), for instance, people might refrain from declaring their drug habits compared to those in more liberalized systems (for example, Portugal and Uruguay). Furthermore, drug policy research surveys are also likely to miss out on some of the most vulnerable sectors of society, including unhoused individuals and prisoners (Stevens 2011).

Seventh, our book does not consider surveys addressing the social acceptability and perceived harmfulness of illegal psychoactive substances. This may represent an important limitation because scholarly studies have shown that attitudes about drugs (for example, disapproval of consumption and perceptions of risk of harmfulness) are often relevant determinants of use (Bachman, Johnston, and O'Malley 1998; Smart and Pacula 2019). On the other hand, we do not measure the population's knowledge about changes in the legal framework. Pacula and colleagues (2005) note that research rarely considers the levels of knowledge in the community about the laws regulating illegal drugs, despite that such understandings can have consequences on certain patterns of drug consumption.

Finally, the timeframe of this book also faces additional methodological challenges. As mentioned before, the periods covered by this study vary from case to case, depending upon the moment in which the new liberalization policy was adopted. Since it is highly possible that reforms of drug laws may be slow to have an impact upon behaviour (Stuart et al 1976), caution is needed in interpreting the findings of the policies that have been recently implemented (that is, Argentina and Uruguay) as they may not illuminate long-term effects. Research has shown that time between the passing of the law and its implementation varies considerably between states (Weinberger, Wyka, and Goodwin 2022). The impacts, in other words, often depend on the provisions of the law and the time it takes to influence the new liberalized markets (Smart and Pacula 2019).

Organization of the book

This book is composed of an introduction, six chapters, and a conclusion. Each chapter, except for the literature review, offers a broad panorama of one drug control policy, each representing a different stage in the drug liberalization spectrum. We start each chapter by tracing back the origins and evolution of each drug policy alternative, helping readers to understand more accurately the contexts in which drug reforms occur as well as their estimated impacts. We later describe the main features of each approach to illicit psychoactive substances, paying special attention to the norms, institutions, and actors in charge of their implementation. In the third section of each case study, except for criminalization, we evaluate the impacts of drug liberalization reforms over the years.

Chapter 1 presents an integrative literature review of the available empirical evidence from a variety of scientific studies and reports addressing the impacts of different drug policy reforms around the world on consumption patterns. Specifically, the chapter focuses on how changes in the legal status of use and possession of small amounts of illicit drugs affect use rates and market-associated factors such as price, availability, and purity. Since the existing scholarly literature has extensively revolved around the reduction or elimination of criminal sanctions, this first review assesses major empirical findings in that single direction. Furthermore, each section includes a brief review of works analyzing principal contextual factors influencing drug use patterns.

Chapter 2 complements the literature by addressing key scholarly works exploring the implications of drug policy reform on health and crime, respectively. The first section of the empirical works reviewed focuses on adverse health consequences such as infectious diseases and overdose deaths. After reviewing studies dedicated to chronic and acute health problems related to the use of illicit drugs, Chapter 2 looks at scholarly works analyzing the various ways changes in the legal status of use and possession of small amounts of illicit drugs affect crime and, to a lesser extent, incarceration rates. Similar to Chapter 1, broader contextual factors are also briefly reviewed.

Chapter 3 introduces the drug policy of prohibition and criminalization in the US. Starting from the years prior to the sanctioning of the Harrison Act of 1914 until the end of the Trump administration (2017–2021), the first section explores the evolution of punitivism throughout different critical junctures. This chapter also reviews some of the international implications – in terms of both the multilateral framework and the foreign policy efforts – of the US anti-drug crusade overseas. The second section describes the main features of US drug policy today, paying special attention to the country's normative and institutional architecture at the federal level. The chapter concludes with a brief evaluation of drug consumption patterns, market-associated factors, and health and security harms attributed to the use of various illegal psychoactive substances during the peak of criminalization. Since several states have adopted various drug liberalization policies over the years, this chapter neither seeks to empirically evaluate the impacts of criminalization nor includes a control group in the analysis.

Chapter 4 presents the first case study, Argentina, a country that adopted the subtler liberalization reform (that is, depenalization) analyzed in this book. The chapter begins with an evaluation of Argentina's drug policy from the early twentieth century until the depenalization of illicit drugs in 2009. Since the criminal offense of possession of drugs is still typified in the penal code, the analysis of Argentina's institutional architecture developed in the second section primarily revolves around the role of law enforcement and the judiciary power, actors that have implemented the depenalization scheme. The third section of this chapter evaluates the likely impacts of the reform on the country's drug consumption patterns and associated harms. To pinpoint more accurately the effects of depenalization, this chapter contrasts Argentina's indicators over time with trends witnessed in other Latin American countries, namely Brazil and Panama.

The analysis of Portugal is conducted in Chapter 5. Starting from the initial drug legislation passed in 1924 until the 2001 reform, this chapter explores the policy alternative of decriminalization. The second section presents the main features of decriminalization policy, paying special attention to the role of dissuasion commissions. The third section assesses the evolution of the patterns of drug consumption and other market-associated factors, together with relevant empirical information in the realms of health and security, including data on overdoses, infectious diseases, homicides, drug-related crimes, and incarceration rates. Statistical evidence from other European countries that did not undergo a major drug policy reform (that is, France and Germany) during the timeframe of the analysis is also evaluated in the final section. The conclusion presents an evaluation of the major strengths and weaknesses of Portugal's drug reform.

Chapter 6 addresses the most radical policy reform of this book: the case of Uruguay. The first part presents a brief historical background of Uruguay's path to legalization. The second section focuses on the institutional architecture behind the country's drug policy, paying particular attention to the changes established to implement and monitor the newly legalized cannabis market created in December 2013. The last section evaluates the estimated impacts of the legalization of cannabis, exploring prevalence, drug seizures, price and potency, adverse health effects, violence, crime, and incarceration rates in Uruguay. To estimate variation if there had been no legal changes in the status of consumption and possession of cannabis, Brazil and Panama are incorporated as a control group in our comparison. The final section presents the conclusions and future challenges for Uruguay in the forthcoming years.

The book concludes with a cross-examination of all case studies on their various levels of drug liberalization. Specifically, we review the historical trajectories of Argentina, Portugal, and Uruguay as well as our main findings. Also, we discuss the lessons learned and some specific policy recommendations about the likely effects of parting from criminalization and redirecting towards alternative liberalization paradigms.

1

The Legal Status of Drugs and Consumption Trends

Scholarly works systematically evaluating problems associated with the use of psychoactive substances are relatively recent (Edwards 1991; Edwards and Babor 2012; Babor et al 2017). The search for patterns and generalizations based on accumulated scientific evidence on drug use and public policy only began to develop in the 1970s (Edwards 2002). New epidemiological research tools, technological innovations, institutional growth, education programs, funding opportunities, specialized journals, professional societies, public recognition, and political support were all influential at this stage of development (Babor 2002). The emergence of the interdisciplinary 'addiction field', merging psychological, biomedical, and social perspectives, together with different nonacademic sources, illustrates the ambition to move the study of drugs 'from faith to science' (Heather et al 1992).

As the field consolidated, different disciplinary subgroups and research areas started to emerge, including those concentrated on policy, health, and harm. Drawing from the contributions of scholars, practitioners, activists, and decision-makers, a cumulative scientific base created new opportunities for the analysis and implementation of drug policy. As Babor and colleagues (2010) note, direct evidence allowed the study of the implications of various reforms in comparison with places and times where no intervention was accomplished. Drug policy reforms in countries like the Netherlands, Italy, Spain, the Czech Republic, Belgium, Germany, and Portugal, along with other subnational jurisdictions such as South Australia, Alaska, and Amsterdam, informed the new works dedicated to evaluate the effects of shifting from criminalization to other forms of noncriminal penalties.

Despite the growing literature, scholarly studies rigorously comparing the effects of drug policy are rather scant (Reinarman, Cohen, and Kaal 2004; Stevens 2011). In particular, research analyzing how transformations within the criminal justice system impact drug use patterns and their associated societal costs is still largely concentrated in a limited number of countries (Babor et al 2010). Theoretical frameworks guiding drug policy research are also limited (Moore and Rhodes 2004; Stevens et al 2019). Disagreement among specialists about research methods and data collection also illustrates the tensions in the field (Best et al 2003). Works revolving around similar phenomena have produced contrasting results. Kleiman, Caulkins, and Hawken (2011, 24) note that 'case studies of drug reform tend to be a bit like Rorschach tests, with the meaning read into the picture by the observer'.

What is the evidence base of drug policy research? What have we learned from drug policy reforms worldwide? The integrative literature review developed in Chapter 1 and 2 of this book evaluates the available theoretical and empirical evidence from a variety of scientific studies and reports addressing the implications of different drug policy reforms around the world. Specifically, this chapter focuses on how changes in the legal status of use and possession of small amounts of illicit drugs affect consumption patterns. Since the literature has commonly revolved around the reduction or elimination of criminal sanctions, this review assesses major findings in that single direction.

It is worth pointing out, however, that these are not the only aspects of policy that influence drug-related problems. Within the three broad categories of prevention, treatment, and enforcement, different governmental instruments beyond criminal sanctions have impacted the configuration of illicit drug markets, public health, and security (Kilmer 2002). Furthermore, a growing literature also shows how actions and factors that are not officially considered drug policy affect consumption and other drug-related patterns (MacCoun and Reuter 1998; Moore 2001; Korf 2002; Reuter and Stevens 2007; Room et al 2010; Stevens 2011). Boyum and Reuter (2001), for example, claim that social policies aimed at tackling poverty, chronic unemployment, public housing, disability, family breakdown, and child abuse may be equally effective in reducing drug-related harms.

This caveat aside, the review of the literature presented here is organized in two sections, each showcasing different sides and consequences of policy reforms related to the use and possession of small quantities of illicit drugs. The first section discusses major theoretical considerations underlying drug policy reform. It pays attention to the main theories informing research among both prohibitionists and advocates of drug policy reform. The second section addresses the way flexibilization or elimination of criminal penalties and their enforcement affect patterns of illicit drug use and other market-associated factors. Special emphasis is given to the conditions of availability, price, and, to a lesser extent, the purity and potency of psychoactive substances.

The legal status of drugs and the patterns of consumption

Illegal drugs are commodities. Similar to other sectors of the economy in which goods and services are traded among different parties, illicit drugs markets are fundamentally governed by the interaction of supply and demand. Given some degree of availability, therefore, it is expected that some individuals will consume drugs; but how intensively, for how long, and in what specific contexts they do so differ from one user to another (Moore 2001). Variations over time and across different socioeconomic and demographic groups indicate that the patterns of drug use are a complex phenomenon (MacCoun and Reuter 1998).

Yet illicit markets, like their legal counterpart, can be deliberately influenced through different state actions. As Beckert and Dewey (2017) claim, legal definitions have been a crucial device in the hands of public institutions to shape and influence the structure and extent of illicit markets. The prohibition of drugs, in particular, has been the centrepiece of legislative and administrative institutions at the national and subnational levels to minimize or prevent consumption and other drug-related harms since the early twentieth century. The suppression of drug consumption through criminal law has indeed reached every corner of the world through the three United Nations conventions currently in force: the Single Convention on Narcotic Drugs of 1961, the Convention on Psychotropic Substances of 1971, and the United Nations Convention Against Illicit Traffic in Narcotic Drugs and Psychotropic Substances of 1988 (Nadelmann 1990; Krajewski 1999; Levine 2003; Bewley-Taylor 2012).

The theoretical foundations for the study of the different ways in which illicit behaviours are influenced by legal sanctions are numerous and fragmented. Nevertheless, the rational choice perspective of modern economics has dominated most of the prohibitionist accounts in drug policy research. Based on microeconomic principles, various proponents of criminalization emphasize how the availability, the price, and the deterrent effects of punishment influence patterns of drug consumption (MacCoun and Reuter 2001a). If the demand is sensitive to price, harshly enforced criminalization is expected to increase the value of drugs above free-market levels, affecting the consumers' willingness to pay for the commodity. Similarly, criminalization is also likely to lead to the production of more potent psychoactive substances because higher potency reduces the bulk and the risk associated with distribution (McCoy 1991; Rasmussen and Benson 1994; Thornton 1998; Room et al 2010).[1] It is not surprising that drug policy reform advocates have historically maintained that legalization could lessen the harms associated with drug consumption as markets can deliver less-potent psychoactive substances (Smart et al 2017). In the long term, the economic theory further suggests, high or increasing prices, low availability, and the so-called nonmonetary costs associated with perceptions of health harms, criminal sanctions, and social penalties affecting opportunities in areas such as employment and housing limit the use of drugs (Pacula 2010).[2]

As an application of the rational choice paradigm of contemporary economics, modern deterrence theory complements the microeconomic principles by focusing on the decision to commit crimes (MacCoun 1993). Drawing on the political philosophy of Beccaria (1764) and Bentham (1789), this theoretical perspective assumes that criminals are rational actors expecting to maximize their own well-being through illegal means. Becker (1968), for example, argues that individuals weigh the expected utility of a criminal act against the possibility of being sanctioned. The implications of modern deterrence theory for drug policy are straightforward: threatening to arrest or incarcerate users for possessing or using illicit drugs may induce people to cease or reduce consumption. Conversely, the prevalence, frequency, and quantity of drug use are likely to increase if punishment is absent.

Various studies have provided alternative explanations to untangle how changes in the legal status of drugs affect use. MacCoun and Reuter (2001a) offer a comprehensive analysis of seven mechanisms by which prohibition or the flexibilization of drug laws impact the levels of consumption. In addition to availability, price, and fear of formal sanctions laid out by rational choice perspectives, the authors identify another four alternative pathways: the symbolic threshold effect, the forbidden fruit effect, the stigmatization effect, and the mediating effects of informal social control factors.[3] Unlike the dominant paradigm, these mechanisms were developed in the fields of sociology and psychology, suggesting that human behaviour, including the decision to use illicit drugs, is also affected by nonlegal norms. According to social-psychological research, informal personal and social norms are relevant because they may influence the effectiveness of laws (MacCoun and Reuter 2001a)

Prior empirical work

Early cannabis depenalization efforts in the US

The first empirical studies evaluating the effects of changes in the legal status of cannabis on use rates were conducted during the 1970s, after different legislatures in the US shifted from strict prohibition to other forms of penalties.[4] The analyses of some of the 12 states that depenalized cannabis between 1973 and 1978 provide contrasting results.[5] While various studies show that the flexibilization or elimination of criminal penalties had no major impacts on the patterns of drug use in Oregon (Drug Abuse Council 1974) and Maine (Maine Office of Alcoholism and Drug Abuse Prevention 1978), the findings corresponding to Ohio (Spitzner 1979) and California

(Budman 1977) indicate modest increases among different segments of the adult population. In the case of California, however, Mandel (1987) provides alternative results, arguing that the Moscone Act, the bill that lowered the penalties for cannabis possession, did not increase consumption. As Single (1989) notes, a major limitation of these evaluations was the lack of control groups to estimate consumption rates in the absence of legal changes in the status of use and possession of the substance.

Stuart, Guire, and Krell (1976) added complexity to the first studies by conducting a controlled comparison of drug policy reform in Ann Arbor, Michigan. The so-called 'decriminalization ordinance' reduced the penalty for possession of small amounts of cannabis to a fine payable in the same manner as a parking ticket. By comparing data with controlled communities that underwent no legal changes, they find that Ann Arbor students' use of cannabis was not affected in any way by the new statute moderating drug penalties. The study even shows that the use of hard drugs declined slightly during the two years in which the possession of small quantities of cannabis was relatively penalty free.

The findings of different cross-state comparisons conducted a few years later were consistent with the pioneering study of Stuart and his colleagues (Johnston, O'Malley, and Bachman 1981; Maloff 1981). After reviewing the surveys of some of the states that changed the legal status of cannabis during the 1970s, one of the empirical evaluations concludes that 'consumption appears to be unaffected, or affected minimally by decriminalization' (Maloff 1981, 321). Indeed, only Saveland and Bray (1981) found higher levels of cannabis consumption in states that moderated their penalties, although these patterns were reported before and after the amendment of the domestic legislation. The first cross-state comparisons, in other words, showed no alarming consequences after different legislatures lessened the sanctions for possession and use of cannabis in the mid-1970s.

Using more recent data, different econometric analyses based on hypothetical modelling have produced mixed results. A first group of studies found no significant estimated increases in cannabis use after changes in drug policy (DiNardo and Lemieux 1992; Thies and Register 1993; Pacula 1998). Pacula (1998), for example, demonstrates the insignificance of decriminalization on cannabis demand, contending that it is law enforcement and not the penalties themselves what influence users' behaviour. Based on similar methodological approaches, other quantitative studies show that legal changes in the status of cannabis have a positive and statistically significant effect on consumption rates (Safer and Chaloupka 1995; Chaloupka, Grossman, and Tauras 1998; Chaloupka et al 1999; Saffer and Chaloupka 1999). In line with this second group of scholars, Farrelly and colleagues (2001) find that higher penalties for cannabis possession discouraged use in the last 30 days but did not affect the frequency of consumption.

Yet scholars have cast doubt on the validity of these cross-sectional econometric studies. According to Babor et al (2010, 171), the estimations of these early quantitative analyses are 'conflicting' because they offer weak causal evidence, a limitation allegedly not present in other natural experiment works. Apart from their methodological approach, other shortcomings highlighted in the literature review developed by Babor and colleagues (2010) include an overemphasis on formal statutory changes, often downplaying the relevance of cannabis prices and law enforcement practices as critical control variables. Pacula, Chriqui, and King (2003), for instance, demonstrate that the impacts of legal penalties on cannabis consumption rates are influenced by the way in which the law is enforced and the citizens' limited knowledge of the legislation. Pacula and colleagues (2003, 2005, 2017) also claim that studies conducted in the US were often not robust enough because the policy differences between states obscured the explanatory power of comparative analysis. Not surprisingly, other studies have included actual penalties or enforcement risks instead of the legal status of drugs as complementary determinants of the prevalence or the frequency of use in the US (Reuter and Kleiman 1986; Reuter 1989; Reuter and Haaga 1989; DiNardo 1993; Farrelly et al 2001; DeSimone and Farrelly 2003; Pacula and Lundberg 2014).[6]

Since the responsiveness of drug use to price variations is often understood as another fundamental determinant of the effectiveness of drug policy, a complementary group of economic studies has gone beyond the analysis of policy variables such as the legal status of drugs or enforcement risks and explored the different ways in which price changes affect consumption patterns in the US. Although some proponents of legalization have claimed that addictive substances are not sensitive to price, the empirical relationship between changes in the monetary value of different illicit drugs and prevalence or frequency of use has been investigated since Nisbet and Vakil's (1972) pathbreaking study of cannabis consumption among students at the University of California, Los Angeles.

Estimates of the price elasticity of drug demand in the US vary from study to study.[7] A vast economic literature reviewed by Pacula (2010), nevertheless, shows that juvenile cannabis initiation (Pacula et al 2001; DeSimone and Farrelly 2003; Pacula, Chriqui, and King 2003; Jacobson 2005); regular (past month) use (Nisbet and Vakil 1972; Williams et al 2004; Clements and Zhao 2009); and, to some extent, heavy use (Pacula and Kilmer 2003) are sensitive to changes in the monetary price of cannabis.[8] For instance, a meta-analysis of numerous quantitative studies conducted by Gallet (2014) finds that the elasticity corresponding to cannabis ranges between -0.28 and -0.31.[9] Another group of relevant academic works has revealed that cocaine (Caulkins 1995; Chaloupka et al 1998; Grossman and Chaloupka 1998; Saffer and Chaloupka 1999; DeSimone and Farrelly

2003; Williams et al 2006) and heroin (Caulkins 1995; Saffer and Chaloupka 1999; Olmstead et al 2015) consumption are also, to a greater or lesser extent, price responsive.

Yet Davis, Geisler, and Nichols (2016) argue that estimating the elasticity of demand for an illicit good such as cannabis or cocaine is problematic since information about purchases on black markets is not systematically recorded. Consequently, data are commonly gathered from different surveys, where participants provide information about their consumption behaviour. Still estimates are annual or at best quarterly, whereas drug markets adapt more quickly (Caulkins 2007). Along similar lines, Pacula and Lundberg (2014) cast doubt about the relevance of the price elasticity literature in the current legalization debate, arguing that many scholars naively draw on their findings to substantiate a particular position regarding a change in the legal status of drugs. According to Pacula and Lundberg (2014, 2), these scholars are 'unaware that the responsiveness of consumption to price can depend on where in the distribution of marijuana users the sample is drawn'.

Coffee shops and cannabis depenalization in the Netherlands

Unlike the reforms adopted in the US, in the Netherlands the national government has been directly involved in the formulation of drug policy, even though local authorities have retained some freedom during the implementation (Korf et al 2001).[10] Sylbing and Persoon (1985) conducted one of the first empirical evaluations on the impacts of the revised Opium Act of 1976, a legislative change that led to a substantial reduction of penalties for drug possession.[11] In their review of three different nationwide surveys of cannabis use, Sylbing and Persoon (1985) show that consumption increased approximately 10 per cent between the late 1970s and 1983. Despite the reported growing incidence, the scholars contend that cannabis use did not reach epidemic proportions in the country.

Various studies conducted during the late 1980s and early 1990s yielded different results, indicating a substantial decline in the use of cannabis after the 1976 drug policy reform in the Netherlands (Engelsman 1989; Nadelmann 1989; Alexander 1990). Similar to Sylbing and Persoon (1985), these empirical studies relied on national surveys, non-incorporating control groups to assess drug use across other European countries that did not undertake a policy reform. The conclusions raised at the local level suffer from similar methodological limitations. Cohen (1995), for example, shows that cannabis use in the last month and last year respectively remained stable in Amsterdam. Although life prevalence increased between 1987 and 1994, a pattern adjudicated to measurement considerations, the scholar notes that greater tolerance did not lead to any intensification of use patterns.

Adopting a more sophisticated methodological approach, MacCoun and Reuter (1997, 2001a, 2001b) examine the Netherlands's life prevalence rates between 1970 and 1996. They reveal that cannabis consumption grew from 1992 to 1996, even though this trend was not directly attributable to the country's drug policies because comparable increases were registered across the control groups: the US and Oslo. Between 1984 and 1992, however, prevalence rates in the Netherlands increased among youth, whereas usage levels were either fixed or decreased in the two other cases analyzed. According to MacCoun and Reuter (1997, 2001a, 2001b), the Dutch escalation of cannabis use during this first period was a consequence of commercial promotion and sales rather than depenalization itself.[12]

Korf (2002) questioned MacCoun and Reuter's (1997, 2001a, 2001b) conclusion that commercial access through coffee shops was associated with growth in cannabis use in the Netherlands. Despite the empirical evidence showing that drug policy reforms went along with changes in cannabis availability and prevalence rates, Korf (2002) argues that regulating the market through law enforcement has a marginal or no effect on the levels of consumption. In her analysis, other factors such as general developments among the young population, which makes marijuana use more or less fashionable and acceptable, explain the simultaneity of ups and downs in consumption rates in relation to stages in the depenalization process. Along similar lines, Abraham (1999) focuses on distinct address density municipalities and their diverse 'lifestyles' to elucidate variations in the levels of drug use across different cities in the Netherlands. In this study, the frequency with which respondents visit clubs, discotheques, and bars correlates to address density and to drug use prevalence, thereby suggesting that national-level figures mask relevant differences between specific local areas.

More recently, Reinarman, Cohen, and Kaal (2004) cast doubt on the relevance of drug policy by comparing the levels of consumption in Amsterdam and San Francisco. They find that the most experienced people who use drugs organize their consumption based on their own subcultural etiquette or practices and less on laws or policies. According to the authors, informal norms and rules about when, where, why, with whom, and how to use cannabis are determinant in understanding consumption patterns. In another cross-sectional comparison, Reinarman (2009) discovers more similarities than differences across the contrasting drug control regimes of Amsterdam and San Francisco, suggesting that cannabis use is an embedded cultural practice not easily reached by drug policy. The limited impacts of variations in the levels of punishment or the reclassification of drugs on prevalence rates was also stressed by Degenhardt et al (2008) and Reuter and Stevens (2007).

Other scholarly studies have explored the effects of depenalization on cannabis potency and prices respectively (MacCoun and Reuter 1997;

Pijlman et al 2005; Hazekamp 2006). In addition to prevalence and patterns of use, MacCoun (2011) compares market indicators in the Netherlands with Europe and the US. He finds that cannabis prices have remained high even though depenalization was expected to produce the opposite outcome.[13] Following Caulkins and Lumbibao's (2010) estimates, MacCoun (2011) shows that drug prices in the Netherlands and the US are comparable on a purity-adjusted basis, but the latter would be lower on a per-gram basis. According to MacCoun (2011), the Dutch hybrid regime, which merges prohibition at the production and trafficking levels with de facto legalization at the consumption level, serves to keep prices from dropping. In other words, high prices are likely to explain why Dutch patterns of use are typical for Europe and even lower than expected in a full-scale legalization scheme.

Prohibition with civil penalties in Australia

The adoption of 'infringement' or 'expiation' notices in South Australia in 1987, the Australian Capital Territory in 1992, the Northern Territory in 1996, and Western Australia in 2004 provided additional evidence for scholars evaluating the impacts of drug policy reforms.[14] Yet no conclusive evidence exists on the impacts of the so-called prohibition with civil penalties (Sutton and Hawks 2005; Room et al 2010), a scheme that maintains the illegality of small-scale possession, use, and cultivation of cannabis but replaces formal prosecution for an infringement notice.[15] Despite that before-and-after studies indicate that decriminalization did not lead to significant changes in the patterns of cannabis consumption, more recent econometric analyses have provided mixed estimations.

The first comprehensive study reviewing national population surveys in South Australia was conducted by Ali and colleagues (1998). In their evaluation of the Cannabis Expiation Notice (CEN), they find that lifetime cannabis use in South Australia rose between 1985 and 1995, echoing national trends. Despite the degree of increase in consumption in South Australia being greater than the country's average, the authors claim that the CEN policy could not have been solely responsible for the increments since similar upsurges occurred in the Tasmania and Victoria states, where there were no changes in the legal status of the substance. In addition, Ali and colleagues (1998) show that South Australia reported neither greater increases in cannabis use among young adults aged 14 to 29 nor variance in weekly consumption vis-à-vis the rest of the country.

Donnelly and colleagues (1999, 2000) reached the same conclusions. Since Victoria and Tasmania, districts that had maintained a strict prohibitionist approach, reported a significant growth in cannabis use above the national average, South Australia's 10 per cent increase between 1985 and 1995 was not attributable to the CEN scheme. These results were broadly consistent with early analyses of the region's use patterns after the moderation of penalties (Christie 1991; Donnelly, Hall, and Christie 1995). Moreover, other works focusing on schoolchildren also confirm that cannabis use in South Australia remained stable despite the adoption of the CEN scheme (Neill, Christie, and Cormack 1991; Donnelly et al 1992).

The legal system in South Australia did not appear to have a significant impact on subsequent cannabis consumption either. By comparing the social effects of strict prohibition in Western Australia and civil penalties in South Australia, Lenton and colleagues (1999a, 2000) find that neither conviction nor the infringement notice deterred subsequent cannabis use. They reveal, for example, that 70.6 per cent of the offenders in Western Australia and 91.2 per cent of the expiators in South Australia reported that their cannabis use was 'not at all' affected one month after the penalty (Lenton et al 2000). Despite the limited relevance of both types of penalties on subsequent use patterns, other studies have shown that minor cannabis offences under the new policy increased as a result of the greater ease with which the CEN could be issued (Christie and Ali 1995; Ali et al 1998). In other words, decriminalization seems to have produced a 'net-widening' effect, where more people come under state control because police discretion to detect and process cannabis possession tends to increase.

Other works explore the impacts of decriminalization across other Australian regions. In a study of the Australian Capital Territory's new drug policy that came into effect in 1992, McGeorge and Aitken (1997) demonstrate that cannabis consumption rates among students from the Australian National University in Canberra remained stable between 1992 and 1994. The inclusion of students from the University of Melbourne, located in Victoria, strengthened the scholars' conclusions about the limited impact of decriminalization on cannabis use (McGeorge and Aitken 1997). Along similar lines, Fetherston and Lenton (2007) show that both lifetime and past 12-month use of cannabis in Western Australia declined between 2002 and 2007. They contend, nevertheless, that this trend began before 2004 when the infringement notice system came into effect and appears consistent with national trends.

More recently, Damrongplasit, Hsiao, and Zhao (2010) adopted a different methodological design to estimate the impacts of decriminalization on cannabis smoking behaviour in Australia. By using both parametric and nonparametric approaches, they observe that living in a decriminalized state increases the probability of smoking cannabis by 16.2 per cent. The findings of Damrongplasit, Hsiao, and Zhao (2010) are consistent with prior econometric studies in the field (Cameron and Williams 2001; Zhao and Harris 2004). Williams (2004), on the other hand, demonstrates that decriminalization only increases the likelihood of cannabis use among males over the age of 25. According to Williams (2004), the lack of general evidence of a positive association between decriminalization and cannabis use suggests that the expected costs of engaging in illegal activities are smaller for this age group because they discount the future more heavily.

Closely associated with the legal status of drugs, other studies have explored the ways in which price influences consumption patterns in Australia. Similar to the evidence available from the US, van Ours and Williams (2007) discover that low cannabis prices are associated with early initiation use of the substance, whereas the decision to quit is not price sensitive. In their analysis, the initiation elasticity ranged from -0.31 to -0.70. Along similar lines, Bretteville-Jensen and Williams (2011) also find cannabis price to be negatively associated with initiation for individuals under the age of 18. They sustain that decriminalizing marijuana shifts the age distribution of uptake towards younger age groups while leaving the proportion of those who start using the drug unchanged. This relationship is particularly relevant given that cannabis prices in Australia have decreased substantially, even faster than the monetary value of other primary products (Clements and Zhao 2009).

Decriminalization of illicit drugs in Portugal

Unlike the Australian experience, Portugal has decriminalized the use, acquisition, and possession of all types of illicit drugs at the national level. Greenwald (2009) offered one of the first assessment of the European country's policy reform. In a hotly debated document published by the libertarian think tank Cato Institute, Greenwald contends that decriminalization did not cause adverse effects on drug usage rates. The study shows that while lifetime prevalence remained roughly the same for various age groups or experienced a slight increase among adults, use rates among the population aged 15–19 declined. In line with the work of other scholars in the field (Quintas and Arana 2017), the Open Society Foundation, in a report authored by Domosławski (2011, 5), also argues that Portugal's decriminalization did not materialize in an 'explosion in drug consumption'. The document presents as the most relevant outcomes: (i) a decrease in the level of drug use in the most sensitive age group (15–19), (ii) the recidivism rates staying relatively low, and last (iii) the consumption of heroin remaining more or less at the same levels of 2001–2002.

Yet alternative evidence has questioned decriminalization's alleged positive impacts. As a response to Greenwald's (2009) report, Pinto Coelho (2010) highlights that lifetime prevalence among the general population increased for every category. The 20–24 age group, for example, experienced a 50 per cent growth between 2001 and 2007. Along similar lines, the White House's Office of National Control Policy (2010) also casts doubt on the validity of the results documented by the Cato Institute. Based on data published by the

European Monitoring Centre for Drugs and Drug Addiction (EMCDDA), the White House (2010) reports increases from 2001 to 2007 in lifetime prevalence rates for cannabis, cocaine, amphetamines, ecstasy, and LSD for the Portuguese general population and for the 15–34 age group in particular. The same factsheet also indicates rises in cocaine and LSD past-month use rates among the general population as well as increases in cannabis, cocaine, and amphetamine consumption in the 15–34 age group.

Since the variation in Portugal's drug use rates can be attributed to a different number of variables or contextual factors, Hughes and Stevens (2010) added complexity to the analysis by incorporating two control countries: Spain and Italy. Building upon their previous briefing report published by the Beckley Foundation (Hughes and Stevens 2007), they find slight growth in lifetime and last-year use in all age groups above 19 for almost all illicit substances reported. According to Hughes and Stevens (2010), however, Portugal's upward trend was not a direct consequence of the 2001 decriminalization policy since the three European countries experienced similar consumption patterns. As the scholars put it, 'The congruity with the other data from neighbouring nations provides little evidence that any apparent increases were directly attributable to the decriminalisation' (Hughes and Stevens 2010, 1006).

In another peer-reviewed article, Hughes and Steven (2012) compare the reports elaborated by Greenwald (2009) and Pinto Coelho (2010) and argue that the lack of consensus over the effects of decriminalization derives from the selective use of evidence. They show, in particular, how the misuse of data generated clear misconceptions about drug use, deaths, and other trends among European countries. Additional methodological concerns have been raised by Laqueur (2014). In a critical appraisal of the before-and-after comparative analysis, the scholar minimizes the impacts of decriminalization on drug-related consumption behaviour, arguing instead that changes were already taking place before 2001. The most dramatic transformation, Laqueur (2014) maintains, was not the legislation itself or the consumption patterns following the reform, but the change in the court system practices regarding the imposition of the criminal law for cases connected to drug trafficking.

Félix, Portugal, and Tavares (2017) address some of the alleged limitations of the before-and-after studies by using Abadie and Gardeazabal's (2003) synthetic control method for comparative analysis. In their econometric model, they demonstrate that decriminalization was not harmful, but it contributed, among other things, to the reduction in the amount of heroin and cocaine seizures and the number of drug-law offenses. The finding of limited or no harm caused by decriminalization is consistent with the works of other Portuguese scholars (Pombo and da Costa 2016; Félix and Portugal 2017). Félix and Portugal (2017), for example, show that drug prices did not drop after the policy change, questioning the classical argument that softer drug law enforcement leads to lower prices and ultimately to higher consumption and dependence.

Commercial cannabis legalization in the US

Finally, the evidence on countries or states that recently legalized the use of cannabis beyond medical purposes is far from conclusive.[16] Kerr, Lui, and Ye (2018) assess the impacts of state-level cannabis legalization policies in the US at the aggregate level. They find that liberalization reforms in effect by 2015 do not affect cannabis use patterns among the general population, which is consistent with recent research (Weinberger, Wyka, and Goodwin 2022) and studies focusing on youth consumption (Dills, Goffard, and Millon 2017).[17] According to Kerr, Lui, and Ye (2018), policy changes are likely to occur in response to attitudinal variations within states and to have effects on behaviours more generally in the US. Anderson and colleagues (2019) focus on high school students (grades 9–12) and show that consumption in the past 30 days declined after the legalization of cannabis for recreational purposes. The trend found by the authors seems to be associated with the difficulties of obtaining cannabis, as many drug dealers have been replaced by licensed dispensaries that require proof of age, making its access more restricted for that age group.

Mason et al (2015) and Estoup et al (2016) conducted the first two studies evaluating the effects of recreational cannabis laws in Washington State. While Mason and colleagues (2015) show that liberalization policies do not affect the likelihood youth will use cannabis, Estoup et al (2016) discover no significant impacts on adolescent cannabis consumption patterns. Their findings are consistent with current research in the state across different samples (Kerr et al 2018; Mosher and Akins 2020). Dilley and colleagues (2019) claim that Washington State's cannabis use among students in the 8th to 10th grades actually declined after legalization. Contrasting this first group of studies, Miller, Rosenman, and Cowan (2017) argue that students at Washington State University experienced a significant increase in cannabis use after legalization, with female, black, and Hispanic undergraduate students leading the upward trend. Most importantly, their findings suggest that the reported increase in cannabis consumption at Washington State University is above the linear trend and the two national samples used as counterfactuals. Focusing on the adult population, Everson and colleagues (2019) add complexity to the analysis by considering geospatial factors. They show that cannabis use did not significantly change immediately after legalization, but it increased subsequently as a result of greater access to retailers. Larger increases occurred in areas located around 18 miles of a cannabis retailer and especially within 0.8 miles.

Questions about the potency and price of drugs also proliferated after Washington State legalized the recreational use of cannabis. Consistent with certain expectations and research in the field (Kleiman 2016; Caulikins et al 2018), Smart et al (2017) show that the value of cannabis fell sharply under the new legal framework, with a coefficient of price variation that stabilized at around 0.3. Nonetheless, the market response to legalization reported by Hunt and Pacula (2017) is slightly different. They find that the relaxation of restrictions in Washington State's cannabis markets did not reduce prices within the four- to five-month window following legalization, although this behaviour is not necessarily indicative of the long-run effects.[18] Other scholarly works go beyond and demonstrate that even though consumer cannabis demand was price inelastic in the short term, it became price elastic within a few weeks of the reform (Hansen, Miller, and Weber 2017). The potency, on the other hand, also changed after legalization. According to Smart and colleagues (2017), the potency went up, exceeding the national average THC level for cannabis.[19] This pattern clearly contradicts the argument raised by different advocates and proponents of legalization such as Cowan (1986) and Buckley (1996), who have long claimed that prohibition and tougher law enforcement practices increase the potency of drugs and legalization would lead markets to deliver safer and less-potent products (Smart et al 2017).

Cerdá and colleagues (2017) extended the analysis to Colorado, the other state in the US where recreational cannabis was legalized in 2012. They reveal that cannabis use in Washington increased 2.0 per cent and 4.1 per cent from 2010–2012 to 2013–2015 among students in the 8th and 10th grades, whereas consumption rates decreased by 1.3 per cent and 0.9 per cent over the same period in states that did not legalize the substance. No significant differences, however, were found in cannabis use among 12th graders in Washington State or for adolescents of any age in Colorado (Cerdá et al 2017). The findings in Colorado are remarkably relevant given that the retail prices of cannabis have dropped since legalization (Subritzky, Lenton, and Pettigrew 2020). A more contemporary study also developed by Cerdá and colleagues (2020) indicates that past-month cannabis use and past-month frequent cannabis use grew only among adults 26 years or older across the first four US states that passaged recreational consumption legalization laws: Colorado, Washington State, Alaska, and Oregon.

In the case of Oregon, empirical evaluations have produced mixed results. In two different studies, David Kerr and colleagues (2017, 2018) assess the effects of recreational cannabis legalization among college students. In their first research article, they find that increases in rates of 30-day cannabis use were stronger among Oregon students than their peers in states that did not legalize the psychoactive substance, but only within the subgroup of those who reported heavy alcohol use (Kerr et al 2017). The association with contextual factors such as alcohol misuse disappears in the second article, as Kerr, Bae, and Koval (2018) show that legalization in Oregon was associated with increased rates of past-month cannabis use and frequency of use among young adult college students compared to nonlegalization states. In another recent study, Rusby et al (2018) demonstrate that Measure 91, enacted in 2015, had no significant effect on the initiation of cannabis use for young nonusers, although increases were registered among those who were already consumers.

According to Smart and Pacula (2019), studies conducted after the legalization of recreational use of cannabis at the state level are subject to several limitations. On the one hand, estimating the impacts of legalization from the day the law was effective is problematic since retail stores have consistently opened one or two years later. Since states have recently conducted marijuana policy reforms, assessing the long-term impacts is also limited by data covering a short span of time. On the other hand, Smart and Pacula (2019) also highlight that the three states that legalized recreational cannabis use had robust medical markets already in place, meaning that the environment may conflate heterogeneity in the control group of states that did not implement a cannabis policy reform.

Other scholarly works conducted at the subnational level in the US have recently evaluated subtler policy reforms such as decriminalization.[20] Grucza and colleagues (2018), for example, assess the intended and unintended consequences of cannabis decriminalization policies adopted in Massachusetts, Connecticut, Vermont, Rhode Island, and Maryland between 2008 and 2014.[21] They find that state-level decriminalization was not associated with increases in cannabis consumption in either aggregate or individual terms. Although the prevalence levels were notably higher in the five states, those patterns were already present before the drug policy reforms. The so-called second wave of decriminalization within the US was also evaluated by Miech and colleagues (2015). By focusing on the case of California, their research demonstrates that consumption in the West Coast state increased after the enactment of Senate Bill 1449 in 2010. Their findings indicate that Californian 12th graders became 25 per cent more likely to have used cannabis in the past 30 days compared to the same population in other states.

State-led cannabis legalization in Uruguay

Contrasting with the reforms adopted at the subnational level in the US since 2012, the legalization of cannabis in Uruguay is a nationwide and noncommercial drug policy controlled by the government. Since the new legislation was enacted in December 2013, only a limited number of scholarly works have analyzed how changes in the legal status of cannabis have affected the country's consumption patterns. Cruz, Boidi, and Queirolo (2018), for example, suggest that cannabis legalization had no significant impact in lifetime prevalence, although their study was not designed to measure changes in drug use patterns. In a recent contribution, Laqueur and colleagues (2020) use a generalization of the synthetic control method to compare survey data from Montevideo and regions in the interior of Uruguay post-legalization (2014–2018) and post initial implementation (2015–2018) to a synthetic counterfactual constructed using a weighted combination of 15 control regions in Chile. They find that legalization did not increase use among adolescents in the short term.

While cannabis legalization may not have changed the country's consumption rates, it could affect the ways users access the psychoactive substance. Queirolo, Álvarez, Sotto, and Cruz (2023) demonstrate that people in Uruguay still obtain cannabis from illicit sources despite the new regulatory framework establishing three legal mechanisms (that is, growing at home, forming or/and being part of a cannabis social club, and buying the product at licensed pharmacies). Therefore, they contend that strict cannabis regulation could be an obstacle for users to abandon the black market completely, suggesting that the implementation or other special aspects of legalization reforms matter (Queirolo et al 2023).

Other drug policy reforms

Meanwhile, evaluations of the impacts of subtler and more volatile drug policy reforms like the reclassification of cannabis in the UK[22] (Nicholas, Kershaw, and Walker 2007; Reuter and Stevens 2007; UK Drug Policy Commission 2008; Room et al 2010; Stevens 2011; Braakmann 2014; Braakman and Jones 2014), decriminalization of soft and hard drugs in Italy[23] (Solivetti 1994, 2001; MacCoun and Reuter 2001a), Spain[24] (MacCoun and Reuter 2001a; Gamella and Jiménez Rodrigo 2004), and the Czech Republic[25] (Zábransky et al 2001; Čecho et al 2017; Červený et al 2017; Zeman, Štefunková, and Trávníčková 2017), or countries that recently approved more ambitious policies such as the legalization of the recreational use of cannabis such as Canada[26] (Hawley, Gobbo, and Afghari 2020; Hawke and Henderson 2021; Nguyen, Mital, and Bornstein 2022) have produced mixed results. The evidence, however, is often limited or preliminary and long-term assessments are necessary.

Cross-national and meta-analyses

The last two groups of studies have conducted cross-national regressions and meta-analyses testing the impacts of cannabis liberalization policies on consumption patterns. On the one hand, Shi, Lenzi, and An (2015) find that drug policies such as depenalization and partial prohibition are associated with higher levels of regular cannabis use among adolescents. Yet the results of this first cross-national study were contested by Stevens (2019), who claims that Shi, Lenzi, and An (2015) misinterpreted their own findings due to methodological limitations with their statistical model and the exclusion of available data (for example, Sweden). Along the same lines, Gabri and colleagues (2022) show that changes in cannabis legislation do not increase the odds of consumption among young Europeans. By contrast, they argue that use rates appeared to grow in countries without policy changes but decrease after both decriminalization and depenalization of cannabis-related crimes (Gabri et al 2022).

Meta-analyses and systemic reviews, on the other hand, indicate that states that legalized the recreational use of cannabis, at both the national and subnational levels, witnessed little or no increases in adolescent use (Melchior et al 2018; Smart and Pacula 2019). In the literature review of quasi-experimental studies conducted by Smart and Pacula (2019), they also reveal that research testing the impacts of liberalization policies within the US suggests potential increases in college students' use and the still unknown effects on other psychoactive substance consumption.

Conclusions

Scholarly studies systematically evaluating the different ways in which changes in the legal status of use and possession of small amounts of illicit drugs affect consumption patterns are relatively recent. Empirical assessments are largely concentrated in a few countries and most of the literature revolves around cannabis reclassification in one single direction: from criminalization to other forms of noncriminal penalties.

The review of the first studies evaluating the impacts of cannabis liberalization policies adopted early in the US produced mixed results. Single-case studies, controlled comparisons, and econometric analyses depict different landscapes of the reforms conducted at the state level since the 1970s. Although no clear agreement exists on the effects of cannabis depenalization on consumption rates, the evidence on price elasticity seems to be more consistent: Use patterns are expected to be sensitive to changes in the monetary prices of cannabis. Similar patterns were reported for the cases of cocaine and heroin. The findings may suggest that the impact of drug policy reform within the US is indirect and complex, as statutory changes by themselves do not explain variation in consumption patterns unless the mechanism of price also experiences fluctuations. Studies focusing on law enforcement, on the other hand, have also produced divergent results, showing different effects of actual penalties, risk of arrest, and seizure on drug demand. More recently, evaluations of recreational cannabis reforms at the aggregate level report either a limited impact or decreasing use rates among adolescents and the general population. At the state level, however, the evidence is not conclusive. Research evaluating the reclassification of cannabis in Washington State, Colorado, and Oregon reveals little or no increases in adolescent use after legalization, whereas the impact among the adult population is less straightforward. The evidence on prices and potency, the reduced number of works reviewed notwithstanding, suggests that cannabis legalization leads to price decreases and higher potency.

Research evaluating drug policy reform in the Netherlands shows that cannabis depenalization did not result in any substantial intensification of use patterns. While early academic studies did not include control groups, later methodological developments allowed scholars to demonstrate that several mechanisms mediate the relationship between cannabis consumption rates and drug policy reform, including the commercial models of coffee shops, informal norms and rules, cultural values, and the youth lifestyle. Similar to the US, the literature also shows that high prices are likely to affect consumption rates. The evidence suggests that a relatively high monetary value due to strict prohibition at the production and trafficking levels exerts influence on the country's use patterns despite changes in the legal status of use and possession of small amounts of cannabis.

In the case of Australia, the evidence overwhelmingly indicates that the CEN scheme had a limited impact on cannabis use. The before-and-after studies, strengthened by the contemplation of control groups, show that consumption across different age groups was not dependent on the adoption of the so-called system of 'prohibition with civil penalties', despite complementary studies suggesting that cannabis offenses increased as part of the net-widening effect. More recently, econometric studies contrasted prior findings, demonstrating that living in a decriminalized state actually increases the probability of cannabis consumption. The available literature also reveals that cannabis use is price sensitive for the Australian case, especially in terms of early initiation. This finding is particularly relevant given the downward trend of cannabis prices reported in the country.

The evidence on Portugal's drug policy reform shows that fears of increasing consumption did not materialize. Despite the first reports showing mixed results, more sophisticated methodological approaches that include control groups overwhelmingly demonstrate that decriminalization did not lead to higher use rates. Empirical studies indicate that other anticipated negative outcomes such as higher numbers of seizures and lowering prices, factors that could be associated with growing drug demand, did not happen. Although recent research casts doubt on the relevance of changes in the legal status of drugs, arguing that other mechanisms such as the practices of the court system have greater explanatory power, the evidence indicates that decriminalization did not result in an increase in drug use.

Despite Uruguay's drug policy reform being too recent to draw definitive conclusions, the available evidence suggests that cannabis legalization had no significant impact on lifetime prevalence rates and consumption among adolescents. The latter finding is important because the commercial legalization model adopted in several states across the US since 2012 is often associated with the opposite policy outcome, especially among the youth population. Of course, the short-term impacts of Uruguay's drug policy reform need to be substantiated by new data and additional comparative research in the future.

In summary, the evidence shows that the feared drug-related 'chaos' following liberalization policies has not materialized. The evaluative record for drug policy reform, however, seems inconsistent in establishing the impacts on consumption reviewed in this chapter. The associated effects vary depending on the case study rather than on the nature of the drug policy itself (that is, depenalization, decriminalization, or legalization), suggesting that contextual factors play a critical role in understanding illicit drug markets. Methodological differences, the selective use of evidence, data availability, and the interpretation of information have all exacerbated the wide disagreement in the field. In spite of the emerging consensus in specific areas such as the relationship between liberalization reforms and price or youth consumption, roughly 50 years of drug policy research demonstrates that there are no linear pathways following changes in the legal status of drugs.

2

The Legal Status of Drugs and Health and Crime

Under certain conditions, the use of illicit substances can have adverse effects in areas such as public health and security. Drug consumption can be associated with health problems such as infectious diseases or even overdose deaths and can also exacerbate criminal activity in some circumstances. Indeed, the connections between drug use and adverse health problems and crime, respectively, are numerous and complex. This second part of the integrative literature review evaluates the available empirical evidence from a variety of scientific studies and reports addressing the health and security implications of drug policy reforms around the world. Unlike the impacts on consumption, scholarly works evaluating the intricate connections between drug policy reform and health and crime are relatively limited and tend to be concentrated in high-income countries.

This chapter is organized as follows. The first section begins with a short analytical discussion of some of the dangers associated with illicit drug use. It then analyzes the impacts of drug policy reform on the health domain; that is to say, the patterns of drug use that are likely to produce adverse health consequences. Since drug policy also entails state interventions to provide health care and welfare support, this section also takes into consideration complementary health and social services aimed at discouraging dangerous or problematic consumption patterns. After reviewing studies dedicated to chronic and acute health problems related to the use of illicit drugs, including overdoses and different infectious diseases, the third section discusses major theoretical considerations around the so-called 'drug-crime nexus'. The chapter then focuses on key empirical evidence from scientific studies exploring how changes in the legal status of use and possession of small amounts of illicit drugs affect crime and, to a lesser extent, incarceration rates. Similar to Chapter 1, each section also includes a brief review of works analyzing broader contextual factors that are likely to influence drug-related problems.

The legal status of drugs and adverse health consequences

Assessing the extent of a country's drug problem requires more than estimating the number of users (MacCoun and Reuter 1998). Certain patterns of drug use are likely to produce adverse health consequences, for the individual themselves but also for society at large. While key epidemiological indicators such as simple prevalence rates provide a first glance at drug consumption patterns in a given territory, there is no clear-cut data on the severity of the health damage associated with the use of illicit substances (Hall, Degenhardt, and Lynskey 2001). The harmful effects of drug consumption are also difficult to untangle from the contexts of their use and the consequences of drug control policies. For example, the risk of fatal heroin overdoses is associated with different factors, including the route of administration, the purity of the supply, the combination with other drugs, and the availability of naloxone in ambulances.[1] Similarly, the spread of HIV and infectious diseases among people who use heroin is also affected by the presence or not of needle exchange programs.

Not surprisingly, wide disagreement and controversy exist among both medical and nonmedical specialists over the dangers associated with illicit drug use. Definitions of what constitutes 'adverse' or 'problematic' as well as their quantitative characterizations commonly differ from study to study. Participants in debates are often selective in highlighting the particular dimensions of drug-related harms underpinning their proposals, suggesting that evaluations and comparisons 'are largely a task of judgment rather than arithmetic' (MacCoun and Reuter 2001a, 111). As Best and colleagues (2003) point out, the selection of empirical evidence, the availability and interpretation of information, and the various ways secondary outcomes such as crime, employment, or blood-borne disease are attributed to drugs affect how the dangers and risks of consumption are estimated.

Jaffe (1985) developed an initial typology for evaluating the dangers associated with drug use. His study identifies several factors influencing the severity of health problems, namely the type of drug, the dose, the route of administration, the general setting, and the user's expectations and experiences. According to Jaffe (1985), addiction and the problematic use of drugs is an extreme case of consumption that is not qualitatively, but rather quantitatively different from compulsive drug use. In a meta-analysis study, English et al (1995) reviewed the literature published prior to 1993 and identified the attributable fractions of different causes of mortality and morbidity associated with the use of illicit drugs. Within the causes of death and principal diagnoses identified as illicit drug-related conditions, English and colleagues (1995) distinguish between (i) those directly attributable to opiates, (ii) those directly attributable to other illicit drugs, (iii) those attributable to unclassifiable injecting drug use, and (iv) other related causes such as road injuries, suicide, and drug psychoses.

Other scholars have focused on broader contextual forces when examining the adverse consequences of drug use (MacCoun and Reuter 1998; Stevens 2011). Moore (2001), for example, claims that the social environment influences the dimension and characteristics of the drug problem in three ways. First, the environment is important because 'background' conditions such as poverty, racial discrimination, and family deterioration are likely to affect both the location and shape of the underlying propensity to use drugs. Second, the social environment is relevant because 'foreground' conditions such as the number of close friends and relatives using drugs, how conveniently available drugs are, and the meaning of consumption in their local milieu can all impact the patterns of use. Finally, the environment also influences the mechanisms that transform any given pattern of drug use into adverse social consequences, including crime or severe health harms such as contracting AIDS.

More recently, Babor and colleagues (2010) take a broad 'public good' perspective on illegal drug use, focusing on mortality and morbidity statistics. They distinguish, in particular, five morbidity and mortality types: (i) overdose, (ii) other injury, (iii) noncommunicable physical disease, (iv) mental disorders, and (v) infectious disease. Besides drug use itself, Babor and colleagues (2010) identify a variety of social, environmental, and behavioural risk factors that influence the ways in which morbidity and mortality are associated with illicit drug use, including housing status or injection behaviour. Similarly, Degenhardt and Hall (2012) distinguish four types of adverse health effects of illicit drug consumption: (i) acute toxic effects (that is, overdose), (ii) acute effects of intoxication (such as, accidental injury and violence), (iii) development of dependence, and (iv) adverse health effects of sustained chronic and regular use (that is, chronic diseases like cirrhosis, blood-borne bacterial and viral infections, and mental disorders).

International organizations have also invested considerable resources to standardize data on harmful illicit drug use. The former United Nations Drug Control Programme,[2] for example, identified 'problem drugs' based on the demand for treatment, emergency room visits, drug-related morbidity (that is, HIV/AIDS and hepatitis), mortality, and other drug-related social ills (Darke, Degenhardt, and Mattick 2006). Along similar lines, EMCDDA measures the seriousness of the drug problem on the basis of five specific epidemiological indicators: (i) the prevalence of drug use in the general population and among the school-going population, (ii) the prevalence estimates of problem drug use, (iii) the demand for treatment on account of drug use, (iv) the infectious diseases related to drug use, and (v) drug-related deaths.

Prior empirical work

The available evidence suggests that only a limited number of those who use illicit substances become problematic users (Babor et al 2010; Stevens

2011). Despite media outlets and politicians often exacerbating the magnitude of problematic consumption, most individuals who start using illicit drugs desist by their own will, without medical treatment or coercion within the span of five years (MacCoun and Reuter 2001). According to the latest Global Burden of Disease (GBD) study (2019), drug use disorders caused approximately 128,082 deaths and 18.1 million disability-adjusted life years (DALYs), accounting for 0.7 per cent of global DALYs in 2019.[3] Although the all-age DALY rate due to drug use disorder has increased since the 1990s, it still ranks 57th among Level 3 causes for global deaths and 38th for DALYs (GBD Collaborative Network 2019).[4] Legal drugs such as tobacco account for 8.71 million deaths and 229.77 million DALYs globally (He et al 2022). The figures associated with illicit drug use are even less relevant if other global risks of mortality are considered, including deaths from ischaemic heart disease (9,137,791) and strokes (6,552,724) (GBD Collaborative Network 2019).

Yet under certain circumstances people who use drugs may experience severe health consequences, including ill health and death. Various studies, most of them conducted in high-income countries, have shown that the adverse effects of cannabis consumption are relatively modest compared to those of other psychoactive substances (Peacock et al 2018; Hall 2020). Although the World Health Organization (WHO 2016) highlights some long-term negative health outcomes such as cognitive impairment, mental disorders, cardiovascular disease, chronic obstructive pulmonary and respiratory disease, and some cancers, the evidence suggests that users seeking treatment for cannabis dependence experience less severe consequences than those present among problematic users of other drugs such as alcohol or opioids (Hall and Pacula 2010; Degenhardt and Hall 2012). Cannabis is indeed not capable of causing immediate death, whereas other psychoactive substances such as opiates and cocaine can be deadly by producing asphyxiation or cardiac arrest correspondingly (Stevens 2011).[5] Combining illicit drugs such as opioids with Central Nervous System depressants such as alcohol or benzodiazepines is also a common cause of drug-related deaths (Darke and Zador 1996; Warner-Smith et al 2001). Furthermore, there are other illnesses associated with the use of certain types of illicit drugs, including HIV, hepatitis C virus (HCV), and hepatitis B virus (Darke, Degenhardt, and Mattick 2006).

A relatively limited number of scholarly works have evaluated the ways in which specific health harms are associated with changes in the legal status of drugs. Broadly speaking, prohibitionists commonly contend that drug policy reforms aimed at softening the legislation are likely to increase problematic drug consumption, whereas critics anticipate that users under a more flexible legal framework such as decriminalization or legalization would no longer be considered deviant and consequently would not continue to secondary deviance and problematic drug use (Korf 2002). These hypotheses, nevertheless, have not been widely tested since major changes in the legal status of drugs are rather recent (Hall 2020; Hall and Lynskey 2020). Moreover, most analyses exploring the acute health harms of drug policy reform have often been conducted in high-income countries where data are systematized (WHO 2016).

Dutch coffee shops

In the Netherlands, research shows that coffee shops or proximity to these authorized retailers do not encourage heavier cannabis consumption (MacCoun 2011; Wouters et al 2012). MacCoun (2011), nonetheless, finds that users of cannabis in the Netherlands are more likely to be admitted to treatment than elsewhere in Europe, although it is possible that the country's higher treatment rates do not reflect a greater treatment demand under a depenalization scheme but a more generous and proactive health policy. During the late 1980s, for instance, around 60–80 per cent of Amsterdam's total population of problematic users were reached by some type of assistance (Engelsman 1989). Alternative explanations suggest that first-time admissions to drug treatment in the Netherlands between 2000 and 2015 were associated with changes in cannabis potency and not with prevalence (Freeman et al 2018). Under these circumstances, changes in the legal status of cannabis are likely to have limited or indirect impacts on problematic drug use.

The most recent trends in Europe seem to corroborate the limited relevance of the legal status of cannabis in the Netherlands. Montanary and colleagues (2017) demonstrate that the overall treatment demand for cannabis-related problems across the 22 European countries analyzed has increased since 2003. In 2014, for example, cannabis was the main drug used as reported by 46 per cent of all new clients entering treatment, with the Netherlands not being among the first five countries in the regional ranking. Even the latest patterns informed by van Laar and colleagues (2020) in the annual report sponsored by the National Drug Monitor, which shows that the number of patients admitted to hospitals with a problem related to cannabis, cocaine, or opiates increased between 2015 and 2018, are not likely to be unique to the Netherlands, but are rather another illustration of a trend observed in Europe.[6]

State cannabis liberalization policies in the US

The impacts at the subnational level were also evaluated by different scholarly works. In the US, Model (1993) uses statistical information collected by the Drug Abuse Warning Network to measure the effects of changes in drug penalties on substance abuse crises between 1975 and 1978. The findings demonstrate that the liberalization reforms adopted across the 12 so-called 'decriminalization states' were associated with increasing hospital emergency room episodes involving cannabis consumption. Interestingly, the number of incidents related to other drugs were significantly reduced after the change of the legal status of cannabis, suggesting that the reduction of penalties may have precipitated the substitution of other drugs for cannabis (Model 1993).

More recently, Cerdá and colleagues (2020) explore the effects of the legalization of recreational use of cannabis in Colorado, Washington State, Alaska, and Oregon. They find that the cannabis liberalization policies adopted between 2012 and 2015 resulted in slightly greater cannabis use disorder (CUD) prevalence rates among adolescents. This increase among all 12-to-17-year-old respondents was 25 per cent higher compared to the same age group in states that did not legalize the recreational consumption of cannabis. They also discovered a similar trend among respondents aged 26 years or older, showing that past year CUD increased from 0.90 per cent to 1.23 per cent. According to Cerdá and colleagues (2020), the enhanced potency of cannabis products available in the market after the adoption of legalization policies could contribute to understanding the upward CUD trends across the four states.

Studies exploring cannabis-related hospitalization in specific states draw similar conclusions. Wang and colleagues (2017), for example, show that hospitalizations, emergency department visits, and regional poison centre calls linked to cannabis exposure increased after legalization in Colorado, which is consistent with prior research (Maxwell and Mendelson 2016). By looking at cannabis-related public health indicators between time periods before and after Colorado's drug policy reform in 2009, Davis et al (2016) also evaluate the health effects of changes in the legal status of cannabis. They demonstrate that hospital discharges coded as cannabis-dependent increased 1 per cent per month (95 per cent confidence interval [CI] = 0.8, 1.1, probability [p] < 0.001) from 2007 to 2013, whereas poison centre calls rose 0.8 per cent per month (95 per cent CI = 0.2, 1.4, $p < 0.01$) after 2009. Research shows that cannabis-related encounters and hospitalizations increased following legalization even when compared to similar episodes associated with alcohol (Calcaterra et al 2019). Additional health impacts linked to cannabis legalization for recreational purposes assessed by different scholars include increases in cyclic vomiting syndrome hospitalizations (Bhandari et al 2019), mental health diagnoses in emergency visits with cannabis-related diagnostic codes (Hall et al 2018), maxillary and skull base fracture attributed to falls (Sokoya et al 2018), and severe burns due to THC extraction from cannabis plants using butane (Monte, Zane, and Heard 2015).

Darnell and Bitney (2017) report slightly different patterns in the case of Washington State. They show that cannabis abuse treatment admissions were not affected by the enactment of I-502, the bill legalizing limited possession for adults and private consumption of nonmedical cannabis, as well as its licensed production and sale. Treatment admissions, indeed, fell as a percentage of all admissions in Washington State in recent years, although there is no evidence indicating that legalization motivated this change (Darnell and Bitney 2017). Estoup and colleagues (2016) also find insignificant impacts on adolescent problematic drug use in Seattle, Washington State. In a study conducted with a sample of students enrolled in five high schools in the greater Seattle area, they maintain that legalization did not increase the frequency of cannabis use among students even though they experienced higher levels of perceived risks and increased negative consequences post drug policy reform.

The impacts of Oregon's cannabis legalization on heavier consumption were explored by Kerr, Bae, and Koval (2018). Despite their finding that the sporadic use of cannabis one to five days in the past month in Oregon increased after liberalization vis-à-vis states that did not legalize the psychoactive substance within the US, heavier and problematic consumption did not experience an upward trend. Kerr, Bae, and Koval (2018), in particular, demonstrate that prevalence rates did not rise with consumption of 10 or more days during the past month. Nonetheless, they warn about the necessity of contemplating regional and subpopulation differences, policy heterogeneity, secular changes in substance use, and impacts over time.

Since the potential harms associated with cannabis are largely attributable to long-term heavy consumption, different scholars highlight the limitations of studies conducted in the US (Hall, Degenhardt, and Lynskey 2001; Hall and Lynskey 2020). According to Caulkins (2017), a long-term national legalization policy in the US would replace the problems of crime and black markets with potentially acute health harms. Caulkins (2017) claims that the legalization of cannabis for recreational purposes is likely to create 40 billion additional hours of intoxication, with roughly half of the consumers meeting the medical criteria for substance use disorder. The potential consequences of a cannabis policy reform in the US are nonetheless expected to impact the markets only decades after its full implementation. National legalization, in Caulkins' (2017, 50) own words, could generate 'a problem of potentially excessive consumption of a "temptation good" whose acute effects are performance degrading, not performance-enhancing'.

Yet cannabis legalization laws are likely to impact the use rates of other drugs in different ways. Various studies show that certain drug liberalization policies adopted in the US have presented social benefits such as reducing opioid analgesic overdose mortality (Bachhuber et al 2014) or opioid problematic use and deaths related to painkillers (Powell, Pacula, and Jacobson 2018). Wen and Hockenberry (2018), for example, demonstrate that recreational cannabis laws adopted within the US were associated with a 6.38 per cent decrease in opioid prescribing rates. In their quantitative analysis, the estimated lower rate of opioid prescriptions associated with the new legal status of cannabis in Alaska, Colorado, Washington State, and Oregon was particularly concentrated in Schedule II of the Controlled Substance Act scheduling (-7.79 per cent; 95 per cent CI, -14.73 per cent to approximately -0.85 per cent).

The Portuguese decriminalization of illicit drugs

Although the use of drugs is still prohibited under decriminalization, the removal of criminal penalties for the possession of drugs is likely to have consequences on consumption disorders. In Portugal, for instance, Pombo and da Costa (2016) conducted a before-and-after empirical study to evaluate the impacts of the country's 2001 drug policy reform on heroin problematic use trends. Their findings indicate that treatment demand declined 37 per cent and drug patients became older and better educated under decriminalization. Despite that, users entering treatment reported more cocaine use, HIV infections decreased while incidences of HCV remained stable. Consistent with prior scholarly works in the field (Negreiros and Magalhães 2009), Félix, Portugal, and Tavares (2017) extend the analysis to other psychoactive substances and demonstrate that the number of clients entering treatment decreased as well as drug-related deaths and the incidence of problematic users among HIV-positive individuals.

Hughes and Stevens (2010) developed a more sophisticated methodological approach and incorporated Italy and Spain as a control group in their analysis. They show that the prevalence of problematic drug use in Portugal, particularly intravenous consumption, declined between 2001 and 2007, whereas Italy and Spain witnessed the opposite trend. Significant reductions were also reported in mortality, HIV, HCV, and tuberculosis rates. In the case of drug-related deaths, despite the three nations showing declines, the downward trend in Portugal was more pronounced than in Italy and Spain. Unlike the results presented by Pinto Coelho (2010), the decline in drug-related deaths is consistent with other empirical evaluations (Greenwald 2009; Hughes and Stevens 2012). However, Hughes and Stevens (2010) note that reductions in opiate-related deaths, perhaps the major driver of the reform, are not likely to reflect simply the effects of decriminalization, but rather a large increase in the provision and uptake of treatment, especially low-threshold opiate substitution programs.

Notwithstanding decriminalization seems to have positive health impacts among problematic users of hard drugs, the evidence for less dangerous drugs like cannabis is the opposite. By conducting a retrospective observational study, Gonçalves-Pinho, Bragança, and Freitas (2019) find that the number of hospitalizations with a primary diagnosis of psychotic disorders and schizophrenia associated with cannabis use increased 29.4 times between 2000 and 2015. From all these hospitalizations, those with a secondary diagnosis of cannabis use rose from 0.87 per cent in 2000 to 10.60 per cent in 2015. According to Gonçalves-Pinho, Bragança, and Freitas (2019), the growth of secondary diagnosis codification in administrative hospital databases and/or the increasing cannabis consumption rates among the Portuguese population likely explains the rise on psychotic disorder hospitalizations.

Other cannabis policy reforms

Subtler drug policy reforms are also likely to adversely impact health. The UK Drug Policy Commission (2008), for example, examines how the reclassification of cannabis affected the number of hospital admissions with cannabis as the main drug. The report finds that treatment for problematic consumption among adults increased from 6,700 in 2003–2004 to 13,087 in 2007–2008. The upward trend was particularly relevant among young people, as the number of admissions of individuals under the age of 18 increased from 3,800 to 11,582 during the same period. The report also reveals that there was also a steady rise in hospital admissions related to mental illness caused by cannabis. According to the UK Drug Policy Commission (2008), neither the increase of individuals in treatment nor the growth in the number of patients with cannabis-related mental and behavioural disorders necessarily reflect greater problematic use. By contrast, the trend is likely the result of better detection practices, more provision for treatment, or even the long-term effects of prior peaks in cannabis use. In their smaller scale research, Kelly and Rasul (2014) estimate the impacts of the depenalization policy introduced between 2001 and 2002 in Lambeth, London.[7] They report a sharp increase of hospital admissions related to the use of hard drugs with concentrated impacts among younger cohorts. Although Kelly and Rasul (2014) do not properly test the so-called 'gateway hypothesis', they show that policy reforms that affect the marijuana market are associated with relevant repercussions for individuals consuming harder drugs.

Yet the health consequences of drug consumption may also reflect the social marginalization of users. Structural factors such as poverty, inequality, lack of access to housing, and lower education are likely to mediate the impacts of policy reforms. Scholarly works have shown that the harmful patterns of drug consumption are often concentrated in socioeconomic deprived populations (Wilkinson 1996; Wadsworth et al 2004; Seddon 2006; Wilkinson and Pickett 2008; Stevens 2011) while drug-related deaths in high-income countries have a greater impact on the poor (Marmot and Wilkinson 1999). The evidence suggests that the likelihood of overdose is higher among unhoused users of drugs (Galea and Vlahov 2002), and unstable housing also increases the odds of seroconversion of HIV to AIDS among people who use injectable drugs (Strathdee et al 1997; Corneil et al 2006).

The legal status of drugs and crime

There are other harms associated with the use of psychoactive substances beyond the health domain and security is perhaps one of the most relevant. The connection between drugs and crime has been widely present in the public mind for many years. The conventional wisdom, often shaped by media outlets and politicians, suggests that problematic drug use is a major driving force behind criminal behaviour. The so-called 'drug-crime nexus' has exerted increasing influence among government officials around the world, affecting policymaking in different public areas such as criminal justice, security, and health.

The drug-crime nexus, however, is not imaginary. Since buyers and sellers of illicit drugs cannot resolve their disputes through public institutions such as courts or law enforcement, the use of violence, at least as a last resource, is always a possibility (Mayntz 2017). Empirical evidence also suggests that drugs and crime are frequently found together at the individual level. Several scholarly works, for example, have demonstrated that people who use drugs exhibit significantly higher average crime rates than nonusers (Chaiken and Chaiken 1990; Nurco, Hanlon, and Kinlock 1991; Harrison and Gfroerer 1992; Yacoubian and Kane 1998; French et al 2000; Bennett, Holloway, Farrington 2008). Additionally, the same person may commit five times as many offenses under the influence of drugs than when sober (MacCoun and Reuter 2001a). Moreover, a high proportion of the prison population are users of drugs (Lurigio and Swartz 1999). According to Bean (2008), data suggest that heroin users, perhaps more than individuals consuming other types of illegal psychoactive substances, are likely to follow these criminal patterns.

Despite drugs and crime being intertwined in a plethora of ways, their interaction is more complex than often portrayed by conventional wisdom and policy thinking (Seddon 2000; Keene 2005; Hughes and Anthony 2006; Allen 2007; DerGhougassian and Cutrona 2015). The fact that drugs and crime are correlated does not indicate that there is a causal relationship (Goode 1997). Most people who use illicit drugs are not engaged in other forms of criminal behaviour despite their strong statistical association. As MacCoun, Kilmer, and Reuter (2003) note, the causal influences between illegal drug use and crime are neither deterministic nor unconditional. The vast majority of users are not criminally active, and the drug-crime nexus varies across individuals, substances, situations, and over time.

As an attempt to untangle the complex relationship between drugs and crime beyond conventional wisdom, research in fields such as political science, sociology, criminology, and even health sciences have developed different theoretical models and conceptual tools. Goldstein's (1985) seminal work is often cited as the one of the first theoretical attempts aimed at understanding how drugs and violence are connected. His tripartite typology divides the relationship between the two phenomena into three specific types: psychopharmacological, economic-compulsive, and systemic. The psychopharmacological model suggests that individuals may become excitable, irrational, and violent after using drugs such as alcohol, stimulants, barbiturates, and phencyclidine. The economic-compulsive model, on the other hand, indicates that people who use drugs, particularly those using expensive substances such as heroin and cocaine, engage in crime to obtain money to support their problematic behaviour. Finally, in the systemic connection, violence is perceived as intrinsic to the involvement in the drug trade. In the last model, market interactions generate aggressive patterns of behaviour, including turf wars over the territory between rival organizations, competition among criminals, violent retaliation, and contract disputes (Goldstein 1985).

Yet Goldstein's (1985) pathbreaking work does not necessarily exhaust the possible ways in which drugs and crime are associated. Although theories on the drug-crime connection often build upon his tripartite model, the focus of Goldstein's (1985) work is violence and not crime. As Goode (1997) claims, albeit sometimes intertwined, these are conceptually different phenomena. Based on this analytical distinction, the theories explaining the relationship between drugs and crime can be divided into three major groups: (i) those that suggest that drug consumption leads to criminal behaviour, (ii) those that claim that crime causes drug use, and (iii) those that maintain that drugs and crime are related to other factors.

The first strand of relevant theorizing posits that drug use leads to crime, suggesting that criminal behaviour is likely to develop with high consumption rates. Drawing on Becker's (1968) economic theory of crime, the 'enslavement' approach is perhaps the most representative approximation within this group. It holds that problematic users turn to crime when the costs of using drugs cannot be afforded with a regular and legitimate job (Goode 1997). Similar to Goldstein's (1985) economic-compulsive model, income-generating crimes such as theft, burglary, and robbery result from addictive behaviours. The so-called psychopharmacological explanations provide an even simpler causal relationship to illuminate the roots of criminal behaviour. Whether the effects of drug consumption are direct or linked to specific situational factors, this approximation maintains that certain chemical properties of drugs are likely to generate negative behavioural outcomes such as crime (Bennet and Holloway 2005). That is to say, individuals may eventually become excitable, irrational, and violent as a result of either short- or long-term drug ingestion (Goldstein 1985).

A second group of theories reverses the logic and claims that crime comes first and problematic use follows. Despite this approximation being less relevant in the literature, several scholars have identified crime as a causal mechanism behind the consumption of psychoactive substances. According to Collins, Hubbard, and Rachal (1985), there are two specific pathways leading to drug abuse: financial and reciprocal. While the first mechanism suggests that crime provides the financial resources needed to engage in expensive drug use, the second indicates that drug consumption is not etiologically important to criminal behaviour as the two factors reinforce each other. The relevance of the criminal 'lifestyle' is consistent with the work of scholars such as Auld, Dorn, and South (1986). In a study conducted during the mid-1980s, they maintain that young people involved in the 'irregular economy' due to impoverished conditions eventually come into contact with the supply and use of illicit drugs. As part of their lifestyle, heroin consumption becomes episodic and irregular rather than an enslaving condition (Auld, Dorn, and South 1986). The use of drugs, for example, could be perceived as a 'chemical recreation' that individuals use to celebrate the successful commission of a crime (Menard, Mihalic, and Huizinga 2001).

Other scholarly works posit that both of these models are somehow correct but claim that the relationship between drug consumption and crime could be bidirectional (White and Gorman 2000). In the 'reciprocal model', as identified by Bennet and Holloway (2005, 2007), drug use may cause crime and crime may cause drug use. The connection, in other words, is not unidirectional but more complex and could even change depending on the circumstances. Rather than one factor causing the other and vice versa, research has also shown that it is possible that the relationship could lead to intensification. Huizinga, Menard, and Elliot (1989), for instance, contend that once drug use and serious delinquency are initiated, polydrug consumption contributes to the maintenance of criminal behaviour.

The notion of causality underlying both groups of theories has been extensively challenged. Scholars have pointed out that the relationship conceived by their proponents, particularly in the first case, is mechanical and derives from a static deterministic conception of human action (Seddon 2000; Simpson 2003; Keene 2005). The empirical testing underlying their theoretical assumptions has been also called into question (Kleiman, Caulkins, and Hawken 2011). Fagan (1990), for instance, claims that there are fundamental differences between psychoactive substances in their association with aggression. He further states that the effects of intoxicants also change based on the amounts used per unit of body weight, tolerance, and genetic or biological predisposition.[8] As Parker and Newcomer (1987, 347) put it in their study of heroin use and crime, 'There are likely to be variations in the drugs–crime relationship in different localities at different times for different drugs'.

Not surprisingly, the third strand of relevant theorizing adds complexity to the relationship between drugs and crime. By rejecting the disciplinary tradition based on causation and determinism, scholars within this group contend that either a third variable mediates the drug-crime nexus or that both phenomena are influenced by a complex set of factors. Gottfredson and Hirschi (1990), for example, claim that it is not drug consumption that causes crime or vice versa but rather a specific psychological feature: the absence of self-control. When examined more closely, Keene (2005) agrees that psychological factors mediate the relationship between drugs and crime. Beyond individual influences, drug consumption and crime may also have common environmental driving forces. In this variant approach, the user is no longer perceived as the real problem as attention shifts to a set of underlying socioeconomic conditions that disproportionately affect a significant majority of users with problematic consumption patterns (Buchanan 2004). This view, therefore, emphasizes that crime and drug consumption coexist in a complex settings of problematic behaviours. A variety of structural factors, including social exclusion (Foster 2000), inequality (Hughes and Anthony 2006; Wilkinson and Pickett 2008; Stevens 2011), houselessness (Manzoni et al 2006), family problems (Dembo et al 1994), or aspects intrinsic to drug markets (Grogger and Willis 2000; Darke 2010) are likely to shape the scale and distribution of drug use and crime.

Prior empirical work

The empirical association between drug use and crime can be determined in different ways. As Bennett and Holloway (2005) point out, research can look at the proportion of users who commit crimes or the proportion of criminals who consume drugs. The frequency with which people who use drugs violate the law or criminals consume illicit substances can also illuminate the relationship between the two phenomena. To a greater or lesser extent, the first two groups of theories build their assumptions on these methodological approaches.

The samples, however, may not be representative of the universe being studied. Huizinga, Menard, and Elliot (1989) claim that studies drawing on preselected drug-using or delinquent populations are ill-prepared to make general inferences due to the population's limited representativeness. The lack of control groups clearly exacerbates this methodological shortcoming. Evaluations of the general population, on the other hand, may be useful for estimating general drug consumption trends but the low incidence of drug use and crime in these samples limit their effectiveness in assessing the relationship between psychoactive substances and criminal behaviour (Gandossy et al 1980). Furthermore, it is also possible that drugs and crime are part of a complex setting of correlated variables and problematic behaviours. While some quantitative studies take the drug-crime nexus further and include in their regression models additional intervening variables, the underlying socioeconomic forces are particularly visible through sociological and anthropological investigations.

Methodological caveats aside, several underlying assumptions have shaped the existing empirical literature in the field. Following Goode (1997), proponents of criminalization commonly contend that severe penalties for drug consumption and trafficking take criminals out of the streets and dissuade potential offenders from breaking the law, positively impacting crime rates. Prohibitionists such as Inciardi (1999), for instance, draw on the psychopharmacological link to claim that increases in drug use following legalization are likely to lead to rising crime rates due to the impact of psychoactive substances on the users' brains. As noted by Stevens (2011), the enslavement theory and economic-compulsive model have been also utilized to justify criminalization. Specifically, their supporters often maintain that the limited number of people using drugs due to the adoption of prohibitionist policies would decrease the level of crime (Stevens 2011).

Those in favour of legalization, by contrast, claim that drug liberalization policies will reduce crime in different ways. In addition to the elimination of drug possession for recreational purposes as a criminal offense, proponents of legalization often refer to both the economic-compulsive and the systemic model to substantiate their arguments. Babor and colleagues (2010) claim that the so-called legalizers believe that the removal of criminal penalties is likely to decrease the amount of acquisitive crime committed by problematic users as well as the violence related to drug markets. While falling prices is the mechanism underlying the first estimated effect of legalization, gang wars and other types of violent confrontations are expected to disappear if criminals are deprived of the high profits from illegal markets.

Notwithstanding the drug-crime nexus has been extensively discussed in the media, politics, and society in general, Goldstein's (1985) tripartite model and related theories have rarely been tested empirically (MacCoun, Kilmer, and Reuter 2003; Stevens 2011). Despite it being a fruitful area of academic inquiry, the scholarly literature evaluating how policy changes influence the relationship between drug use and criminal behaviour is particularly scant (McBride, VanderWaal, and Terry-McElrath 2003; Dragone et al 2019). Only a limited number of studies have empirically tested how depenalization, decriminalization, or legalization affect the various ways in which crime and drug consumption are related. Most of the studies revolve around cannabis liberalization policies adopted in the US, especially after several states recently legalized its medical and recreational use.

Cannabis liberalization policies in the US

Even though the evidence on the effects of drug liberalization policies on crime in the US comes mainly from research on medical cannabis laws,[9] an increasing number of academic studies focus on recreational legalization. Dills, Goffard, and Miron (2017) conduct one of the first analyses at the aggregate level, showing that both early and recent cannabis liberalization policies had a minimal impact on youth criminal behaviour.[10] Despite the evidence suggesting that legalization is associated with increased petty crimes such as shoplifting, they claim that cannabis liberalization in general does not significantly affect self-reported criminal behaviour. This is consistent with the work of Maier, Manes, and Koppenhofer (2017), who reveal a lack of relationship between states that depenalized cannabis and crime rates.[11] They even show that states that changed the legal status of cannabis experienced a significant reduction in all crimes (except murder), although fluctuations were not attributable to drug policy reform. Huber III, Newman, and LaFave (2016), however, report slightly different results. Unlike the effects of medical legislation evaluated in their peer-reviewed article, they reveal that the 15 states that adopted a cannabis depenalization scheme between 1970 and 2012 experienced approximately 65,000 and 9,300 additional burglaries and robberies respectively. Focusing on the cases of Colorado, Oregon, and Washington State, Stamm and Murphy (2019) also observe that both violent and property crime increased in the years following the legalization of recreational cannabis. Since Stamm and Murphy (2019) do not include a control group in their analysis, crime patterns are nonetheless not attributable to drug policy reform.[12]

At the county level, research in the US has also produced mixed results. Dragone and colleagues (2019) find no evidence that cannabis legalization in the state of Washington led to increasing crime rates. On the contrary, they demonstrate that rapes and property crimes drop substantially on the Washington side of the border compared to Oregon before legalization and relative to the pre-reform period. Although their analysis is limited to drug-related offenses, Hao and Cowan (2020) show that cannabis possession arrests rose roughly 30 per cent in counties neighbouring the states of Colorado and Washington. By considering the spillover effects of drug policy reforms, they contend that law enforcement efforts to penalize cannabis in criminalizing states are complicated by neighbouring states' choices to legalize the recreational use of the substance. A similar study conducted by DeAngelo, Gittings, and Ross (2018) in specific jurisdictions within Los Angeles County also demonstrates that 'low priority initiatives', a policy that instructs police to de-emphasize law enforcement against minor cannabis possession offenses, resulted in fewer arrests for possession in adopting areas relative to non-adopting ones.

Since commercial legalization is materialized through the operation of retail dispensaries, a final strand of empirical research conducted within the US has focused on neighbourhood security. In the case of Denver, Colorado, for example, studies reveal that an additional cannabis outlet leads to a reduction of a variety of disaggregated categories of crimes (Burkhardt and Goemans 2019; Brinkman and Mok-Lamme 2019). Hughes, Schaible, and Jimmerson (2019), however, show the exact opposite results. Drawing on the routine activity theory[13] (Cohen and Felson 1979) and broken windows theory[14] (Kelling and Wilson 1982), they find that, except for murder and auto theft, recreational cannabis outlets are associated with statistically significant increases in neighbourhood crime rates and disorder. Research in Denver also indicates that the spillover effects of dispensaries can even affect the areas adjacent to where cannabis is legally sold (Freisthler et al 2017). Focusing on Seattle, Bellevue, and Tacoma, Washington State, Thacker and colleagues (2021) report similar patterns after the opening of legal retail outlets. They claim, however, that increases in crime are generally quite small, casting doubt as to whether any specific policy action is warranted.

Portugal's decriminalization of illicit drugs

Hughes and Stevens (2010) evaluate the impacts of Portugal's decriminalization on different crimes. Between the periods 1995–1999 and 2000–2004, they observe a 9 per cent increase in crimes strongly linked to drugs, with street robberies, theft from motor vehicles, and theft of motor vehicles leading the ranking. Other forms of theft such as assaults and robberies of post offices and theft from homes and businesses experience the opposite trend (Hughes and Stevens 2010). Homicides, on the other hand, fluctuated after the implementation of decriminalization, rising in the aftermath of drug policy reform and returning to 2001 levels by 2011 (Stevens et al 2019). Nonetheless, the lack of clear crime patterns distinct from those of neighbouring European countries suggests that Portugal's crime fluctuations are not directly attributable to decriminalization (Hughes and Stevens 2010; Laqueur 2014). In the realm of drug offenses, the available evidence is less ambiguous. Laqueur (2014) shows that the drug offender prison population dropped significantly after 2001–2002, although she claims that the buildup of Portugal's incarcerated population is likely explained by the embracing of de facto practices already present among criminal courts rather than by decriminalization itself. According to Quintas and Arana (2017), by reducing the burden on the criminal justice system, law enforcement is able to direct its policing resources towards other forms of crime.

Depenalization efforts in the UK

Unlike the cases of legalization or decriminalization, where there is practically no room for interpretation of the law, depenalization often paves the way for greater police discretion. Empirical evaluations of subtler drug policy reforms thus consider an additional critical dimension: law enforcement.

Adda, McConnell, and Rasul (2014), for example, measure the impact on crime of cannabis depenalization in the London borough of Lambeth. Based on administrative records of the Metropolitan Police Service between 1998 and 2006, they claim that an experiment unilaterally introduced by the local police in 2001, known as the Lambeth Cannabis Warning Scheme, led to the reduction of the total number of crimes despite an increase of cannabis-related offenses. According to Adda, McConnell, and Rasul (2014), depenalization caused a behavioural response from law enforcement in two different dimensions: the reduction of penalties for being caught with marijuana and, more importantly, the relocation of police efforts and resources towards nondrug crimes. The limited or inexistent impacts of depenalization on crime were also reported at the national level. By using individual-level panel data for England and Wales from 2003 to 2006, Braakman and Jones (2014) show that crime rates were not affected by the 2004 reclassification of cannabis. Although property crimes for the 15-to-17-year-old group slightly increased, a pattern attributed to low-level crimes, Braakman and Jones (2014) claim that no major transformations of criminal or risky behaviour were observed in their study.

Conclusions

The review of the literature evaluating the relationship between changes in the legal status of drugs and adverse health consequences suggests that information is often poorly quantified, at least when compared to other studies focusing on simple drug consumption patterns. Relevant indicators such as the potency of drugs, for example, have been widely unexplored. Most of the evidence is concentrated in high-income countries and revolves largely around cannabis-related harms. Scholarly research in this field also suffers from time-related limitations. Since the potential harms associated with drugs are largely attributable to long-term heavy consumption, the empirical assessments of recently adopted drug policy reforms may not be totally illustrative of major health complications.

The evidence in the Netherlands suggests that there is no direct association between heavy cannabis consumption and coffee shops or proximity to these authorized outlets. Research indicates, however, that cannabis users in the country are more likely to be admitted into treatment than elsewhere in Europe. Since higher treatment rates do not necessarily imply that the demand for medical assistance grew as a result of depenalization, some scholars identify greater cannabis potency or a more generous and proactive health policy as possible driving forces. More recent empirical evidence also suggests that problematic consumption, measured by the number of drug-related hospital admissions, is not unique to the Netherlands but rather another example of a general trend observed in Europe.

The UK provides another possibility to evaluate the health impacts of depenalization, even though the reclassification of cannabis is considered a subtler drug policy reform compared to the Dutch version. The available evidence reveals that hospital admissions related to mental illness caused by cannabis rose after depenalization. Furthermore, treatment for problematic cannabis consumption also increased, particularly among younger cohorts. A similar upward trend was reported in terms of hard drugs, suggesting that cannabis control policies are likely to affect individuals using other illicit drugs such as cocaine, crack, heroin, crystal-meth, LSD, ecstasy, or methadone. Further exploration is warranted in future studies to test if the statistical association between cannabis consumption and other drugs is likely to validate or invalidate the gateway hypothesis.

In Portugal, the evidence overwhelmingly shows that decriminalization had a positive impact on most of the country's drug-related health indicators. Research reveals that problematic drug use, especially intravenous consumption, decreased following the 2001 reform. Both single-case studies and controlled comparisons also demonstrate a significant drop in the number of HIV infections as well as drug-related deaths. Except for the case of cannabis, where the evidence is mixed, hospitalizations decreased substantially after decriminalization. Scholars claim, however, that the improvement in drug-related indicators is intimately linked to the provision and uptake of treatment rather than the law reform itself.

Unfortunately, scholarly research on other states that have decriminalized the use of cannabis is limited. In Australia, for example, studies at the subnational level have only evaluated the impacts of the system of expiation notices on cannabis frequency of use, while treatment, hospitalization, and long-term drug-related harms remain widely unexplored. Still the available evidence shows mixed results. While research indicates that changes in the legal status of cannabis did not affect the frequency of its consumption, alternative accounts demonstrate that the decriminalization framework adopted in some of the Australian states and territories favoured higher cannabis consumption levels.

In the US, by contrast, the empirical evidence is relatively robust. Research on the impacts of cannabis liberalization policies adopted since the 1970s shows that depenalization was associated with increasing hospital emergency room episodes. This is consistent with recent research in the field. Despite the impacts varying from state to state, studies predominantly confirm that hospitalizations, emergency department visits, and regional poison centre calls are likely to increase after recreational cannabis legalization. The evidence on problematic use is less conclusive, however. While some studies show that CUD prevalence rates, particularly among adolescents, increased after drug policy reform, other accounts report the opposite results for both adolescent and young adult college students.

Finally, only a limited number of studies have empirically tested how changes in the legal status of drugs affect criminal behaviour. Even though the drug-crime nexus has been in the spotlight among media outlets and politicians across the world, the empirical evidence available about the different ways in which these phenomena are related is still scarce. Most of the scholarly works revolve around medical and recreational cannabis liberalization policies adopted in the US or other high-income countries.

In the US case, the evidence at the state, county, and neighbourhood levels is far from conclusive. Aggregate-level analyses revolve around both cannabis depenalization and recreational legalization, showing three different outcomes following drug policy reform: in some cases crimes increased, in others they decreased, and in still others there was no evidence of substantial change. Research focusing on specific counties, on the other hand, reveals that rapes and property crimes dropped after recreational cannabis legalization, whereas the evidence on drug possession offenses is mixed. Finally, the most detailed information is found at the neighbourhood level. Despite evidence indicating that additional cannabis outlets lead to a reduction in crime, a slightly greater number of studies find the opposite result. That is to say, research demonstrates statistically significant increases in neighbourhood crime rates as well as spillover effects in areas adjacent to new legal cannabis outlets.

The Portuguese experience suggests that crimes strongly linked to drugs such as street robberies, theft from motor vehicles, and theft of motor vehicles increased after decriminalization, although the evidence is relatively insignificant to attribute these fluctuations to drug policy reform. In fact, research shows that other forms of theft such as assaults and robberies from post offices experienced the opposite trend after 2001. Furthermore, studies demonstrate that Portugal's decreasing drug offender prison population is associated with the adoption of different practices that were already present before decriminalization.

The ways in which law enforcement practices changed as a result of liberalization drug policies were also evaluated in the UK. At both the national and local levels, the empirical evidence, albeit limited, suggests that depenalization had insignificant impacts on different types of crime. Interestingly, studies also indicate that the reclassification of cannabis at the local level transformed law enforcement practices, as police efforts and resources were eventually reallocated towards nondrug crimes.

3

The US and the Origins of Criminalization

Between April 1991 and June 1992, several individuals were sentenced to lengthy prison terms after trying to sell crack cocaine to Pamela Mersky, an undercover agent working for the US Drug Enforcement Administration (DEA) in Boston and its suburbs (US Court of Appeals 1994). Among the individuals sentenced to mandatory prison was Paulita Cadiz, a young pregnant woman with no criminal record. According to the investigations, the 18-year-old woman went for a 10-minute car ride with a drug dealer who asked her to meet the undercover agent. Pamela Mersky recorded Cadiz offering to approach the drug dealer's car before the DEA officer went to another nearby vehicle to purchase crack cocaine (Brelis 1992). Even though Cadiz pleaded innocent, arguing that she was not aware of the illicit transaction, she received a mandatory 10-year prison sentence for aiding the drug dealer. The imprisonment of first-time offenders was not an extraordinary event in the US by the time Cadiz received her sentence. In 1992, drug offenders accounted for over half of federal prison population (Miller and Freed 1994). Similar to Cadiz, about 36 per cent of those prisoners could be classified as 'low-level' drug offenders (Roth 1994). Reports show that the prison population with no criminal history in 1992 were serving 2.5 times as long as their 1985 counterparts (Katz and Durham 1994).

In an effort to draw attention to the stringency of the US criminal justice system during the 1990s, especially in terms of mandatory minimum sentences, President Bill Clinton's attorney general, Janet Reno, ordered the Department of Justice to conduct a study on nonviolent drug offenders incarcerated in the US (Katz and Durham 1994). 'It does not help to send someone off to prison for three years, pluck them out of the community and then plunk them back down', Reno said in an interview (as cited in Wilkinson 1993). Although the report she requested demonstrated the highly punitive and disproportionate nature of the US criminal justice system,

Reno's attempts to transform it, as has happened during most administrations so far, were rather limited.

The US federal drug policy has barely changed over the last 40 years (Reuter 2013). Since the enactment of the Harrison Act in 1914, the executive branch, Congress, and a growing federal bureaucracy have gradually contributed to the escalation of a fully-fledged 'war on drugs'. The most recent estimates suggest that the US has spent more than US$1 trillion since President Richard Nixon announced to the American people at a press conference in 1971 that illicit drug abuse was the country's 'public enemy number one'. Stringent sentencing laws and hardline enforcement have resulted in the world's largest prison population, accounting for approximately 2.3 million people behind bars – around one-fifth incarcerated for a drug law violation (Martin et al 2019).

Overseas, the US has also sponsored the adoption of a set of policies that promotes the expansion of the military's role in fighting drug trafficking (Rosen 2014; Cutrona 2017). Striking 'at the supply side of the drug equation', as President Nixon (1971) claimed, became Washington's top priority in Latin America. Since the unveiling of Operation Intercept, the first modern attempt to stop illicit drugs at their source, the US has spent billions in waging a war on drugs abroad. Colombia, for example, received almost US$8 billion over a decade, becoming the world's third largest recipient of US military aid, surpassed only by Israel and Egypt (Bagley 2012). By the 1990s, these programs were central to Washington's foreign policy, accounting for more than 92 per cent of US military and police aid to the Western Hemisphere (Andreas and Nadelmann 2006).

This chapter traces back the origins and evolution of the US criminalization policy still prevailing at the federal level. Since Washington's punitive efforts have also shaped the criminalization of drugs worldwide, this chapter briefly discusses key foreign policy interventions at both the multilateral and bilateral levels. It also explores the country's major trends of illicit drug use, health harms associated with consumption, and drug-related security concerns between 1980 and 2012, a phase of increased criminalization that anticipated drastic liberalization reforms adopted at the state level.

This chapter proceeds in three main sections. The first part addresses in more detail the origins and evolution of the US's punitive policy against illicit drugs, from the years prior to the sanctioning of the Harrison Act of 1914 to the end of the Trump administration, when various states had already liberalized cannabis at different levels. The second section describes the main features of the US drug policy today, paying special attention to its normative and institutional architecture at the federal level. The final section explores major trends associated with illicit drug use during the peak of punitivism. We present an analysis of various indicators such as prevalence, drug-related pathologies, overdoses, homicides, incarceration, and other relevant data.

It is important to highlight that this chapter is not placing criminalization under empirical scrutiny, but rather intends to understand patterns associated with illicit drug use and other policy trends under a punitive landscape. The chapter concludes by evaluating the strengths and weaknesses of the US drug policy prevailing at the federal level.

The empirical evidence provided in this chapter is subject to various methodological caveats. Unlike the Argentinian, Uruguayan, and Portuguese cases, the US federal drug policy has been characterized by continuity rather than change – cannabis[1] liberalization initiatives were developed at the state level and are not widely discussed here. This chapter, therefore, neither evaluates the impacts of criminalization nor relies on comparative data or a control group to provide an estimate of the effects if there had been no criminalization of use and possession of illicit drugs. Though beyond the scope of this chapter, the ongoing cannabis liberalization reforms adopted in several states could help to mitigate this difficulty. To learn more about these alternatives, the so-called 'bifurcation' of US drug control policy (Stevens 2011) and the exploration of its impacts are briefly reviewed in Chapters 1 and 2 of this book.

The emergence of the punitive model

By the early twentieth century, most psychoactive substances were legal in the US. Even though state and municipal legislation was gradually passed from coast to coast after San Francisco forbade smoking opium in 1875, the sale and consumption of drugs were not prohibited by federal law (Goode 1997). Other than tariffs, no formal restriction was placed upon importation, and psychoactive substances such as cocaine and heroin were widely available within the US territory. Either prescribed by doctors or purchased in groceries, drugs became a popular item among citizens due to a long-standing acquiescent attitude privileging the consumer's choice and self-treatment (Bertram et al 1996). For example, a six-ounce glass of a popular soft drink like Wiseola, Celery-Cola, or Koca-Nola – at the time three of Coca-Cola's larger competitors in the national market – contained approximately two milligrams of cocaine (Spillane 1999).

Yet counterdrug legislation at the local level was widely ineffective in curbing consumption due to different law enforcement problems. By 1900, the US harboured approximately 250,000 problematic users and drug consumption became a great challenge to medical and legal institutions (Musto 1973). Notwithstanding psychoactive substances were present across practically every socioeconomic stratum, problematic users were often identified with different foreign groups and internal minorities (Reinarman and Levine 1997). For example, while opium and its derivates were associated with the Chinese population entering the US during the second half of the nineteenth century, cocaine (crack cocaine) and cannabis – or 'marijuana' as it was coined to highlight the drug's 'Mexican-ness' – were commonly linked to African Americans and Mexicans, respectively. This, of course, contributed to exacerbating anti-immigrant sentiments.

Concerns about drug use in the US started growing fast at the beginning of the 1900s. The *laissez-faire* attitude, favouring individuals' self-administration, gave way to a greater awareness of the harmful potential of drugs. Moral entrepreneurs, particularly American missionaries returning from Asia, began to pressure the federal government, urging them to avoid the negative consequences of other countries' drug trade (Andreas and Nadelmann 2006). Physicians and pharmacists, whose professional consolidation involved the regulation of patent medicines, reinforced the importance of instituting controls to drug availability and misuse. The supply and prescription of drugs appeared more feasible as concerns among the general population spread. Bertram and colleagues (1996) note that the emergence of a punitive consensus among actors was rooted in the puritanical strain in American culture, commonly based on the original ideas of rural nineteenth-century Methodism, Baptism, Presbyterianism, and Congregationalism.

The role of organizations such as the American Pharmaceutical Association and the American Medical Association became visible with the enactment of the District of Columbia Pharmacy Act in 1906. By protecting registered pharmacists from those without a license or door-to-door peddlers, the law prohibited the free sale of habit-forming drugs such as opium, morphine, cocaine, and chloral hydrate. The enactment of the Pharmacy Act, together with the belief that the US had a moral obligation to develop a national law before asking other countries to do the same, paved the way for the first proposed federal legislation (Musto 1973). The Foster Bill, introduced in the House of Representatives in 1910, was the direct antecedent of the Harrison Act. The lack of consensus among drug-trade leaders, however, doomed the initiative to failure.

Before it materialized at home, the US was already leading an international crusade to prohibit the trade of opium. In 1909, 13 countries were represented in the Shanghai Opium Commission, an international body trying to raise awareness of the dangers associated with opium consumption (Manuel 2021). The US delegation was led by physician Hamilton Wright, and Charles Henry Brent – the Episcopal Church's first missionary bishop of the Philippines – was the chairman of the meeting. Although nothing tangible came out of the Shanghai summit as the resolutions were merely recommendations, the US effectively set the foundation for the multilateral end of opium trade (Musto 1973).

Conditions for the approval of a federal drug control legislation were already in place by the end of 1914. The US government not only succeeded in pressuring other countries to sign the International Opium Convention at The Hague in 1912 (the first multilateral agreement with binding commitments), but it also reached a final compromise among different interest groups at home. The Harrison Narcotics Tax Act was passed by the National Congress on 17 December 1914, regulating for the first time the production, importation, and distribution of opiates and coca products. As Goode maintains (1997), the bill did not technically outlaw drugs, but it required that lawful manufacturers and dispensers were registered and taxed. Since prescribing psychoactive substances concerned states' rights, the federal government used instead its taxation powers to impose the law (Chawla 2004). In this context, unregistered drug distributors such as saloonkeepers could be easily prosecuted in the US. The main purpose was to contain psychoactive substance transactions within a legitimate medical realm (Courtwright 2015). Over the years, however, a series of rulings by the US Supreme Court determined that medical maintenance was illegal (Inciardi 1992).

The second and third Hague International Opium Conferences of 1913 and 1914 proved the US's growing influence worldwide. Although major powers like Great Britain, the Netherlands, and Portugal, who were directly involved in nonmedical opium trade, were largely unwilling to drastically restrict poppy cultivation and trade, the contracting powers agreed to control and regulate opium within their respective territories. Most importantly, the regulation of opium marked the strengthening of the international system and the birth of the contemporary drug control regime (Bewley-Taylor 2012).

Attention shifted to the alcohol problem during the 1920s. Nevertheless, the prohibition of certain types of beverages did not prevent many states from criminalizing the sale and possession of cannabis. Since the substance was finally withdrawn from the Harrison Act's final version, the only federal regulatory law before 1937 was the Pure Food and Drug Act of 1906, which required that cannabis had to be marked on the label of any drug sold to the public (Musto 1973). Yet the landscape changed by the mid-1930s, when Harry Anslinger, the 'drug czar' in charge of the newly created Federal Bureau of Narcotics (FBN), joined the battle of different governors, attorneys, and law enforcement officers in the country's Southwest (Bertram et al 1996). Perceiving it as a source of crime and deviant behaviour, law enforcement linked cannabis consumption to Mexican immigrants. Despite the presence of budget constraints to enforce the law, the National Congress echoed the anxiety of different interest groups and enacted the Marijuana Tax Act on 2 August 1937.

Public concerns about drugs changed with the onset of the Cold War. Accused of destroying Western society, illicit drugs were commonly tied to the 'communist threat' during the 1950s. Organized crime and juvenile delinquency, in particular, raised numerous moral questions, absorbing media attention. Harry Anslinger seized the opportunity and pressured for harsher drug legislation. In addition to the Boggs Act of 1951, which drastically increased penalties for cannabis use, Congress passed the Narcotic Control Act of 1956. According to McWilliams (1990, 116), the bill created 'the most punitive and repressive anti-narcotics legislation ever adopted by Congress'. Not only were the minimum and maximum penalties for all drug offenses increased, but also the death penalty could be imposed on any adult who sold heroin to minors.

The punitive paradigm entered a relative impasse during the 1960s. Different social forces emerged to challenge the mainstream approach sponsored by the FBN, supporting instead a medical perspective on psychoactive substances. In the midst of the 'hippie' counterculture that popularized drug use, the Johnson administration (1963–1969) reacted to the country's increasing consumption rates by passing the Narcotics Addict Rehabilitation Act of 1966. The new legislation said that 'addiction' was a mental illness, allowing people who used drugs to opt for treatment as a pretrial civil commitment instead of prosecution. The budget for treatment and prevention expanded from US$59 million in fiscal year 1970 to US$446.8 million in 1975 (Bertram et al 1996). By merging the FBN and the Bureau of Drug Abuse Control, President Johnson also created, in 1968, the Bureau of Narcotics and Dangerous Drugs.

After a period of relative inattention, the battle against illicit drugs revived during the Nixon administration (1969–1974). Drugs were transformed into a central policy concern and the voices against the punitive paradigm lost momentum. The president's hardline approach was confirmed in June 1971, when he openly declared that 'drug traffic is public enemy number one domestically in the US today and we must wage a total offensive, worldwide, nationwide, government-wide, and if I might say so, media wide' (Epstein 1990, 178). Between 1970 and 1975, counterdrug expenditures increased around 650 per cent, climbing from US$43 to US$321 million (Bertram et al 1996). Major legislative initiatives such as the Comprehensive Drug Abuse Prevention and Controlled Substances Act of 1970, which combined different laws into one statute and placed psychoactive substances under federal jurisdiction, accompanied Nixon's war on drugs. Furthermore, in 1973 Nixon created the DEA, a single-mission federal agency that has a presence in almost every country in the world.

On the international front, a couple of years earlier, in 1969, the US had launched Operation Intercept, the first modern initiative to stop drug trafficking at the source. By deploying approximately 2,000 customs and border patrol officers along the country's southern border, Washington advanced the largest peacetime search and seizure operation thus far (Carpenter 2003). This initiative complemented the US' efforts at the multilateral level. While the international trade became the first target of the United Nations, the system evolved to cover the supply side, beginning with organic drugs and ultimately incorporating psychotropic substances (Chawla 2004). The US played a key role in leading the 'strict control' coalition during the meetings that resulted in the multilateral agreements (McAllister 2000). Levine (2003) argues that the United Nations' 1961 Single Convention on Narcotic Drugs and the Convention on Psychotropic Substances of 1971 reflected Washington's main concerns and the country's internal epidemics.[2]

Neither of the presidents who immediately followed Nixon, Gerald Ford (1974–1977) and Jimmy Carter (1977–1981), continued with his hardline approach to drugs. Both administrations softened the anti-drug rhetoric, and the 'war' was virtually desecuritized or removed from the top of the national security agenda. The presence of more permissive attitudes towards drugs in different parts of the US emerged throughout the mid- and late 1970s. Not surprisingly, the rates of acceptance of the occasional use of certain types of drugs also increased, especially among youth (Carpenter 2003). Despite the de-escalation of the presidential rhetoric and the appearance of more tolerant attitudes, the expansion of the federal anti-drug apparatus continued. Between 1977 and 1981, the drug law enforcement budget increased from US$382 million to US$855 million (Bertram et al 1996).

Still, major transformations were accomplished at the state level. While some jurisdictions discussed the legalization alternative, the legislatures of 12 states shifted from strict prohibition to other forms of penalties: Oregon in 1973; Alaska, Colorado, and Ohio in 1975; California, Maine, and Minnesota in 1976; Mississippi, New York, North Carolina, and South Dakota in 1977; and Nebraska in 1978 (MacCoun and Reuter 2001).[3] Although these states are commonly referred as 'decriminalization states', these jurisdictions retained some of their original cannabis criminal offences (van het Loo et al 2003). As Single (1989, 462) notes, the 'decriminalization' laws in the US 'were much less radical than their name implies … they merely involved the elimination of jail terms for first offenders, which had already been an unusual sentence for most cases'.

The war on drugs escalated as never before with the arrival of Ronald Reagan in the Oval Office (1981–1989). The explosion of crack cocaine consumption and the related violence strengthened the plea for a more aggressive approach against illicit drugs. The president reacted by declaring 'an all-out war on big-time organized crime and the drug racketeers' (Marion 1994, 147). Even his wife, Nancy Reagan, joined the crusade and launched the 'Just Say No' campaign, encouraging children to reject experimenting with illicit drugs. Major institutional transformations accompanied Reagan's hardline approach in the US. The entire federal intelligence apparatus became engaged in counterdrug efforts and even the military's participation was ultimately secured by the amendment of the Posse Comitatus Act in 1981 and 1988, respectively, when Congress introduced different exceptions.[4] Moreover, in 1982 Vice President George HW Bush was appointed as the official in charge of the South Florida Task Force, the first of several agencies of this kind inaugurated to coordinate drug enforcement within the US.

In the legislative realm, in 1986 Congress passed the Anti-Drug Abuse Act, establishing new mandatory minimum prison sentences for certain drug offenses.[5] The bill was approved only weeks after Len Bias, a rising basketball star playing at the University of Maryland and signed by the Boston Celtics, died of a drug overdose at age 22, sparking new fears and countless media stories. Only two years later, the Anti-Drug Abuse Amendment Act of 1988 established the policy goal of a 'drug-free America' while also creating the Office of National Drug Control Policy (ONDCP). As William J Bennett (1989), the first US drug czar of the institution, maintained, the main goal of Washington's drug control policy during those years was to take drug users off the streets and deter new users from becoming deeply involved in that activity. Under these circumstances, public attitudes toward illicit drugs became less accepting. Surveys showed, for example, that only 21.8 per cent of college freshmen supported the legalization of cannabis in 1985, compared to 52.9 per cent in 1977 (Astin, Green, and Korn 1987).

Domestic developments were exacerbated by structural changes in the political economy of illicit drugs. The growing power of international drug cartels abroad and the fact that almost all illicit drugs circulating in the US were cultivated and processed in Latin America and the Caribbean reaffirmed Reagan's decision to intervene internationally (Bagley and Tokatlian 2007). In 1986, through National Security Directive 221, the president declared drug trafficking a national security threat, authorizing military and intelligence agencies to become involved in counterdrug efforts. In this context, federal spending in this realm skyrocketed from US$1.2 billion in 1981 to more than US$5.7 billion by the end of the 1980s (Carpenter 2003). The Andean Ridge, in particular, became the main target of Washington's escalating interdiction policies.

The war on drugs accelerated with the thawing of the Cold War. In his first televised national address as president, George HW Bush (1989–1993) called drugs 'the greatest domestic threat facing our nation today'. National initiatives such as the '1033 program', which distributed surplus military equipment to law enforcement agencies fighting against drugs, were rapidly launched. Furthermore, the arrival of the Republican president consolidated the US' emphasis on targeting the supply side of the political economy of illicit drugs. The Andean Initiative, designed to empower Latin American military and police forces to carry out counterdrug initiatives, drastically increased the US' foreign assistance. In 1990, for instance, a five-year aid package totalled US$231.6 million, of which all but US$48.6 million was designated for the police and military forces (Isacson 2005). By the end of the 1990s, the US international counterdrugs programs represented more than 92 per cent of all US military and police aid in the Western Hemisphere

(Andreas and Nadelmann 2006). According to Carpenter (2003), the US-led war on drugs emerged as a substitute for the fading communist threat.

Although the Clinton administration (1993–2001) attempted to deescalate the war on drugs, advocating for treatment for users instead of incarceration, most of the changes were limited to style and rhetoric. Neither the law enforcement budget nor the institutional architecture was significantly transformed during Clinton's two terms in office despite his attempts to downsize the federal drug bureaucracy and the search for new treatment initiatives within the criminal justice system (Bertram et al 1996).[6] On the contrary, concerns about illicit drugs and crime compelled Clinton to sign the 1994 Violent Crime Control and Law Enforcement Act into law, expanding mandatory minimum sentences and establishing a federal 'three-strikes' provision.[7] In effect, the new legal framework led to a new spike in the prison population. Since violence was no longer perceived as a domestic phenomenon, in 1995 the president also issued Decision Directive 42. By defining transnational crime as a national security threat, Washington opened the gates for a greater involvement in the drug affairs of several Latin American countries. The most illustrative supply-side strategy was Plan Colombia, approved at the end of the Clinton administration. The new security aid package accounted for US$7.5 billion, of which roughly US$1.3 billion was provided by the US government.

President George W. Bush (2001–2009) took office after strongly criticizing Clinton's approach to illicit drugs. During his election campaign, the Texas governor proposed to allocate US$2.7 billion to prevention and treatment programs, asserting that in the last seven and a half years, fighting drug abuse had ceased to be a national priority (Neal 2000). Nevertheless, terrorist attacks of 11 September 2001 made the war on drugs far less of a priority, and the US counterdrug strategy eventually became part of the war on terrorism (Andreas and Nadelmann 2006). Washington was no longer fighting against drug lords or guerrilla groups but against 'narco-terrorists'. Between 2000 and 2012, the US provided US$13.9 billion in military assistance to Latin America and the Caribbean, with 83 per cent going towards programs intended to limit the supply of illicit drugs (Isacson 2015). In this context, Colombia became the world's third largest recipient of US military aid, surpassed only by Israel and Egypt (Pizarro and Gaitán 2006). The administration's domestic efforts, of course, were widely subordinated to the antiterrorist crusade abroad. 'It's important for Americans to know that trafficking of drugs finances the world of terror, sustaining terrorists … if you quit drugs, you join the fight against terror in America', the president openly claimed (The White House 2001). The continuation of different interdiction initiatives at the source, coupled with his warlike rhetoric, did not prevent Bush from focusing on the demand for illicit drugs. In 2002, the president reiterated that the fight against drug use was at the centre of his agenda (Bush 2002). The Strategic Prevention Framework, for example, created an infrastructure that connected several prevention efforts at federal, state, local, and nongovernmental levels. In 2007, the president supported many of these projects by allocating US$79.2 million through the Drug Free Communities program (The White House 2006).

After calling the war on drug 'an utter failure' in 2004, the Obama administration (2009–2017) raised expectations among advocates of drug policy reform. The first change came in 2010, when Barack Obama signed the Fair Sentencing Act. By reversing the provisions of the 1986 Anti-Drug Abuse Act, he eliminated the mandatory minimum sentence for simple possession of crack cocaine and increased statutory fines (US Sentencing Commission 2015). With its implementation, the sentencing disparity between crack and powder cocaine offences was drastically reduced. The new legislation cut the ratio from 100:1 to 18:1 (Kleiman, Caulkins, and Hawken 2011). The Democratic president also lessened or eliminated the sentences of hundreds of nonviolent drug offenders, arguing that 'America is a nation of second chances'[8] (Obama 2015). The Synthetic Drug Abuse Prevention Act of 2012, on the other hand, placed different types of cannabinoids, stimulants, and hallucinogens into Schedule I of the Controlled Substances Act. As a response to the US' growing heroin and prescription opioid epidemic, Obama also signed the Comprehensive Addiction and Recovery Act in 2016. Focused on public health instead of criminalization, the bill aimed at strengthening prevention, treatment, and recovery efforts with an allocation of over US$181 million. For the first time since the Carter administration, the US was devoting more resources to public health than law enforcement and other agencies in charge of different interdiction programs (Lopez 2017).

Yet the most significant changes were developed at the state level, when Colorado and Washington State legalized the recreational use of cannabis in November 2012. Though the Department of Justice remained silent during the voting phase, Attorney General Eric Holder adopted an active approach once the ballot measures were enacted by voters. Through the Cole Memorandum, the Obama administration discouraged federal prosecutors from pursuing cannabis-related criminal cases in states that had softened their drug use policy.[9] Starting with Washington State and Colorado in 2012, several states began to legalize the use and possession of cannabis. The federal government, however, was reluctant to adopt a more flexible approach. President Obama admitted that 'legalization is not the answer' and 'the U.S. will not be going in this direction' (Calmes 2012).

The Trump administration (2017–2021) reinstated several initiatives associated with the war on drugs. Amid the country's opioid crisis that in 2016 alone caused more than 42,000 deaths, and in 2020 took the lives of about 100,000 people, Donald Trump also made it clear during his presidential campaign that building a border wall to stop the flow of illicit drugs from the south would be a policy priority. Once in office, Trump not only increased the funds allocated to tackle the opioid crisis, but also proposed more resources in the areas of interdiction and law enforcement, including US$18 billion to build the wall and a US$400 million increase for the DEA (The White House 2020). Furthermore, Trump appointed as his attorney general Jeff Sessions, who openly opposed pro-cannabis legislation. In January 2018, Sessions rescinded the Cole Memorandum that stated that the Department of Justice would not prosecute state-compliant cannabis-related activity. Although Trump casts his drug control efforts as victories, including restrictions on opioid prescriptions, with the declaration of the opioid crisis as a public health emergency and the pressure to curtail China's exports of illicit fentanyl into the US, he faced several drug-related challenges during the end of his administration. More specifically, the decreasing number of opioid overdoses was overshadowed by a drastic rise in deaths due to synthetic opioids such as fentanyl as well as those involving cocaine and psychostimulants (Hedegaard, Miniño, and Warner 2020).

In a context marked by continuity rather than change, the most radical drug policy reforms in the US happened at the state level. As of this writing, in 2023, a total of 23 states, two territories, and the District of Columbia have approved the recreational adult use of cannabis. Adopting a commercial model, most of these states have allowed licensed for-profit firms to produce, process, and distribute cannabis for adult users within the state jurisdiction (Pardo 2020). Other drug policy alternatives adopted in the US include the use of medical cannabis and the decriminalization of the possession of small amounts of the psychoactive substance. Furthermore, in 2020, Oregon became the first state to decriminalize psilocybin, a Schedule I psychedelic, and legalize it for therapeutic use.

US drug policy and its institutional foundations

Federal laws regulate the possession, trafficking, and manufacturing of illicit drugs. The Controlled Substances Act[10] places all psychoactive substances under federal legislation into one of five schedules, based upon its medical use, potential for abuse, and safety or dependence liability.[11] Notwithstanding states have created their own statutory frameworks, drug control is primarily under federal jurisdiction. In the states that have not decriminalized cannabis or psychedelics, or where a drug offense is related to other psychoactive substances, individuals accused of violating federal legislation are commonly prosecuted. Moreover, sentencing discretion from judges has been removed by different drug laws, not allowing for the options of probation or parole (Levine 2003). Except for defendants with felony or misdemeanour nonviolent cases, which can be referred to drug courts,[12] offenders are under the purview of the federal criminal system.

Federal agencies are in charge of enforcing national controlled substance laws across all states and territories, although the majority of suspects arrested for drug offenses are handled by law enforcement agencies and courts at the state level (Sacco 2014). The DEA is primarily responsible for enforcing drug legislation. The institution, within the Department of Justice, has approximately 226 offices organized in 21 divisions throughout the US territory, working in partnership with state and local agencies (DEA 2021a). Other federal institutions such as the Federal Bureau of Investigation (FBI), the Marshals Service, the Bureau of Alcohol, Tobacco, Firearms, and Explosives, the Postal Inspection Service, and agencies at the Department of Homeland Security participate and support federal drug investigations while also making drug arrests. Overseas, the DEA has about 86 offices in 67 countries around the world (DEA 2021a). Other agencies such as the Customs Service and the FBI have officers in US embassies, helping with drug control efforts in foreign countries (Babor et al 2010).

The participation of other institutions such as the military is more limited, at least domestically. The 1878 Posse Comitatus Act outlaws the armed forces from developing law enforcement initiatives except where expressly authorized by the Constitution or Congress. As Kopel (2000) maintains, however, several loopholes and new legislation, including the 1981 'drug law' exception and the 1988 'omnibus drug bill', have increasingly authorized the participation of the armed forces in certain types of counterdrugs efforts. Even though the military's direct involvement is not legally allowed, under the new organizational scheme soldiers may assist different law enforcement agencies in surveillance and other drug-related activities, providing military equipment, and offering training for domestic security personnel and operations.

The coordination of all federal agencies implementing US drug policy, both domestically and internationally, is the responsibility of ONDCP. Created by the Reagan administration through the Anti-Drug Abuse Act of 1988, the organization also leads the development of the consolidated federal drug control budget and develops the National Drug Control Strategy, a document outlining each administration's counterdrugs efforts elaborated annually. The director of ONDCP, known as the country's drug czar, is the principal advisor to the president on drug control issues. The position is appointed by the president with the approval of Congress. The current director of ONDCP is Rahul Gupta, a physician with experience in the area of public health.

Yet state and local governments often play a larger role in drug control initiatives compared to their federal counterpart. Even though single-mission agencies, similar to those present at the national level, were created over the course of the years, most of them have been gradually replaced by a large array of institutions having substantial roles but not specializing in drugs. With states and cities deprived of local drug czars, their authority tends to be dispersed and fragmented (Boyum and Reuter 2005). Since local governments bear most of the administrative burdens and costs of executing federal control legislation or unfunded mandates, they are more inclined towards innovation (Bagley 2015). However, Kleiman and Smith (1990) note that local policymakers have historically lacked accurate city-by-city data on drug-related activity, counteracting the effectiveness or assessment of their counterdrug efforts. Yet this situation seems to be changing rapidly as a result of the states' increasing autonomy in designing their respective drug control policies, as illustrated by the new cannabis liberalization wave.

On the international front, the State Department has traditionally served as the principal counterdrug agency (Isacson 2005). Within this institution, the Bureau for International Narcotic and Law Enforcement Affairs, previously known as the Bureau for International Narcotics Matters, has been in charge of developing policies and programs to combat drugs and crime, playing an important role in the training of partner nations' security forces. The International Narcotics Control program, in particular, has controlled most military aid under the Foreign Assistance Act of 1961. Other US agencies involved internationally include the Department of Justice, the Defense Department, the DEA, the CIA, the Pentagon, and the unified combatant commands.

In short, the US federal institutional architecture criminalizes users to discourage illegal drug consumption. Rather than promoting prevention, treatment, or other demand-side strategies, federal efforts have been focused instead on law enforcement (MacCoun and Reuter 1998). Underpinned by a warlike narrative demanding a 'drug-free America', law enforcement has dominated budgetary allocations over the years. Defining drug habits as morally wrong, the rationale behind the US classic model suggests that criminal penalties and punishment are effective deterrents. Tougher enforcement, on the other hand, is likely to increase prices and reduce availability, its advocates commonly suggest. Not surprisingly, US drug control policy is the most relevant international example of criminalized drug prohibition (Levine 2002).

Criminalization in practice

Since the modern phase of the war on drugs gained momentum, various presidential administrations have claimed success in their counterdrugs efforts, both domestically and internationally. President Nixon, for example, told a conference of judges, prosecutors, educators, and police officers that the US had 'turned the corner on drug addiction' (The New York Times 1973,

20). Similarly, William J. Bennett said that Washington was 'on the road to victory' in the war on drugs, stressing that the country was 'beginning to break its interest and habit on drugs' (Savage 1990).

This section explores illicit drug consumption trends and their associated harms since the modern phase of the war on drugs accelerated in 1980 until the first cannabis legalization reforms adopted in 2012 at the state level. Before addressing some key epidemiological surveys and other drug-related indicators in the realms of health and security, it is useful to mention that some of the studies conducted in the US suffered major methodological transformations during this period. Hence, in cases where disparities in the collection and processing of data can affect the comparability of trends, this section narrows down the analysis to the periods 1990–2012 and 2000–2012.

Illicit drug use patterns

The US is the world's most lucrative market for illicit drugs. Recent estimates suggest that Americans spend approximately US$150 billion on cannabis, cocaine, heroin, and methamphetamine in a year (Midgette et al 2019). Illicit drugs sold in the US are predominantly produced and trafficked from Latin America. The cannabis consumed in the US has been historically grown in Mexico, Colombia, and Jamaica, although an increasing share is now provided domestically, particularly after several states legalized its recreational use. While cocaine is supplied by countries in the Andean Ridge, heroin is cultivated on poppy farms in Mexico and, to a lesser extent, Colombia. Synthetic opioids such as illicitly manufactured fentanyl, which combined with heroin, cocaine, methamphetamine, or alcohol is especially lethal, were originally produced in China and transit through the Mexican territory into the US. New developments suggest that criminal organizations operating in Mexico, especially the Sinaloa and Jalisco New Generation cartels, are now dominating the fentanyl supply after China put the substance under a controlled regime in 2019 following Washington's diplomatic pressure (Kamp, Córdoba, and Wernau 2022). The bulk of the manufacture of other synthetic drugs such as methamphetamine also takes place in Mexico, displacing the US domestic supply.

The US has witnessed at least four major drug 'epidemics' during the second half of the twentieth century: heroin in the late 1960s, cocaine powder in the mid-1970s, crack cocaine in the 1980s, and methamphetamines during the 1990s and early 2000s. Nevertheless, due to the increasing number of overdoses, the ongoing synthetic opioid crisis is often referred as a new epidemic (Ciccarone 2017). Though there have been other health crises, heroin, cocaine, and methamphetamines probably accounted for 90 per cent of the social costs associated with illegal drug use in the US by the mid-2010s (Bagley 2015).

Drug consumption in the US is measured by two regular surveys: The National Survey on Drug Use and Health (NSDUH), previously known as the National Household Survey on Drug Abuse (NHSDA), and Monitoring the Future (MTF). While NSDUH tracks consumption among the general population (noninstitutionalized residents of the US aged 12 or older),[13] MTF focuses mainly on high school students. As Boyum and Reuter (2005) note, however, both mechanisms fail in identifying patterns of heavy drug use, particularly because problematic users are often socially isolated and beyond the reach of general population surveys. Moreover, unlike legalization or decriminalization settings, where users' inclination to report tends to be greater, the stigma associated with illegal activities such as consumption may have a negative impact on the results' accuracy, although this is likely changing, in part due to drug liberalization policies adopted in several states.

Caveats aside, the last estimates before the first states in the US started adopting different types of legalization reform suggest that approximately 23.9 million people used illicit drugs, corresponding to 9.2 per cent of the total population aged 12 or older (Substance Abuse and Mental Health Services Administration [SAMHSA] 2013).[14] Cannabis (7.3 per cent) was the most consumed psychoactive substance, followed by cocaine[15] (0.6 per cent) and hallucinogens[16] (0.4 per cent). Methamphetamines and heroin, on the other hand, were used by approximately 0.2 per cent and 0.1 per cent of the population, respectively. Other relevant forms of illicit drug use, which in some cases registered higher prevalence than the so-called 'traditional psychoactive substances', include inhalants as well as the misuse of prescription stimulants, tranquilizers or sedatives (including benzodiazepines), and pain relievers (SAMHSA 2013).[17]

The long-term picture indicates that prevalence rates for all illicit drugs increased since the inception of the first epidemiological studies, peaking in the late 1970s and then falling substantially during the 1980s (SAMHSA 1990; Mieczkowski 1996).[18] Consumption continued to decrease or remained relatively stable during the 1990s, with most indicators finishing the decade well below the figures registered in the late 1970s (SAMHSA 1999). Yet increasing initiation rates among the youth population suggested that the use of illicit psychoactive substances was changing across several states in the US. This trend became a major preoccupation among government officials during the end of the Clinton administration, favouring the expansion of the sample size of the National Household Survey on Drug Abuse in 1999 (Gfroerer 2018).

The lifetime prevalence (LTP) reveals slightly different patterns. Increases in consumption rates were almost constant, peaking in the late 1980s and 1990s. Following the upward trend, the 2000s witnessed new increases. The LTP of all illicit drugs among the population aged 12 or older has expanded by almost 10 percentage points, increasing from 38.9 in 2000 to 48.0 in

2012.[19] The latest National Survey on Drug Use and Health (SAMHSA 2013) data released by SAMHSA before the first two states, Colorado and Washington State, legalized recreational cannabis demonstrates that the LTP of all illicit drugs among the general population was above the figures of the late 1980s and early 1990s, when use rates oscillated between 36 and 37 (SAMHSA 1990, 1995).

Last-year (LYP) and last-month (LMP) estimates are more effective in evaluating recent consumption trends, as increases in LTP among adults are expected due to higher levels of use in the earlier decades of people who are ageing (Mieczkowski 1996). Graph 3.1 demonstrates that both measures decreased during the 1980s and then increased steadily during the 2000s and early 2010s, reaching their highest levels in 2012, when the US registered a LYP and LMP of 16.0 and 9.2, respectively (SAMHSA 2021).

Since changes in measurement for some illicit drug categories affected the comparability of data, Graph 3.2 disaggregates psychoactive substances into cannabis, cocaine, heroin, and LSD. Use rates registered a drastic decrease during the 1980s or remained relatively stable (like heroin). There were minor changes during the 1990s. Except for the LYP and LMP of LSD, all illicit drugs experienced increases between 2000 and 2012. This is the case of cannabis, a substance that registered increases of 1.1 and 2.5, a trend that continued after the first states legalized the substance (SAMHSA 2021). Nevertheless, in 2012, the prevalence of various illicit drugs seemed to be below the levels of the late 1970s, when consumption reached a historical

Graph 3.1: LYP and LMP of all illicit substances among population aged 12 or older by year

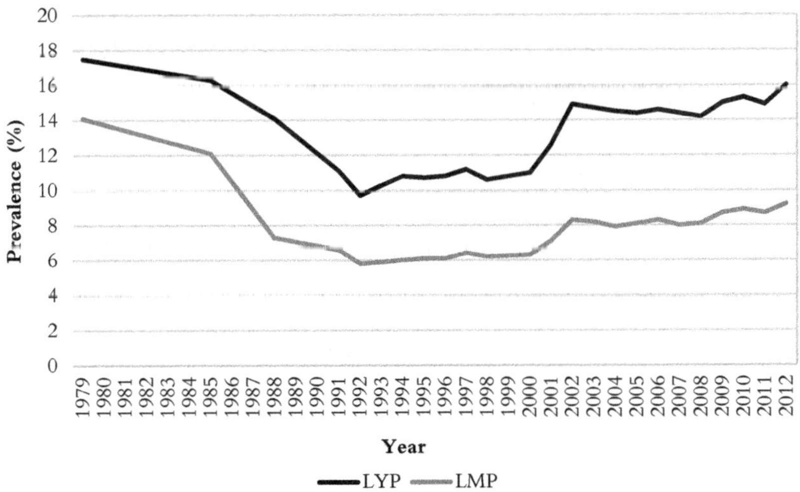

Source: Authors, based on SAMHSA (1995, 2013–2002)

Graph 3.2: LMP among population aged 12 or older, by drug type and year[20]

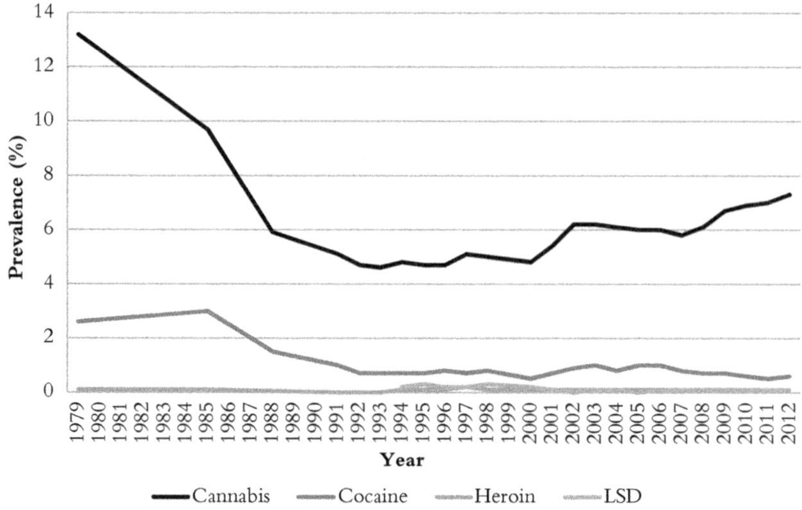

Source: Authors, based on SAMHSA (1995, 2002, 2019, 2021)

peak (SAMHSA 1999, 2013). Cannabis and cocaine, for example, registered lower prevalences in 2012 compared to 1979. The past-year and past-month use rates of any illicit drug were also higher in 1979. The only exception to this trend was heroin, which displayed a higher LYP in 2012 (SAMHSA 1999, 2013).

Special attention needs to be paid to the initiation of substance use or the use of particular illicit drugs for the first time during a person's lifetime. As noted in the introduction of this book, these figures often reveal long-term consumption trends among the population.[21] According to SAMSHA (2013), the illicit drugs with the largest numbers of recent initiates in 2012 were cannabis (2.4 million), pain relievers (1.9 million), and tranquilizers (1.4 million). Far behind were other psychoactive substances such as ecstasy (869,000), stimulants (676,000), and cocaine (639,000) (SAMSHA 2013).

The NSDUH report reveals that the number of initiates followed the LYP and LMP trends registered during the 1980s, although increases were already noticeable in the second half of the decade. The upward trend continued during the 1990s for almost all illicit psychoactive substances. The 2000s, however, witnessed major changes. Except for heroin, the number of individuals who reported first using or misusing cannabis, cocaine, heroin, and LSD slightly decreased between 2000 and 2012. Nevertheless, caution is required in the interpretation of data. Unlike the consumption rates reviewed earlier, the number of people initiating the use of illicit drugs does not take into consideration variations in the size of the population over time.

Looking at prevalence rates throughout the years, it seems clear that criminalization was not totally effective in preventing the use of psychoactive substances in the US. Despite that last-year and last-month illicit drug use rates fell after peaking in the late 1970s, the relative stability of the 1990s did not last long. Except for the LYP and LMP of LSD, all illicit drugs registered new increases during the 2000s and early 2010s. Certainly, the first cannabis legalization reforms were adopted in a context of increasing use rates. In most of the cases, however, these increases were not large enough to bring US consumption rates above the levels of the late 1970s.

Market-related trends

The main goal of the US supply-side strategy has been to drive up the street prices of psychoactive substances, especially cocaine and heroin, making them scarce at home through different law enforcement initiatives (US House of Representatives 2009). In the long term, high prices and low availability, together with the negative perceptions of health harms associated with consumption, the deterrence effects of punishment, and other social penalties, are believed to limit the use of illicit drugs (Pacula 2010).

How has the drug market evolved in the US under criminalization? What have been the variations of market-associated factors like the price and potency of illicit drugs? What patterns of law enforcement activity can we observe? This section explores the trends of seizures, price, and potency of illegal drugs before the first legalization reforms.

Seizures

Most illicit drug seizures in the US happen at formal ports of entry, especially at the southwestern border. The bulk is confiscated on land, followed by air and sea, respectively (Congressional Research Service 2019). Nonetheless, psychoactive substances that are produced or manufactured domestically or those that are not seized at the US ports of entry or at other trafficking points may be later confiscated by different law enforcement authorities. While the primary agency in charge of seizing illicit drugs entering the US territory is Customs and Border Protection (CBP),[22] other federal, state, local, and tribal law enforcement agencies – some of which do not necessarily focus on specific drug-related crimes – are also involved in domestic illicit drug confiscations.

Since there is no central database gathering all the information on illicit drug seizures from different law enforcement authorities, policymakers and the media commonly rely on reports published by CBP (Congressional Research Service 2019). We also base our analysis on the data provided in these reports. Broadly speaking, the available evidence demonstrates that law enforcement authorities seized approximately 1.3 million kg of cannabis in 2012, followed by cocaine (27,000 kg), methamphetamines (9,000 kg), and heroin (2,000 kg) (Congressional Research Service 2019).[23]

Data gathered by the United Nations Office on Drugs and Crime (UNODC) (2022) reveal that psychoactive substances registered higher confiscations before the first cannabis legalization reforms were adopted compared to the figures exhibited during most of the 1990s. While confiscations of cannabis and heroin trended upward since the early 2000s, seizures of cocaine and methamphetamines experienced several fluctuations. Nonetheless, the total amount of confiscations in 2012 was clearly higher than that registered in 1990, the first year with available information. Interestingly, seizures of illicit drugs started declining after 2012 – a trend likely driven by a drastic decrease in cannabis confiscations due to state-level legalization reforms (CBP 2022).

Not surprisingly, the literature analyzing whether seizures of illicit drugs in the US affects consumption is far from conclusive. MacCoun and Reuter (2001) contend that drug seizure is an imperfect indicator to assess drug consumption patterns because it depends upon at least three specific factors: (i) the quantity shipped, (ii) the care taken by traffickers and dealers to protect their shipments, and (iii) the stringency of law enforcement measures. Moreover, various quantitative analyses have found that the self-reported perceived availability has little or no causal effect on drug use patterns, suggesting that US supply reduction strategies have a limited potential to affect the market (Bachman et al 1988; Bachman, Johnston, and O'Malley 1998). Caulkins (1999), by contrast, demonstrates that variations in perceived availability of cannabis and cocaine affect drug use rates among youth, although he maintains that additional longitudinal studies examining the relevance of supply factors are warranted.

Prices

The price of illicit substances is closely related to their availability and hence to enforcement. Prices are also influenced by other factors such as the distance from the supply countries and purchasing power. For example, heroin is two and a half to three times more expensive than cocaine in the US, whereas in Asia and Eastern Europe the ratio is exactly the opposite (Babor et al 2010). Furthermore, scholars have demonstrated that other factors such as changes in drug marketing (Rhodes et al 2002) or transformations in communication and transportation networks (Stares 1996) can also affect the retail price of psychoactive substances. Thus, it is possible for overall prices to drop even if enforcement rigour increases (Caulkins and Reuter 1998).

Notwithstanding the relevance of the demand and other cost components affecting prices, US drug policy has been mostly focused on the supply of psychoactive substances. Specifically, Washington, DC's drug control spending seeks to restrain supply primarily through prices, unless it is able to make psychoactive substances scarce (Caulkins 2001). Yet the evidence suggests that the threshold level of low availability and high prices under which drug consumption becomes highly unlikely is difficult to achieve through drug law enforcement (MacCoun and Reuter 2001). Various scholars have shown the limited ability of US-led interdiction efforts overseas (Reuter, Crawford, and Cave 1988; Rydell and Everingham 1994) and enforcement activities at home (Reuter and Kleiman 1986; DiNardo 1993) to affect the prices of illicit drugs in the long run.

Price data most commonly used in academic research are published by the DEA's System to Retrieve Information from Drug Evidence (STRIDE) (Caulkins 2007). The ONDCP, for example, has drawn on STRIDE to trace the fluctuation of prices over the years. The White House's office shows in a recent report that the price of cocaine and heroin fell steadily during the 1980s, whereas cannabis experienced the opposite trend, reaching a peak in 1991 (ONDCP 2004). By the mid-1990s, while cocaine and heroin prices – after adjusting for inflation – were about one-third of their 1981 levels, cannabis almost returned to the value registered in the early 1980s (MacCoun and Reuter 2001).

UNODC complements STRIDE's data by elaborating a synthesis of the information gathered from other reporting units. The evidence reveals that retail prices of cocaine adjusted for purity and inflation remained relatively stable, whereas heroin decreased substantially till 2007 and then trended upward for three consecutive years (UNODC 2022).[24] Nevertheless, their prices seem to be well below the levels registered during the 1980s, when cocaine and heroin were sold on the street at approximately US$750 and US$3,260, respectively (ONDCP 2015).[25] Cannabis price trends, on the other hand, are more difficult to gauge because several states have created different price frameworks. Swanson and Gamio (2015), for instance, claim that the value of cannabis differed in 50 states and eight major cities of the US.

Given the US's stringent law enforcement efforts during periods where street drug prices decreased, especially in the 1980s when the war on drugs escalated as never before, it seems unlikely that a greater emphasis on this aspect of drug control policy could reverse the trend (Hagan 2001). In this regard, Caulkins and Reuter (2010) claim that prohibition plus a base level of law enforcement can drive prices above the levels of a legal market, but the costs of expanding law enforcement beyond this point to further increase the price of drugs are extremely high. Arguing that the US is far into the region of diminishing returns, Caulkins and Reuter (2010) suggest that toughness could be focused instead on the most violent and noxious forms of illicit drug dealing.

Furthermore, while there is robust evidence showing that price changes affect drug use, impacts on other outcomes are less clear (Hughes, Hulme, and Ritter 2020). In the health realm, for example, Caulkins (2001) finds that fluctuations in prices are associated with variations in the number of hospital emergency department mentions of cocaine and heroin. Along similar lines, Dhaval (2006) demonstrates that heavy or chronic drug consumption is negatively related to drug prices across 21 large US metropolitan areas. In his panel data methodology, the elasticity of the probability of a cocaine and heroin mention with respect to own price is estimated at -0.27 and -0.10, respectively.

Potency

Illicit drug markets are often characterized by delivering low-quality goods and services, primarily because of the absence of an authority or third party capable of enforcing contracts through legal means (Babor et al 2010). Certain illicit drugs such as cocaine and different types of heroin are often diluted and/or adulterated throughout the distribution chain (Moore 1973). Due to the risks associated with trafficking and distribution, illegality and stringent law enforcement are expected to lead to the production of more potent psychoactive substances. While increasing drug concentration per volume benefits the trafficker by making the illegal product easier to conceal, it is likely to punish the consumer by making drug dosages less predictable (Hagan 2001).

Data on illicit drug purity are invaluable but challenging (Caulkins 2007). Similar to the prices of illicit drugs in the US, most of the available information comes from STRIDE. In the case of cannabis, for example, the percentage of THC has increased steadily since the mid-1990s, going from 3.96 per cent in 1995 to 12.27 per cent in 2012 (National Institute on Drug Abuse 2021). In fact, the levels of THC before several states started legalizing the substance are far from the historical means registered in the US during the 1980s and 1990s, when the potency of cannabis never exceeded 5 per cent (Smart et al 2017). According to Mahamad and colleagues (2020), a THC potency above 20 per cent can represent a serious public health concern, as high concentrations of THC have often been associated with greater dependency (Freeman and Winstock 2015), adverse psychological and cognitive problems (Volkow et al 2014), and other health complications.

The potency of cocaine and amphetamines followed slightly similar patterns during the last years before the legalization reforms. Starting in the early 2010s, the potency of methamphetamines increased substantially (DEA 2016, 2021b). The purity of cocaine also trended upward during the same period of time. After a drastic decrease registered in the mid-2000s, the purity of cocaine at the retail level slowly started to increase starting in 2010 (UNODC and EUROPOL 2021). The retail purity of heroin, by contrast, remained relatively stable over the years, oscillating between 30 per cent and 39 per cent (DEA 2021b).

Broadly speaking, the evidence suggests that tougher enforcement has not resulted in price increases on psychoactive substances such as cocaine and heroin. The purity of various illicit drugs, however, increased before the first cannabis legalization initiatives were adopted in 2012, a pattern not clearly identifiable in the case of heroin. These contradictory signals, especially when viewed through the lens of a rational choice perspective, warrant future research attention among scholars studying drug policy reforms.

Adverse health effects

Surveys of illicit drug use in household and school populations serve as one of the primary sources of information about problematic consumption and its impacts on public health. In order to estimate the magnitude of drug use disorders in the US, the NSDUH asks a series of questions to assess dependence on or abuse of illicit drugs in the past year. Data on both substance use disorder (SUD) and treatment at a specialty facility are particularly relevant when estimating the negative impacts of illicit drug consumption.

SUD occurs when recurrent consumption of alcohol or other drugs causes clinically significant impairment, including health problems, disability, and failure to meet major responsibilities at work, school, or home. In 2012, approximately 22.2 million people aged 12 or older had at least one illicit drug use disorder in the past year, accounting for 8.5 per cent of the population. Cannabis ranked first with 4.3 million people, followed far behind by pain relievers and cocaine with 2.1 and 1.1 million, respectively (SAMSHA 2014). Out of the total people with SUD, nearly 2.5 million had received any substance use treatment in the past year (SAMSHA 2014).

The evidence shows that the number of people with SUD in the US remained relatively stable from 2002 to 2012, the years in which NSDUH followed the same criteria to measure drug dependence (SAMHSA 2015, 2019).[26] More specifically, the estimates indicate that SUD rates among the population aged 12 or older have oscillated between 2.5 per cent and 3.0 per cent. Despite the last figures seeming to be below the levels registered in 2002 (that is, 3.06 per cent), variation has not been substantial over the course of the years.

NSDUH also presents information on substance use treatment. Data are divided between people having a need for treatment and those who received it at any location, including hospitals, emergency rooms, private doctor's offices, or prison. Regarding the second measurement, the 2013 report shows that in 2012, 4 million people or 1.5 per cent of the population

Graph 3.3: Received any substance use treatment in the past year among the general population by year[27]

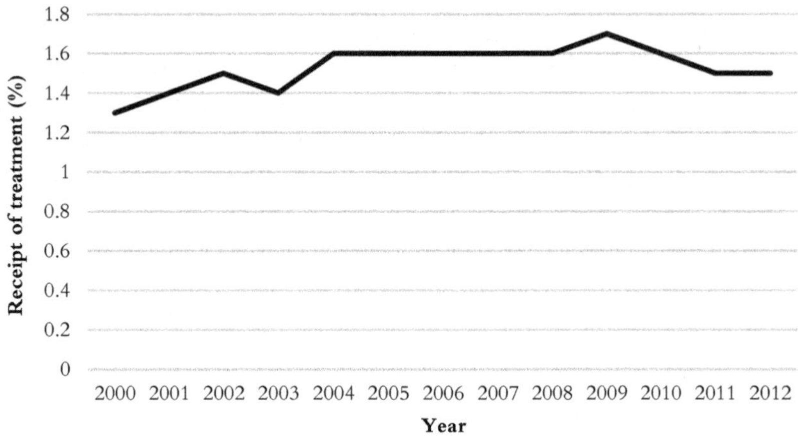

Source: Authors, based on SAMHSA (2021–2002)

received any substance use treatment in the past year (SAMSHA 2013).[28] As shown in Graph 3.3, this percentage has remained relatively stable since 2000 despite the prevalence rates of several psychoactive substances trending upward. Unfortunately, NSDUH did not include questions asking whether respondents had received treatment for a problem related to substance use before the 2000s (SAMHSA 2002), which certainly limits the analysis of long trends of problematic use in the US.

Drug-related viruses and infectious diseases, on the other hand, comprise other consequences of the consumption of certain psychoactive substances. HIV and AIDS remain a persistent problem in the US. The long-standing ban on the use of federal funds for needle and syringe exchange programs (NSEPs), which was only reversed in 2009 under the Obama administration, has likely affected the infection rates among people who inject drugs (PWID).[29] In 2012, for instance, 35,937 individuals received an HIV/AIDS diagnosis (Centers for Disease Control and Prevention [CDC] 2013). Out of the total population diagnosed in the US, 3,026 were PWID, accounting for about 8 per cent of HIV/AIDS detections in the country (CDC 2013). These figures are well above the average registered since the early 1980s (Graph 3.4). Yet improvements in detection mechanisms may also explain the low number of diagnoses in the early 1980s. In 1986, for instance, HIV/AIDS infections among PWID represented around 17.2 per cent of total detections, whereas in 2012 this percentage decreased to 6.3 per cent. This comparison suggests that the incidence of illicit drugs in HIV/AIDS infections could have been higher in the past despite the reduced number of diagnoses registered.

Graph 3.4: Estimated HIV/AIDS infections among people who inject drugs by year

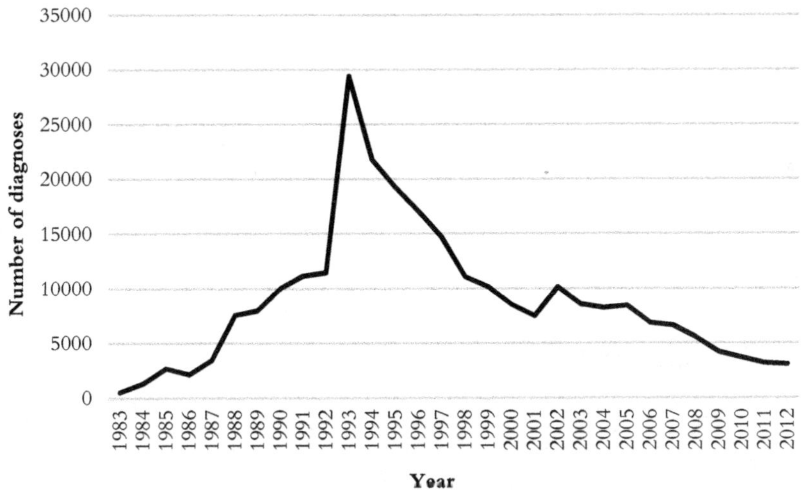

Source: Authors, based on CDC (2005, 2009, 2019, 2020, 2021)

Harm reduction policies are still limited in the US. Even though the Consolidated Appropriations Act of 2018 permits the use of funds from the Department of Health and Human Services to support NSEPs, federal funds cannot be allocated to purchase needles or syringes. Meanwhile, evidence reveals that PWID experience comparatively higher risks than other people with HIV infection. According to Mitsch, Hall, and Babu (2016), PWID have the shortest life expectancy after a HIV diagnosis and around 40 per cent of the detections among PWID are classified as severe disease (that is, stage 3 AIDS). Research also indicates that the lack of HIV highly active antiretroviral therapy, a medication regimen used to treat and control human immunodeficiency virus type 1, is a critical factor contributing to advanced immunosuppression and mortality among PWID with HIV infection (Montaner et al 2010).

Overdoses

Deaths from drug overdose have increased steadily in the US since the 1980s (Graph 3.5).[30] From 1980 to 2012, the number of deaths per 100,000 inhabitants skyrocketed from 1.1 to 13.1. Faster increases were experienced during the new century. In 2012, for example, the US registered 41,502 drug overdose deaths, representing a 138 per cent increase from 2000. During the same period, the age-adjusted rates for drug-poisoning deaths involving opioid analgesics more than tripled (Warner, Hedegaard, and Chen 2014).

Graph 3.5: Drug overdose deaths per 100,000 inhabitants by year[31]

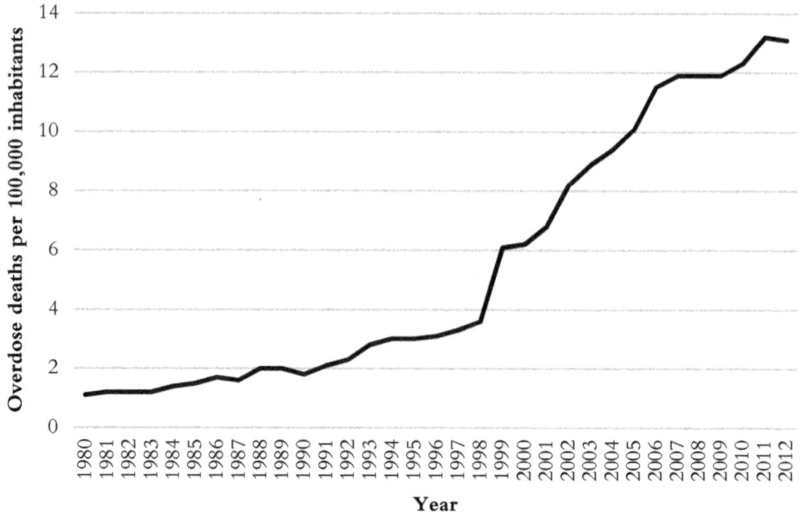

Source: Authors, based on Hedegaard, Miniño, and Warner (2020), Darakjy et al (2014), and CDC (2022)

Not surprisingly, it is more likely that someone living in the US will die from a drug overdose than from a car accident (Rosen 2021).

Overall, the evidence reveals that the number of people with SUD and those who received treatment remained relatively stable before the first legalization initiatives were adopted. HIV infections, by contrast, experienced a substantial increase and a later decrease, remaining in 2012 above the levels of the 1980s. Hence, the country's growing overdose rates could be connected to various factors such as the use of more dangerous drugs, higher potencies, or the adulteration and/or mixing of psychoactive substances. The DEA (2021), for example, maintains that traffickers continue to mix illegal drugs as part of their strategy to increase their profits and/or avoid law enforcement. Under these circumstances, the limited relevance of harm reduction strategies such as drug consumption rooms, drug-checking services, or NSEPs becomes critical to understand the lethality of drugs in a country where criminalization has largely prevailed.

Drug-related violence

The US harbours a population highly concerned about insecurity (Garland 2001; Chevigny 2003; Simon 2007; Wacquant 2009). Since Richard Nixon securitized drugs and declared them 'public enemy number one', a long-standing association between drugs and criminal behaviour has been forged in the public mind. Even before the war on drugs escalated during the mid-1970s, illicit drugs were widely identified as the main driving force behind insecurity. As already noted, underlying the expansion of the federal state apparatus and the country's counterdrug legislation since the early twentieth century was the widespread fear of substance abuse leading to criminal behaviour.

Even though various studies have shown that a proportion of crime could be attributable to illicit drug consumption, the relationship is neither simple nor linear (Goode 1997; Seddon 2000; MacCoun, Kilmer, and Reuter 2003; Keene 2005; Hughes and Anthony 2006; Allen 2007). Since we have already reviewed the literature on the drug-crime nexus in Chapter 2, in the remainder of this section the intentional homicide rate, particularly murders that occurred during a 'narcotics felony', is used as the main indicator for drug-related violence in the US. Surveys of prison inmates are also provided as a complement to untangle the drug-crime nexus.

The US Department of Justice uses two nationwide data collection systems to track detailed information on homicides: the FBI's Uniform Crime Reporting (UCR) Program and the Bureau of Justice Statistics' National Crime Victimization Survey. Although both statistical measures have gone through a number of changes over the years, the complementary information of each program provides valuable insights and a comprehensive overview about the nature, trends, and impacts of homicides in the US.

The FBI's estimates show a long-term decline in the number of national homicides per 100,000 inhabitants since the last peak experienced in the early 1990s, when murder rates almost reached the levels of the early 1980s. This trend also continued during the 2000s (Graph 3.6). According to the 2012 UCR report, the US registered a total of 14,827 offenses under the category of murder and nonnegligent manslaughter, corresponding to a rate of 4.7 homicides (UCR 2012). Notwithstanding these figures are slightly above the levels observed in 1957, the year with the lowest rate recorded in modern US history, homicide rates have decreased substantially since the beginnings of the 1970s, 1980s, and 1990s, when murders per 100,000 inhabitants exceeded 9 per cent.

Despite periods of growing hysteria, homicide rates in the US have escaped from the continent's long-term patterns of violence, particularly since the 2000s, when Latin America and the Caribbean became the world's most homicidal region (UNODC 2019). Indeed, the US has registered the third or fourth lowest murder rate in the Americas, only ranking behind countries like Canada, Chile, and Argentina (UNODC 2019). Other crimes such as robbery and larceny-theft experienced a similar trend between 1980 and 2012. While robbery rates declined from 251 to 113, larceny-theft rates decreased from 3,167 to 1,965 (UCR 2021). Unlike the fears that justified some of the most stringent criminal policies in the US throughout the

Graph 3.6: US homicide rates by year

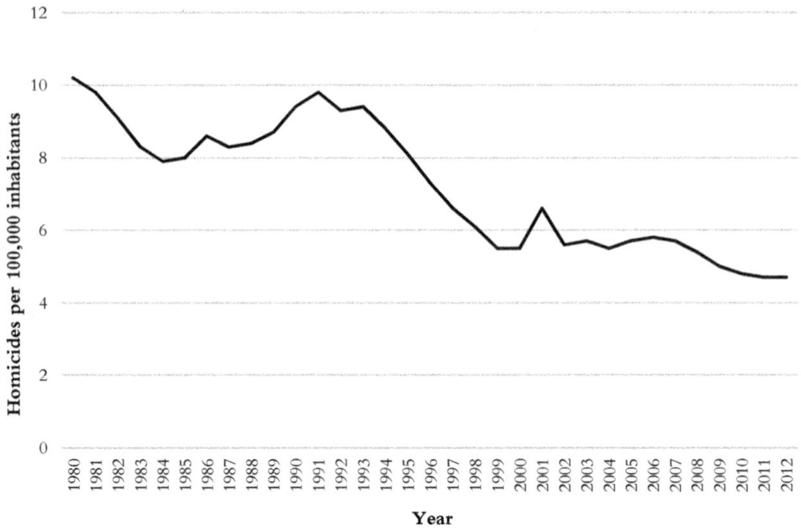

Source: Authors, based on Bureau of Justice Statistics (2007), UNODC (2021b), UCR (2021), and Cooper and Smith (2011)

decades, these figures illustrate the long-term patterns of the 'great American crime decline' (Zimring 2007).

UCR also provides information on the proportion of homicides that are drug related. According to the FBI, murders that occur specifically during a drug felony, such as drug trafficking or manufacturing, are considered drug related. Broadly speaking, drug-related homicides increased during the 1980s and trended downward in the following decade. Between 2000 and 2013, they followed the general trend depicted in Graph 3.6. After some fluctuations, drug-related homicides reached a peak in 2006 and then declined (UNODC 2019; UCR 2021).

Data on drug-related homicides are more robust than on other offenses, especially because murders are likely to be reported, are easily measurable, and tend to be thoroughly investigated. Nonetheless, statistics on this field illustrate some of the general difficulties of quantifying the drugs-crime relationship. As the Bureau of Justice Statistics remarks, the FBI does not include as a drug-related homicide a murder that occurs during a robbery or a burglary committed by someone under the influence of drugs. Neither is considered a homicide that occurs during a robbery committed to obtain money to buy drugs. In these specific cases, the crime is officially recorded in terms of its relationship to the most serious offense only, and robbery and burglary are more serious than drug trafficking according to the FBI's offense classification criteria (BJS 1994).

Alternative methodological approaches have been developed to elucidate the ways in which crime and drugs are related. The Survey of Inmates in State Correctional Facilities, more recently known as the Survey of Prison Inmates, has produced national statistics on state and federal prison populations across a variety of domains, including but not limited to drug consumption.[32] The US government has developed seven national surveys so far (1974, 1979, 1986, 1991, 1997, 2004, and 2016).[33] Since 1991, the first year of measurement, the percentage of inmates who reported committing their current offense to obtain money for drugs has increased in the federal prison system while fluctuating at the state level (Table 3.1). Along similar lines, the proportion of offenders who admitted committing their crime while under the influence of psychoactive substances has remained stable in state institutions while steadily increasing at the federal level (Table 3.2). As noted in Chapter 2, however, these indicators also suffer from some difficulties in quantifying the connection between drugs and crime. Neither the so-called economic compulsive crime nor the influence of drugs demonstrates how crime and drugs interact nor the context under which they occur.

The tough on-crime policy has emphasized the use of incarceration to counter violence in the US. After 40 years of the modern phase of the war on drugs, the US has incarcerated its citizens at a rate that is nearly five times the world average (Bagley 2015; Rosen and Cutrona 2023). Even larger countries like China and India have smaller populations in prisons and jails.[34] According to the BJS (2022), approximately 1,570,397 adults were incarcerated in 2012

Table 3.1: Percentage of inmates who reported committing offense to get money for drugs

Year	Federal	State
1991	10%	17%
1997	16%	19%
2004	18.4%	16.6%

Source: Authors, based on Bureau of Justice Statistics (1994, 2004)

Table 3.2: Percentage of inmates who reported committing crime under the influence of drugs

Year	Federal	State
1991	17%	31%
1997	22%	33%
2004	26%	32%

Source: Authors, based on Bureau of Justice Statistics (1994, 2004)

under the jurisdiction of federal and state prisons. To put it another way, nearly 480 people for every 100,000 inhabitants were behind bars in state and federal facilities that year (BJS 2021). Followed by the Russian Federation, Rwanda, the Virgin Islands, Cuba, and Georgia, the US held the world's biggest total incarceration rate during the years of harsher drug laws at the federal level (Institute for Crime and Justice Policy Research 2023).

Drug offenses have had a disproportionate impact on the prison population in the US. Between 1980 and 2012, the number of people sentenced for drug charges in federal and state prisons skyrocketed from 4,900 to 98,900 and from 19,000 to 210,200, respectively (Drug Policy Facts 2022). While drug convictions are a defining characteristic of the federal prison system, accounting for nearly half of the sentenced prisoners, around 15 per cent of those under the jurisdiction of state correctional authorities are convicted of a drug offense as their most serious crime (BJS 2019). Interestingly, unlike other offense types, the total number of prisoners for drug charges at the state level began to decrease before the first cannabis legalization reforms adopted during the early 2010s, suggesting that law enforcement procedures shaped the prison population regardless of the changes in the legal status of drugs. Research has demonstrated that de facto practices of the court system regarding the imposition of the criminal law can anticipate drug policy reforms such as decriminalization (Laqueur 2014). At the federal level, on the other hand, the US did not witness a decrease in the prison population for drug offenses, showing the pervasive effects of criminalization before the wave of cannabis legalization began at the state level, starting with Washington State and Colorado in 2012.

Unequal drug laws and biased law enforcement have produced profoundly uneven outcomes in terms of race and ethnicity in the US (Tonrym 1995; Chesney-Lind 2002; Travis 2002). Although the gap has narrowed over the past decade, the racial and ethnic makeup of prisons continue to be considerably different from the country's demographics (Wacquant 2009; Johnson, Golub, and Dunlap 2008; Levine 2009). According to a document from the Drug Policy Alliance (2015), African Americans comprise nearly 40 per cent of the population incarcerated in state or federal prison for drug law violations, even though their drug use rates are not different from those of other races. Latinos, on the other hand, make up about 17 per cent of the US population, but comprise 20 per cent and 37 per cent of the people in state and federal prisons for drug offenses. Alongside the large and uneven number of people incarcerated for violation of the drug laws, the US has witnessed the expansion of less visible punishments such as disenfranchisement, withdrawal of student loans and welfare benefits, restrictions on driving licenses, and exclusion from different occupations. Not surprisingly, the consequences of drug offences have disproportionately affected women, African Americans, and Latino Americans (Stevens 2011).

Even though the government has gradually shifted its drug policy towards a more comprehensive approach, a significant amount of the money is devoted to supply reduction strategies. To put it another way, in 2012, 62.5 per cent of the resources available went to law enforcement, interdiction, and international initiatives, whereas prevention and treatment programs represented only 37.5 per cent of the federal drug control budget (ONDCP 2013). These figures are relevant given that the federal drug control budget jumped from about US$1.5 billion in 1980 to US$24.5 billion in 2012 (ONDCP 2013, 2021).

Conclusions

In one major policy shift at the federal level, the Biden administration announced on 6 October 2022, changes to end the US's 'failed approach' to cannabis. The president granted a full, complete, and unconditional pardon to thousands of citizens convicted of simple possession under federal law, calling governors to follow his lead with state offenses across the jurisdictions that have not decriminalized cannabis. Biden also directed various federal agencies to review the classification of the psychoactive substance in a clear attempt to remove cannabis from Schedule 1 of the Controlled Substances Act, a category that also regulates other illegal drugs such as heroin and LSD.

Critics fear, however, that the White House's announcement is too narrow to reverse a highly punitive approach still prevailing at the federal level. The pardon, for example, did not consider the situation of individuals convicted in states even though local courts prosecute most US cannabis offenses, especially across the states that have not decriminalized the psychoactive substance. Noncitizens who were not lawfully present in the US at the time of their criminal offense were also excluded from the executive action announced in October 2022. Most importantly, the presidential pardon will not protect individuals from facing federal cannabis possession offenses after the date of the proclamation, meaning that the future still resembles what the US has done with this psychoactive substance since simple possession became a crime in the 1970s.

At the time of the writing of this book, Maryland and Missouri had legalized the recreational use of cannabis in the 2022 midterm elections. The reform of the cannabis policy was also on the ballots of North Dakota, South Dakota, and Arkansas, states that already allowed the medical use of the psychoactive substance but did not approve the initiative. As a result, the recreational use of cannabis is now legal in 23 states, Guam, and Washington, DC. Furthermore, Colorado became the second state – after Oregon in 2020 – to legalize psychedelics after its residents voted to approve Proposition 122. The initiative is intended to decriminalize and regulate hallucinogenic substances found in mushrooms listed in Schedule 1 of the Controlled Substances Act.

Liberalization, however, has not been the norm in the US. In this chapter we traced the roots of the US's punitive approach towards illicit psychoactive substances, starting from state and municipal legislation in the late nineteenth century until the adoption of the Harrison Act in 1914. Highly punitive laws have been accompanied by a growing federal bureaucracy to combat illicit drugs. At the international level, the US also played a leading role in creating the first multilateral framework (that is, the International Opium Convention at The Hague) to restrict the trade of certain psychoactive substances such as opium. Despite certain impasses, the US' stringent model accelerated during the 1970s, when the war on drugs at home was complemented by several security initiatives abroad – especially in Latin America – focused on the supply side of the political economy of illicit drugs. Even the multilateral system echoed the US' efforts to criminalize and prohibit psychoactive substances. Yet criminal penalties and punishment, underpinned by a warlike narrative, have proved to be largely ineffective deterrents against the consumption of drugs and its associated problems.

The federal government did not break the population's interest in and habits with drugs, as William J Bennet claimed it would in the late 1980s. The US harbours the world's most lucrative market for illicit drugs. After a substantial decline witnessed in the 1980s and early 1990s, consumption levels started to increase during the 2000s. The LTP of all illicit drugs was in 2012 above the levels of the late 1970s, when consumption rates in the US reached a historical peak. LYP and LMP have also trended upward since the 1990s, although both use rates are below the levels of the late 1970s. Except for the LYP and LMP of LSD, all illicit drugs experienced increases between 2000 and 2012, and substances such as heroin registered even higher rates than the late 1970s. Furthermore, some illicit psychoactive substances were purer in 2012 than 40 or more years ago. The available evidence also indicates that the demand for illicit drugs did not subside despite seizures trending upward, suggesting that the federal emphasis on law enforcement aimed at increasing the monetary prices of illegal substances has been far from successful. Actually, the prices of dangerous illicit substances such as cocaine and heroin are well below the levels of the late 1970s and early 1980s.

Certain patterns of drug use have also led to adverse health consequences. Although the number of people with SUD and the demand for substance use treatment in the US remained relatively stable between 2000 and 2010, the steady increase in the number of drug overdoses has become a major preoccupation in the US. From 1980 to 2012, the number of deaths per 100,000 inhabitants skyrocketed from 1.1 to 13.1.

Yet the US has escaped from the continent's long-term patterns of violence. Homicides and other crimes such as robbery and larceny-theft are well below the levels registered during the 1980s. Even though surveys conducted across several correctional facilities suggest that the incidence of illicit drugs in criminal behaviour has increased among federal prisoners, the evidence is still inconclusive regarding the drug-crime nexus. Drug offenses, nevertheless, have had a disproportionate impact on the prison population. As a result of the tough-on-crime policy, the number of people sentenced for drug charges in federal and state prisons escalated substantially between the early 1980s and 2012. However, this upward trend seems to be coming to an end after several states started liberalizing their drug policies, a phenomenon also witnessed at the federal level.

The US drug policy, in other words, has been far from effective in curbing drug consumption and some of its associated harms. Although it would be a mistake to attribute drug use increases and other related problems such as increasing overdoses to prohibition and criminalization, especially because states still retain a lot of power when designing their drug policies and there may be other factors affecting the trends analyzed, the punitive federal approach has failed to at least prevent the damage. Under these circumstances, questions about the historical emphasis on law enforcement and incarceration rather than prevention or treatment are likely to proliferate among a society increasingly aware of the negative impacts of more than 100 years of the war on drugs.

4

Depenalization in Argentina

In the first days of February 2022, 23 people were reported lifeless and about 70 others were hospitalized in Buenos Aires due to the consumption of adulterated cocaine. This unprecedented event and the recent cases of drug-related violence in Rosario, the country's third most populous city, reopened the conversation about Argentina's drug policy. According to Baisotti (2022), since the COVID-19 pandemic the drug trafficking landscape has been shifting, confrontations among criminal organizations have resurfaced, the drugs sold on the streets are of alarmingly low quality, and there is a higher demand for illicit psychoactive substances.

Argentina is taking a more important role in the political economy of illicit drugs. The psychoactive substances enter the territory through two main routes. Cocaine comes mainly from Bolivia through the northern area, passing through the provinces of Jujuy and Salta, and then is distributed in the south to major cities and tourist destinations. Argentina was for many years considered only a transit country for drugs trafficked to feed the European market particularly. Yet, in recent years, drug violence in certain provinces and increases in illicit drug consumption have presented important public health and security challenges. Like other countries in South America, Argentina departed slightly from the long-established drug prohibitionist regime. Under the Supreme Court of Justice's Arriola ruling of 2009, the personal use of all illegal drugs was partially liberalized.

This chapter explores the case of depenalization in Argentina. As discussed in the introduction of this book, we refer to depenalization as a drug policy that still considers the possession and use of psychoactive substances a criminal offense typified under the law, yet the legislation is not always enforced in certain stages of the criminal justice system. Another particularity of this policy, especially in the case of Argentina, is that the non-punishable quantities of drugs are not specified by a new law and the determination for compliance is left to the authorities.

The analysis of the Argentinian depenalization case presents its challenges. Since there is not a homogenous implementation of the drug policy across the country, its application depends merely on the criteria of security forces and judges. Moreover, the data we base our analysis on, especially the comparison with the control groups, derive primarily from United Nations Office on Drugs and Crime (UNODC) statistics. Although there are established metrics for countries to follow to present the data to the international organization before publication, the information provided can sometimes be flawed and the quality of the data can be rated low when assessed by experts (ARQ Report 2018). The case, however, has been understudied and its assessment is worth exploring. Building on the literature, we analyze Argentina in an attempt to expand our understanding of different forms and executions of drug policies.

This chapter is organized into three main sections. The first part presents an overview of the evolution of Argentina's drug policy, from the early twentieth century until the depenalization of psychoactive substances in 2009. After evaluating major policy transformations throughout the years, the second section examines the current institutional and normative architecture developed to tackle the country's drug-related problems. The third section analyzes the estimated impacts of Argentina's depenalization reform. Final remarks are offered in the conclusion.

Drug policy reform in historical perspective

As it happened in most countries around the world, psychoactive substances were still legal in Argentina in the early twentieth century. Despite no restrictions other than administrative regulations being imposed domestically, the drug market remained relatively small, with consumption mostly limited to the upper social classes (Corda and Rossi 2016). By the early 1900s, however, the government faced growing pressure from various local actors to criminalize certain practices, favouring national legislation and the country's decision to sign the Protocol of Powers.[1]

The first hints of Argentina's drug regulation date back to 1924, when the National Congress passed Law 11.309. The bill was presented by Congressman Leopoldo Bard to amend Article 204 of the Penal Code. For the first time, under this bill, the smuggling of psychoactive substances and alkaloids into the country was criminalized. The new legislation also penalized the sale of these substances without a medical prescription with a sentence of up to two years in prison. Two years later, during the Marcelo T. de Alvear administration (1922–1928), Law 11.331 was introduced, reforming the Penal Code once more and broadening the legal framework to penalize the 'illegitimate' possession of psychoactive substances and alkaloids.

The public debate shaping drug policy lost momentum after the sanctioning of Law 11.331. Despite the National Congress discussing a project presented in 1942 to repress the possession of psychoactive substances 'intended for trade or supply' (Gómez 2013),[2] drug-related issues were not a priority among high-ranking government officials and society in Argentina. With Washington, DC's efforts concentrated on alcohol prohibition and US federal agencies experiencing budget constraints following the legalization of alcoholic beverages, the international system did not exert much pressure on countries like Argentina to legislate on drug-related matters.

It was only after the second half of the twentieth century, when Argentina faced several military coups, that illegal drugs appeared on the national political agenda once again.[3] During the military dictatorship that governed Argentina from 1966 to 1973, the security apparatus expanded, and drugs were framed as a national security threat. In the political discourse, drugs were considered the 'new enemy within', establishing a direct link between radical political militants, drug trafficking, and consumption (Manzano 2015, 37). According to Touzé (2006), users were often depicted as dangerous and rebellious, an idea and image generated mainly in the US and disseminated throughout Latin America.

Following the country's ratification of the United Nations Single Convention in 1963, the military dictatorship expanded even more the categories of drug-related activities considered crimes. In 1968, for example, Law 17.567 was passed reforming Article 204 of the Penal Code, punishing the production, contraband, and sale of drugs with prison sentences of up to six years. It was the only time in Argentina's history that a criminal law explicitly excluded the possession of psychoactive substances for personal consumption as a crime (Corda 2011). Nonetheless, since the law was a product of a military dictatorship, it was repealed in 1973.[4]

Drug policies in Argentina started to toughen significantly during the early 1970s, mirroring the punitive rationale carried by the US under the Nixon administration (1969–1974). By 1974, during the government of María Estela Martínez (1974–1976), Argentina passed Law 20.771, the first legislation fully dedicated to drugs.[5] Law 20.771 imposed new penalties for the production, trafficking, and commerce of illegal psychoactive substances, establishing that drug offenses fell under the country's federal jurisdiction. Most importantly, Article 6 criminalized the illegitimate possession of drugs for personal use with imprisonment of one to six years. Argentina's harsh legislation was accompanied by the creation of state-led agencies aimed solely at combating illegal drugs. These included the *División de Narcóticos* (Narcotics Division) created in 1971, the *Comisión Nacional de Toxicomanía y Narcóticos* (National Council of Toxicology and Narcotics) established in 1972, and the *Centro Nacional de Reeducación Social* (National Centre of Social Reeducation) created in 1973. According to López Rega, the minister of Social Welfare and chief of the *Alianza Anticomunista Argentina* (Argentine Anticommunist Alliance),[6] guerrillas were 'the main drug users in Argentina. Therefore, the anti-drug campaign will be an anti-guerrilla campaign' (Blum 2003, 205).

The Supreme Court of Justice's jurisprudence also contributed to the toughening of Argentina's drug policy before the transition to democracy in 1983. The *Colavini* ruling, the first participation of Argentina's Supreme Court in this matter, confirmed the constitutionality of the criminalization of the possession of psychoactive substances for personal consumption acknowledged in Article 6 of Law 20.771.[7] The 1978 national decision compared 'drug addiction' with events such as 'wars' and 'plagues', and associated users with different illegal activities such as 'delinquency' and 'insurrection' (Touzé 1996). In effect, the latter illustrates the general ambiance during Argentina's last military dictatorship (Touzé 1996). A few years later, the 1981 *Valerio* ruling reiterated the Supreme Court of Justice's unambiguous jurisprudence and declared criminal penalties for illegal drug possession for personal use to be constitutional.

The return to democracy in Argentina brought a gradual reversal of the repressive policies of the 1970s. As Manzano (2015, 61) claims, 'Wide segments of Argentines thought that it was possible and desirable to rethink the drug problem, thanks in part to its association with authoritarian projects'. The image of users started shifting, deconstructing the idea from 'consumers as criminals' to 'consumers as patients'. This set a differentiation between traffickers and problematic users, meaning that psychoactive substances were no longer considered a national security threat associated with guerrilla insurgency.

Under the Raúl Alfonsín administration (1983–1989), the rhetoric changed, focusing on prevention while also legitimizing health care provisions for users (Camarotti, Kornblit, and Di Leo 2010). An example of the new efforts was the creation, in 1985, of the *Comisión Nacional para el Control del Narcotráfico y el Abuso de Drogas* (Drug Abuse and Drug Trafficking Control National Commission [CONCONAD]). Under the direct control of the Ministry of Health and Social Welfare, the newfound organization noted in its first document that 'the national government decided to face the problem of drug trafficking and abuse, taking advantage of the possibility of fighting it from a preventive perspective' (CONCONAD 1986). Along these lines, the national government launched different prevention initiatives. Through Law 23.358, for instance, schools and the media were instructed to include information about the adequate prevention of problematic use on their curriculum and programming, respectively.

The Supreme Court's jurisprudence also changed after the democratic transition. The 1986 *Bazterrica* ruling[8] declared the unconstitutionality of Article 6 of Law 20.771, reversing the criteria followed during the last dictatorship in the *Colavini* and *Valerio* decisions. Enrique Petracchi, a Supreme Court judge at the time, stated:

> Our country is emerging from 50 years of political vicissitudes, during most of which prevailed the authoritarianism and intolerance in the

> rules of social organisation; they have put at serious risk the possibility of placing us as a nation within the framework of the ideals which gave foundation. That succession of authoritarian periods was characterised by the proliferation of prohibitions as a resource to control social relationships … the damage it can cause to the current Argentine society any impairment to the system of individual freedoms is surely less risky than that posed by the social danger of drug addiction. (Supreme Court 2009)

During this time, debates around legalization pervaded the political discourse, calling for a reform of the country's drug policy. In 1986, the Radical party congressmen Adolfo Gass and Fernando Mauhum presented the first project proposing the decriminalization of *coqueo* (coca chewing) and drug possession for personal use.[9] The legislative initiative, discussed in the Argentine Senate, promoted the development of similar projects.[10] One, for example, was presented by Lucia Alberti, Matilde Fernández de Quarracino, Néstor Golpe, and Ricardo Felgueras and suggested a multidisciplinary approach instead of a one-fits-all paradigm as a better solution to tackle the country's drug problem (Página/12 1988). Most of the proposals favouring drug policy reform were anchored to Article 19 of the Argentinian Constitution, which establishes that 'the private actions of men that in no way offend public order or morality, nor injure a third party, are reserved only to God, and are exempt from the authority of the magistrates' (Constitución de la Nación Argentina 1994, Article 19).

Yet the most relevant transformation happened a few months after the Peronist President Carlos S. Menem (1989–1999) took office. In October 1989, the National Congress passed Law 23.737, replacing the 1974 drug legislation.[11] The bill was presented by the Radical party congressman Lorenzo Cortese and retained most of the language on drug trafficking-related crimes. Nonetheless, the length of sentences already established increased, from four to 15 years in prison.[12] Most importantly, Law 23.737 criminalized the possession of drugs for personal use, thereby reversing the essence of the *Bazterrica* ruling of 1986. In cases of possession of small quantities of cannabis, the bill's Article 14 clearly states that 'the prison sentence will range from one month to two years when a small quantity of drugs and other circumstances suggest unequivocally that possession is for personal use' (Ley 23.737, Article 14). Under this law, however, a prison sentence could be interchangeable with treatment or prevention courses. This health provision was included to avoid an open contradiction of the Supreme Court's ruling.

A few months before the enactment of Law 23.737, the national government created another institution to be in charge of the country's drug control policy, the *Secretaría de Programación para la Prevención de la Drogadicción y la Lucha contra el Narcotráfico* (Secretary for the Prevention of Drug Addiction and the Struggle Against Drug Trafficking [SEDRONAR]).[13] The new national agency's mission merged the security and health fields, handling both drug consumption- and drug trafficking-related issues simultaneously. Despite the dual focus, the organization was particularly attentive to the security realm and Secretary Alberto Lestelle's personal inclination towards a *mano dura* (iron fist) approach against drug traffickers rapidly permeated SEDRONAR's mission and work (Cutrona 2017, 2019). In 2017, under Decree 33, the institution changed its name to *Secretaría de Políticas Integrales sobre Drogas de la Nación Argentina* (Secretariat of Comprehensive Drug Policies of the Argentine Nation). Nevertheless, the acronym SEDRONAR was kept because of its national and international recognition (Cutrona 2017, 2019).

The Supreme Court followed the national government's approach to illicit drugs. Through the 1990 *Montalvo* ruling, Argentina's highest judicial court reversed the *Bazterrica* precedent adopted during the Alfonsín administration, reaffirming the jurisprudence put forward by the dictatorship in 1978 and 1981, respectively.[14] According to the Supreme Court's new ruling, 'The possession of psychoactive substances, whatever their quantity, is a punishable conduct according to Article 14, the second part of Law 23.737, and such reasonable punishment does not affect any right recognised by the Fundamental Law' (Ley 23.737 1989, 2).

During this time, the image of people who use drugs as criminals was reinstated. Menem radicalized his narrative, framing illicit psychoactive substances as a national security threat. Newspaper headlines often portrayed the views of different high-ranked government officials, demanding the adoption of repressive policies to combat drug trafficking. In the political discourse, the consumption of various illegal drugs was said to be 'jeopardising Argentina's lifestyle' (Malamud-Goti 1994, 16). President Carlos S. Menem himself contributed to the growing hysteria around illegal drugs by openly requesting the application of the death penalty for drug traffickers operating in Argentina (Alaniz 2000). In 1995, the National Congress passed Law 24.424, sanctioning the self-cultivation of psychoactive substances with one month to two years in prison. The new national legislation punished the offenses by applying Articles 17, 18, and 21 of Law 23.737.

Years later, during the economic and social crisis of 2001–2002, drug issues almost disappeared from the political agenda.[15] In addition to the lack of policies aimed at dealing with the country's increasing prevalence rates, the apathy of the national government was reflected by the minor involvement of SEDRONAR. While Lorenzo Cortese was in office (2000–2002), the secretary almost disappeared, registering the lowest budget allocation in Argentina's history (Burzaco and Berensztein 2014). Additionally, in October 2001, SEDRONAR stopped paying allowances to 380 problematic users who had no other means to access medical treatment. The situation worsened when Cortese resigned in January 2002, leaving the institution without a director. At the end of 2002, SEDRONAR had no budget and rumours that the organization would eventually dissolve quickly spread throughout the country (Barbano 2002).

The National Congress also overlooked discussing drug policy alternatives in Argentina during the early 2000s, except for the introduction of a project aimed at decriminalizing the possession of illicit drugs for personal consumption. The legislative initiative, presented by the Socialist congressman Eduardo García in 2003, also attempted to diminish the compulsory harmful handling of people who use drugs by various government-led institutions. Despite the official support of nonprofit organizations such as the *Asociación de Reducción de Daños de Argentina* (Argentinian Harm Reduction Association), the legislative project was never considered.

As the economic, social, and political situation slowly improved, the Néstor Kirchner administration (2003–2007) found some room to promote new structural reforms. Notwithstanding Argentina's drug law originally established that offenses falling under Law 23.737 belonged to the Federal Justice's magistrates, in 2005 the National Congress passed the so-called *desfederalización* (decentralization) framework. Under the new framework, provincial prosecutors were allowed to deal with minor drug offenses. Law 26.052 left the Federal Justice to focus on major trafficking crimes. The bill's Article 2 establishes that 'offenses defined and punished by this law are the competence of the Federal Justice except for those provinces and the Autonomous City of Buenos Aires, which chose to assume jurisdiction by law' (Ley 26.052 2005). In this context, Argentina's drug control policy stopped being exclusively a federal matter, and with this the country's jurisdictional powers, the map of relevant actors, and other institutional practices were drastically transformed after the sanctioning of Law 26.052.

The *Frente para la Victoria* (Front for Victory), the political party led at the time by President Cristina Fernández (2007–2015), Néstor Kirchner's wife, created the *Comisión Nacional Coordinadora de Políticas Públicas en Materia de Prevención y Control del Tráfico Ilícito de Estupefacientes, la Delincuencia Organizada Transnacional y la Corrupción* (National Coordinating Commission of Public Policy on the Prevention and Control of Drug Trafficking, Organised Crime, and Corruption). The commission, established by Decree 1.359/2009, overlapped with SEDRONAR's main functions. This created a parallel institutional infrastructure dedicated to the fight against illegal drugs in Argentina. The incompatibility between the two institutions gained greater visibility when the commission drafted a decriminalization project, a drug liberalization alternative rejected by the authorities of SEDRONAR (Burzaco and Berensztein 2014).

Two years later, the National Coordinating Commission of Public Policy on the Prevention and Control of Drug Trafficking, Organised Crime, and Corruption was formally transferred from the chief of the Cabinet of Ministers to SEDRONAR (La Nación 2012). The institutional transformation during the Cristina Fernández administration continued. In 2013, health and security drug-related matters, originally overseen by SEDRONAR, were separated into two different national agencies. Under the new organizational framework, the recently created Ministry of Security was put in charge of drug supply and trafficking issues, whereas SEDRONAR continued to deal with prevention and assistance of people who use psychoactive substances.

A pivotal point in Argentina's drug policy came in 2009, after a case involving three individuals detained and sentenced for cannabis possession reached the Supreme Court. Based on the right to individual privacy acknowledged in Article 19 of the Argentinian Constitution, the *Arriola* ruling declared unconstitutional the second paragraph of Article 14 of Law 23.737, which criminalizes the possession of psychoactive substances for personal consumption. More specifically, the ruling reads: 'It is declared unconstitutional the legal provision insofar as it incriminates the possession of illegal drugs for personal consumption carried out under conditions that do not pose a specific hazard or damage to rights or property of a third party' (Constitución de la Nación Argentina 1994, Article 19). Along these lines, Carmen Argibay, one of the Supreme Court's judges at that time, claimed that drug possession for personal use does not provide any reasons to affirm that the accused have carried out anything more than a private act or that they have offended public morals or the rights of others (Supreme Court 2009). According to Bergman (2018), since the ruling does not specify names or permitted amounts of allowed psychoactive substances, it strikes down the authority's intervention in personal use for all illegal drugs.

Following the Supreme Court's ruling, the adoption of two policies suggested that Argentina was getting closer to a structural change in the legal status of drugs. On the one hand, the government adopted the *Programa Nacional de Educación y Prevención sobre las Adicciones y el Consumo Indebido de Drogas* (National Program for the Education and Prevention of Addictions and Drug Abuse), an initiative launched under the umbrella of the Ministry of Education. On the other hand, the National Congress passed in 2010 Law 26.657, also known as the Mental Health legislation. The new legal framework recognized that problematic consumption must be addressed as an integral part of the country's mental health policies. In addition, Law 26.657 also discouraged hospitalization as the main intervention strategy to treat problematic consumption, promoting instead programs where people who use drugs can receive treatment without losing ties with their families, friends, and the community in general. Altogether, these policy initiatives collided directly with the main tenets of Argentina's drug law.

The *Arriola* ruling eventually sparked the drug policy debate once again. The National Congress was at the forefront of a reform. In addition to the proposal presented by incumbent senator Anibal Fernández,[16] other six projects proposing the decriminalization of drugs were put forward between 2011 and 2012. The authors of the legislative initiatives came from different political parties and included Vilma Ibarra; Diana Conti; Victoria Donda; Adriana Puiggros, Adela, Segarra, and María del Carmen Bianchi; Ricardo Gil Lavedra and Manuel Garrido; Fabián Peralta, Gerardo Milman, María Linares, Omar Duclós, and Margarita Stolbizer.

Unlike previous times, the attempt to liberalize Argentina's drug control policy was supported by the national government. In 2008, during the presentation of a national survey on the public use of illicit drugs, President Fernández stated: 'I do not like addicts to be sentenced as if they were criminals. Those who must be sentenced are those who sell the substance' (Cutrona 2017, 103). Fernández also admitted that she was 'waiting for the project', referring to the proposal to amend the drug law on which the National Coordinating Commission was working (Guagnini 2008). Moreover, SEDRONAR's secretary at the time, Rafael Bielsa, agreed to the need for a revision of the punitive paradigm (Ruchansky 2012). He stated at a meeting with a local office of the United Nations: 'The [Supreme] Court said in the Arriola ruling that possession for personal use of a certain amount of marijuana is not punishable, and the executive power is obligated to coordinate the legal right with the court and to make changes in the positive law' (as cited in Gallo 2012).

The legislative reform, nevertheless, never materialized. Despite the parliamentary consensus in favour of decriminalization, illustrated by the elaboration of a common draft by the main political parties within the Chamber of Deputies, the bill was not approved. The absence of broad social support and the forthcoming midterm legislative elections shifted the focus of the national debate towards other topics. According to Cunial (2018), the role of the Catholic Church was decisive in this regard, as the institution used its 'authority' in the field of drugs and the electoral context to condition the original project proposed by the ruling party. Illustrative of this point was the organization of a 'youth march' in which Cardinal Jorge Bergoglio, who would become the Pope, rejected the decriminalization project, identifying those who promoted the legislative initiative as 'the merchants of death' (La Nación 2012).

The election of Mauricio Macri (2015–2019) to the presidency in 2015 brought the decriminalization debate to a halt. Similar to the other two main candidates competing in the general elections, the political discourse of the leader of the *Cambiemos* (Let's change) coalition subordinated practically all aspects of the country's drug policy to the security field, understanding that psychoactive substances are closely related to crime and delinquency (Cutrona 2018). The drug problem, in other words, was presented as an existential threat, relegating other relevant policy-making aspects such as treatment and human rights to a secondary role. Not surprisingly, the president's first drug policy initiative was to declare a year-long 'state of security emergency', transforming drug trafficking into public enemy number one once again.

Interestingly, one of the few initiatives incompatible in part with the punitive approach promoted during the Macri administration came from the National Congress. In March 2017, the Senate passed the Medical Marijuana Law. The bill established a regulatory framework for scientific research on the cannabis plant and its derivatives, enabling therapeutic access to these substances to certain patients. Law 27.350 also created the *Programa Nacional para el Estudio y la Investigación del Uso Medicinal de la Planta de Cannabis* (National Program for the Study and Research of the Medicinal Use of the Cannabis Plant) and the *Registro Nacional Voluntario* (Voluntary National Registry) to coordinate the application of the new legislation.

Yet Law 27.350 spurred some criticism. The social organizations behind the plan, including *Mamá Cultiva*, Cannabis Medicinal Argentina, and other groups formed by mothers of children with different pathologies, highlighted legal loopholes and ambiguities in the original legislation. They also objected to the decree regulating the new law approved by the president in September 2017. According to a document published by the *Consejo Nacional de Investigaciones Científicas y Técnicas* (National Council for Scientific and Technical Research [CONICET]) in 2020, by limiting the use of medicinal cannabis to cases of refractory epilepsy, the regulation ignored other relevant pathologies such as cancer, rheumatism, fibromyalgia, and chronic pain. On the other hand, self-cultivation, one of the main drivers of the promoters of the project, was excluded by only allowing imports, an expensive alternative difficult to access for most individuals in Argentina. Regarding this point, Valeria Salech, then president of *Mamá Cultiva*, declared that the regulation left many families 'adrift', as the new legal framework still considered them 'criminals' liable to sentences of up to 15 years in prison (Centenera 2020).

Despite certain advances in drug policy, there is still concern and debate over the implementation of some of the liberalization reforms. The Argentinian state has promoted contrasting policies to deal with illegal drugs. The defence of human rights, the liberal jurisprudence of the Supreme Court of Justice (not always present), and the progressive approach of certain political elites have coexisted with a punitive drug legislation, the sustained growth of the prison population for drug-related offenses, and the highly repressive practices of the security forces (Cutrona 2021). Under these circumstances, there is a grey area between the Supreme Court's depenalization ruling and its execution. Human rights organizations have pointed out glitches in the judicial system when reporting on consumption crimes. These are attributed to poor investigations and errors in police procedures (Centro de Estudios Legales y Sociales 2018).

Depenalization: Law enforcement rules

Argentina's drug policy privileges criminal prosecution as its main control tool (Corda and Rossi 2016). Law 23.737 punishes every stage of the drug commodity chain with imprisonment. While the production, manufacturing, and trafficking of illicit psychoactive substances (Article 5) are penalized with prison sentences of four to 15 years, possession (Article 14) is punishable with one to six years. Nevertheless, when possession is considered for personal consumption (Article 14, paragraph 2), Argentina's drug law reduces sentences by one month to two years. In cases of problematic use, imprisonment penalties could be replaced by rehabilitation or other alternative medical treatments (Articles 17 and 18).

As already mentioned, however, the *Arriola* ruling declared unconstitutional the second paragraph of Article 14 of Law 23.737. After the Supreme Court of Justice's latest jurisprudence on the subject, judges in Argentina have the authority to decide whether the quantity and circumstances of drug possession qualifies as 'personal use' and/or 'affect third parties'. This situation, therefore, has created a grey area in which not only lower courts but also different law enforcement agencies, which initiate most of Argentina's prosecutions, have the responsibility for interpreting the context surrounding the detention of an individual with possession of illicit drugs. Argentina's depenalization, in other words, is granted by jurisprudence and not by law.

Under the current legal framework, drug violations are considered federal crimes. Despite decentralization having changed the national scheme by allowing lower courts and state law enforcement agencies to deal with minor drug offenses, the bulk of the prosecutions conducted in Argentina are overseen by federal courts and national law enforcement agencies. The federal agencies with drug-related responsibilities are the *Policía Federal Argentina* (Argentine Federal Police), the *Gendarmería Nacional Argentina* (Argentine National Gendarmerie), the *Prefectura Naval Argentina* (Argentine Naval Prefecture), and the *Policía de Seguridad Aeroportuaria* (Airport Security Police). The armed forces, on the other hand, are not allowed to participate in domestic security affairs such as counterdrug initiatives despite several presidential administrations bypassing the legal framework since the return to democracy in 1983.[17]

Individuals detained by orders of federal or national[18] courts are sent to the *Servicio Penitenciario Federal* (Federal Penitentiary System [SPF]). The SPF oversees 32 out of the 308 detention facilities operating in Argentina

(Dirección Nacional de Política Criminal 2018). Out of the country's total population incarcerated for illicit drug offenses, roughly 60 per cent are held in the SPF. The *Sistema Penitenciario de la Provincia de Buenos Aires* (Penitentiary System of the Buenos Aires Province) follows the ranking with approximately 20 per cent, whereas the remaining state prisons hold the rest of the population imprisoned for drug-related offenses nationwide (Corda 2011). These percentages have varied considerably over the course of the years, particularly after the National Congress passed the decentralization scheme in 2005.

In 2013, when the Ministry of Security took control of supply and trafficking issues, SEDRONAR was left with the responsibility of focusing on the demand for psychoactive substances. Under the umbrella of the chief of the Cabinet of Ministers, the institution implements prevention and treatment programs across the country, an activity developed in coordination with the 23 provincial governments and the *Ciudad de Buenos Aires* (autonomous City of Buenos Aires [CABA]). Likewise, the National Census of Treatment Centres registers public and private institutions providing treatment. To assist users, SEDRONAR offers grants and subsidies channelled through organizations and programs such as *Comunidades Terapéuticas* (Therapeutic Communities), *Casas de Atención y Acompañamiento Comunitario* (Attention and Community Accompanying Houses), *Dispositivos Integrales de Abordaje Territorial* (Comprehensive Territorial Approach Devices), and *Dispositivos de Tratamiento Comunitario* (Community Treatment Devices) (SEDRONAR 2019).

In 2020, SEDRONAR had an independent annual budget estimated at $1,707 million Argentinian pesos (approximately US$6.09 million) (Ministerio de Economía 2020). Official reports show that the institution's allocation of funds has grown substantially over the course of the years, in both nominal and relative terms. While nominal increases are mostly explained by Argentina's rampant inflation, relative fluctuations suggest that drug-related issues have gained political salience. Table 4.1 demonstrates that SEDRONAR's budget, as a percentage of all the jurisdictions' allocations, has increased exponentially since 2014.

The *Consejo Federal de Drogas* (Federal Drug Council [COFEDRO]) brings together the representatives and government authorities working in the field of drugs from each of the 23 provinces and CABA. The main goal of the institution is to agree on and coordinate different public policies for the prevention and treatment of problematic consumption based on local and regional experiences in the field. Despite COFEDRO remaining relatively inactive during a couple of years, it still meets regularly in different provinces under the auspices of SEDRONAR.

Argentina has experienced numerous changes in its drug policy. Many actors, political parties, and ideologies have had a great impact on its evolution

Table 4.1: SEDRONAR budget 2007–2020[19]

Year	SEDRONAR	% of total
2007	19	0.017
2008	29	0.018
2009	33	0.014
2010	48	0.017
2011	64	0.017
2012	80	0.015
2013	102	0.016
2014	128	0.014
2015	279	0.022
2016	556	0.035
2017	739	0.031
2018	1,133	0.039
2019	1,292	0.030
2020	1,707	0.035

Source: Authors, based on Ministerio de Economía (2020)

throughout the years. Since depenalization was reached in 2009 under a Supreme Court of Justice ruling and not under a new national law, there are some inconsistencies in its application. What have been the estimated impacts of depenalization in Argentina? Have consumption patterns changed over the years? What effects has it had on the country's security and public health? We explore these questions in the following section.

The estimated impacts of depenalization

Touzé et al (2008, 5) maintain that 'the analysis of the context of severe economic, social, and political crises that Argentina experienced is of significant importance to comprehend the policies, services, and practices of drug use during the decade between 1994 to 2004'. Some key events include wars, revolutions, political transitions, and economic collapses, which, according to Touzé and colleagues (2008), produced an increase of great scale in the number of users of injectable drugs and other high-risk practices associated with illicit drug consumption.

After the many ambivalences in Argentina's drug policy, some degree of liberalization came with depenalization. More than a decade has passed since the last Supreme Court ruling, and despite constant pressure to decriminalize, different social and political forces keep pulling the country towards punitivism. Have subtle reforms like depenalization affected Argentina's illicit consumption patterns and other drug-related harms? We start our analysis of the estimated impacts of the 2009 *Arriola* ruling by looking at changes in drug use trends, seizures, drug prices, and purity pre- and post-policy change. We later examine health-related impacts such as the transmission of viruses and infectious diseases as well as the demand for treatment. Last, we explore the area of security by observing the evolution of intentional homicides, robbery and theft rates, and prison population.

To complement our analysis, we compare the Argentinian trends with a control group, composed of Brazil and Panama. Choosing a control group in the South American region was not an easy task. Almost all countries have liberalized at least at some level the use of certain psychoactive substances – especially cannabis – for recreational purposes. Some exceptions include Guyana and Suriname, where such substances have remained criminalized. Unfortunately, due to the lack of national surveys in these countries, year gaps, and methodological differences in the collection and processing of data, it was extremely difficult to establish a truly precise comparison.

In Panama, the recreational use of psychoactive substances is criminalized, although flexible penalties may be applied to problematic users (Penal Code, Article 320) (Organization of American States [OAS] 2019). Between 2007 and 2012, different reforms to the penal code broadened the typology of drug offenses and increased criminal penalties, equating some of them to homicides, femicides, and contract killings (Rodriguez Blanco and Cumbrera Diaz 2017). Brazil, on the other hand, decriminalized the use of illegal drugs for personal use in 2006 (Lei 11.343, Article 28).[20] Although its legal framework differentiates between users and traffickers, the specific volume of drugs in possession that separates the two actors is not determined by law. Like Argentina, there is a high level of uncertainty in the practice of law where there is not a defined line that differentiates simple from aggravated possession and the distinction is left to the officials' or judges' discretion (OAS 2019). This has created an 'ambiguous' drug policy, one of 'conservative progressive intention' (Rodriguez 2022). This situation, in conjunction with other factors such as political and social conservatism, has led to the continuation of a highly punitive application of their drug laws, making the policy of decriminalization an inconsistent and ineffective approach that does not keep people who use drugs out of the criminal justice system. Not surprisingly, OAS notes that in Brazil 'the unauthorised possession of substances for personal consumption is considered a criminal offense' (OAS 2019, 19).

For comparative purposes, different databases were used to assess Argentina's illicit drug prevalence, mainly looking at the national surveys periodically published by SEDRONAR. When comparing Argentina to the control group, statistics from OAS or UNODC were used to make a sound analysis of data scrutinized under the same methodological framework. Likewise, the data were adjusted to the corresponding part of the analysis. For this reason, some figures might differ when analyzing Argentina individually and in a regional comparative perspective.

Drug consumption trends

Under the umbrella of SEDRONAR, the *Observatorio Argentino de Drogas* (Argentinean Observatory of Drugs [OAD]) is the institution in charge of producing and systematizing epidemiological, statistical, and geographical information on drugs. Before its creation in 2005, empirical data were scattered and unorganized, thereby hampering the comparability and use of studies. Efforts to gather information and assess the magnitude of the consumption and abuse of psychoactive substances in Argentina have been carried out by SEDRONAR with the support of the *Dirección Nacional del Observatorio Argentino de Drogas* (National Directorate of the Argentine Observatory of Drugs). In conjunction with UNODC and the Inter-American Drug Abuse Control Commission (CICAD/OEA), the Inter-American Observatory of Drugs provides technical and financial support to South American countries within the Sub-regional Information and Research System on Drugs in Argentina, Bolivia, Chile, Ecuador, Peru, and Uruguay. The objective of this regional initiative is to strengthen the National Drug Commissions and their national observatories, with the purpose of generating data and updating information about the drug consumption trends in each country (SEDRONAR 2017c).

In Argentina, national studies on the use of psychoactive substances in the population aged 12 to 65 were conducted in 2006, 2008, 2010, and 2017, sharing common methodological specificities, which makes them compatible to the data produced at the regional level. These four epidemiological studies aimed to shed light on the associated risks of drug consumption, as well as gather relevant background information related to public policies and progress in prevention strategies, treatment, and control of the supply of different psychoactive substances (SEDRONAR 2017c).[21]

Drug consumption in Argentina has become an area of concern for policymakers. Observing the life prevalence of various illegal drugs, cannabis shows the highest consumption levels, which doubled after 2010, increasing from 8.1 to 17.4 per cent in 2017. Cocaine's prevalence presents its highest rates in 2006, following a downward trend in 2008 and 2010. Seven years later, in 2017, its consumption nonetheless increased 2.7 percentage points. Even though at a much lower scale, the rest of the illicit psychoactive substances seem to follow a similar trend. For example, the consumption of inhalants decreased after 2006, maintaining lower prevalence rates between 2008 and 2010, and then increased in 2017.

Based on the available data, we observe that lifetime prevalence for most of the psychoactive substances registered a rise after depenalization in 2009, excluding heroin which stayed at the same rate. The increments were not evident right after the policy change but a few years later. The most noticeable is the case of cannabis use, and cocaine at a lower scale. However, most of the other illicit psychoactive substances that show increments after depenalization also experienced greater rates of consumption during the pre-policy reform years (that is, 2006). That is, Argentina witnessed higher levels of use before policy change in most illicit drugs except for cannabis.

The most recent national study conducted in 2017 reports that about 1,482,165 Argentinians had used cannabis at least once during the last year and 245,936 had started using the psychoactive substance. Compared to 2008, the year prior to the reform, the annual incidence of cannabis use in 2017 is 2.1 times higher (Graph 4.1). Among those who had consumed cannabis once in their life, about 41 per cent had continued use during the last year (SEDRONAR 2017b). Between 2008 and 2017, the last-year prevalence (LYP) of cocaine also increased from 1.0 per cent to 1.5 per cent. Among people who used cocaine during the last 12 months (292,052), almost half of them (48.6 per cent) reported their consumption to be frequent, 37.6 per cent reported occasional usage, and 13.8 per cent accounts for experimental use (SEDRONAR 2017b). The LYPs of all other illicit psychoactive substances evaluated in the report also present increases, except for coca base paste, which decreased slightly, and inhalants, which stayed at the same level.

The last-month prevalence (LMP) presents patterns similar to the lifetime prevalence (LTP) and LYP (Graph 4.2). The most substantial increase is also reflected in cannabis usage, not right after depenalization but eight years later. Prevalence grew 8.5 percentage points from 2008 to 2017, reaching

Graph 4.1: Argentina's LYP among the general population by drug type and year

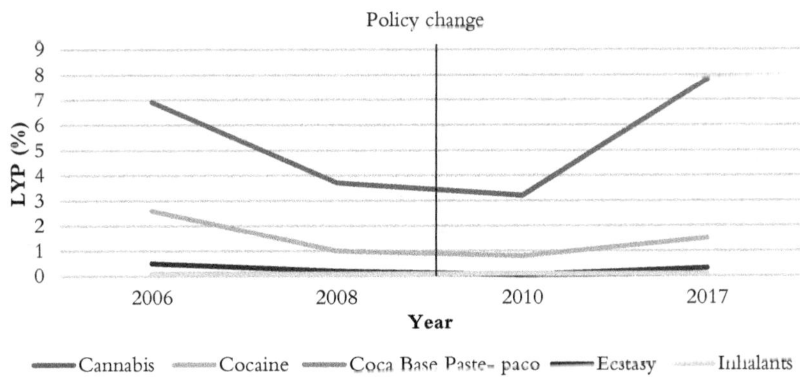

Source: Authors, based on SEDRONAR (2017)

Graph 4.2: Argentina's LMP among the general population by drug type and year

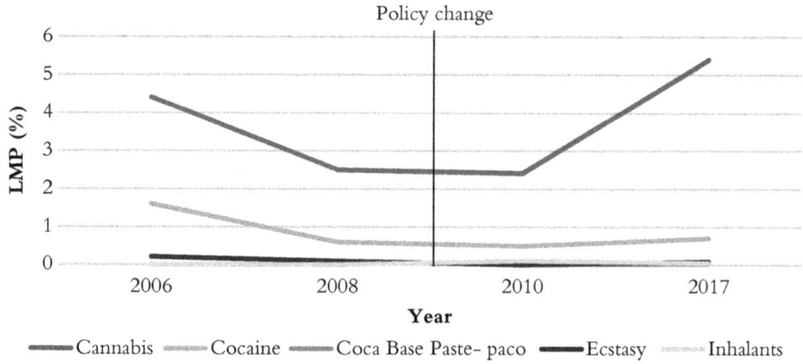

Source: Authors, based on SEDRONAR (2010, 2017b)

higher rates compared to pre-policy reform figures. Between 2008 and 2017, cocaine consumption increased, by 1.5 percentage points, as did inhalants, by 0.05 percentage points. Coca base paste, by contrast, presents a minor decline of 0.02 percentage points, whereas ecstasy does not register changes in the levels of consumption during the same period.

As observed in the other prevalence measurements, consumption increased in all substances after depenalization. Cannabis, in particular, presents an important level of growth compared to other illegal drugs' increases. However, putting cannabis aside, then as with the other prevalence measurements analyzed previously, cocaine, coca base paste, and ecstasy experienced higher rates of consumption in 2006 compared to 2017 when depenalization was fully operational.

In terms of last-month frequency of cannabis consumption, the overall use (56.6 per cent) in Argentina is mainly occasional. The national surveys also demonstrate that 6.2 per cent use the psychoactive substance experimentally, while 236,820 consumers (16 per cent) stated that they used cannabis on a daily basis. Frequent use is concentrated in men between 18 and 34 years old, most of whom are working adults (72 per cent) and high school graduates (67 per cent). In Argentina, 278,689 (18.8 per cent) of users display patterns of problematic consumption (SEDRONAR 2017a).

Illicit drug consumption by age group and initiation age

As mentioned in previous chapters, the age of initiation is a good indicator to predict future drug use patterns and the associated risks. The available evidence suggests that the younger the person starts the consumption of drugs, the greater the possibility of facing health risks in the future

(National Institutes of Health 2021). Comparing the data from 2006 (before depenalization) and 2017,[22] in three (18–24, 25–34, and 35–49) out of the five age groups, there is an increase in cannabis LTP after the depenalization reform. In the 18–24 cluster, lifetime prevalence increased from 22.2 in 2006 to 29.3 in 2017. In the 25–34 age group prevalence increased from 22 to 26.8 during the same years as the 35–49 group increasing from 13.6 in 2006 to 15.5 in 2017. The most evident growth is shown in the 18–24 cohort, followed by the 25–35 age cluster (SEDRONAR 2010, 2017b).[23]

In our analysis, we pay close attention to the 12–17 age group since it is considered the cohort most vulnerable to developing future health-related problems, including substance abuse or dependency (Bretteville-Jensen and Williams 2011). In the case of Argentina, there are two positive notes to take into consideration. One is that the rates of prevalence of this age group are among the lowest. The second is that although consumption rates increased after 2010 (in all age groups), they are lower compared to 2006. Likewise, the bottom-most rates of LTP are shown in the 50–65 age group, declining 6.3 percentage points from 2006 to 2017.

According to a SEDRONAR (2017a) report, of the individuals who started cannabis consumption at age 17, 30 out of 100 show abusive use and about 46 per cent report frequent consumption. Among the individuals who started cannabis use at 25, 6 out of 100 users present problematic use or substance abuse, and 19 per cent consume the psychoactive substance frequently. To put it differently, the evidence clearly indicates that the earlier the initiation age of cannabis consumption, the greater the probability the user will develop a substance use problem in the future.

In terms of the LTP of cocaine by age group, the historical trends in Argentina indicate that in all age groups cocaine life prevalence is higher post-reform (2017) compared to pre-reform rates (2008), suggesting that depenalization can increase the use of a psychoactive substance often associated with high overdose rates – a trend experienced in the US (Tardiff et al 1996; Coffin et al 2003; Darke, Degenhardt, and Mattick 2006) and, more recently, in Europe (Sanchez et al 1995; European Monitoring Center for Drugs and Drug Addiction 2003) and Australia (Darke et al 2005). While more significant increases are present in the ages between 18 and 49, the lowest growth is shown in the 12–17 age cluster. Nevertheless, as in all the use measurements – except for cannabis – analyzed here, in 2006 Argentina presented higher life LTP rates compared to the ones post-policy change in all groups.

More generally, the lifetime prevalence of all illicit drugs also registered drastic increases in the years following the reform. The most significant growth is observed among Argentinians in the 18–24 and 25–34 age groups. These increases took place after depenalization in 2009, reaching levels of 30.1 per cent and 27.5 per cent in 2017 compared to 17.7 per cent and

17.4 per cent in 2008, respectively. Similarly, the 35–49 age group also presents noticeable increments, rising 8.4 percentage points from 2008 to 2017. Consumption within the 12–17 group also shows increases but at lower rates compared to ages 18–49, rising 6.1 percentage points from 2008 to 2017 (SEDRONAR 2010, 2017b).

The annual initiation age for cannabis, cocaine, and ecstasy usage among Argentinians also experienced transformations. The initiation age for cannabis from 2008 to 2017 changed slightly, averaging about 18.4 years old. For cocaine and ecstasy, it increased from 18 to 20 years and 20 to 22 years correspondingly (SEDRONAR 2017b). This means that individuals are initiating cannabis, ecstasy, and cocaine consumption at an older age, suggesting that depenalization has contributed to limiting the probability of younger cohorts using illegal psychoactive substances for the first time.

Argentina's cannabis and other illegal drugs use patterns in the Latin American context

Drug usage in South and Central America has been escalating at considerable rates during the last decade (CICAD 2019), posing great challenges in terms of public health and security and furthering the conversation about alternative drug policy options. Most countries in South America have opted to liberalize at some level the possession and use of psychoactive substances for recreational purposes. The most extreme case is Uruguay, the first country in the world to fully legalize the consumption of cannabis. The Uruguayan case is fully explored in Chapter 6. This section compares drug consumption patterns in Argentina with those in Brazil and Panama, our control group. The purpose is to assess if changes in consumption patterns in Argentina have been influenced by the depenalization reform or if these fluctuations correspond to more general or regional trends.

Among the South American countries, Argentina is the country with the third highest LYP of cannabis consumption at 8 per cent, just after Uruguay (9.5 per cent) and Chile (14.5 per cent), representing one of the major cannabis markets in the region. Despite that the survey years do not exactly match in each of the cases analyzed in this chapter, the prevalence of the rest of the South American countries is well below the averages registered in Chile, Uruguay, and Argentina, often oscillating between 1 and 4 per cent (CICAD 2019).[24]

Disappointingly, the amount of data available to conduct our analysis as precisely as intended is tightly limited for reported consumption rates. The data used for the comparison are gathered from UNODC records for methodological uniformity. The evidence shows that the LYP rates of cannabis consumption increased in Brazil and Argentina, although in the latter country the increment is more notable. In the case of Brazil, consumption increased only 0.21 percentage points from 2005 to 2012, whereas in Argentina it grew 4.4 percentage points from 2008 to 2017. Panama, by contrast, presents a decrease of 0.43 percentage points from 2003 to 2015 (UNODC 2019).

Cocaine is a popular illicit drug in South America, placing the region as one of the highest consumers in the world with 2.8 million users. Brazil, in particular, is the largest cocaine market in South America. The evidence indicates that LYP of cocaine in Brazil and Argentina present increases. Brazil displays an increase of 1.48 percentage points from 2005 to 2012 and Argentina grew by 0.67 percentage points from 2008 to 2017. That is to say, cocaine consumption in Brazil is rising at a faster rate compared to the rest of the countries. Like with cannabis, Panama is the only case that shows a decrease – of 1.1 percentage points – from 2003 to 2015 (UNODC 2019).

Last, Brazil and Argentina also register increases in the LYP of ecstasy consumption, yet the growth rates in this case are not as substantial. In Brazil, ecstasy consumption increased 0.05 percentage points from 2005 to 2012 and in the case of Argentina it increased 0.23 percentage points from 2011 to 2017 (UNODC 2019). As happened with the other illicit drugs, Panama witnessed a decline of 0.36 percentage points from 2003 to 2015.

There are some parallels in the consumption patterns of Brazil and Argentina. Both South American countries witnessed increases in cannabis, cocaine, and ecstasy prevalence rates following Argentina's depenalization, which may point to a regional trend rather than the impact of drug policy reform. Regardless of the degree of drug liberalization, the general tendency for two of the three cases (but also observed among other countries in the region) seems to be the increase in use rates. Indeed, Panama and Brazil, although they have closely similar drug policy practices, present opposite tendencies. In this context, it is hard to pinpoint depenalization as the sole guiding force behind Argentina's increasing drug consumption patterns.

Market trends

In Argentina, some of the large-scale counterdrug efforts have had an outward focus on targeting international drug trafficking without really looking at the inward dynamics where traffickers are feeding the domestic market (Daugherty 2015). As Argentina becomes an important actor in the South American drug supply chain, there are indications of a higher flow of drugs in the country coming from Bolivia and Peru and destined for the European market and, to a lesser extent, West Africa. In this section we explore fluctuations in drug seizures, drug prices, and purity before and after depenalization.

Drug seizures

Cannabis seizures in Argentina significantly increased after depenalization in 2009, reaching historical levels in 2018 with the confiscation of 256,411 kg of the psychoactive substance (Table 4.2). Cocaine appropriations have fluctuated since 2008, although they ended 2019 (10,534 kg) below pre-reform levels (12,112 kg). Ecstasy seizures increased considerably after depenalization. Hashish confiscations reached a peak in 2013 (11 kg) and have since reduced significantly compared to 2008, the year prior to depenalization. Methamphetamine experienced a rise after the drug policy change, showing its highest seizure amounts in 2016 (51 kg) and then falling the following years to just 3 kg in 2018, below pre-liberalization levels (UNODC 2019).

Since the *Arriola* ruling in 2009, there has been an increase in the amount of cannabis and ecstasy seized in Argentina, whereas the rest of the psychoactive substances experienced the exact opposite trend. Yet the overall increase may suggest that law enforcement agencies have reinforced their counterdrug efforts towards trafficking activities following the Supreme Court's depenalization of consumption. It is interesting to observe that drug seizures dropped dramatically in 2010 and 2011, the first two years right after Argentina's drug policy reform. Evidence from other countries shows

Table 4.2: Annual drug seizures in Argentina (kg)

Drug/Year	Cannabis	Cocaine	Heroin	Ecstasy	Hashish	Methamphetamine
2006	87,526	6,502	33	6	2	0
2007	89,940	7,533	0	18	0	0
2008	107,530	12,112	15	3	40	20
2009	**91,869**	**12,643**	**0**	**37**	**20**	**0**
2010	36,294	238	6	26	0	0
2011	28,680	:	:	5	:	9
2012	129,058	10,462	2	:	35	17
2013	127,510	:	:	:	105	19
2014	140,645	:	:	:	4	21
2015	206,755	6,972	0	:	0	0
2016	160,633	8,446	:	:	0	51
2017	175,028	15,790	9	:	2	26
2018	256,411	12,001	0	25	0	3
2019	187,618	10,534	11	:	:	:

Source: Authors, based on UNODC (2019)

that drug liberalization laws are not automatically translated into practice (Belackova et al 2017). Factors such as limited knowledge about the new legal framework (Burris et al 2004), personal views and experiences (Greer et al 2022), or low education standards (Arredondo et al 2017) among law enforcement officers can affect the implementation of drug policy reforms. Furthermore, confusion about the new legal framework among law enforcement officers could also affect their policing practices.

As an attempt to sort out other driving forces behind seizure fluctuations, in Graph 4.3 we look at the regional trends and compare cannabis and cocaine seizures with the control group. Similar to Argentina, cannabis seizures in Brazil have been constantly increasing since 2013, reaching its highest peak in the last 14 years with 350,314 kg confiscated in 2019. During the last decade, Brazil has become a major player in the drug trafficking landscape in the South American region as well. It serves as a key transit country for cocaine trafficked to Europe (Garzón Vergara 2008). Powerful gangs such as the *Primeiro Comando da Capital* (First Command of the Capital) or *Comando Vermelho* (Red Command) have broadened and strengthened the domestic market to secure economic gains (Lessing 2017; Wolff 2019). In addition, President Bolsonaro's iron fist approach strengthened enforcement efforts, likely leading to more drug seizures. Although data are not available for several years, compared to Brazil and Argentina, cannabis seizures in Panama do not represent significant amounts despite the fact that it also shows a slight increase in 2018 and then a decline in 2019 to 12,900 kg.

Looking at cocaine seizures, we observe the opposite pattern (Graph 4.4). Argentina's cocaine seizures are relatively low compared to the control group, averaging about 6,000 kg a year. The highest amount seized since 2005 was 15,896 kg in 2017, after which seizures declined again to finish 2019 below pre-reform levels. Panama presents especially high rates of cocaine confiscations between 2007 and 2010, ranging from 102,000 kg to 98,000 kg.

Graph 4.3: Annual cannabis seizures in Brazil and Panama in relation to Argentina (kg)

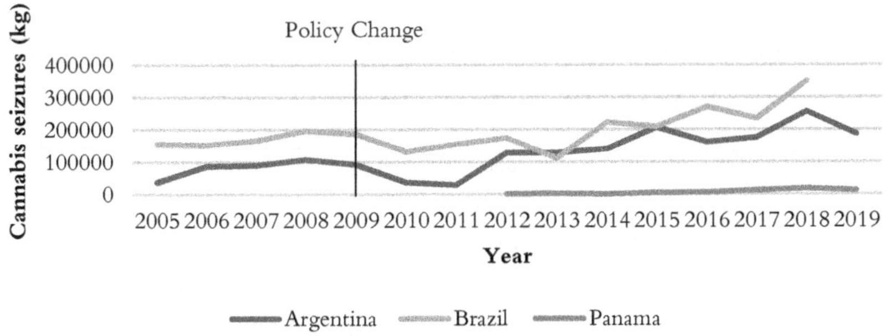

Source: Authors, based on UNODC (2019a)

Graph 4.4: Annual cocaine seizures in Brazil and Panama in relation to Argentina (kg) by years

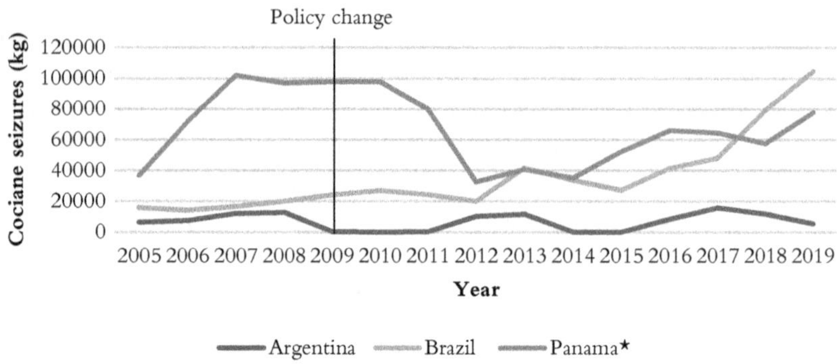

Source: Authors, based on UNODC (2019a)

Since then, the number of secured amounts has been decreasing but remains higher than those of Argentina. Similarly, Brazil's cocaine confiscations show a remarkable increase from 2017 to 2019, going from 48,047 kg to 104,581 kg, and even surpassing Panama's figures during those years.

Like Brazil, Panama has become a popular territory for drug traffickers, particularly for Colombian criminal organizations. Due to its geographical position, it serves as a corridor that connects producers of cocaine in South America and the trafficking routes through Central America towards the US. The country is also a safe haven for money laundering and criminal organizations take advantage of the high levels of corruption, which facilitate their illicit activities (Yagoub 2017). Other factors such as better logistics, infrastructure, and the local market may be responsible for the availability of drugs in a particular territory, more so than drug policy changes.

Price and purity

As mentioned at the beginning of this chapter, the high potency and poor quality of psychoactive substances sold and currently circulating on the Argentinian streets have caused dozens of casualties. Most victims are from vulnerable and poor communities, which paints a picture of the nature of the drug market in Argentina and how it is evolving. Price and purity of a drug are influenced by, among other things, its place of origin. The geographical proximity to a source country can translate to lower drug costs and higher quality of psychoactive substances (Baisotti 2022). Argentina shares a border with Bolivia, a major source country but also a transit route for the cocaine trafficked primarily from Peru and, to a lesser extent, Colombia. Route 34, also known as the '*ruta blanca*' (white route), connects Bolivia's southern region with the province of Salta, one of the main entry points for cocaine in Argentina. Route 11 plays an analogous role with regard to cannabis trafficking from Paraguay.

In this section, we observe changes in drug prices before and after Argentina's 2009 depenalization reform, and compare it with Brazil and Panama to look for regional trends. The ideal unit of analysis would be retail prices adjusted for purity and inflation, as this metric reflects what buyers pay for their purchase provided that pure grams is what they are actually looking for based on their economic power. Unfortunately, the overall quality of the information received by the UNODC is low for this measure (ARQ Report 2018). Therefore, the analysis on drug prices presented here is neither purity nor inflation adjusted. This is particularly relevant in the case of inflation, as Argentina registered in October 2023 an interannual inflation rate of 142.7 per cent (Instituto National de Estadística y Censos 2023).

Table 4.3 displays cannabis prices in Brazil and Panama in relation to Argentina. In Brazil, between 2005 and 2018, cannabis prices more than tripled. In Panama, the value of cannabis also increased after 2005. Similarly, Argentina shows higher prices in 2019 (US$2,700) compared to 2006 (US$2,500), the last year of data available before the Supreme Court depenalized the recreational use of psychoactive substances in 2009 (UNODC 2010, 2019; SEDRONAR 2010). In other words, the increases in the price of cannabis appears to be part of a regional trend and not so much related to the flexibilization of drug policy.

Cocaine prices present slightly different trends among the three Latin American countries. On the one hand, Brazil and Panama have registered

Table 4.3: Cannabis prices in Brazil and Panama in relation to Argentina (kg/US dollars) by year (retail price not adjusted for purity and inflation)

Year/Country	Brazil	Panama	Argentina
1997	900	:	:
1998	:	80	500
2004	:	:	1,500
2005	150	50	400
2006	:	:	2,500
2013	1,000	:	:
2015	:	2,500	:
2016	210	2,500	940
2017	:	2,500	2,000
2018	550	:	7,130
2019	:	800	2,700

Source: Authors, based on UNODC (2010, 2019) and SEDRONAR (2006)

Table 4.4: Cocaine prices in South America in relation to Argentina (kg/US dollars) by year (not adjusted for purity and inflation)

Year/Country	Brazil	Panama	Argentina
1996	2,500	:	:
1998	:	2,500	2,200
2005	3,000	2,500	4,800
2015	:	:	:
2016	:	4,500	900
2017	:	4,500	1,620
2018	8,800	:	3,300
2019	:	:	2,280

Source: Authors, based on UNODC (2010, 2019) and World Drug Report (2018)

important increases, doubling or tripling the figures from 2005 to 2018 and 2017, correspondingly. Argentina, on the other hand, experienced a substantial decline after depenalization in 2009, from US$4,800 in 2005 to US$2,280 in 2019 (UNODC 2010, 2019; World Drug Report 2018) (Table 4.4).

For years, Argentina offered some of the cheapest cocaine in the region. Nevertheless, the quality of the drugs that are sold in the domestic market is relatively low. Analyses performed on seized cocaine in some cases demonstrated that its purity was not higher than 11 per cent to 25 per cent (Infobae 2009). While this situation may not have substantial adverse health consequences in countries that have adopted harm reduction strategies like Portugal, in Argentina depenalization itself does not prevent users from suffering overdoses or other drug-related problems. In effect, the stories of the individuals who died in February 2022 after consuming adulterated cocaine could have been different if Argentina had created a socio-sanitary structure or implemented specific harm reduction programs such as drug checking services[25] and drug consumption rooms.[26]

Our analysis shows that drug prices for cannabis and cocaine took different directions after depenalization in Argentina in 2009. Cannabis got more expensive, and cocaine became two times cheaper. The regional trend marks that the prices of cannabis and cocaine are increasing, whereas Argentina presents opposite trends in the value of cocaine. As shown in Chapter 1, scholarly studies have found that high prices can limit drug use (Pacula 2010). Yet in the Argentinian case, the impact of price variation on consumption patterns has not been linear. In the case of cannabis, for example, prices increased following depenalization, but users of the psychoactive substance were not deterred. In the case of cocaine, by contrast, consumption increased after policy change in a context where the psychoactive substance sells more cheaply. Most importantly, although cocaine is less expensive, the younger age cluster presents one of the lowest increments in consumption rates and also the initiation age has increased despite changes in the legal status of psychoactive substances.

Contrary to the expectations raised by some advocates of criminalization and prohibition, cannabis prices increased after the *Arriola* ruling. This effect, however, is not unique to Argentina, as a similar occurrence happened in the Netherlands, where cannabis prices remained high despite the adoption of depenalization (MacCoun 2011). Yet in the case of the Netherlands, high prices seem to have deterred individuals from cannabis use, whereas in Argentina consumption keeps growing. In other words, the Argentinian experience suggests that criminalization of the supply and its impact on the prices of drugs cannot be used by policymakers as a mechanism to control consumption.

Adverse health consequences

Most of Argentina's drug-related deaths are caused by tobacco and alcohol (SEDRONAR 2019). Fatalities caused by infectious diseases associated with the use of psychoactive substances were about 1,463 in 2017, which represents 9.4 per cent of all drug-related deaths. According to a report conducted by SEDRONAR in 2017 on mortality rates related to psychoactive substance consumption, about 15,500 deaths were totally or partially attributed to drug use, a rate of 54.9 per 100,000 inhabitants. Most of these casualties are caused by cardiovascular disease or neoplasms. Regarding viruses, HIV accounted for 5 per cent (145) of all deaths attributed to psychoactive substances. Overdose deaths were 100 that year (0.4 per 100,000 inhabitants).

Consumers who inject drugs are 22 times more prone to contracting an infectious disease than the general population (Montain et al 2016). As already noted in Chapter 2, practices such as sharing of syringes, the usage of objects for intranasal ingestion, sharing bowls where a substance has been heated or diluted, and the use of water already used to rinse others' syringes, among other things, can lead to the rapid propagation and transmission of serious infections such as HIV. In Argentina, the number of people living with HIV has been steadily increasing since 2000. In 2000, cases among the Argentinian population numbered 59,000, thereafter showing steady growth until it reached 140,000 infected people in 2019 (Ministerio de Salud 2019). While the increase in HIV cases is a continuation of a trend already established before depenalization, growth rates have slowed compared to the figures registered before the 2009 *Arriola* ruling.

A report published by SEDRONAR in 2019 on mortality related to the consumption of psychoactive substances stated that between 2016 and 2018,

98 per cent of HIV cases reported in Argentina were sexually transmitted and only 0.8 per cent of men and 0.2 per cent of women were infected by using injectable drugs. This is a relatively low incidence rate, as the prevalence of HIV among people who inject drugs (PWID) in some countries can be as high as 80 per cent (Aceijas et al 2004). The substance that is consumed the most under this modality in Argentina is injectable cocaine with a LTP of 63.3 per cent among the 25–49 age group, 10.2 per cent among the 50–65 age group, and 1.6 per cent in the younger cluster (12–17). The total number of drug-related deaths due to infectious diseases during the same period of time was estimated to be around 1,463 cases, and 5 per cent of those were from HIV 2019 (Ministerio de Salud 2019).

One of the greatest challenges that Argentina faces is the high percentage of late diagnoses that were uncovered in the last HIV/AIDS and sexually transmitted infection survey published by the National Health Ministry in 2019. Most of the late diagnosed cases are the ones related to the use of injectable drugs and the sharing of syringes. Between 2013 and 2014, for example, 53 per cent of men infected with HIV through shared needles had a late diagnosis. In 2018, the rate was found to be 62 per cent. Official reports suggest that late diagnosis is leading to a myopic view of the real magnitude of the problem. In 2013 alone, the rate of late diagnosis of all cases of HIV transmitted through drug use in males was 53 per cent, and in 2018 it was 62 per cent (Ministerio de Salud 2013, 2019).

Infectious diseases that are commonly transmitted through drug consumption practices such as hepatitis B and C have decreased in Argentina (Ministerio de Salud 2019). Between 2004 and 2011, for example, the number of people who tested positive for hepatitis B was 69,986 (2.18 per cent) and 20,478 (0.64 per cent) for type C. Between 2012 and 2018, hepatitis B decreased 40 per cent compared to the previous period with 4,298 cases (1.30 per cent), and type C declined 46 per cent with 11,435 cases (0.34 per cent) (Ministerio de Salud 2019).

Public policies aimed at assisting people who use drugs began to be relevant within governmental institutions in Argentina at the beginning of the twentieth century. At that time, the National AIDS Program and SEDRONAR issued the 351 Resolution, which recommended to the Ministry of Health the adoption and implementation of programs reclassifying drug usage as a health problem. Other bills were presented in the Chamber of Deputies in 2003, urging the adoption of this approach. Entities that collaborate in harm reduction efforts are primarily nongovernmental organizations and local programs financed by international sources (Ministerio de Salud 2013). Harm reduction plans have been developed mainly in Buenos Aires and Rosario. The programs not only consist of syringe exchange or substitution of opiates, but they also guarantee access to information and prevention. However, unlike in other drug liberalizing countries explored in this book such as Portugal, no systematic programs for people who use drugs have been created at the national level that are consistent and lasting.

In comparison with Argentina and Panama, Brazil presents higher numbers of people living with HIV, though the country harbours a larger population (Graph 4.5). Specifically, sexually transmitted diseases account for most cases. Transgender people are estimated to have an HIV prevalence rate of 30 per cent, gay men 18.3 per cent, PWID 5.9 per cent, and prisoners 4.5 per cent (Joint United Nations Programme on HIV/AIDS 2019). The Brazilian government began implementing a needle exchange program in 1994. Assessments of the program since its implementation have shown a reduction in the prevalence of HIV among PWID. Although the overall number of people living with HIV is steadily increasing, the prevalence of the virus among PWID has declined significantly (Inciardi et al 2006; Lindenmeyer Guimaraes et al 2015).

In Panama, on the other hand, the number of people living with HIV has increased through the years. Compared to Argentina and Brazil, the Central American country maintains a lower number of infected people. Nevertheless, recent reports indicate that injecting illicit drugs in Panama is one leading cause of HIV infections transmitted in the 15- to 44-year age group (Sanchez 2021), thereby presenting important long-term social and economic risks for the country.

Demand for treatment

There are three national surveys dedicated to assessing drug treatment demand and consumption in Argentina: the *Estudio Nacional sobre Perfiles de Pacientes en Tratamiento por Consumo de Substancias Psicoactivas* (National Study on

Graph 4.5: People living with HIV in Brazil and Panama in relation to Argentina by year

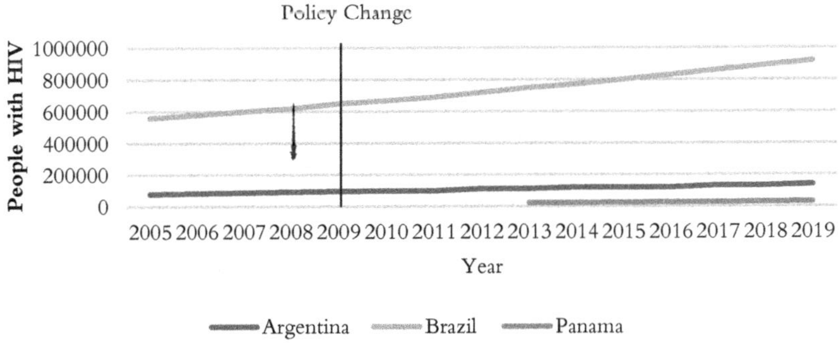

Source: Authors, based on Ministerio de Salud (2019), and OAS (2010)

Patients' Profiles in Treatment for Consumption of Psychoactive Substances), conducted in 2004, 2010, and 2019. These are the most comprehensive reports for understanding demand for treatment in the country. Cocaine was the drug responsible for the most people seeking treatment from 2004 (15.2 per cent) to 2019 (50 per cent). Before depenalization in 2004, cannabis was the drug that drove most people to look for treatment, but the distribution shifted from 19.5 per cent in 2004 to 8.9 per cent in 2019. The next psychoactive substance that drives people to seek treatment is paste base or *paco* with a share of 4.4 per cent in 2004 and 17.7 per cent in 2019. Crack is another drug that has shown an upsurge on demand for treatment, increasing from 0.1 per cent in 2004 to 11.8 per cent in 2019. Inhalants, ecstasy, LSD, and heroin present variations. The percentages for motivation for treatment for these drugs are relatively low and oscillate between 0.1 per cent and 0.4 per cent (SEDRONAR 2019).

Demand for treatment in Argentina has decreased since the adoption of depenalization (Table 4.5). This decline was particularly evident in the years following the Supreme Court's ruling, when treatment demand decreased approximately 22 per cent. The downward trend was nonetheless reversed in 2019 as the number of people in treatment increased again. However, despite these last increments, the demand for treatment in 2019 was still below pre-reform levels. To some extent, this latest fluctuation seems to reflect the country's drug use patterns over the years.

Illegal drug-related deaths

The use of illegal substances can lead to accidental or self-inflicted overdoses and other unintended consequences (Darke, Degenhardt, and Mattick 2006). Table 4.6 shows that Argentina's psychoactive substance consumption related death rates present fluctuations over the course of the years, ranging from .78 to .35 between 2005 and 2019.[27] Following depenalization in 2009, the rate of illegal drug-related deaths increased, almost doubling by 2014. Since

Table 4.5: Demand for treatment in Argentina by year

Year	Number of people in treatment
2004	149,841
2008	27,369
2011	21,252
2017	18,195
2019	25,690

Source: Authors, based on OAD (2004, 2019)

Table 4.6: Argentina's illegal drug-related deaths per 100,000 inhabitants by year[28]

Year	Rate of deaths
2005	.78
2006	.77
2007	.21
2008	.19
2009	**.65**
2010	1.02
2011	:
2012	:
2013	:
2014	1.25
2015	.66
2016	.64
2017	.72
2018	.51
2019	.35

Source: Authors, based on SEDRONAR (2010, 2019) and World Bank (2018)

2015, however, the rate of deaths has continuously dropped, reaching its lowest point in 2019.

The number of illegal drugs related deaths per 100,000 inhabitants in Argentina almost doubled in the years right after depenalization, yet the rate significantly decreased in the following years. The data are not desegregated but the incidence could be due to both direct causes such as overdoses and indirect causes such as traffic accidents. In 2017, for example, almost one third of drug-related deaths were by overdose. An analysis conducted by the Observatory of Addictions and Problematic Consumption of Buenos Aires (Informe final 2021) finds that traffic accidents are the second leading cause of death among people between 15 and 34 years old and 3 out of 10 drivers (28 per cent) have suffered an accident under the influence of a psychoactive substance. The most common drug used by the drivers involved in accidents was alcohol (25.1 per cent), followed by cannabis (3.6 per cent) and cocaine (2.0 per cent). Yet of great concern is also the availability of low-quality drugs that have recently killed dozens of Argentinians. Increase of consumption, the access to low-quality drugs, and the still illegal nature of these substances may be keeping problematic users in the shadows. Consumers can be exposed to dangerous situations while getting illegal substances from dealers, making it more unlikely they will seek treatment. A rise in illegal psychoactive substance related deaths can be attributed as well to the late detection of viruses such as HIV.

Notwithstanding drug consumption increased after depenalization, the policy does not seem to have affected the rates of HIV or infectious diseases transmitted using certain drugs. This is in part attributable to the low prevalence of injectable illicit drugs such as heroin. Nevertheless, demand for treatment declined after the country's drug policy reform. The substance that drives the most people to treatment is cocaine. The rates of drug-related deaths post-reform, on the other hand, have increased. There are several factors that may be contributing to this outcome, including that access to and use of low-quality drugs have already taken the lives of dozens. There are other indirect reasons such as traffic accidents. In effect, driving under the influence of psychoactive substances has become one of the main causes of traffic accidents in Argentina. In other words, despite cocaine raising some concerns regarding problematic use, the liberalization of all drugs for personal consumption has not led to boosts in the problematic use of most psychoactive substances.

Crime and violence

Another important indicator for assessing the impact of a drug policy is security. Has depenalization affected the security realm in Argentina? In this section, we explore some key indicators usually assessed to measure violence such as intentional homicide rates, robberies, and theft at the national level, and then we compare them to Brazil and Panama.

In Argentina, the *Sistema Nacional de Información Criminal* (National System of Criminal Information [SNIC]) compiles annual data from the 23 provinces and CABA, representing the most comprehensive national studies on crime. The official reports by the *Dirección Nacional de Política Criminal* (Criminal Policy National Directorate) shed light on the growing violence witnessed since the early 1990s in Argentina. Indeed, the country's overall crime rates have increased significantly over the course of the years, reaching historical levels during the 2001–2002 economic and social crisis. The country has not only faced violent times in certain cities such as Rosario, but Argentina has been also on the verge of economic and social collapse on repeated occasions.

Yet Argentina has registered relatively low homicide rates (Flom 2023). Following the economic and social debacle that led to the resignation of Fernando de La Rúa in December 2001, homicide rates decreased almost by half from 2002 to 2019. In 2002, Argentina's levels of violence reached its peak with a rate of 9.7 homicides per 100,000 inhabitants. After depenalization in 2009, homicide rates started to ascend again, but overall violence has followed a downward trend to finish in 2018 below pre-reform levels (UNODC 2019). As noted in Chapter 3, Argentina has even registered fewer homicides per 100,000 inhabitants than high-income countries like the US.

Yet violence is not equally distributed in Argentina. While in Rosario and places in CABA murders and drug-related crimes have increased exponentially over the years, most cities and provinces still exhibit European homicide levels. In 2013, for instance, Rosario registered 21.8 homicides per 100,000 inhabitants, four times more than the national average. Despite the salience of violence in certain areas of the province of Santa Fe, both the national and provincial governments have failed to contain the territorial competition among criminal organizations fighting to control the profits of the illegal drug economy (Cutrona 2021). According to the MPA (2021), 44.7 per cent of the 358 homicides in the province of Santa Fe in 2021 were directly motivated by conflicts within the illegal economy and by different criminal organizations.

The Latin American context has been far more complicated, as the region is known for its exceptionally high levels of violence. According to a report by the World Bank (2018), the homicide rates position Latin America as the most violent region globally, averaging 23.9 homicides per 100,000 inhabitants in 2012, more than double the rates of Africa (9.4), North America (4.4), Europe (2.9), and Asia (2.7). It is not surprising, therefore, that both cases in the control group present higher homicide rates than Argentina (Graph 4.6).

Yet the three cases, albeit with different magnitudes, reflect similar trends. There is not a specific change that indicates that the liberalization of Argentina's drug policy had a visible impact on this measurement. It is important to highlight that the last year we are using to analyze the data in our cases is 2019. The Covid-19 pandemic and the adoption of stringent

Graph 4.6: Homicide rates per 100,000 inhabitants in Brazil and Panama in relation to Argentina by year

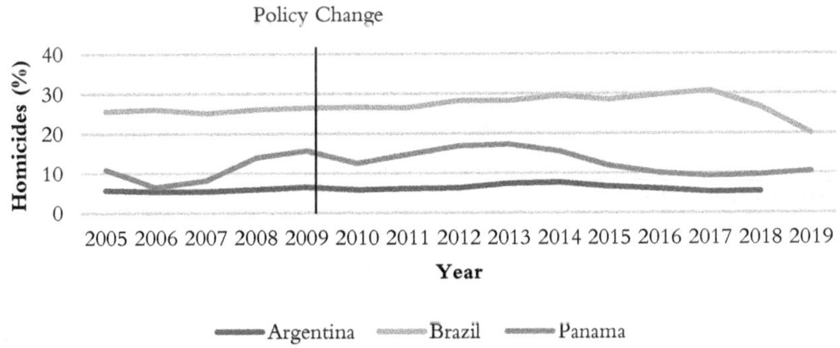

Source: Authors, based on UNODC (2019)

lockdown policies could have impacted most of our analysis at different levels. Nevertheless, the region's intentional homicide rates seem to be slowly returning to pre-pandemic levels after some of the world's longest and strictest Covid-19 lockdowns were gradually lifted (InSight Crime 2022).

Robbery and theft

In 2019, crimes against property in Argentina reached a rate of 2,179 cases per 100,000 inhabitants, a 13.6 per cent increase with respect to the previous year. Of the various crimes that comprise this variable, robberies are foremost with 48 per cent, followed by theft with 34 per cent. According to UNODC (2019), robberies increased from 914 to 1,069 per 100,000 inhabitants from 2005 to 2019. The most noticeable increase occurred from 2008 (a year before depenalization) to 2014, though data comparability is limited because the Fernández administration stopped publishing security statistics in 2009. The rates went down between 2017 and 2018, and then increased again in 2019 (Table 4.7). In general, robbery rates appear to be higher after 2009. Scholars note that factors such as poverty, inequality, and social exclusion in the context of the pre-pandemic economic fall could have played a relevant role in the country's increase in crime (Kessler and Assusa 2021).

Argentina's robbery rates figure among the highest in Latin America and also in comparison to the control group. More specifically, the country's rates of robbery double and triple those of Brazil and Panama, respectively. Yet Brazil's robbery rates have also followed a mostly upward trend since 2006 (475), reaching 807 in 2017 and 561 in 2019. Similarly, Panama presents increases during the same period, although at lower levels than Brazil.

Contrary to robbery, theft rates have been declining in Argentina (Table 4.8). In 2008, in a pre-depenalization context, theft rates were at 709 per 100,000 inhabitants compared to 673 in 2014 and they continued to decline, reaching a rate of 625.5 in 2018, which is the last year of measurement. Looking at the control group, Brazil's theft rates present an upward trend since 2011, reaching 1,052.3 in 2018. In contrast, Panama's rates declined from 544.7 in 2014 to 320 in 2019. That is, Panama reflects lower theft rates compared to the other countries.

Observing these contending figures from countries with different approaches to drug policy, there is no clear suggestion that crime rate fluctuations, in particular robbery and theft, are linked to the liberalization of Argentina's drug policy. Although there are year gaps in the data, theft rates do not seem to have been impacted by depenalization since they do not present any critical shift before and after the 2009 Supreme Court's *Arriola* ruling. Instead, Argentina's security challenges are likely associated with structural factors such as weak institutions and corruption, school dropout, income inequality, social exclusion, accelerated urban growth, draconian

Table 4.7: Robbery rates in Brazil and Panama in relation to Argentina by year

Year/Country	Argentina	Brazil	Panama
2005	980	:	152
2006	908	475	158
2007	934	488	172
2008	1,002	487	184
2009	:	470	224
2010	:	552	228
2011	:	550	261
2012	:	492	266
2013	:	504	228
2014	1,209	633	251
2015	1,097	758	206
2016	1,074	771	192
2017	989	807	243
2018	1,216	696	:
2019	1,131	561	:

Source: Authors, based on UNODC (2019)

crime control policies, and broader transformations within the political economy of illicit drugs in Latin America.

Drug law violations

Data from the SNIC (2020) show that violations of Law 23.737 have increased significantly during the last years. In 2017, for instance, there were 47,656 crimes registered, while there were 61,746 in 2018 and 98,036 in 2019 (Table 4.9). One offense behind these sudden increases is simple possession of psychoactive substances for personal consumption, which grew more than 50 per cent from 2018 to 2019. Other crimes following this trend include simple possession and import diversion of psychoactive substances, showing a 33 per cent increase. Possession or delivery of drugs grew by 50 per cent, cultivation and production quadrupled, and other crimes in violation of Law 23.737 account for 22,224 in 2019 – a difference of 5,477 from the previous year. A drug-related crime that marks a decrease in cases is psychoactive substance smuggling, which fell from 1,400 crimes in 2017 to 554 in 2019.

After the reform, not only has the violations of Law 23.737 grown, but drug-related sentences have more than doubled (Graph 4.7). In 2008, in a

Table 4.8: Theft rates in Brazil and Panama in relation to Argentina by year

Year/Country	Argentina	Brazil	Panama
2008	709.09	972.1	472.3
2009	:	923.8	507.6
2010	:	706.5	501.3
2011	:	628.1	497.4
2012	:	715.08	538.5
2013	:	887.77	536.7
2014	673.26	:	544.7
2015	631.27	:	475.7
2016	620.86	:	395.9
2017	579.65	1109.05	451.9
2018	625.49	1052.33	395.6
2019	:	:	320

Source: Authors, based on UNODC (2019)

Table 4.9: Violations of Law 23.737 by year[29]

Drug-related Crime	2017	2018	2019
Simple possession of psychoactive substances for personal consumption	21,260	28,585	52,647
Other crimes in violation of Law 23.737	11,503	16,747	22,224
Simple possession of psychoactive substances	8,276	8,224	12,219
Commercialization and delivery of psychoactive substances	4,455	6,056	6,519
Import diversion of psychoactive substances	41	20	1,439
Possession or delivery of psychoactive substances	262	644	1,299
Cultivation and production of psychoactive substances	275	222	821
Smuggling psychoactive substances	1,400	955	554
Organization and finance of psychoactive substances	99	173	208
Collusion with psychoactive substances	85	120	107
Total	**47,656**	**61,746**	**98,037**

Source: Authors, based on SNIC (2020)

pre-depenalization context, sentences for drug law violations accounted for 1,666 and reached 3,934 by 2017, increasing 2.4 times. Minor traffickers such as 'drug mules' predominate among those sentenced.[30] In this particular setting, sentence rates for women and non-citizens, which are usually used as mules and are situated at the lowest levels of the organizational structure of

Graph 4.7: Sentences for drug law violations in Argentina by year

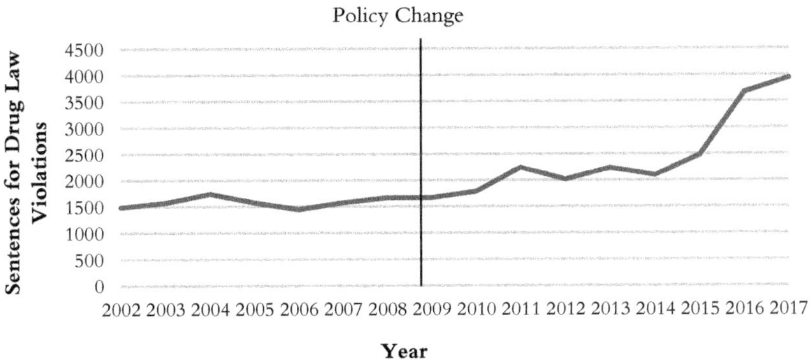

Source: Authors, based on SNEEP (2018)

different drug trafficking groups, have heightened. They are mostly detained and processed under illegal substance possession charges. This has become the main cause of incarceration among women in Argentina (National Statistical System on the Execution of the Sentence [SNEEP] 2018).

More recently, the number of drug-related cases filed in the federal justice system has remained stable, presenting between 20,000 and 24,000 cases annually (CELS 2018). However, the cases recorded at the provincial justice systems that adopted the decentralization Law 26.052 reflect higher figures every year. This illuminates the discrepancies in the application of depenalization at the federal and provincial justice levels. At the national level, a low number of the cases initiated for drug crimes were taken to trial from 2010 through 2017, accounting for only 8 per cent of the cases processed (CELS 2018). Most individuals convicted for drug-related crimes committed a minor nonviolent offense. In some cases, they were first offenders and were incarcerated mainly for simple attenuated possession for personal consumption (Di Nicola 2020). Although the jurisdiction at the federal level oversees more severe crimes on the supply side such as drug trafficking, in 2016, 86 per cent of the drug-related sentences given were for four years or less and 4 of every 10 sentences were releasable crimes (CELS 2018). The following year, in 2017, 65 per cent of the sentences for drug law violations were for four years, meaning that this trend of lowering sentences seems to be continuing in today's Argentina (SNEEP 2018).

The prison system

Penitentiary institutions in Argentina are situated at the federal and provincial levels. The Federal Penitentiary System is directed by the Ministry of Justice and Human Rights, and the Provincial Prison System is mandated by the provincial-level governments, and they function under their own institutions. Among the two penitentiary systems, 308 detention units and 62 centres belong to the Buenos Aires Penitentiary Service, the Federal Penitentiary Service has 32 centres, and the rest of the provinces total 214 units throughout 23 provinces. The latter houses all of the prison population that is incarcerated for nonfederal crimes (Procuración Penintenciaria de la Nación 2019). In this particular institutional setting, the Argentinian justice system's plurality creates a complex structure in which the two levels function under slightly different policies and legal schemes.

With the adoption of depenalization, it is expected for the prison population in Argentina to decrease, at least in the number of people incarcerated for possession of drugs for personal consumption. Since 2005, the country's general prison population experienced a constant upward trend from 55,423 inmates to 94,883 in 2018; that is, from a rate of 142.5 to 216.2 per 100,000 inhabitants.[31] In 2018 (the last year reported), there was an increase of 11 per cent in relation to the previous year, 2017, with 85,283 incarcerated people or a rate of 194.1.[32] In a report by the *Sistema Nacional de Estadística sobre Ejecución de la Pena* (SNEEP 2018), it is shown that the Buenos Aires province maintains the highest incarceration rates in the country, accounting for nearly 45 per cent of the total. The report also notes that the prison population is mainly composed of young men; that is, more than 60 per cent are younger than 33 years.

The most common charges for people incarcerated in Argentina are robberies and attempted robberies with 37,535 reported cases in 2018. The second most common crime is violation of the country's drug law (Law 23.737) with 15,216 prosecutions, accounting for 16 per cent of the total incarcerated population. Third is malicious homicide with 12,419, followed by rape with 11,547. In 2018, drug-related crimes showed a 24 per cent increase in relation to 2017.[33] Our findings are consistent with the work of Maier, Mannes, and Koppernhofer (2017), who observes no attributable correlations (except for murders) between drug liberalization and crime trends across several states in the US that depenalized cannabis. Along the same lines, Assa, McConnel, and Rasul (2014) also found limited or no impact of depenalization schemes on crime rates in the London region of Lambeth.

It is evident that the depenalization scheme adopted in 2009 did not prevent people who use drugs from being prosecuted. It did not prevent them from being incarcerated either. As shown in Table 4.10, the number of people behind bars for infringement of Law 23.373 skyrocketed between 2016 and 2020. In this context, the prison population incarcerated for the possession of psychoactive substances has not decreased following the reform. By contrast, after a first decline in 2017, the number of inmates behind bars for drug possession increased substantially (SNEEP 2020, 2021). Based on

Table 4.10: Incarcerations for violation of Law 23.737 in Argentina by year

Violation typology/ Year	2016	2017	2018	2019
Infringement of Law 23.373	1,371	3,867	8,439	8,405
Possession	2,739	1,298	1,768	2,163
Commercialization	4,262	3,910	3,258	3,778
Traffic	794	1,540	1,249	1,126
Other	1,310	1,664	502	1,192

Source: Authors, based on SNEEP (2016, 2018, 2019, 2020)

the number of sentences for drug law violations, this increase does not seem to be new but rather the continuation of a historical trend that we are unable to quantify due to the absence of disaggregated data. As a result, the number of people incarcerated for minor drug-related cases continues to increase despite the goal of the Supreme Court's ruling being exactly the opposite. Hernan Olaeta (2022), the head of Argentina's Criminal Policy National Directorate, mentions that there a couple of points to consider when looking at the typification on the violations of Law 23.737. The first is that some of the individuals imprisoned in any of the categories might have been sentenced for more than one crime. Second, the data gathered are mainly from the prison population of federal penitentiaries. Other cases of drug law violations may be in commissaries or house arrests. These cases, as a result, might not be included in some national reports, obscuring Argentina's statistics.

Prison rates in South and Central America in relation to Argentina

Latin America harbours a rising population incarcerated for illegal drug offenses. Surveys demonstrate that drug offenders comprise approximately 16 per cent of the total inmate population, although the actual figures are much higher since drug crimes are under federal jurisdiction and some surveys do not include federal prisons (Bergman and Fondevila 2021). In the South American region, Brazil presents the highest rate of prison population per 100,000 inhabitants with 337, followed by Uruguay with 322.3 in 2017. In Argentina and Brazil, prison population rates have been steadily growing (Graph 4.8). In Panama, by contrast, the rates have fluctuated since 2005, presenting a decline in 2008 and then a continuous growth peaking in 2015 (488). In the following years, however, the rates in Panama started to decrease and then slightly increased again in 2019 to finish with 427 inmates per 100,000 inhabitants (UNODC 2019a).

Graph 4.8: Rates of prison population in Brazil and Panama in relation to Argentina by year

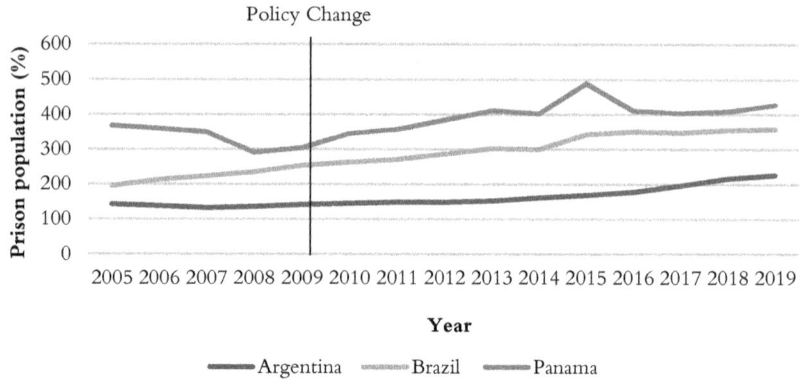

Source: Authors, based on UNODC (2019a)

In Brazil, the drug law enacted in 2006 by Lula da Silva, a centre-left president, proposed a more liberal and less punitive drug policy by eliminating prison sentences for drug consumers but reinforcing them for traffickers. Nonetheless, in Brazil there is a lack of a clear criteria to differentiate the consumer from the trafficker and the distinction is left to police officers on the streets and judges in courts. Not surprisingly, scholars have described the Brazilian legal framework as an example of criminalized drug prohibition (Rodriguez 2022). This has led, among other things, to sentences that are highly racially and socially biased, reflected in a prison population that is 67 per cent black. Furthermore, law enforcement has focused on minor drug offenses. In São Paulo, for example, half of the individuals incarcerated for drug-related charges are behind bars for possession of no more than 40 grams of cannabis (Salvadori 2021).

Panama, on the other hand, presents the highest prison rates compared to Argentina and Brazil. Panama's drug policy has given greater relevance to criminal punishment to control drug consumption and other associated harms. Under these circumstances, crimes against collective security constitute the fourth offense mostly committed in the country. This includes crimes against the integrity of a person. By 2015, for instance, 3.5 per cent of detainees were arrested for this crime; among them 73 per cent were drug-related crimes and 66 per cent were specifically for illicit drug possession. In effect, the offense has a conviction rate of 40 per cent, even higher than for other crimes such as homicide with 21 per cent or rape with 24 per cent (Cumbrera Diaz and Rodriguez Blanco 2016).

Notwithstanding comparability is relatively limited due to missing data and sampling differences, the countries with harsher drug policies present higher rates of incarceration, but still all cases witnessed increases. Not surprisingly, the Argentinian prison population has grown but at a lesser rate compared to Brazil and Panama. While in Panama the 'law in the books' mostly explains this trend, in Brazil it is the consequence of not having a clear typification of drug law violations, with well-defined definitions between the consumer, the trafficker, and specific drug quantities allowed. In Argentina, by contrast, the unsuccessful depenalization to lower the country's prison rates can be blamed mainly on its practice and not on indistinct legal taxonomies.

Conclusions

Argentina has experienced numerous changes in its drug policy. Ideologies and actors, both national and international, have had a great impact on its evolution. During most of its history, the country joined the US-led crusade that emphasized the construct of drugs as a 'national enemy', presenting the problem as an existential threat and reinforcing the processes of criminalization, stigma, and social discipline (Touzé 1996). Law 20.771, passed in 1974, was the first penal rule focused specifically on psychoactive substances that positioned them within the 'national security' framework, placing consumption, possession, trafficking, growing, and selling as federal crimes. The punitive approach to drugs was finally materialized in 1989, when the National Congress passed the current drug legislation (that is, Law 23.737). However, following several comings and goings, finally in 2009, with the *Arriola* ruling, Argentina's Supreme Court of Justice depenalized the possession of all illicit drugs for personal consumption. In this chapter we have evaluated the historical trajectory followed by Argentina as well as the estimated impacts of depenalization in three particular realms: prevalence, health, and security.

In terms of consumption, LTP, LYP, and LMP of most psychoactive substances present increases after depenalization. Cannabis has experienced the most alarming growth, almost doubling after the policy reform, followed by cocaine at a lower rate. There are some exceptions such as coca base paste, whose LYP and LMP slightly decreased. Heroin displays no change in LTP, and neither do the LMP of inhalants and LMP of ecstasy. There are some parallels in the consumption patterns of Brazil and Argentina. Both countries have witnessed increases in cannabis, cocaine, and ecstasy prevalence rates following Argentina's depenalization, which may point to a regional trend rather than a direct effect of the reform. Panama and Brazil, although they have similar drug policy practices, present opposite tendencies. In this context, it is hard to pinpoint depenalization as the guiding principle behind drug consumption fluctuations in Argentina.

Argentina's LTP for cocaine and all illicit drugs increased in all age groups. Nevertheless, there are some positive notes when it comes to the age of consumption. First, the youngest age cluster (12–17) presents among the lowest rates of consumption and prevalence which are today below pre-depenalization levels. Second, the initiation age has increased for cannabis, cocaine, and ecstasy. The available evidence clearly indicates that people try illicit psychoactive substances for the first time at an older age. This upward trend is particularly visible in the years after drug liberalization. That is to say, the flexibilization of drug policy in Argentina has not shifted the initiation age to younger individuals nor has it boosted the usage in younger groups.

Notwithstanding the lack of data limits the comparison between the pre- and post-drug reform contexts, the majority of Argentina's population use cannabis and cocaine on an occasional or recreational basis. Frequent use is concentrated in men between 18 and 34 years old, most of whom are working adults and high school graduates. In Argentina, only 278,689 users (18.8 per cent) are associated with patterns of problematic drug consumption (SEDRONAR 2017b).

Drug prices in cannabis and cocaine took different directions after Argentina's depenalization reform in 2009. While cannabis increased in market value, cocaine became two times cheaper. The regional trend marks that the prices of cannabis and cocaine are increasing, whereas Argentina presents opposite trends in terms of cocaine. In the Argentinian case, drug prices do not seem to reflect an impact on consumption in the case of cannabis, but the decrease in cocaine prices has possibly affected use oscillations. In other words, cannabis prices increased, but consumption was not affected. On the contrary, it grew significantly after depenalization. In the case of cocaine, consumption also increased after the policy change in a context where the substance sells more cheaply, probably because of price decreases in the Andean region and the drug's increasingly low quality in Argentina. Most importantly, although cocaine is less expensive, the younger age cluster presents one of the lowest increments in consumption rates. Contrary to the expectation that drug prices drop after liberalization reforms, the price of cannabis and other illicit psychoactive substances in Argentina increased after the *Arriola* ruling.

Other market-associated factors also present contrasting trends. On the one hand, cannabis seizures increased in the post-reform years. Cocaine seizures, on the other hand, declined after depenalization. This trend, however, is not likely affecting the consumption of the psychoactive substance. Furthermore, Argentina's declining cocaine seizures seems to be unique, since in Brazil and Panama cocaine seizures have increased. Factors such as the development of new trafficking routes and the size of the local market may be responsible for the market size for drugs in a particular territory, more so than drug control policy changes.

In terms of the likely effects of depenalization on the health realm, HIV cases in Argentina show a continuous upward trend, although there is no evident impact of drug policy change in explaining this fluctuation given the limited use of injectable drugs. Moreover, most of the individuals with HIV were infected through social encounters and only a small percentage of cases are drug related. Compared to Brazil and Panama, in Argentina the number of people infected by drug usage is low and does not present an alarming trend. The main challenge is the high percentage of late diagnoses, which can lead to a myopic view of the real magnitude of the problem. Infectious diseases such as hepatitis B and C are declining. Demand for treatment also decreased after depenalization, suggesting that Argentina's growing prevalence rates do not have major health consequences. Since most of the use is still occasional or recreational, depenalization has not aggravated the risks associated with problematic consumption. This trend likely explains why the number of illegal drug-related deaths increased after depenalization. That is to say, the data are not desegregated and several of the incidents registered could be due to indirect causes such as traffic accidents.

In assessing violence, the rate of homicides in Argentina is going down at the national level, and there were no major shifts post-policy change. However, homicide rates during the COVID-19 pandemic started to increase and many of the homicides registered are attributed to organized crime (Baisotti 2022). In addition, there are indications that in some provinces such as Santa Fe a high percentage of the murders are attributed to confrontations among criminal organizations. Similarly, crime rates' fluctuations, in particular robbery and theft, are not likely linked to Argentina's drug policy liberalization. Though there are year gaps in the data, neither theft nor robbery rates seem to have been impacted by depenalization since they do not present any critical shift before and after the 2009 Supreme Court's *Arriola* ruling. Additionally, the situation in Brazil and Panama is worsening compared to Argentina. Under these circumstances, the evidence suggests that Argentina's security challenges are likely associated with structural factors such as weak institutions and corruption, school dropout rates, income inequality, social exclusion, accelerated urban growth, draconian crime control policies, and broader transformations within the political economy of illicit drugs in Latin America and the Caribbean.

One of the main purposes of liberalizing drug policies is to relieve overpopulated prisons to cut down on the expenses this generates in order to reallocate resources towards other areas such as health and fighting organized crime. However, Argentina's depenalization reform did not lead to the reduction of the prison population. In fact, sentences related to drug law violations have more than doubled, a trend motivated by an increasing number of cases registered at the provincial level following decentralization. What is more, the number of people incarcerated for possession of psychoactive substances did not decrease despite the adoption of depenalization. It is evident that even after Argentina's reform the persecution of minor drug-related crimes continues and that there is a disconnect in the application of the *Arriola* ruling at the federal and provincial levels. As a result, the country's prison population for minor drug-related cases continues to increase despite the Supreme Court's decision to depenalize the recreational use of illicit drugs in 2009.

Argentina is a good example for policymakers and students to understand the complexity of the processes, at various levels (that is, social, economic, governmental), that come with drug policy change. As our observations suggest, although depenalization in Argentina has shown some successes, it has failed to meet most of the expectations. Furthermore, the South American country does not mirror more organized depenalization experiences such as those adopted in countries like the Netherlands. This indicates that the act of adopting a more liberal drug policy does not guarantee success in its implementation. The Argentinian case shows that policy change by itself is not sufficient; there is a need for regulatory mechanisms, more rigorous implementation, to convey a more effective impact. Possibly, better results rely on amending the conflict between the law and jurisprudence, as the persecution of consumers continues, and attention has not shifted to harm reduction efforts or the targeting of powerful drug trafficking organizations. Since the *Arriola* ruling there has been no other major change in the legislative realm except for the legalization of cannabis for medical purposes in 2017. Nevertheless, the dialogue has been reactivated due to the casualties of dozens of Argentinians who used adulterated cocaine. Yet the presence of more pressing problems such as inflation, devaluation, and poverty limit the possibilities for any attempt to reassess where the *Arriola* ruling stands and where it needs to go, in terms of deeper liberalization and better implementation of Argentina's drug policy.

5

Decriminalization in Portugal

Portugal anticipated many of the greatest political transformations in Western Europe (Léonard 2016). After leaving behind the monarchical regime that characterized the region during the nineteenth century, it became one of the first republics in 1910.[1] Although it was the last European power to accept the independence of its African colonies, Portugal was involved in the first uprisings that ultimately led to Africa's decolonization process in the 1950s. Most importantly, the *Revolução dos Cravos* (Carnation Revolution) in 1974, which overturned the longest dictatorship in Western Europe during the twentieth century, paved the way for the 'Third Wave' of democratization throughout much of the developing world (Huntington 1991).

In July 2001, Portugal also became one of the first countries in the world to decriminalize the consumption, acquisition, and possession of all types of illicit drugs. The so-called conservative, isolationist, and Catholic European country broke with the prevailing punitive paradigm, placing illicit drugs and psychotropic substances outside the criminal justice system framework. Focusing on prevention, treatment, harm reduction, and other social regulation initiatives gradually launched by the Ministry of Health, Portugal thus became a world pioneer in drug liberalization policies.

Opponents and advocates of drug liberalization policies have provided alternative evidence, pointing to the benefits or drawbacks of decriminalization. Where is Portugal after more than 20 years of the radical drug policy reform? What are the most significant consequences of this transformation on the local drug market, the population's health, and the country's crime rates? Based on this evaluation, is decriminalization a successful alternative to the prevailing punitive paradigm? By analyzing the Portuguese case, this chapter seeks to identify the estimated impacts of decriminalization on drug consumption levels and other trends in the health and security realms, respectively.

The chapter is organized in three main sections. Starting from the initial drug legislation passed in 1924 until the enactment of decriminalization in 2001, the first section traces back the origins of Portugal's drug policy. The second section explores the main features of decriminalization, paying special attention to the role of dissuasion commissions. In order to fully understand the consequences of this radical policy shift, the third section assesses the evolution of the patterns of drug consumption and other market-associated factors, together with relevant empirical information in the health and security spheres. Statistical evidence from other European countries such as France and Germany is also analyzed in the final section. The conclusion presents an assessment of the major trends, strengths, and weaknesses of Portugal's decriminalization policy.

Caution is required in the interpretation of data. This chapter relies on findings from a series of recent statistical studies, but its primary purpose is not to offer causal explanations. Similar to the other two case studies in this book, Argentina and Uruguay, the main methodological constraint of this analysis is the absence of a control comparison. These limitations, when data are available, are partially mitigated by contrasting the evolution of Portugal's drug-related indicators with other European countries that did not undertake policy reform. Although further methodological difficulties arise in generating cross-national comparisons, particularly because information systems among European countries are multimethod and multisource (Mounteney et al 2015), the incorporation of a control group of countries that did not change the legal status of psychoactive substances (that is, France and Germany) during the timeframe of the analysis helps to pinpoint more accurately the possible effects of the decriminalization policy.

The road to decriminalization

Portugal's legal system has been widely influenced by the punitive paradigm enforced at the multilateral level. Yet the country's interests during the early twentieth century were not totally compatible with the US's punitive efforts overseas. By the 1900s, the Kingdom of Portugal, also known as the Portuguese Empire, played a significant role in the political economy of opium. It controlled, among other territories, a thriving poppy cultivation in Macau. Its participation in the opium industry explains why the Kingdom of Portugal was reluctant to adopt stringent measures to regulate this psychoactive substance during the International Opium Convention in 1911–1912 (Musto 1973).

The first drug legislation was passed in 1924 during the last years of the *Primeira República Portuguesa* (First Portuguese Republic), a period often described as the 'transition' between the Kingdom of Portugal and the *Estado Novo* (New State).[2] Law 1.687 was born as an attempt to comply with the main requirements of the 1912 First International Opium Convention. Regulated by Decree 10.375, the country's earliest legal system restricted the import of opium, cocaine, and their derivates to doctors and scientists, respectively. The *Direcção General de Saúde* (General Health Office) was the national institution in charge of authorizing the acquisition of different psychoactive substances by pharmacies, drugstores, or scientific organizations in the country.

Portugal's drug policy after this first antecedent became increasingly shaped by the authoritarian rule. Only a few months after the establishment of the *Ditadura Nacional* (National Dictatorship) in May 1926, more restrictions and heavier penalties were adopted through Decree 12.210. Despite the conservative nature of the *Estado Novo*, the authoritarian regime established by António de Oliveira Salazar in 1933, the country's next major legislation approved in 1963 promoted a relatively flexible approach to psychoactive substances.[3] Law 2.118, also known as *Lei de Saúde Mental* (Mental Health Law), framed problematic use as a psychological illness and established treatment alternatives, although it did not create institutions to tackle the problem (Intervention Service in Addictive Behaviors and Dependencies [SICAD] 2020b). In 1970, however, Portugal reintroduced new punitive measures against the use of illicit drugs. Decree-Law 420 'updated' prior legislation by categorizing psychoactive substances. The production, trafficking, and consumption of illicit drugs were punishable by imprisonment of two to eight years and fines between $10,000 and $100,000 euros (around US$28 and US$280).

Following the *Revolução dos Cravos*, the provisional government that overthrew the *Estado Novo* created in 1975 the *Centro de Estudos da Juventude* (Center for Youth Studies) and *Centro de Investigação Judiciária da Droga* (Center for Drug Judicial Investigation), the first national institutions aimed at tackling Portugal's drug problem.[4] According to Decree-Law 792, the *Centro de Estudos da Profilaxia da Droga* (Center for the Study of Drug Prophylaxis) replaced the Center for Youth Studies in 1976, working with the prevention, treatment, and integration of problematic users. By the same token, the *Centro de Investigação e Controle da Droga* (Center for Drug Research and Control), the new organization in charge of fighting drug trafficking activities, substituted the Center for Drug Judicial Investigation. With the adoption of the Portuguese Constitution early in 1976, the country's drug control policy became more predictable and increasingly respectful of the population's human rights. Most importantly, the new institutional architecture gradually created after democratization introduced the notion of decriminalization (Moreira et al 2011).

After ratifying the 1971 Convention on Psychotropic Substances through Decree-Law 430/83, the government of Aníbal Cavaco Silva (1985–1995) launched the first national plan against illicit drugs in 1987. Commonly known as *Projeto VIDA* (VIDA Project), the new initiative was supervised by the Council of Ministers and was intended to reduce the supply and demand of drugs in the country. As Moreira et al (2011) point out, *Projeto*

VIDA also favoured the opening of specialized treatment centres throughout Portugal, all of them operating under the umbrella of the Ministry of Health. Additional innovations included a call for the implementation of AIDS prevention initiatives, a free telephone helpline service, the establishment of drug treatment in prisons, and supply reduction interventions. Interestingly, *Projeto VIDA* was adopted during the government of the *Partido Social Democrata* (Social Democratic Party [PSD]), a centre-right political party, suggesting that the incorporation of progressive and human rights-oriented programs was not limited to Portugal's left-wing politics.[5]

The use of psychoactive substances increased markedly during the 1980s (Soares et al 2017). Intravenous heroin consumption, in particular, became a major concern among public health officials. The number of users was estimated to be between 50,000 and 100,000, representing around 1 per cent of the population (Pombo and da Costa 2016). The country's drug problem gained visibility with the proliferation of open-air markets, where a significant population of users of intravenous heroin obtained illicit drugs (Hughes and Stevens 2010). Rising rates of viruses/infectious diseases such as HIV, AIDS, tuberculosis, and hepatitis C spotlighted the adverse effects of drug use in Portugal.

During the 1990s, the repressive focus on drugs gained momentum. As had happened during most of Portugal's history, Decree-Law 15/93, the country's latest legislation before decriminalization, was issued as an attempt to comply with the 1988 United Nations Convention against Illicit Traffic in Narcotic Drugs and Psychotropic Substances, ratified by Portugal in 1991. Also known as *lei da droga*, Decree-Law 15/93 stipulated the imprisonment of people who used drugs for up to three years, though consumers were 'legally punishable in an almost symbolic fashion' (Decree-Law 15/93). Due to its ambiguity, the criminalization of drug use was not mandatory (Rêgo et al 2021). Yet other signs suggested that Portugal was not following a punitive recipe. During the Cavaco Silva administration, Portugal also embraced harm reduction programs, including the provision of syringes to prevent the contagion of infectious diseases, the adoption of drug substitution programs, and a protocol signed between the Ministry of Health and the Association of Pharmacies to supply methadone (Santos 2004).

Portugal's drug reform was born in the midst of the growing hysteria of the 1990s. Punitive policies, however, were not meeting the expectations. Heroin use reached historical levels, HIV/AIDS continued to proliferate, and the supply of cocaine and new synthetic drugs also increased substantially during the last part of the century (Quintas 2011). Drug-related deaths also followed an upward trend (Portuguese Institute of Drugs and Drug Addiction [IPDT] 2000). Public opinion surveys reflected the centrality of the drug problem, thereby showing that problematic use became the country's top concern in 1997 (Pombo and da Costa 2018). From the

National Parliament to grassroots groups at the local level, several debates were held to discuss different possibilities to confront Portugal's drug-related problems (IPDT 2000).

Contrary to the typical and expected emergency policy response, the *Partido Socialista* (Socialist Party) led by António Guterres (1995–2002), who defeated the PSD after a 10-year tenure, reacted to the population's rising concerns by appointing a committee of specialists to develop a national strategy against drugs.[6] Doctors, sociologists, psychologists, lawyers, and social activists submitted their recommendations in 1998 under a document known as *Estratégia Nacional da Luta Contra a Droga* (National Strategy to Fight Against Drugs). Divided into 12 different drug policy areas, the official report included a more holistic approach with recommendations for international cooperation, legal framework, prevention, treatment, harm reduction, prisons and drugs, rehabilitation, supply reduction and money laundering, research and training, civil society, coordination, and financial resources (Moreira et al 2011). Above all, the document created by the scientific committee also proposed the decriminalization of personal drug use as a national policy.

Almost three years later, after the Parliamentary Committee on Drugs and the Council of Ministers formally approved the National Strategy to Fight Against Drugs, the socialist government adopted the *Plano de Ação Nacional de Luta contra a Droga e a Toxicodependência – Horizonte 2004* (National Action Plan for the Fight Against Drugs and Drug Addiction – Horizon 2004). In addition to setting the country's drug-related objectives, the National Action Plan established the budget and institutional architecture developed to confront Portugal's illicit drug problems during the following years.

By the end of 2000, during António Guterres' second term in office, the Portuguese parliament passed Law 30/00, decriminalizing the acquisition, possession, and consumption of all types of illicit drugs. The cornerstone of the National Strategy to Fight Against Drugs was complemented by Decree-Law 130-A/01 and Decree-Law 183/01. While the former legislation regulates the functioning of the *Comissão de Dissuasão para a Toxicodependência* (Dissuasion Commission), the latter created different harm reduction programs and socio-sanitary structures. More specifically, the drug-checking services and drug consumption rooms, albeit developed slowly over the years, became critical harm reduction initiatives accompanying Portugal's decriminalization scheme (European Monitoring Centre for Drugs and Drug Addiction [EMCDDA] 2019c).

Furthermore, in order to centralize the country's drug control policy, Decree-Law 269-A/2002 merged the *Serviço de Prevenção e Tratamento da Toxicodependência* (Drug Addiction Prevention and Treatment Service) and the *Instituto Português da Droga e da Toxicodependência* (IPDT) and created the *Instituto da Droga e da Toxicodependência* (Institute of Drugs and Drug

Addiction [IDT]). The new drug control institution was nonetheless replaced in 2011 by the *Serviço de Intervenção nos Comportamentos Aditivos e Dependências* (SICAD 2020c).

Yet during the last decade Portugal witnessed the resurgence of different punitive measures that partially reversed the country's liberalization policy adopted in 2001. In 2008, for example, the Supreme Court of Justice reestablished drug consumption as a crime in cases where the quantity confiscated exceeds the average use of 10 days. This ruling, 8/2008, was endorsed by the Constitutional Court in 2014 through judgment 587 (Rêgo et al 2021).[7] According to SICAD (2020a), the number of convictions for drug use increased substantially after the ruling 8/2008, suggesting that the impacts of decriminalization were largely shaped by the role of the judiciary power.

Decriminalization and the role of dissuasion commissions

The Portuguese attitude towards the drug problem has shifted from punitivism to a comprehensive public health-oriented approach, with prevention and treatment at the centre stage (Félix, Portugal, and Tavares 2017). Under Portugal's decriminalization policy, drug acquisition, possession, and consumption are prohibited but sanctions are taken outside the framework of criminal law. While these actions are treated as administrative offenses, trafficking and cultivation are still considered crimes under the provisions of Decree-Law 15/93. Specifically, Law 30/00 stipulates the average dose for '10 days of use' as the formal limit separating consumption from trafficking activities.[8] The threshold quantities, however, are often indicative rather than binding. In practice, the police determine what a person intended to do with the substances in their possession. For example, an individual caught selling an amount of drugs considered legal for personal use would be referred to court regardless of the quantity (Domosławski 2011).

The dissuasion commissions, regulated by Decree-Law 130-A/01, are the centrepiece of decriminalization. Aimed at preventing the consumption of drugs and psychotropic substances, the dissuasion commissions replaced Portugal's criminal courts (Soares et al 2017). Under the umbrella of the Ministry of Health, there is one dissuasion commission per each of the country's 18 continental districts. They are composed of three specialists, nominated by the Ministry of Health, the Ministry of Justice, and the government, respectively. Law 30/00 establishes that one of the institution's members shall be a legal expert, whereas the other two shall have expertise in the field of problematic consumption (for example, doctors, psychologists, sociologists, and social services workers). Its chairman, appointed by the government, is responsible for the coordination of drug control policies within each of Portugal's dissuasion commissions.

Dissuasion commissions receive people who use drugs referred by the police or courts when individuals caught with no more than ten doses demonstrate that psychoactive substances were destined for personal consumption. Around 90 per cent of the cases are refereed by the two main agencies,[9] the *Polícia de Segurança Pública* (Public Security Police) and *Guarda Nacional Republicana* (National Republican Guard), whereas courts are the origin of 10 per cent of the proceedings (SICAD 2018a). Though participation is not enforced by law, the attendance rate is high (Silvestri 2020).

After the individual is interviewed by a group of specialists, dissuasion commissions offer targeted advice and support based on each individual's circumstances. Users can also receive different administrative sanctions, including monetary fines, financial donations, social work, privation of social benefits, banning from the exercising of a certain profession or occupation, and even travel restrictions. While newcomers appearing before the commission are often exonerated from regular proceedings and drug-dependent individuals do not receive financial fines, non-problematic users may be sentenced to pay either a fine or a nonpecuniary penalty. Ranging from approximately 25 to 530 euros, which represents the minimum monthly wage, monetary fines are rather light (Cabral 2017).

Complementary to Portugal's decriminalization policy, new harm reduction measures were launched in 2001. Through Decree-Law 183, the national government created programs and socio-sanitary structures for the prevention, treatment, and reinsertion of problematic users (Santos 2004). The Portuguese harm reduction strategy includes offices to support problematic users, shelters, syringe exchange programs, street support teams, low-threshold methadone maintenance, drug consumption rooms, and drug-checking services. Although many harm reduction programs were not new, before decriminalization they were mostly isolated and experimental (Barbosa 2009). For instance, the use of methadone and syringe exchange programs were already in place before Portugal reformed its drug policy in 2001, whereas other initiatives such as drug consumption rooms were launched later. Portugal currently harbours three of these harm reduction establishments: two located in Lisbon and one in Porto (Correia 2022).

The coordination of the Portuguese drug policy, including its goals and implementation, is in charge of the *Conselho Interministerial* (Interministerial Council), a body chaired by the prime minister that counts with the participation of the national drug coordinator and each of the ministers. One level below, the *Comissão Técnica do Conselho Interministerial* (Interministerial Technical Committee), chaired by the national coordinator and composed of government representatives, supports and advises the Interministerial Council. Replacing the IDT, SICAD is the institution in charge of promoting the reduction of drug use and the prevention of problematic behaviours. Finally, the *Conselho Nacional para os Problemas da Droga, das Toxicodependências e do Uso Nocivo do Álcool* (National Council for the Problems of Drugs, Drug Addiction and Harmful Use of Alcohol) is in charge of advising the Portuguese prime minister and other members of the national government on alcohol- and drug-related matters.

The estimated impacts of decriminalization

Instead of jail, 'we are offering sun, beaches and any drug you like' said Paulo Portas, the leader of Portugal's conservative Popular Party after the enactment of decriminalization in 2001 (New York Times 2001, 7). Becoming a 'drug paradise' for foreigners visiting the European country was not the only outcome predicted by opponents and critics of the initiative. Sceptics also argued that decriminalization leads to a perception of acceptability of illicit drug use, causing increases in consumption, particularly of cannabis (Hughes and Stevens 2010). Even the country's health and security situation would be compromised after Portugal's policy shift, claimed Melanie Phillips, a famous British journalist in a BBC television show (Full Fact 2012).

Where is Portugal after 20 years of decriminalization? What are the impacts of this major policy shift on the country's consumption patterns and drug-related harms in the areas of health and security? This final section assesses the likely effects of decriminalization on drug use rates and other market-associated factors. Since there are other problems attributed to the consumption of psychoactive substances, this part also evaluates adverse health consequences such as overdoses and infectious diseases on the one hand, and homicides, drug-related crimes, and incarceration rates on the other.

In order to disentangle other factors affecting drug-related patterns in Portugal, France and Germany, European countries that did not undertake a radical policy reform during the timeframe of the analysis, are incorporated as a control group. The use and possession of illicit drugs were criminal offenses in France and Germany, respectively (EMCDDA 2019d, 2019e). Although in France prosecution may be waived or simplified in minor cases and Germany has recently passed legislation allowing adults to possess small quantities of cannabis for personal use, in both countries users faced the possibility of incarceration for minor offenses during the timeframe of the analysis (EMCDDA 2019e, 2019f). As noted earlier, comparison results should be interpreted with caution. EMCDDA (2020) notes that in some countries there may exist systematic under-reporting problems, differences in terms of case definitions, and registration processes.

Drug consumption patterns

Since the enactment of decriminalization, the Portuguese government has developed four national surveys on psychoactive substance use (that

Graph 5.1: Portugal's LTP, LYP, and LMP of all illicit substances among the general population by year

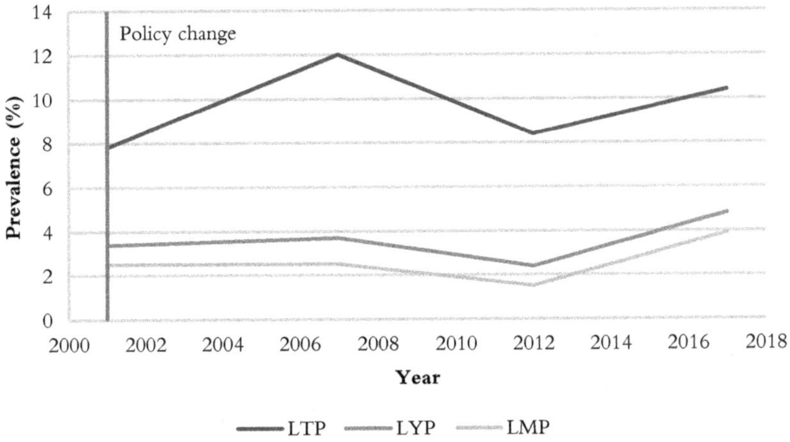

Source: Authors, based on SICAD (2009, 2013, 2020a) and Balsa (2008)[10]

is, *Inquérito Nacional ao Consumo de Substâncias Psicoactivas na População Geral*): 2001, 2007, 2012, and 2016/2017. It follows from the reports that Portugal's lifetime prevalence (LTP) of all illicit substances use has experienced ups and downs since 2001 (Graph 5.1). After registering a peak in 2007, when the country reached a prevalence rate of 12 per cent, the trend went downward thereafter. Still below the levels of 2007, the last report shows an increase of 2 percentage points compared to 2012. That is to say, the country's LTP over almost 20 years of decriminalization expanded 2.6 percentage points (SICAD 2018b).

Unfortunately, 2001 was the first year in which the national survey on psychoactive substance use was conducted. Other studies, however, can help to illuminate Portugal's LTP rates before decriminalization. For example, the Health Behaviour in School-aged Children[11] report published in collaboration with the World Health Organization in continental Portugal shows that LTP of all illicit substances among students (sixth, eighth, and 10th graders) increased from 5.2 per cent to 10.3 per cent between 1998 and 2002 (IDT 2004). With cannabis leading the ranking, the use of all illicit drugs rose before decriminalization (Table 5.1). The European School Survey Project on Alcohol and Other Drugs[12] confirmed the upward trend: the LTP of all illicit drugs among 16-year-old adolescents increased from 12 per cent in 1999 to 18 per cent in 2003 (IDT 2004). Although incorporating data from other studies presents serious methodological challenges, particularly because the age cohorts and the observations covered are widely heterogeneous, Table 5.1 suggests that LTP rates of all illicit psychoactive substances were already rising, perhaps at a faster pace, before Portugal's drug policy reform in 2001.

Table 5.1: Portugal's LTP among students by illicit drug type

Drug	1998	2002
Cannabis	3.8	9.2
Heroin	1.0	1.2
Cocaine	0.9	1.7
Stimulants	2.7	3.5
Ecstasy	:	2.2
LSD	:	1.7

Source: Authors, based on IDT (2004)

Yet measuring drug use at least once in a lifetime is not always effective in assessing recent consumption trends (WHO 2000; EMCDDA 2010; United Nations Office on Drugs and Crime [UNODC] 2010b). In Portugal, for instance, LTP data may also include drug use that took place before decriminalization. Under these circumstances, the 'last year' (LYP) and 'last month' (LMP) prevalence indicators can reflect more accurately the impacts of drug policy reform. On the one hand, last-year drug use among the general population expanded 1.4 percentage points since 2002 (Graph 5.1). Specifically, estimates on annual drug consumption increased from 3.4 per cent to 4.8 per cent between 2002 and 2017 (SICAD 2013, 2018a). On the other hand, LMP increased from 2.5 per cent in 2002 to 3.9 per cent in 2017, echoing the last-year increase rates (Balsa 2008). In other words, both drug consumption indicators grew at a lower rate relative to LTP estimates.

At first glance, Portugal's increases in LTP, LYP, and LMP among the general population are consistent with the findings reported by Pinto Coelho (2010) and the Office of National Drug Control Policy (2010) reviewed in Chapter 1, albeit data suggest that this trend began before decriminalization. Based on information published by EMCDDA and IDT, both reports show that LTP of all illicit drugs increased following decriminalization, a trend also found by Hughes and Stevens (2010), although they do not attribute these fluctuations to Portugal's drug policy reform. These studies, however, only cover up to 2007, the first important peak in Portugal's drug use trends. Most importantly, the methodological design of these two first evaluations does not include a control group, limiting the possibility of establishing cause-and-effect relationships.

Special attention needs to be paid to the 15–24 age group, as the late period of adolescence is commonly identified as the most sensitive one because it often determines the possibility of a person using drugs in the future. According to the four national surveys, the LTP, LYP, and LMP of any illicit drug among the population aged 15–24 remained relatively stable over the course of decriminalization.[13] While the LTP increased 1.6 percentage points between 2002 and 2017, the last-year use rate fell 0.8 percentage points and the LMP did not experience fluctuations (IDT 2009; SICAD 2016b, 2020a). Unlike other estimates, these figures suggest that decriminalization did not have a substantial impact on young people initiating the consumption of illicit drugs.

Cannabis was the most-used illicit drug during this period, followed far behind by cocaine and ecstasy. Except for cannabis, which registered the highest prevalence in 2017, last-year and last-month use rates for cocaine, ecstasy, heroin, LSD, and amphetamine-type stimulants (ATS) have either remained stable or decreased since decriminalization (SICAD 2018b) (Table 5.2). In other words, the general upward consumption trend illustrated in Graph 5.1, which is likely a continuation of old patterns registered at least since the late 1990s, seems to be extensively underpinned by cannabis use rather than by use of other illicit drugs. Furthermore, Table 5.2 also confirms that consumption of heroin, a psychoactive substance commonly associated with premature death in Europe (EMCDDA 2015) and a key driving force behind decriminalization, is trending downward in Portugal.

SICAD also measures the consumption continuity rates, an indicator that shows whether illegal drugs are used one or multiple times. Interestingly, the proportion of individuals who have consumed cocaine, heroin, and ecstasy throughout their lives and declare that they have used this same substance in the last year declined between 2001 and 2017.[14] Except for heroin, which experienced a minor increase in the last national survey on psychoactive

Table 5.2: Portugal's LYP and LMP among the general population by drug type and year

LYP						
Year	**Cannabis**	**Cocaine**	**Ecstasy**	**Heroin**	**LSD**	**ATS**
2001	3.3	0.3	0.4	0.2	0.1	0.1
2007	3.6	0.6	0.4	0.3	0.1	0.1
2012	2.7	0.2	0.3	<0.1	0.2	<0.1
2017	5.1	0.2	0.1	0.1	<0.1	<0.1
LMP						
Year	**Cannabis**	**Cocaine**	**Ecstasy**	**Heroin**	**LSD**	**ATS**
2001	2.4	0.1	0.2	0.1	<0.1	0.1
2007	2.4	0.3	0.2	0.2	0.1	0.1
2012	1.7	0.1	0.2	<0.1	0.1	<0.1
2017	4.3	0.1	<0.1	<0.1	N/A	N/A

Source: Authors, based on SICAD (2018b)

Graph 5.2: Portugal's consumption continuity rates among the general population by drug type and year

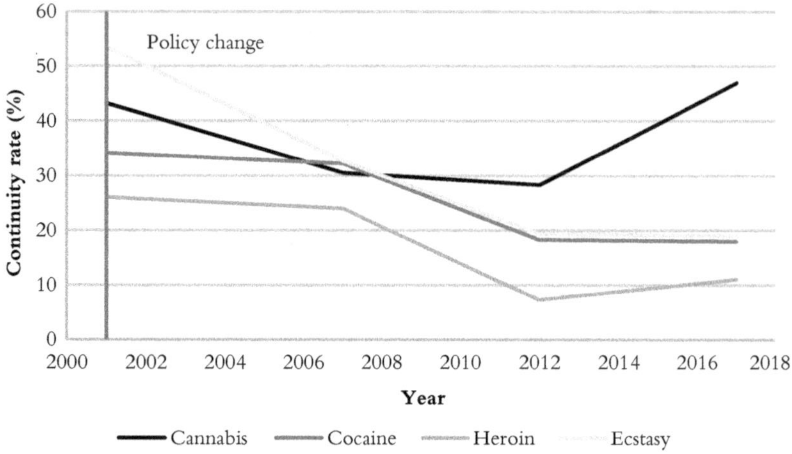

Source: Authors, based on SICAD (2013, 2020a) and IDT (2006)

substance use, the downward trend has been sustained among all the so-called hard drugs (Graph 5.2). Cannabis, by contrast, is the only psychoactive substance whose latest consumption continuity rates are above the levels of the 2001 reform. To put it differently, Graph 5.2 demonstrates that the frequency of consumption has not intensified during the decriminalization period, suggesting that liberalization has limited ability to increase the harms associated with the abuse of illegal drugs.

Dissuasion commissions

Portugal's consumption trends can be also illustrated by the activity of dissuasion commissions. Between 2002 and 2019, Portugal's dissuasion commissions registered a total of 144,111 proceedings. Rising from 5,580 cases in 2002 to 9,353 in 2019, the number of appearances before these institutions increased steadily until 2017 and began to decrease thereafter (IDT 2006; SICAD 2013, 2020a).[15] The last official report shows that the vast majority of the individuals referred to administrative processes are single males, accounting for 92 per cent and 90 per cent of the cases. While 50.9 per cent of the individuals under proceedings are under the age of 24, 27.7 per cent of the cases are between 25 and 34 years old. Out of the total population appearing before dissuasion commissions, 54.9 per cent have a job and 18.3 per cent are unemployed, whereas around 23.5 per cent are identified as students. Likewise, roughly 5 per cent of the individuals referred to the administrative process appear more than once in a year, suggesting that the recurrence rate remains low (SICAD 2020a).

Cannabis accounts for 83 per cent of the total proceedings in Portugal, followed far behind by cocaine and heroin with 7 per cent and 4 per cent, respectively. Administrative processes involving more than one drug represent 6 per cent of the total (SICAD 2020a). Nevertheless, the distribution of drugs involved in each administrative process has varied significantly since dissuasion commissions began to operate in 2001. While cannabis proceedings slowly increased after the enactment of decriminalization, the percentage of heroin-related administrative processes decreased drastically. Specifically, heroin proceedings lowered from 26.39 per cent in 2002 to 3.82 per cent in 2019. Administrative processes involving cocaine remained relatively stable (IDT 2007; SICAD 2012, 2020a). The activity of dissuasion commissions, in other words, seems to confirm the consumption patterns depicted in Table 5.2.

Since the goal of the ruling is to prevent the consumption of psychoactive substances rather than punish users, sanctions have remained a minor outcome. In 2019, for example, approximately 19 per cent of the 8,150 commission rulings imposed punitive sanctions, whereas 80 per cent and 1 per cent were suspensive and absolving resolutions, respectively (IDT 2007; SICAD 2012, 2020a). This trend, however, has been slowly reversed since the enactment of decriminalization. Between 2001 and 2019, the percentage of punitive sanctions has tripled. Although sanctions increased before the 2008 Supreme Court decision, the upward trend seems to reflect the rise of punitivism noted by Rêgo and colleagues (2021).

Portugal's drug use patterns in the European context

Europe is an important market for illicit drugs. With drugs supplied either from other regions, particularly Latin America, North Africa, and West Asia, or from domestic production, consumption increased in many European countries during the first years of the twenty-first century (UNODC 2009). Available data suggest that use of cocaine entering from the Andean subregion is trending upward, whereas heroin consumption remains stable with low rates of initiation (EMCDDA 2018a). Cannabis consumption among young adults also expanded during the same period (EMCDDA 2019a). Production, on the other hand, is mostly limited to cannabis, whose supply seems to have displaced imports, and some synthetic stimulants like ecstasy, which are also manufactured for export. Moreover, some illicit psychoactive substances and chemical precursors are transited through Europe and destined for other continents (EMCDDA 2018a).

Compared to other members of the European Union (EU), Portugal's consumption rates are relatively low (Table 5.3). Although survey years do not match for each of the countries, it is evident that Portugal's LTP and LYP for any illicit drug among the general population are below the

Table 5.3: LTP, LYP, and LMP of any illicit drugs among the general population in the EU

Country	Year	LTP	LYP	LMP
Austria	2015	24.6	6.7	2.7
Belgium	2013	15.8	5.1	N/A
Bulgaria	2016	11.2	5.7	2.6
Croatia	2015	20.3	8.3	5.3
Cyprus	2016	12.3	2.2	1.3
Czechia	2017	31.2	9.5	2.2
Denmark	2017	39	7.1	3.5
Estonia	2008	21.3	6.5	2
Finland	2014	22.2	7.2	2.7
France	2017	45	11.5	N/A
Germany	2015	27.7	6.6	3.4
Greece	2015	11.2	2.9	1.3
Hungary	2015	9.9	2.3	1.2
Ireland	2015	30.7	8.9	4.7
Italy	2017	33.3	10.6	5.6
Latvia	2015	11.3	4.6	2.2
Lithuania	2016	11.5	3.1	1.3
Luxembourg	2014	34.7	6.2	2.8
Malta	2013	1.4	N/A	N/A
Netherlands	2017	28.2	11	6.8
Norway	2017	24.8	N/A	N/A
Poland	2014	16.4	4.7	2.2
Portugal	2016	11.7	5.4	4.4
Romania	2016	10.9	5.8	2.8
Slovakia	2015	16.6	4.7	2.3
Slovenia	2012	16.1	4.5	2.4
Spain	2017	36.3	11.9	9.6
Sweden	2016	15.6	9.4	3

Source: Authors, based on EMCDDA (2019a)

Note: Bold indicates countries that are part of the control group.

average, whereas the last-month use rates are slightly above (EMCDDA 2019a). In effect, except for Germany's LMP, the control group registers higher LTP, LYP, and LMP estimates relative to Portugal. In several measures, France and Germany even double or triple the Portuguese prevalence rates (EMCDDA 2019a).

A closer examination of France and Germany reveals that the LYP and LMP of cannabis, the only psychoactive substance whose consumption has increased in Portugal during decriminalization, either rose or remained practically at the same levels between 2000 and 2017 (EMCDDA 2019a). On the one hand, Portugal registered an increase of 1.8 percentage points in the LYP of cannabis, a lower escalation than France (2.6) but higher than Germany (0.1). On the other hand, Portugal's last-month use growth (1.9) was lower than only France (2.1), as Germany registered a decrease of 0.2 percentage points. In other words, increases in cannabis use rates in Portugal are not likely attributable to decriminalization but are rather indicative of broader trends within the political economy of illicit drugs in Western Europe.

As noted, Portugal's last-year and last-month use of psychoactive substances other than cannabis have either remained stable or decreased since decriminalization. Nonetheless, in France fluctuations followed different patterns. In the case of cocaine, for example, Portugal's LYP decreased 0.1 percentage points between 2001 and 2017, a pattern also witnessed in Germany, whereas France registered an increase of 1.4 percentage points (EMCDDA 2019a).[16] While last-month use remained stable in Portugal and Germany, respectively, it increased 0.1 percentage points in France, even though there are several missing values in the dataset for this particular country (EMCDDA 2019a). Ecstasy, LSD, and ATS consumption rates also exhibited similar patterns. While in Portugal LYP and LMP remained stable or slightly decreased after the adoption of the decriminalization policy, fluctuations in France and Germany also included slight or moderate increases (EMCDDA 2019a). Unfortunately, there is no accurate information available on trends of heroin use rates in France and Germany.

In short, data from the control group suggest that the overall increase of Portugal's LTP, LYP, and LMP of all illicit drugs among the general population are not attributable to decriminalization. The upward trend not only seems to have begun before drug policy reform, but was also experienced in France and, to a lesser extent, in Germany. This is consistent with the findings of Hughes and Stevens (2010), who compared Portugal's use patterns over the course of decriminalization with those of Spain and Italy, countries that also observed increases after 2001. Furthermore, this disaggregated analysis of each illicit drug also shows that the prevalence of only cannabis increased, echoing trends in the control group. Even the LYP and LMP of any illicit drug among those aged 15–24, a population that may suggest future use trends, remained stable or slightly decreased during decriminalization.

Market trends

Changes in the legal status of drugs can also affect the supply of drug markets and law enforcement activity (MacCoun and Reuter 2001). In addition to formal penalties, variations in seizures and prices of illicit psychoactive substances are likely to influence consumption patterns. Since the impacts of policy reforms are often indirect and complex, other market-associated factors such as the potency of drugs can also experience changes after the adoption of decriminalization.

Drug seizures have witnessed significant fluctuations in Portugal during the last 20 years. Official reports indicate that a total of 34,284 kg of illicit drugs were seized in 2000, the year prior to decriminalization, whereas in 2019 the amount of drugs confiscated dropped to 14,309. By contrast, the number of ecstasy tablets climbed from 25,496 to 34,161 during the same period (IDT 2004, 2008; SICAD 2014, 2020a) (Table 5.4). The overall decrease was driven mainly by hashish, as seizures of other psychoactive substances such as cocaine and marijuana rose between 2000 and 2019.[17] Confiscations of heroin, on the other hand, seem to have decreased substantially since 2001. According to Félix, Portugal, and Tavares (2017), the decline in seizures, which in their statistical model is particularly evident for heroin, would have been less accentuated in the absence of decriminalization. They argue that the downward trend is likely the consequence of changes in law enforcement practices, as police officers shifted their focus from people who use drugs to the supply side of the market (Félix, Portugal, and Tavares 2017).

The Portuguese drug seizure declines seem to have developed in line with the rest of the European region (EMCDDA 2019a). Although the number of observations does not entirely match with Portugal, the EMCDDA (2019a) database shows that Germany experienced similar fluctuations during the post-decriminalization period, with marijuana and cocaine availability trending upward and hashish and heroin showing exactly the opposite pattern.[18] Still, unlike Portugal, Germany increased the overall number of kilograms seized compared to pre-reform levels. In France, on the other hand, the quantity confiscated increased for all the psychoactive substances. Of course, there are difficulties in collecting reliable data about the structure of illicit markets compared to other indicators such as prevalence rates (Félix, Portugal, and Tavares 2017).

According to SICAD (2018a), most of the hashish and cocaine seized in Portugal come from North Africa and South America, respectively. While Morocco is the main source of hashish followed far behind by Spain, cocaine comes from Brazil, Paraguay, and Chile. Even if these countries do not produce or manufacture cocaine, they serve as transshipment territories. Heroin, on the other hand, is mostly trafficked from Mozambique and the Netherlands. Ecstasy seizures in Portugal suggest that the synthetic drug

Table 5.4: Police seizures (kg) under the drug law by year and drug type[19]

Year	Hashish	Marijuana	Cocaine	Heroin	Ecstasy
1998	5,575	7	625	97	1,127
1999	10,636	66	823	76	31,319
2000	30,467	223	3,026	568	25,496
2001	6,473	235	5,574	316	126,451
2002	7,022	361	3,140	96	222,466
2003	31,556	265	3,017	72	155,492
2004	28,994	119	7,423	99	107,734
2005	28,258	121	18,083	182	118,162
2006	8,458	152	34,477	144	113,835
2007	42,772	133	7,363	62	58,515
2008	61,262	37	4,878	68	70,309
2009	22,966	5,045	2,697	128	8,987
2010	34,774	40	3,244	47	48,370
2011	14,633	108	3,678	73	7,791
2012	18,314	49	4,020	66	73,887
2013	8,689	96	2,439	55	14,554
2014	32,877	108	3,715	39	7,169
2015	2,412	224	6,029	97	50,934
2016	7,068	264	1,047	57	151,275
2017	14,791	410	2,734	29	16,931
2018	4,173	138	5,540	27	196,643
2019	3,235	492	10,567	15	34,161

Source: Authors, based on SICAD (2014, 2020a) and IDT (2004, 2008)

is manufactured within the country and later destined for Brazil (SICAD 2018a). The last report also highlights the growing relevance of Portugal as a transit platform for heroin trafficked from countries such as South Africa to Europe (SICAD 2020a).

The average price of illicit drugs in Portugal also changed over the course of the years. After two decades of decriminalization, each substance's price has fluctuated differently (Table 5.5). Except for marijuana, the value of all illicit drugs decreased substantially relative to the year prior to the reform. The prices of heroin and cocaine, for example, fell approximately 51 per cent and 46 per cent, respectively (IDT 2004, 2007, 2011; SICAD 2018a, 2020a). Since the legal risks were partially removed and law enforcement was

Table 5.5: Average drug price, by year and drug type

Year	Hashish	Marijuana	Cocaine	Heroin	Ecstasy
1998	1.78	2.25	45.63	38.5	11.7
1999	1.09	1.4	40.37	31.33	6.7
2000	4.13	3.83	60.31	49.72	5.98
2001	4.06	3.26	53.51	50.27	6.86
2002	2.45	2.62	38.57	43.78	5.9
2003	2.49	4	41.4	46.8	5.27
2004	2.31	2.66	42.23	46.54	4.5
2005	2.13	3.67	45.11	41.01	3.56
2006	2.18	2.15	45.73	42.17	3.18
2007	3.45	4.7	44.65	37.57	3.2
2008	3.28	5.09	45.56	33.25	2.8
2009	2.99	6.22	47.44	36.62	:
2010	3.59	:	46	35.32	3.68
2011	3.12	:	50.07	35.74	:
2012	3.03	:	48.01	28.04	:
2013	2.9	5.47	47	25.64	:
2014	2.55	6.23	47.81	31.47	4.43
2015	2.5	7.41	48.63	31.61	2.58
2016	2.3	8.21	42.52	26.27	2.96
2017	2.35	6.65	44.05	27.14	2.84
2018	2.66	5.89	43.28	27.71	3.82
2019	2.63	5.27	32.53	24.25	4.91

Source: Authors, based on SICAD (2018a, 2020a) and IDT (2004, 2007, 2011)

expected to soften following decriminalization, the overall fall in drug prices was not totally surprising. Prior scholarly works, however, have predicted the opposite outcome. By using a difference-in-differences statistical model, Félix and Portugal (2017) found that the prices of cocaine and heroin did not decrease after the Portuguese drug reform.

Unfortunately, the prices recorded are unadjusted by quantity and purity. SICAD (2017) highlights that Portugal does not adjust the value of drugs per pure gram and the data about retail prices stopped being registered after the adoption of Law 30/2000, as users were no longer asked by authorities to reveal the value of drugs purchased on the street. As a result, it is not possible to estimate price variations per unit in lower transactions (that is, retail) vis-à-vis higher levels of the market (that is, wholesale). Similarly, the value per pure gram purchases cannot be distinguished from the nominal price.

Caveats aside, the prices of illicit drugs followed slightly different patterns in Germany. As had happened in Portugal, available data show that the retail monetary values of hashish and marijuana in Germany increased since the early 2000s. Nonetheless, Germany also witnessed increases in the prices of cocaine and heroin, illicit drugs whose monetary values decreased significantly in Portugal following the adoption of decriminalization policy (EMCDDA 2019b). The price of ecstasy, on the other hand, also trended downward in both countries. Sadly, the number of missing values in the dataset for the French case is comparatively high, too much so to draw any definitive conclusions.

The purity/potency per gram of each illicit substance sold in Portugal is another relevant indicator of the market's performance, which can also impact the population's health. The evidence indicates that except for heroin, the potency of all illicit drugs has increased since Portugal adopted the decriminalization scheme (Table 5.6). This is evident in the case of cannabis, as the potency of both hashish and marijuana climbed significantly between 2000 and 2019 (EMCDDA 2019a; SICAD 2020a). This ascending trend contradicts the argument raised by some critics of criminalization, who often note that liberalization policies are expected to drive down the potency of drugs, helping to deliver safer psychoactive substances (Smart et al 2017). However, the increasing potency of illicit drugs in Portugal is not likely attributable to decriminalization, as France reported similar patterns (EMCDDA 2019a). Germany also registered increases in the potency of hashish, the only psychoactive substance with available information.

In summary, the evidence indicates that seizures decreased after decriminalization, a trend primarily driven by hashish. Likewise, prices followed a predictable trajectory and decreased after 2000. Interestingly, the monetary value of almost all illicit drugs rose in Germany, suggesting that fluctuations are likely attributable to decriminalization. However, Portugal's use patterns seem to have not been sensitive to changes in the prices of drugs. Except for cannabis, last-year and last-month use of all illicit drugs either remained stable or decreased despite their monetary value dropping substantially. The potency of drugs, on the other hand, experienced increases following decriminalization, echoing the behaviour in France and, to a lesser extent, Germany.

Adverse health consequences

Dramatic institutional changes such as Portugal's decriminalization of illicit drugs are likely to impact not only prevalence rates but also the population's health. Long-lasting and acute health disorders, even overdose deaths, are

Table 5.6: Average potency/purity, by year and drug type

	Hashish	Marijuana	Cocaine	Heroin	Ecstasy
1998	4.3	1.6	65	34.7	15.7
1999	3.7	:	68.9	36.1	:
2000	2.2	0.2	53.3	37	:
2001	5.5	5.2	73.5	34.1	:
2002	2.6	3.1	41.7	15.5	:
2003	6	1.4	39.3	17.2	72.9
2004	6.9	3.5	34.4	18.8	60
2005	5.4	3	32.6	18.5	51
2006	5.8	6.3	44.6	18.9	18.4
2007	6.6	3.9	48.1	25.1	45
2008	7	4.8	48.4	31.9	34.6
2009	7.2	3.8	38.7	32.4	22.2
2010	9.1	5.2	38.9	27.4	39.4
2011	9.3	5.2	33.7	12.8	59.8
2012	11.7	5.4	32.8	11.5	72.4
2013	13.9	6.6	37.3	12.6	77
2014	18	7.8	40.1	14	80
2015	14	8.3	34.6	19.5	88.1
2016	14.8	7.2	40.3	15.5	82.8
2017	11.4	8.3	43.9	15.2	97.9
2018	15.3	8.1	50.1	18.1	130.5
2019	14.3	6.9	59.5	14.8	98.9

Source: Authors, based on EMCDDA (2019b) and SICAD (2020a)

commonly associated with the chronic use of psychoactive substances. Of course, factors such as the quantity and quality of the drugs available, the route of administration, the user's vulnerability, and the general context in which psychoactive substances are consumed can also affect their harmfulness.

Hospitalizations and treatment

Treating drug use as a medical issue rather than as a criminal problem implies, among other things, the provision of different medical services. After a first stage aimed at enhancing the proximity to users through prevention campaigns, the Portuguese strategy encouraged problematic users to undergo programs in treatment centres (Félix, Portugal, and Tavares

Graph 5.3: Number of patients in treatment by year

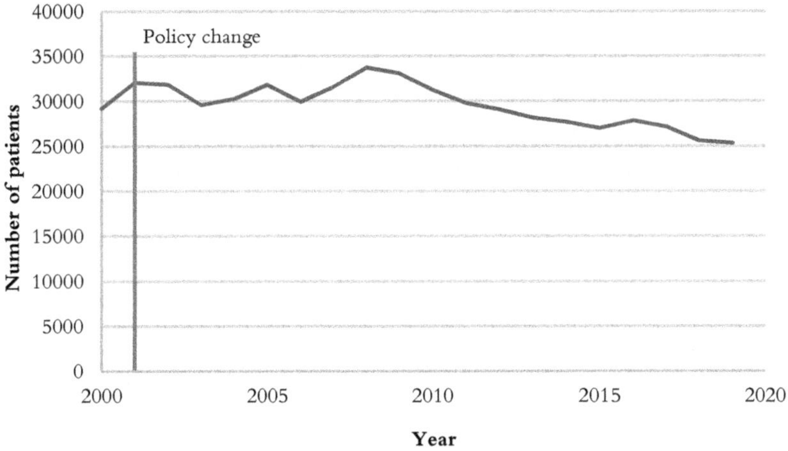

Source: Authors, based on SICAD (2013, 2020a) and IDT (2007, 2009)[20]

2017). According to official reports, the number of drug-related patients has slowly decreased after experiencing a peak in 2008, finishing in 2019 below Portugal's pre-reform levels (IDT 2007, 2009; SICAD 2013, 2020a) (Graph 5.3). More specifically, the number of individuals admitted along the Portuguese public health network dropped by around 13 per cent between 2000 and 2019, showing that decriminalization did not provoke important adverse health effects.[21] This trend is particularly relevant since a key goal of the 2001 reform was to facilitate access to treatment by reducing the social stigma of drug use, meaning that a higher number of patients following the adoption of decriminalization would have not been totally surprising. In other words, these results may also mean that the key goal of reaching users through treatment is not working.

Portugal's decreasing hospitalization and drug treatment rates were also reported by other scholars (Negreiros and Magalhães 2009; Félix, Portugal, and Tavares 2017). According to Pombo and da Costa (2016), drug patients in Portugal, especially those using heroin, were older and better educated compared to those admitted before decriminalization. Other studies, nevertheless, show that cannabis hospitalizations seem to be an exception to this falling trend. Echoing Portugal's rising cannabis prevalence rates reported in Table 5.2, Gonçalves-Pinho, Bragança, and Freitas (2019) find that admissions to hospitals with a primary diagnosis of psychotic disorders and schizophrenia associated with the use of cannabis increased 29.4 times between 2000 and 2015.

Unfortunately, due to changes in the flow of data at the national level, there is no comparable information available for Europe (EMCDDA 2019a).

Data for the period 2000–2013 are missing for the control group. Yet broad estimates indicate that the demand for heroin treatment in Europe has been falling steadily, whereas hospitalizations associated with the consumption of cannabis and cocaine seem to be undergoing the exact opposite trend (EMCDDA 2021). Even though further research is needed to monitor current patterns, the nature of hospitalizations seems to be reflecting major variations in the prevalence of illicit drugs in the entire European region.

Infectious diseases

The spread of drug-related infectious diseases was a major concern driving decriminalization. In 1999, Portugal recorded the highest rate of AIDS associated with the use of illicit drugs in the EU and the second highest prevalence of HIV among injection drug users (Hughes and Stevens 2010). Between 1990 and 1999, for example, the number of drug-related AIDS infections climbed from 46 to 611, representing a 1,200 per cent increase (IDT 2004). This rising trend, however, was drastically reversed after Portugal decriminalized the use and possession of drugs in 2001. Specifically, diagnoses of HIV and AIDS lowered from 1,390 and 566, respectively, in 2000 to 16 and 13 in 2019 (Graph 5.4). Similar to HIV and AIDS infections, other scholarly works have reported decreasing numbers of cases of hepatitis C following Portugal's drug policy reform (Pombo and da Costa 2016).

Portugal's improving records of infectious disease diagnoses developed in line with trends observed in the European region. The last report elaborated by EMCDDA (2021a) shows a substantial decline in the number of HIV and AIDS diagnoses among European countries. Between 2009 and 2019, the only period for which updated data are available, France recorded a steady decrease in HIV and AIDS infections, whereas Germany witnessed exactly the opposite trend in terms of HIV diagnoses (EMCDDA 2021a). Indeed, the total number of diagnoses between the other two European countries are still above the Portuguese rates in 2019 (Table 5.7). Most importantly, Portugal experienced a more pronounced decrease (94.3 per cent) compared to France (57.1 per cent), whereas the sum of HIV and AIDS diagnoses increased in Germany (10.8 per cent), suggesting that decriminalization had a positive effect on the number of infectious diseases in the country.

Unlike treatment and infectious disease patterns, Portugal's drug-induced deaths, commonly referred as overdoses, have experienced different fluctuations.[22] After undergoing a drastic decline following decriminalization, reaching the lowest levels in 2005, the number of overdoses oscillated in an upward direction (Graph 5.5). The last report shows that overdoses in Portugal slightly increased, remaining practically at the pre-reform levels (EMCDDA 2021b). Hughes and Stevens (2010) claim that increases in the post-2005 period can be attributed to changes in measurement practices,

Graph 5.4: Portugal's HIV and AIDS diagnoses by year[23]

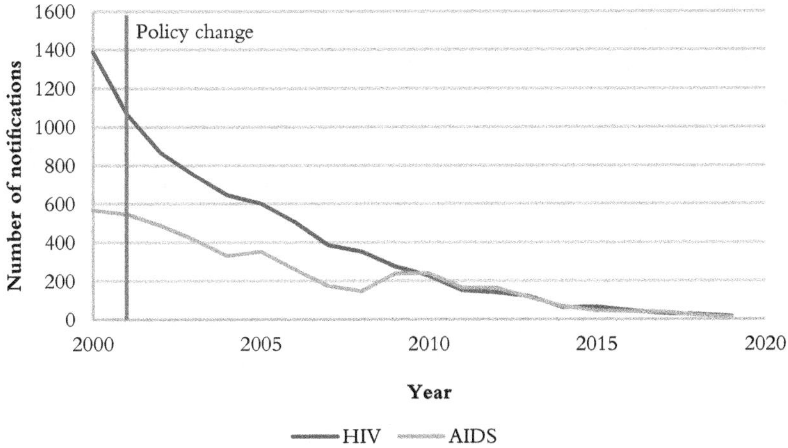

Source: Authors, based on EMCDDA (2021a) and IDT (2007, 2010)[24]

Table 5.7: Portugal, France, and Germany HIV and AIDS diagnoses by year

Year	Portugal		France		Germany	
	HIV	AIDS	HIV	AIDS	HIV	AIDS
2009	275	239	131	58	97	50
2010	227	240	129	60	83	36
2011	151	165	123	62	84	41
2012	142	165	131	45	88	42
2013	121	115	111	42	108	31
2014	63	68	104	30	131	26
2015	64	47	78	31	142	21
2016	46	41	61	19	134	18
2017	32	39	60	12	116	13
2018	27	22	68	19	146	18
2019	16	13	65	16	159	4

Source: Authors, based on EMCDDA (2021a, 2021b)

as the number of toxicological autopsies performed after 2002 climbed significantly.[25] Along these lines, Alcina Correia (2022), the director of SICAD's Monitoring and Information Department, argues that current data are not comparable with the information collected in 2001. Unlike the ongoing methodological approach, data in the past only indicated the presence of illicit psychoactive substances in Portugal's registered

Graph 5.5: Overdoses in Portugal, France, and Germany by year[26]

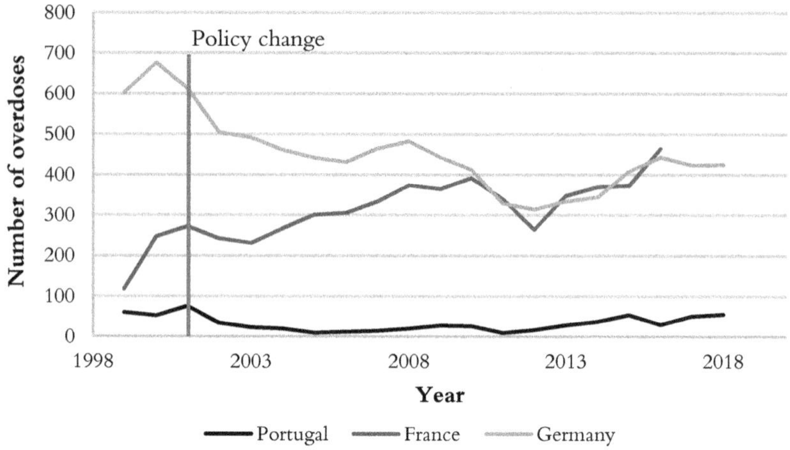

Source: Authors, based on EMCDDA (2021b)

deaths, which were not necessarily associated with overdoses. Likewise, the epidemiology of overdose deaths also changed throughout the years. Overdose deaths are today predominately related to cocaine and not to heroin as they were before. An additional problem noted by Correia (2022) is the presence of new products, some of them synthetic, used to 'cut' the main psychoactive substance before it reaches consumers.

The number of overdoses in Europe have also trended upward (EMCDDA 2021b). Yet France and Germany have experienced slightly different patterns. Germany, on the one hand, followed the Portuguese downward trend after 2000–2001 but sustained it with minor fluctuations till 2012, when the country witnessed a new escalation. France, on the other hand, registered a slow increase in the number of overdoses between 2000 and 2016. Since roughly three-quarters of fatal overdoses in Europe are still linked to the use of opioids, primarily caused by heroin injection (EMCDDA 2021b), variations among countries are likely to illustrate the different stages in the heroin epidemic (Hughes and Stevens 2010). Furthermore, EMCDDA (2018b) also points out that highly potent synthetic opioids such as fentanyl are playing an increasing role in the number of overdoses in some European countries.

Crimes and drug-related violence

The association between illicit drugs and crime is often present in the mind of politicians and the population, exerting influence across different policy-making areas. Although violence was not a major motivation behind Portugal's decriminalization, drug policy reform may still affect crime in various ways. In addition to the offenses of use and possession themselves, violent and property crimes, as well as homicides, can experience fluctuations over the course of a radical drug policy shift such as decriminalization.

Intentional homicides

The *Instituto Nacional de Estatística* (National Statistics Institute) is the Portuguese entity responsible for producing and disseminating official statistics on crime and justice. Notwithstanding more detailed information is published by the Ministry of Justice's *Direção-Geral da Política de Justiça* (Directorate-General for Justice Policy), there are no disaggregated data on drug-related homicides available. At the expense of precision, therefore, the intentional homicide rate is perhaps the most straightforward, measurable, and comparable indicator for measuring violence in Portugal. As UNODC highlights, the core element of intentional homicide is the complete liability of the direct perpetrator, which excludes other types of killings such as those related to war or conflicts, suicides, or self-defence (UNODC 2013).

Portugal's homicides levels have oscillated over the course of the years. Though in 2007 the country faced the highest peak during the last two decades, it never surpassed the average of two intentional homicides per 100,000 inhabitants (UNODC 2021). After almost 20 years of decriminalization, Portugal still registers fewer murders per 100,000 inhabitants than in the pre-reform years (Graph 5.6). In other words, the post-2007 trajectory confirms that the original fears raised by Pinto Coelho (2010) of the Association for a Drug Free Portugal that suggested that the country's homicide rates were growing as a direct result of decriminalization policy did not materialize in the long run.

Portugal's homicide profile displays a similar trend to that observed in the rest of Europe since the early 2000s (UNODC 2021). Fluctuating at a slower pace than the region's average, Portugal's intentional homicides per 100,000 inhabitants decreased from 1.1 to 0.8 between 2000 and 2018. France and Germany also display a steady reduction in their intentional homicide rates during this period, although the downward trend witnessed less pronounced fluctuations in these two countries (UNODC 2021).

Robbery and theft

Other types of crimes sometimes associated with the drug market have also registered a drop in Portugal during decriminalization. Between 2003 and 2017, robbery and theft rates declined from 190 and 988 to 115 and 860, respectively (UNODC 2021).[27] Except for the six-year period from 2008 to 2014, Portugal never surpassed 1,000 thefts per 100,000 inhabitants. Similarly, in 2004 the European country registered a rate of more than 200 robberies

Graph 5.6: Intentional homicide rates in Portugal, France, and Germany by year

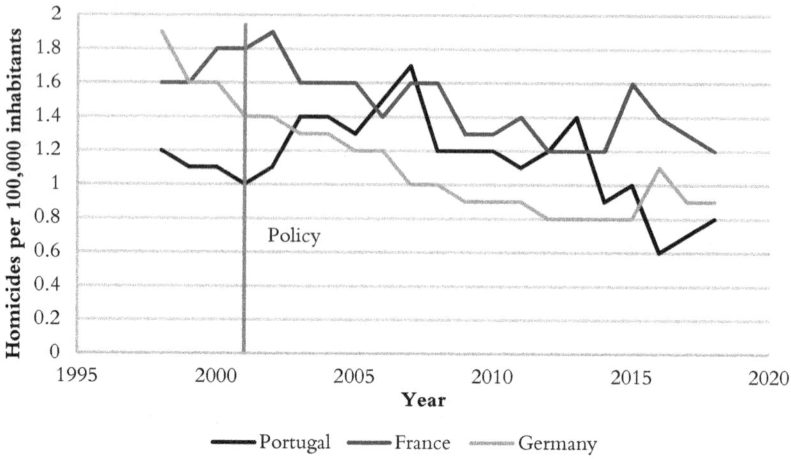

Source: Authors, based on UNODC (2021)

(UNODC 2021). As Redondo and Frerich (2014) point out, Portugal's crime rates are relatively low when compared to the rest of the world.

Notwithstanding the methodological perils of comparing theft and robbery crimes across countries, as governments develop their own reporting mechanisms, police recording strategies vary, and trust in law enforcement affects information, the broad trends witnessed in France and Germany since 2003 suggest that Portugal's downward trajectory was slightly different from the rest. While the three countries experienced decreases in the number of robberies per 100,000 inhabitants, theft rates rose in France to finish in 2017 below post-reform levels. Although it is not possible to attribute Portugal's improving crime records solely to decriminalization, it is clear that the softening of penalties did not have a negative impact on the security landscape.

Drug-related crimes

Yet neither robberies nor thefts shed light on the alleged relationship between drugs and crime. Under these circumstances, the three national surveys on drug use conducted in the prison system (*Inquérito Nacional sobre Comportamentos Aditivos em Meio Prisional*) can be informative in this regard. The last report shows that the number of crimes directly related to drugs decreased 19.3 percentage points between 2001 and 2014, whereas crimes indirectly related to drugs were also at their lowest levels since the adoption of decriminalization. As a result of this downward trend, crimes that do not have any relationship with drugs increased from 27.1 per cent to 47.4 per cent during the same period. According to Torres and colleagues (2016), three possible mechanisms could be operating to move Portugal's criminal landscape away from the drug market: (i) the direct effects of the removal of criminal penalties on drug consumption, (ii) a decrease in both the number of crimes and the use of psychoactive substances, and (iii) an increase of non-drug-related crimes as a result of unemployment as well as the social and economic crisis.

Following Quintas and Arana (2017), it is also possible that law enforcement has redirected their policing resources towards other forms of crime following the decriminalization of drug possession and use. When disaggregated, both drug trafficking crimes and trafficking intended to use psychoactive substances have steadily decreased since 2001. Though the last national survey of the prison population demonstrates that both offenses are still among the top five crimes among Portugal's prison population, their incidence has decreased significantly since the 2001 drug policy reform (Torres et al 2016). Most importantly, both drug trafficking crimes and trafficking intended to use psychoactive substances decreased at a faster pace relative to thefts and homicides, whereas robberies increased during the same period. In other words, the evidence suggests that not only homicide, robbery, and theft rates lowered following decriminalization, but also rates for crimes associated with the use and trafficking of drugs.

Incarceration

The world's prison population has increased over the years. It is estimated that more than 10.2 million people, including sentenced and pretrial prisoners, were held in penal institutions worldwide in 2013, accounting for an average imprisonment rate of 144 inmates per 100,000 of the world population (UNODC 2015). While this trend may be attributable to increasing levels of criminal activity, this is not always the case. Studies have shown that rates of imprisonment and crime may evolve independently of each other (UNODC 2010c). In many countries, for example, individuals convicted of drug-related crimes such as consumption, possession, and trafficking receive longer maximum and minimum sentences than individuals convicted of murder (Rosen and Brienen 2015).

In Portugal, incarceration rates have slightly decreased since the early 2000s. Even if the prison population per 100,000 inhabitants is still below 2003 levels, the first year after decriminalization for which information is available, incarceration rates started increasing in 2008. In 2019, for example, Portugal had more people behind bars per 100,000 inhabitants than France and Germany (Graph 5.7). Not surprisingly, Gomes and Duarte (2018) claim that Portugal, at least in the European context, is considered a punitive country. Nevertheless, Portugal's latest incarceration rates are still

Graph 5.7: Incarceration rates in Portugal, France, and Germany by year

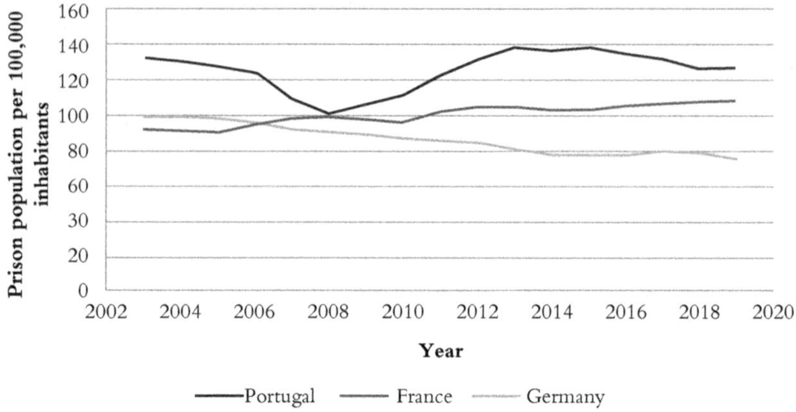

Source: Authors, based on UNODC (2021)

below the average of 166.2 prisoners per 100,000 inhabitants registered in Europe (UNODC 2021).

The prison population for drug violations have also decreased since the adoption of decriminalization (Graph 5.8). More specifically, the number of prisoners went down from 3,829 in 2000 to 1,862 in 2019, representing a 51.3 per cent decline. Since the new legal framework promotes non-incarcerative sanctions, this sharp decrease is not totally surprising. According to Laqueur (2014), the buildup of Portugal's falling incarcerated population is likely the result of de-adoption of de facto practices that were already present among criminal courts rather than the decriminalization policy itself.

Conclusions

Portugal underwent a late modernization process vis-à-vis other European countries (Lains 2007). Despite being an agricultural economy for most of its history, the country anticipated many of the greatest political transformations in Western Europe. Except for the more volatile experiences of Spain, Italy, and the Czech Republic, Portugal became the first country to decriminalize the use and possession of all illicit drugs. Under the umbrella of the Ministry of Health, Portugal has gradually developed a legal and institutional architecture focused on prevention, treatment, and the social reintegration of people who use drugs through harm reduction programs instead of criminalization.

One of the most widely debated aspects of decriminalization has been its impact on consumption. Available evidence indicates that both LYP and LMP of all illicit drugs among the general population expanded 1.4 percentage points, reflecting a continuation of old consumption patterns. Yet this trend

Graph 5.8: Portugal's prison population for violation of the drug law

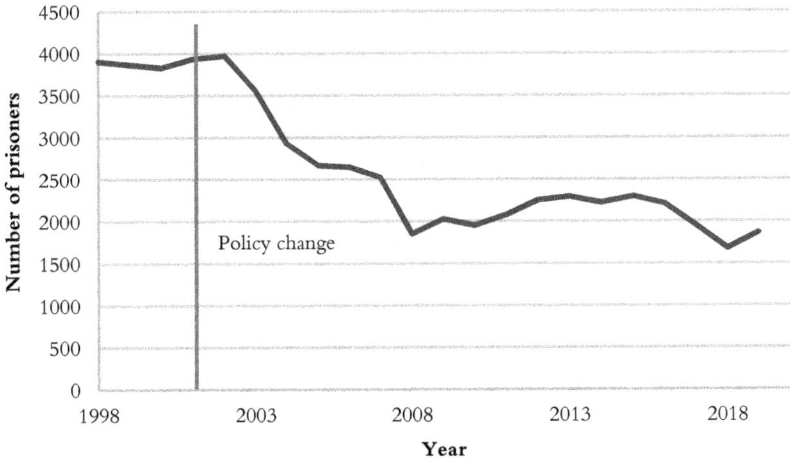

Source: Authors, based on SICAD (2013, 2020) and IDT (2006)

was motivated only by the use of cannabis, as increases were non-existent for all other illicit drugs, including cocaine, ecstasy, and, especially, heroin – the main driving force behind the Portuguese reform and whose chronic use is often linked to premature death. The consumption continuity rates also decreased over the course of decriminalization, suggesting that drug use is less likely to cause health problems. Furthermore, since France and Germany also registered increases in cannabis use rates, the growing prevalence of this psychoactive substance in Portugal is not likely attributable to decriminalization, but rather reflects a regional trend. The evidence also shows that both LYP and LMP of all illicit drugs lowered or remained stable among youth, an age cohort that is often at risk for long-term engagement, implying that the drug policy reform did not have a positive impact on those initiating consumption.

Portugal's declining seizures, a trend that could be associated with changes in law enforcement practices and market size, was witnessed neither in Germany nor in France. The price of illicit drugs except for marijuana, on the other hand, decreased substantially relative to the pre-reform years. Given that LYP and LMP for all drugs except for cannabis remained stable or went down between 2001 and 2017, prices seem to have played a minor role in explaining consumption fluctuations. Interestingly, the monetary value of almost all illicit drugs rose in Germany, suggesting that Portugal's price changes are likely attributable to decriminalization. Yet the way the reform affected the potency of illicit drugs contradicted the argument of some liberalization advocates. In line with trends witnessed in France and, to a lesser extent, Germany, the potency of all illicit drugs in Portugal increased after decriminalization.

Aside from the drug market performance, Portugal's drastic policy shift had some impacts on the population's health. Despite the more solid infrastructure and harm reduction programs, the number of drug-related patients slowly decreased after a peak in 2008, finishing in 2019 below pre-reform levels. Portugal's decreasing hospitalization rates were accompanied by a significant drop in HIV and AIDS infections, thereby reversing the trend experienced during the 1990s. It is highly possible that Portugal's improving records of infectious diseases are attributable to decriminalization and harm reduction policies, as diagnoses in France decreased at a much slower pace and Germany registered an overall increase in the number of HIV and AIDS infections. Unlike treatment and infectious disease patterns, Portugal's rate of overdoses has experienced ups and downs, declining following decriminalization but finishing in 2018 roughly at the same levels as pre-reform. Likewise, the number of drug-induced deaths increased in France, whereas Germany registered fewer of them. More research is needed to untangle the mechanisms behind Portugal's overdose fluctuations, especially the upward trend witnessed after the first decline following decriminalization.

The security landscape also shows positive trends. Similar to France and Germany, Portugal's homicide rates finished in 2018 below pre-reform levels. Robbery and theft rates also went down in the post-decriminalization period. Interestingly, evidence from Portugal's prison population reveals that the numbers of crimes both directly and indirectly related to drugs decreased between 2001 and 2014. The minor role of psychoactive substances is also illustrated by the lower incidence of drug-related crimes relative to thefts, homicides, and robberies. Not surprisingly, Portugal's prison population incarcerated for violation of the drug law dropped significantly following decriminalization, suggesting that the burden on the criminal justice system was reduced, allowing law enforcement to redirect their resources towards other types of crimes.

What are the lessons offered by the Portuguese experience? From our analysis, we observe that since decriminalization, consumption rates of all drugs except for cannabis have either decreased or remained stable. In this case, removing criminal penalties from all drugs did not expand Portugal's drug market or the consumption of more dangerous drugs. After decriminalization, drug consumption patterns have not presented alarming increasing rates. What is more, continuity rates, treatment, and infectious diseases have experienced drastic drops since 2001, whereas overdoses in 2019 remained practically at pre-reform levels. Finally, not only the general crime landscape improved, but also those offenses linked to illicit drugs. In other words, Portugal's experience urges policy-makers considering drug liberalization to ask important questions and decide what matters the most, how much people use drugs or what problems follow from it.

Yet caution is required when assessing the results. Although Portugal's health and security conditions improved following decriminalization, while the patterns of drug consumption did not suffer major setbacks, other key structural factors such as the expansion of the welfare state, the adoption of harm reduction programs, or broader trends experienced within the political economy of illicit drugs in the European region likely affected the impacts of the Portuguese reform. The trajectories followed by the control group highlight the relevance of considering non-policy influences to evaluate drug policy outcomes. As João Goulão, the architect of Portugal's drug policy reform, cautioned, 'It is very difficult to identify a causal link between decriminalization by itself and the positive tendencies we have seen' (Ingraham 2015).

6

Cannabis Legalization in Uruguay

On 25 February 2016, three years after the legalization of cannabis in Uruguay, the local police, dressed in full military gear, delivered the world's first cargo of cannabis plants ever cultivated by a state. Fernando Saicha, then responsible for the growing of cannabis by Simbiosys, one of the first two companies the Uruguayan government hired to oversee the cultivation and supply of the psychoactive substance to pharmacies, stated that he felt he was 'witnessing utopian scenes from a movie' (Garat 2017). In effect, after so many years of prohibition, the South American state was preparing to grow and sell cannabis.

Uruguay might be a small country in territory, with a population of approximately 3.4 million inhabitants, but it has been a big political and social influence in the world, renowned for being in the frontline of progressive policies and a driver of social change in the South American region. For example, in 1927, it became the first Latin American country to grant women the right to vote (Walsh and Ramsey 2016). The nation was also a pioneer in the region to legalize same-sex marriage in 2008. Uruguay has also distinguished itself for having a strong state presence, relatively solid institutions, and low corruption rates. These factors created a fertile ground for the adoption and implementation of a novel drug policy.

Following the progressive trend, on 20 December 2013, the Uruguayan parliament approved Law 19.172, which established the legalization, regulation, and control over production, acquisition, storage, commercialization, and distribution of cannabis by the national government. The legal status of other illicit drugs such as cocaine or heroin, however, did not change. The purpose of the reform was to separate crime and violence associated with 'hard drugs' (that is, cocaine) from the use of 'soft drugs' (that is, cannabis). The language on the law states three main goals: (i) reduce drug trafficking-related violence by taking cannabis off the black market, (ii) promote public health through education and prevention campaigns, and (iii) eliminate the existing legal paradox that allowed for possession but that effectively blocked users from accessing cannabis.

The decision to adopt the revisionist strategy comes, in part, from the high rates of drug-related violence and the failed results of the US-led 'war on drugs' that have shaped the international arena, particularly in Latin America and the Caribbean, since the second half of the twentieth century. As former president and main supporter of cannabis legalization José Mujica (2014) stated during a speech,

> I am convinced of Einstein's advice: When you want to change things and you do the same thing again, nothing changes. We have been repressing and persecuting for so many years and we are getting worse and worse, that we began to think of other alternatives, and that is why I use the term 'experiment.'

In the political economy of illicit drugs, Uruguay has been considered a transit country, especially for cocaine. However, in recent years, it has become a key international drug trafficking hub (DW 2019).[1] Its proximity to cocaine sources and producer countries in the region such as Peru, Bolivia, and Colombia has facilitated the establishment of trafficking routes to Europe, West Africa, and other states in South America such as Brazil and Argentina. Open trade policies with less strict border controls and flexible bank laws also have made Uruguay a place of interest for criminal organizations. The country's cannabis market is estimated to be around 40 tons or US$45.5 million per year (Lissardy 2019).

The initiative for state-regulated cannabis legalization in Uruguay caught international attention. The adoption of the policy has been either highly criticized or praised by global institutions and world leaders. The experiment, if successful, is hoped to become a model for more countries to follow to mitigate the unintended consequences of the conventional punitive paradigm. Yet, the country has faced significant challenges, some due to the lack of experience or nonexistent models available to implement the statewide legalization of cannabis. Assessing the indicators presented in previous chapters, we ask: What are the historical roots of this drug policy alternative? What has happened in Uruguay in the years after legalization? How has the drug market changed after the radical drug policy reform? Is legalization the path to follow to tackle different health and security challenges? Is legalization a more promising drug policy vis-à-vis the mainstream dogmas?

This chapter is divided into five sections. The first part presents a brief historical background on Uruguay's path to legalization. The second section focuses on the institutional architecture behind the country's drug policy, paying particular attention to the changes established to implement and monitor the new legalized cannabis market. Following the structure of the previous chapters, the third section presents an analysis to evaluate the estimated impacts of the legalization of cannabis, exploring prevalence, drug seizures, price and potency, adverse health effects, violence, crime, and incarceration rates in Uruguay. To further our analysis, we also include Brazil and Panama as our control group. The final section presents the conclusions.

The path to legalization

Refocusing the problem of psychoactive substances from a criminal perspective to a noncriminal framework is not an easy task. Although Uruguay made the implementation possible, the pathway to legalization has faced numerous challenges. This section presents a brief account of the drug policy evolution in Uruguay, discussing the process and the social and political context that led to the adoption of Law 19.172 in 2013.

The evolution of drug policy in Uruguay

The evolution of drug policy in Uruguay has transpired through several waves or critical junctures shaped by international and domestic contexts and mechanisms. The specific factors that guided the South American country's drug policy reform range from ideological and social constructs, international regimes vicissitudes, and the rise of powerful drug trafficking organizations to transformations in consumption patterns.

A century ago, during the presidency of Jose Pablo Torcuato Batlle y Ordoñez, a period also known as the 'Batllismo' (1856–1929), Uruguay set the foundation for a welfare state, where the government offered quality free education and health care for all (Garat 2016). During this time, cannabis, cocaine, and opium and its derivatives (morphine and heroin) were used for both medical and recreational purposes and possession of reasonable amounts of drugs destined for personal use was not considered a crime (Graham 2015).

The first drug policy reform in Uruguay took place in 1908 and its main purpose was to target the domestic consumption problem and the availability of psychoactive substances in pharmacies without control mechanisms or regulations. This happened under the administration of Claudio William (1907–1911). He approved a ruling to ban the selling of drugs after a first purchase without the proper medical prescription, meaning that opiates were no longer freely available in drug stores (Marin Gutierrez 2017). Four years later, in 1912, Uruguay joined the international fight against drugs led by the US and signed its first international accord, La Haya Opium Convention of 1912.

A second shift in drug policy came hand in hand with the social construction of drug consumption and the moralistic discourse fashioned by many countries around the world in the early 1900s. During those years in the US, for example, the narrative about drugs was shifting towards criminalization, although psychoactive substances such as cocaine, opium, and cannabis were legal and consumed widely. For political and economic gains, government officials, members of the clergy, and even scientists attributed to drugs the decomposition of the social fabric, especially for youths, leading them to rebellion and ruin (Himmerlstein 1978). Propaganda was created around the idea that cocaine induced African American men to rape white women (Musto 1973), and marijuana was claimed to induce violence among Mexican Americans, calling the drug 'killer weed' or 'drop out drug' that poisoned 'the minds and morals of youth' (Reinarman 1994). As noted in Chapter 3, this construction about drugs would endure for many decades to follow, not only in the US but also around the world. At the same time, however, a parallel movement was emerging in Uruguay. Under the dictatorship of Gabriel Terra (1931–1938), the medical community was highly influential in the propagation of a discourse where drug consumption was considered a 'moral and physical degradation' (Garat 2013, 3).

Uruguay joined the Central Committee of the Board of Directors of the Opium Commission of the League of Nations in 1933. At the end of World War II and the beginning of the US hegemony, the creation of multilateral organizations such as the United Nations became an international instrument to advance the implementation of a global counterdrug effort at the multilateral level, but Uruguay refused to criminalize personal consumption or possession. The inconsistencies in the measures taken at the international level and the ones adopted domestically started to originate law enforcement irregularities among security forces and within the judicial system. In other words, under the law, there was no precision about the differences between a consumer and a drug trafficker. Moreover, there was no clarification on what to consider a 'reasonable amount' in drug possession cases for personal consumption. These discrepancies, in turn, caused internal conflicts in Uruguay on how to balance and manage competing drug policies.

The third wave of reforms took place during the civic-military dictatorship in the 1970s. After President Richard Nixon declared the war on drugs in 1971, the US exacerbated its counterdrug efforts in Latin America and the South American Narcotics and Psychotropic Agreement (ASEP) was signed in 1973. Now the treaty integrated elements of the United Nations' prohibitionist international regime (Graham 2015). The new agreement emphasized regional coordination and repressive measures against drug use, underlining the involvement of security forces to implement it. The ASEP agreed with the US-led war on drugs establishment and strategies and soon the US Drug Enforcement Administration was training the Uruguayan armed forces.

As the US-led war on drugs continued, Uruguay started to move away from the international treaties and underwent some drug policy reforms domestically. The discourse and perception around drug consumption started to change accordingly. A distinction between the conceptualization of consumers as 'addicts' and consumers as 'criminals' was drawn. The purpose of this strategy was to make a better assessment by which to evaluate people who use drugs, in order to provide the proper help or treatment needed. In this setting, what determined if the individual detained for drug possession went to prison or received treatment was the mental state of the detainee, socioeconomic factors, and the gravity of the crime (Garat 2013).

From 1973 to 1985, Uruguay went through one of the darkest periods in its history. On 27 June 1973, during a *coup d'état*, Juan Maria Bordaberry assumed the presidency, quickly built alliances with the military, dissolved the Congress, and proposed the elimination of the popular vote or a representative democracy. The authoritarian regime was responsible for countless violations of human rights, tortures, homicides, exiles, and forced disappearances for deserters and opponents of the newly established civic-military dictatorship. Tensions grew between the military officials and the political leaders, and the dictatorship started to lose force as well as cohesion. In 1980, proposed constitutional reforms giving rise to more political openness to which the authoritarian regime was highly objected were rejected (Schelotto 2015).

In 1985, Uruguay turned to democracy once again. Two years later, in 1987, the Congress created the Special Commission on Drug Addiction with the purpose of exploring the magnitude of drug consumption phenomena. After reconnoitering the dynamics of the policy and some of its negative impacts, questions were raised about the conventional drug policy and its effects (Garat 2013, 2016). The results of the study advocated for a more relaxed and permissive environment for personal consumption. Although the official discourse was changing, the social stigma of drug use in Uruguay during the mid-1980s was still pegged to crime. There was also a strong association of drugs with young people, which at the time became a major social problem. In this context, what followed was an era of repression. Between 1986 and 1987, the Anti-Narcotic Police arrested about 1,470 individuals – most of them high school or university students. The oppressive strategies instigated social movements among the youth led mainly by the *Frente Amplio* (Broad Front)[2] political party that became key in influencing drug reform in Uruguay. Another leading group was The Youth of the Socialist Party, which proposed the legalization of cannabis and the freedom for personal use. Experts started to stress the application and respect to individual sovereignty consecrated in Article 10 of the Constitution. There was also an ideological shift that criticized the idiosyncrasy of the last decade. As a result, in 1998, the Uruguayan legislature approved Law 17.016, which depenalized personal consumption for a 'reasonable quantity' (Galain 2018).

On 13 July 1988, the *Junta Nacional de Drogas* (National Drug Board [JND]) was created in Uruguay with two objectives: to battle drug trafficking and to fight drug abuse. The JND was founded as a collaborative effort among committees and advisors from experts from the different ministries such as Interior, Foreign Affairs, Economy and Finance, National Defense, Culture and Education, Social Security, Public Health, Tourism, and Social Development. It is presided over by the deputy secretary of the Presidency of the Republic, but the one in charge of the organization and coordination of its activities is the general secretary of the National Drug Secretary (Garibotto 2010). The JND was established as an instrument for the creation of a comprehensive drug policy covering everything from the advancement of prevention strategies and problematic use treatments to the repression of drug trafficking, chemical precursors, and money laundering.

Another important juncture began when Uruguay witnessed a sudden rise in drug consumption, especially among a younger sector of the population. It is believed that the upsurge was caused by the affluence in the drug trafficking activities that flourished in South America in the 1990s with the appearance of powerful drug cartels such as Medellín and Cali in Colombia that extended their operations all throughout the continent, increasing easy access to illegal drugs. Traces of Colombian and Mexican drug organizations such as the Juárez cartel in Uruguay showed that the country had become increasingly relevant for international trafficking and money laundering operations. In addition, the appearance of domestic drug lords such as Omar Clavijo Cedrés, one of the most notorious Uruguayan traffickers, shed light on the changing security landscape in the country. The illicit industry started to negatively impact the transparency of institutions and corrupt the social fabric. Once again, it was recognized that a change in drug policy was imperative, to one focused on prevention, treatment, and harm reduction.

As the decade progressed, the division between the prohibitionists and the supporters of decriminalization of personal consumption persisted. In 1998, Uruguay voted for Law 17.016, framed after the model of the United Nations Convention against Illicit Traffic in Narcotic Drugs and Psychotropic Substances of 1988. Under this policy, consumers, producers, and traffickers would be catalogued as criminals. It took 10 years for Uruguay to sign the treaty, meanwhile making some adjustments at the domestic level. Internally, for example, the government did not abolish banking secrecy, did not criminalize the personal use of drugs, and lowered minimum sentences for drug-related offenses (Garat 2016). In addition, Article 31 allowed a 'reasonable amount'[3] for personal use (Ley 19.172 2014).

Uruguay's advancements at the domestic level continued. President Jorge Luis Batlle Ibañez (2000–2005) believed that the war on drugs had floundered and pondered about the possibility of legalizing certain substances and in this way ending drug trafficking. Under his administration, Batlle effected a new drug policy approach focused more on harm reduction towards consumers. The tactic was not well taken by international organizations such as the International Narcotics Control Board (Marin Gutierrez 2017). The minister of the Supreme Court in Uruguay, Gervasio Guillot Martinez (1998–2003), did not support decriminalization but believed it was a good strategy to combat corruption. Despite his scepticism, he went further and proposed the legalization of cannabis. He believed it to be an experiment whose results could be evaluated to assess the viability of more flexible drug policies such as the legalization of other psychoactive substances. The Youth of Frente Amplio studied Martinez's proposal and created the 'Movement for the Liberation of Cannabis'.

Right after *Frente Amplio* took power in 2005, the movement towards cannabis legalization took momentum. The drug use problem was approached as a health issue and the government started building ambulatory centres for treatment. Hospitals were committed to offering quality care for problematic users. A more aggressive strategy was established to fight organized crime and other illegal activities such as money laundering. Congress imposed a limitation on banking secrecy and the Special Court for Organised Crime was created (Garat 2016). President Tabaré Ramón Vázquez Rosas (2005–2010) favoured the stimulation of dialogue around drug legalization. At the international level, Uruguay started to express criticism of the prohibitionist paradigm at the UN narcotic conventions. Under this government, Law 17.835 became a legal instrument to fight drug trafficking and created the *Secretaría Nacional para la Lucha contra el Lavado de Activos y el Financiamiento del Terrorismo* (National Secretary of Anti-Money Laundering)[4] (Marin Gutierrez 2017). According to Queirolo et al (2018), public insecurity opened the window to make cannabis legalization in Uruguay possible. Yet it can be seen as contradictory, since the rise of public insecurity and drug-related crime could have led instead to harsher drug control policies as it often happens in many countries around the world. In addition, the authors also observe that presidential endorsement was decisive in pressing towards legalization.

On 20 June 2012, President José Mujica (2010–2015) and his cabinet presented the 'Strategy for Life and Coexistence' plan. The proposal consisted of 15 points that would lead to the legalization of cannabis. The process would be controlled and regulated by the government with the central purposes of challenging drug trafficking cartels, focusing on security efforts, risk and harm reduction strategies for consumers, and control of quality and potency of the drug (Hetzer and Walsh 2014). The government would be able to protect people who use cannabis by assuring them a safe way to acquire the psychoactive substance while also identifying the habits of consumers to provide treatment. In addition, the government intended to take the profits generated by the informal industry away from organized crime, as the unusual amount of violence in the country was perceived to be linked to their illegal activities. As Mujica stated in an interview: 'I pretend to snatch the market out of the illicit industry … attack it at the source … worse than drug addiction is drug trafficking' (VICE 2016).

Finally, in 2013, the Uruguayan Congress passed Law 19.172, which established the framework for the legalization and regulation of the cannabis market. Following Mujica's proposal, the law's main objective is to 'establish a normative framework that allows for regulation in the cannabis market with the intent to contribute to the reduction of the risks and imminent damage that people consuming cannabis for recreational or medicinal purposes incur' (Ley 19.172 2014, 1). The law also sets other secondary goals such as the reduction of drug-related violence through increasing mandatory sentences for corruption and drug traffickers, the fragmentation of the drug market into 'hard' and 'soft' psychoactive substances, and the promotion of public health through the expansion of treatment opportunities for problematic drug use.

Law 19.172 and its implementation

The implementation of Law 19.172 has not been an easy process. The Uruguayan government did not have any previous experience with drug legalization, not even for medicinal purposes. The lack of antecedents made the process challenging and progress has been slow, but steady. One major challenge was to define how to start supplying cannabis to the pharmacies. Law 19.172 was ratified in 2013, yet the selling of cannabis in registered pharmacies did not start until 2016. The Uruguayan authorities looked outward to foreign models to implement the new legislation. The legalization models from Colorado and Washington State in the US served as bases for the infrastructure needed for a statewide legalization system. Other procedures mirror regulatory measures from the 'coffee shops' in the Netherlands and cannabis social clubs in Spain (Hetzer and Walsh 2014). In the paragraphs that follow, we explore the guiding framework and conditions of legalization in Uruguay, as well as institution building. This section also reflects on the main challenges that Uruguay has faced throughout the legalization process.

Regulation

Creating a framework for legalization and regulation of cannabis is an intricate task. There are many governance issues that play an important role in the judicial system such as production, taxation, price, supply, and the growth of the market. Decisions such as determining a 'safe' amount for regular consumption are highly contended, as well as the potency, type of drugs available, and logistics of distribution. There are other relevant questions to consider, such as: What is the appropriate age for legal consumption? Who will be responsible for growing and distributing the product? How much cannabis should be grown? Who should control and monitor legal consumption?

The regulatory framework consists of legal access to cannabis in three main ways: growing at home, forming and/or being part of a cannabis social club, and buying the product at licensed pharmacies. For the first option, each home grower is allowed to have up to six female flowering cannabis plants that are only for self-consumption and must not exceed 480 grams per year. They must register their plants with the *Instituto de Regulación y Control del Cannabis* (Institute of Cannabis Regulation and Control [IRCCA]). The second option is cannabis social clubs. Each club should be composed of 15 to 45 people, and they can establish a civil association. Registration with the IRCCA and other authorities is required. The club can have up to 99 plants in the same space but cannot distribute more than 480 grams to each of their members annually. Any surplus must be turned over to the IRCCA.[5] The third option is to buy the cannabis at pharmacies. Licensed pharmacies can sell up to 10 grams per week to consumers with or without a prescription. The Uruguayan government is the agency responsible for making cannabis available in pharmacies and providing it at a price that equals or competes with the illegal market.[6] The product sold must be produced by commercial growers approved by the state.[7] To buy at these establishments, consumers must register with the IRCCA (Ley 19.172 2014).

Consumers can have legal access to cannabis through only one of these three options, as the regulations clearly state that acquiring it from more than one of the sources is strictly prohibited (Ley 19.172 2014). Registration can occur only once, and to protect the identity of the user, all personal information that people provide is encrypted following the security standards of financial institutions. Furthermore, some security systems allow buyers to scan their fingerprints at pharmacies, which is linked to the IRCCA database of registered consumers of cannabis.

In 2014, the Uruguayan government hired the first two companies, Symbiosis and ICCorp, to be in charge of the planting, storage, and distribution of 2 tons of cannabis each per year. The growing of the psychoactive substance in Uruguay started in May 2016, three years after the passing of the law, and the companies distributed the product for sale to 16 licensed pharmacies. By the first day, 5,000 people had signed up and within weeks the number of registered consumers rose to 14,000. Two variants of cannabis were launched to the market, *indica* and *sativa*, the latter of which contains low levels of THC and high levels of CBD (IRCCA 2017).[8] As of 2020, there were approximately 50,000 people registered.

An important caveat in this law is that only residents of Uruguay are eligible to purchase cannabis at pharmacies and resale is prohibited. This is to lower the possibilities and the fears of making Uruguay a cannabis tourist destination. In addition, the legalization law prohibits the advertising of cannabis or the promotion of its consumption at any social event, such as concerts or fairs. It includes sanctions for sales to minors and unauthorized production (Hertz and Walsh 2014). Other specifications resemble the law for tobacco smoking or alcohol consumption; that is, smoking cannabis in enclosed public spaces such as bars and restaurants is illegal.

Yet, seven years after legalization, there are still regulatory and implementation gaps. There are issues of control over unregistered cultivation, production, or sale of cannabis outside the legal context, just to mention some. Individuals who participate in the unauthorized production, selling, or trafficking of cannabis will be subject to criminal charges of 10 to 20 years in prison (Graham 2015). Along the same lines, driving under the influence of cannabis continues to be illegal; nonetheless, the exact amount of THC concentration levels that are above the considered allowed amount is yet to be determined.

Institutional reform

As of 2013, the JND served as the only body for drug policy in Uruguay. After the passing of the cannabis law, the government created a new regulatory institution, the IRCCA. The new agency's purpose is to be exclusively in charge of the implementation, evaluation, and monitoring of cannabis legalization. IRCCA was designed to have interagency cooperation; that is, it follows the policy directives of the JND, and it is also linked to the executive branch under the Ministry of Public Health.

The IRCCA is the institution responsible for the revision of applications for individual registration, cannabis clubs, and the licensing of pharmacies, to make sure that every application meets the required qualifications and conditions. Its jurisdiction also includes the inspection of the premises where the cultivation, harvest, production, storage, distribution, and dispensation of cannabis take place, as well as the transportation of the substance and the logistics of distribution. In the case of home growers, a representative from IRCCA can access their homes with either the owner's consent or a judge's order. Besides the monitoring processes, IRCCA also conducts analyses and testing of seeds, plants, and the products sold at pharmacies, to screen if legal and regulatory requirements are being fulfilled. If discrepancies are found, the IRCCA can implement sanctions or penalties including fines, forced closures, and legal action. The institution has full support of the Ministry of the Interior and security forces for implementation purposes (IRCCA 2017).

From the start, the creation of IRCCA came with challenges. It faced budgetary constraints, some processes took a long time to establish, the institution was understaffed, and the lack of experience complicated and slowed down its progress. Nevertheless, the allocation of resources for IRCCA has improved during the past years. On 20 December 2015, the

Vázquez administration signed a bill allotting it 15 million Uruguayan pesos (US$500,000) per year until 2020. It was projected that the IRCCA would have a revenue of about 4 million Uruguayan pesos (US$139,000) to 19 million pesos (US$656,000) by 2019. Besides the governmental budget, IRCCA also charges licensing fees to the companies producing commercial cannabis for sale in pharmacies (Ramsey 2016). This 'variable fee' will not be used for profit, but to keep the cannabis price competitive vis-à-vis the illegal market.[9]

The estimated impacts of legalization

Uruguayan authorities estimate that, so far, the legalization of cannabis has taken about US$22 million out of the illegal market, even though nonofficial transactions still remain lucrative. In 2018, for instance, only one out of three consumers in Uruguay obtained cannabis through the legal options (Lissardy 2019). Other users have chosen not to register due to distrust in the government and the stigma around cannabis consumption.

This section evaluates the legalization of cannabis in Uruguay. As in previous chapters, we assess changes after drug policy reform in the country's consumption patterns as well as other drug-related harms in the realms of public health and security. We evaluate the evolution of different indicators monitoring their patterns before and after legalization in 2013. Since there is not a counterfactual case, we assess indicators over time across other countries with tighter drug policies, namely Brazil and Panama. The purpose is to observe, for example, if consumption patterns in Uruguay are mostly guided by drug policy change or are rather explained by exogenous factors. As noted in Chapter 4, choosing a control group in South America was challenging. Almost the entire region has liberalized at least at some level the use of certain psychoactive substances – especially cannabis – for recreational purposes. Exceptions in Latin America are Guyana and Suriname, where the substances have remained criminalized. Unfortunately, due to a lack of national surveys in these countries, year gaps, and methodological differences in the collection and processing of data, it was extremely difficult to establish a truly precise comparison.

In Panama, the recreational use of psychoactive substances is criminalized, although flexible penalties may be applied to problematic users (Penal Code, Article 320) (Organization of American States [OAS] 2019). Between 2007 and 2012, different reforms to the penal code broadened the typology of drug offenses and increased criminal penalties, equating some of them to homicides, femicides, and contract killing (Rodriguez Blanco and Cumbrera Diaz 2017). In Brazil, on the other hand, the law in the books indicates that the country decriminalized the use of illegal drugs for personal use in 2006 (Lei 11.343, Article 28).[10] Yet, the specific volume of drugs in possession that separates traffickers from users is not determined by law, making decriminalization an unrealized policy. As a result, OAS has noted that in Brazil's de facto policy, 'the unauthorised possession of substances for personal consumption is considered a criminal offense' (OAS 2019, 19).

Moreover, methodological differences must be considered, and results should be interpreted with caution. The Inter-American Abuse Control Commission (CICAD 2019), for example, points to variations in population samples and discrepancies in the indicators as limitations across the surveys conducted in Latin America. Data from *Encuestas Nacionales en Hogares sobre Consumo de Drogas*, CICAD, and the Organisation for Economic Co-operation and Development might have a few points of differences when comparing their measurements. Various datasets were used for different variables and are presented in this work as published by each institution for comparison purposes. There are, however, limitations on the data, particularly when assessing the control group.

Drug consumption trends

To assess consumption patterns, we based our analysis on data presented in the *Encuestas Nacionales Sobre Consumo de Drogas en Población General* (National Surveys on Drug Use in the General Population). These surveys are presented by the JND, created by Executive Power Decree 463/988 with the intent of making the institution responsible for promoting studies to monitor the consumption of drugs in Uruguay. For this reason, the JND created the *Observatorio Uruguayo de Drogas* (Uruguayan Drug Observatory [OUD]), which oversees the designing, data collection, and analysis of drug consumption trends in the country. The first National Prevalence Survey was presented in 1994 and has continued to be published every three to five years.[11] The studies reflect the epidemiological surveillance of the evolution, magnitude, and characteristics of legal and illegal drug consumption in the country, among the 15- to 65-year-old population in cities of 100,000 inhabitants or more.

It is estimated that in 2018, approximately 25,500 people in Uruguay used cannabis daily (JND 2022). Official surveys also indicate that around 48 per cent have consumed cannabis at some point in their lives and continued usage during the last 12 months, whereas the other 52 per cent can be considered former users (JDN 2019). Likewise, data on lifetime prevalence (LTP), last-year prevalence (LYP), and last-month prevalence (LMP) demonstrate a sustained increase in cannabis consumption in Uruguay since 2001, with different growth rates before and after legalization (Graph 6.1).[12]

As shown in Graph 6.1, all prevalence measurements have trended upward since Uruguay reformed its cannabis policy in 2013. LTP, for example, presents an increase of 13.6 percentage points after legalization, going from

Graph 6.1: Uruguay's LTP, LYP, and LMP of cannabis among the general population by year

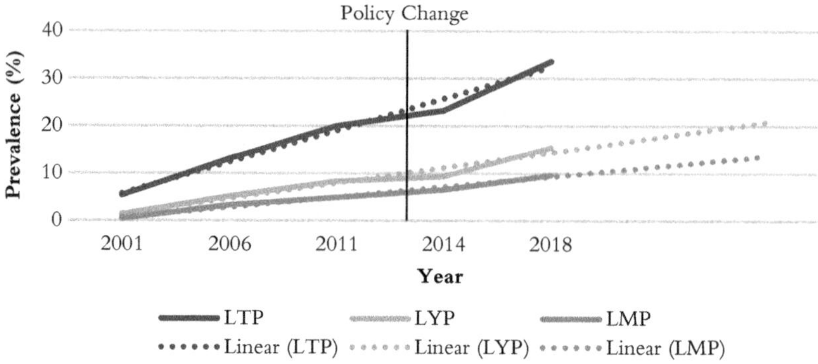

Source: Authors, based on JND (2022)

20 per cent in 2011 to 33.6 per cent in 2018. Similarly, the other two indicators also show increases in cannabis consumption during the same period. While LYP increased 7.1 percentage points, going from 8.3 per cent to 15.4 per cent, LMP grew 4.7 percentage points, increasing from 4.9 per cent in 2011 to 9.6 per cent in 2018.

In general, cannabis consumption among Uruguayans has been steadily increasing since the early 2000s. In line with prior empirical work (Queirolo et al 2018), the average LYP and LMP growth rates in Uruguay do not reflect a significant increase post-policy change, although there are signs suggesting that the pace of increase may be quickening after legalization. In other words, it is still difficult to assess if usage increases are due to the country's liberalization of cannabis, if they are following an already established historical trend, or if there are other underlying mechanisms driving consumption fluctuations.

As already noted, the patterns of drug consumption in younger age groups often serve as a guide for future behaviours and trends. The age groups that have experienced the highest growth rates since cannabis legalization in Uruguay are the 19–25 and 26–35 clusters. The increases among the 19–25 age group after legalization seem particularly alarming. Nonetheless, while the LTP and LYP prevalence among the 19–25 group displays greater increases after legalization, the LMP decelerated compared to the increases registered during the pre-policy reform years, going from 12 percent to 20.8 post reform (Encuestas Nacionales en Hogares sobre el Consumo de Drogas 2001, 2012, 2016, 2018).

The population aged 26–35, on the other hand, experienced the highest and fastest growth rates of all the groups after the adoption of legalization in all three indicators. This upward trend was also witnessed among the youngest cluster (15–18) in LTP, LYP, and LMP after legalization. Unlike the rest of the age groups, the 15–18 age group does not present increases in LMP between 2014 and 2018. In this particular case, our observations align with Laqueur et al's (2020) study on the impact of cannabis legalization in Uruguay on adolescent cannabis use. They demonstrate that the regulatory approach to cannabis supply helps minimize the impact of legalization on adolescent cannabis use.[13] In addition, similar to Rivera-Aguirre et al (2021), we observe that the legalization of recreational cannabis in Uruguay does not appear to be associated with multiyear changes in risky and frequent cannabis use among young people.

Parallel to the trends registered among the younger cluster, the age groups 36–45, 46–55, and 56–65 display lower growth consumption rates after legalization compared to the pre-reform years, oscillating between 3.2 and 0.2 percentage points. The lowest growth in usage on all indicators are present on the last age group (56–65). The three clusters have maintained a relatively stable consumption pattern since before legalization and have experienced increases on the three prevalence indicators at a much slower rate than the three younger groups. As scholarly works conducted in other countries have demonstrated, the older age groups are composed of more experienced people who use drugs that have an established lifestyle; therefore, their consumption habits are often not drastically affected by radical policy transformations like legalization (Reinarman, Cohen, and Kaal 2004).

The data on the evolution of the initiation age of cannabis consumption in Uruguay show that the initiation age experienced an upward trend after 2011 at 18 years and then shifted to 20–21 years in 2018 (Encuestas Nacionales en Hogares sobre el Consumo de Drogas 2001, 2012, 2016, 2018). In spite of easier accessibility, affordability, and legality of cannabis use, individuals are initiating consumption at an older age. Scholars have shown that different mechanisms can influence the initiation age. Anderson and colleagues (2019), for example, demonstrate in their study in the US that use among younger cohorts decreased following recreational cannabis legalization due to the difficulties of accessing the psychoactive substance, as drug dealers were replaced by licensed dispensaries that require proof of age. Regardless of the mechanisms, Uruguay's legalization seems to have contributed to shift the age distribution of uptake towards younger cohorts while increasing the age of those who start using cannabis. This trend, albeit not totally visible today, is likely to impact consumption patterns in the future.

Despite prevalence rates increasing among the general population, the daily use of cannabis among Uruguayans has been declining since legalization, showing a decrease of daily intake by 4.7 percentage points from 2011(14.6 per cent) to 2018 (9.9 per cent). Single intake of the drug, on the other hand, points towards an ascending trend. This tendency appears to have intensified after legalization, reporting at 13.7 per cent in 2018 compared to 8.7 per cent in 2011 (Encuesta Nacional en Hogares sobre Consumo de Drogas 2001, 2012, 2016, 2018). In other words, the evidence suggests that legalization is likely favouring the experimental and recreational use of cannabis while limiting the possibilities of problematic consumption.

Our analysis of Uruguay's frequency fluctuations is consistent with the study of Laqueur and colleagues (2020). In their study of Montevideo and regions in the interior of the country, they did not find a relationship between legalization and self-reported frequency of use. In effect, the evidence proposes that cannabis legalization might give users a greater ease of access and freedom to experiment without any penalties or legal consequences, but the reform is not necessarily associated with major frequency of use changes. The surveys in Uruguay indicate that daily consumption is the least common practice reported by users (JND 2019). Instead, people using cannabis several times during the last year appears to be the constant indicator with the highest rate of frequency, which was higher in 2006 (before the legalization policy took place). According to the JND (2019), almost half of the people surveyed reported initiation and discontinuation of use within the same year and consumed the substance only one or two times after the first experience.

Other drug use

Prohibitionists often rest on the idea that cannabis is a gateway to more addictive drugs (MacCoun and Reuter 2001; MacCoun 2011). Since the 1970s, several scholars have studied the gateway hypothesis, arguing that the early experimentation with soft drugs like alcohol, tobacco, or cannabis eventually lead to the use of more dangerous illicit substances (Kandel 1975; Kandel and Faust 1975; Lynskey, Heath, Bucholz 2003). Has cannabis legalization impacted other drug use patterns in Uruguay? In this section, the prevalence of other drugs such as cocaine, heroin, morphine, and ecstasy are explored.

As happened with cannabis, the consumption of other illegal drugs such as cocaine, hashish, hallucinogens, and ecstasy also have experienced steady increases since 2001 (Table 6.1). Even though all four drugs display increases post-policy reform, the increases seem to be following an already established trend. Broadly speaking, other psychoactive substances such as inhalants, ecstasy, heroin, morphine, and opium display lower magnitudes of consumption, fluctuating between 0.1 per cent and 0.2 per cent.

In this context, the removal of criminal penalties for cannabis consumption has not prompted the usage of other drugs to skyrocket, suggesting that the gateway hypothesis, in this case, cannot be validated, at least at the aggregate level. Since there is no evidence that people who use cannabis in Uruguay turned to the use of hard drugs, the differentiation of markets proposed by the country's drug policy reform seems to be in a way achieved.

Table 6.1: Uruguay's LYP of other drugs among the general population by year

Type of Drug/Year	2001	2007	2011	2014	2018
Cocaine	1.3	4	6.2	6.8	7.8
Hashish	:	1.5	3	2.8	4.1
Hallucinogen	0.6	1.2	2.3	3.1	3.9
Inhalant	0.1	0.6	1.5	0.9	1.4
Ecstasy	0.1	0.7	0.2	:	0.9
Heroin	0.1	0.2	0.2	0.1	0.1
Morphine	:	0.1	0.2	0.1	:
Opium	:	0.2	0.1	0.1	:
Other	:	0.4	0.2	0.3	0.3

Source: Authors, based on Encuestas Nacionales en Hogares sobre Consumo de Droga (2001, 2012, 2016, 2018)

Uruguay's cannabis and other drug use patterns compared to Brazil and Panama

According to the *Informe Sobre Consumo de Drogas en las Americas* 2019 (Drug Use in the Americas) report, published by CICAD, cannabis consumption trends have been rapidly evolving in the Americas. Recent data establish that cannabis use has increased in at least six of the seven countries that conducted drug use surveys in the region. Along with the increase of prevalence, it is also observed as a general trend that initiation of drug use starts at an earlier age. Consumption among the underage population between 12 and 17 years is increasing and has become the age group with the second highest prevalence rates reported (CICAD 2019).

Compared to other countries in the South American region, Uruguay holds one of the highest LYP rates of cannabis consumption during the last year reported with 9.4 per cent in 2014, just below Chile with 14.5 per cent in 2016, and above Argentina with 8 per cent in 2017 (Table 6.2).[14] The prevalence among the rest of the South American countries is far below the average of Chile, Argentina, and Uruguay, oscillating between 4.2 per cent and 0.5 per cent (CICAD 2019).

Looking more closely at the control group, we analyze the LYP of cannabis consumption among the general population in Brazil, Panama, and Uruguay (Graph 6.2). While the United Nations Office on Drugs and Crime (UNODC) offers limited information, the data available signal a decrease in LYP prevalence in Panama, although trends cannot be easily established due to the high number of missing values. Surveys in Brazil also provide limited information, but data suggest instead a slight increase in the country's

Table 6.2: LYP of cannabis consumption among the general population in South America

Country	Year	LYP
Argentina	2017	8
Brazil	**2016**	**2.8**
Bolivia	2014	1.2
Chile	**2016**	**14.5**
Colombia	2013	3.1
Ecuador	2014	0.8
Guyana	2016	4.2
Paraguay	2003	0.5
Peru	2010	1
Suriname	2014	3.3
Uruguay	**2014**	**9.5**
Venezuela	2011	1.8

Source: Authors, based on CICAD (2019)[15]

Graph 6.2: LYP of cannabis consumption in Brazil, Panama, and Uruguay

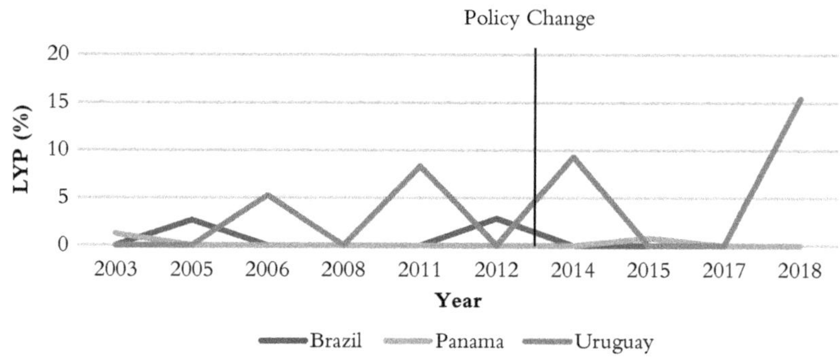

Source: Authors, based on UNODC (2010, 2022)

cannabis prevalence. Still, Brazil's consumption levels are below the average in Latin America, a pattern that scholars find difficult to explain (Jungerman et al 2010; Madruga et al 2022). Compared to Uruguay, however, both Latin American countries exhibit lower and more stable consumption rates even though these differences cannot be directly attributed to the adoption of legalization in 2013.

Cocaine is the controlled substance with the fourth highest rates of consumption worldwide, and its use is mainly concentrated in the Americas, Europe, and Oceania (CICAD 2019). Looking at the LYP of cocaine in the

Graph 6.3: LYP of cocaine consumption in Brazil, Panama, and Uruguay

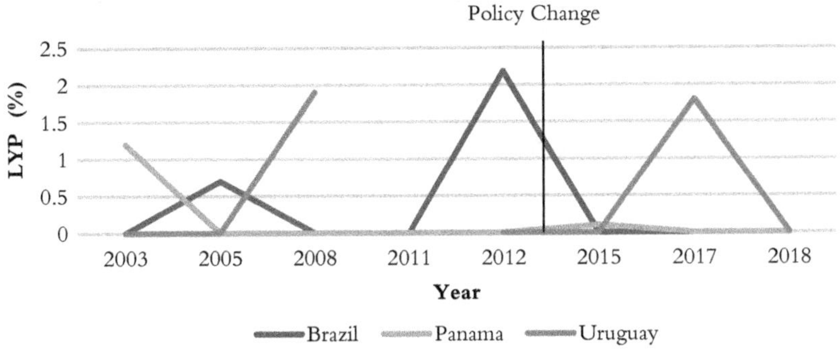

Source: Authors, based on UNODC (2010, 2022)

control group, based on UNODC's database, we observe that Brazil presents growing consumption rates, increasing 1.48 percentage points from 2005 to 2012. Panama, by contrast, experienced a decrease of 1.1 percentage points during the same period. Similar to cannabis, we cannot attribute these fluctuations to policy changes as there are not enough values to make an accurate assessment (Graph 6.3).

The recreational use of ecstasy was popularized during the 1980s, mainly in Europe at electronic music events known as raves. Its consumption later expanded to the US and the rest of North and South American continents. South America, nonetheless, has not experienced significant consumption rates of ecstasy. In effect, consumption rates in Brazil and Panama have remained relatively stable. Compared to the control group, Uruguay presents a noticeable LYP growth of 0.5 percentage points post-policy reform, above the averages of Brazil and Panama, where the ecstasy market did not grow or declined, respectively (UNODC 2010, 2022).

Notwithstanding, the fluctuations cannot be attributed to drug policy reform, especially because the number of missing values is substantial, the consumption of other drugs in the control group and Uruguay seems to have followed slightly different trends after legalization. On the one hand, cannabis and ecstasy prevalence reflects a clearer increase in Uruguay compared to Brazil, whereas in Panama prevalence rates decreased. Cocaine, on the other hand, presents increases in both Uruguay and Brazil, the latter being South America's largest cocaine market (UNODC 2021).

Market trends

The drug market evolves constantly. It is not unusual for trafficking routes to shift, to reopen, or for new ones to emerge. By looking at seizures, prices, and potency, we can observe alternative drug policies impacts, which in turn can influence consumption patterns or other market trends. These mechanisms, especially prices and seizures, are also of paramount importance to understanding the internal dynamics of illegal drug markets (Caulkins and Reuter 1998; Caulkins 2007). The following paragraphs are dedicated to the analysis of changes in drug prices, potency, and seizures before and after policy change in Uruguay.

Price

When the consumption of psychoactive substances is illegal, criminal organizations or drug dealers add a 'security tax' to their products. The tax includes the added value of assuming the risk of injury or incarceration in order to distribute and deliver the product in an illegal context. If the product is legalized, economic theory further suggests, the added tax loses value; therefore, there is more competition, supply increases, and large-scale investment is needed to reduce production costs (Boivin 2014). In other words, more flexible and less harsh drug control policies can lead to a drop in the monetary value of psychoactive substances.

When discussing the future implementation of cannabis liberalization, one of the main goals of Uruguayan policymakers was to lower its retail price to US$1.00 per gram, with the purpose of making it competitive with the black market. Table 6.3 shows that the goal price has not been reached, probably for rentability reasons. The year cannabis was legalized reflects one of the highest prices reported between 2009 and 2019, with a price

Table 6.3: Cannabis price in Uruguay by year (grams/US$) (retail price not adjusted for purity)

Year	Uruguay
2009	4.0
2010	2.9
2011	3.1
2012	2.9
2013	7.3
2014	6.5
2015	5.8
2016	4.0
2017	4.0
2018	4.0
2019	6.2

Source: Authors, based on UNODC (2022)

of US$7.3 per gram. Then the price declined during subsequent years. It is important to notice that although legalization was approved in 2013, the selling of cannabis in pharmacies started almost four years later. Since 2017, the government has been in charge of setting the price of the psychoactive substance. From 2016 until 2018 the reported price was a stable US$4.00 per gram. In 2019, however, the price increased to US$6.2. It is also critical to note that Uruguay has adjusted the potency of the cannabis offered in pharmacies and also has broadened the variety of products available. This may explain changes in cannabis prices.

The trends of cannabis wholesale prices in Uruguay vis-à-vis the control group are slightly different. Panama presents the highest prices compared to the other countries, particularly between 2015 and 2017 when the psychoactive substance was sold at US$2,500 (UNODC 2010, 2019, 2022).[16] Even though cannabis wholesale prices trended downward in the post-reform years, this trajectory was reversed in Uruguay. In 2019, the South American country registered a noticeable increase, more than doubling the wholesale price by kilogram from US$1,250 to US$3,453, respectively (UNODC 2010, 2019, 2022).

The availability of data on the cocaine prices in the control group is highly limited for Brazil and Panama. This presents challenges to conduct a meaningful comparison. Yet the evidence indicates that Uruguay's cocaine wholesale prices per gram have been noticeably higher compared to the control group. Nonetheless, the three Latin American countries showed increases. Uruguay is the country that reports the highest prices since 2010, reaching a value of US$15,500 per kilogram after legalization, compared to prices in Panama of US$4,500 and US$8,00 in Brazil during those years. However, Uruguay presents a decrease in 2019 to US$12,750 (UNODC 2010, 2019, 2022).

Broadly speaking, the evidence indicates that legalization impacted the price of illicit drugs in Uruguay. It was part of the new drug policy framework plan to intentionally lower the price of cannabis to compete with the informal market. In this context, cannabis retail and wholesale prices decreased after legalization, although the trend was partially reversed in 2019. Official reports show that the prices of other psychoactive substances that remain illegal such as cocaine and ecstasy experienced different fluctuations. While cocaine prices increased, the value of ecstasy decreased. In 2009, for example, a tablet of ecstasy in Uruguay was sold at US$110.00, whereas in 2016 and 2017 it was worth US$65.00.

Potency

The potency of illicit substances is another relevant indicator of the market's performance. Unlike other countries where the use of cannabis is still illegal and criminalized or across some commercial legalization frameworks like those adopted in the US since 2012, in Uruguay, the potency of the psychoactive substance is set by the government. After its legalization, IRCCA adjusted the potency of cannabis provided and sold it in dispensaries to meet consumers' demands. Initially, the cannabis offered in pharmacies had a potency of 2.5 per cent THC and 6–7 per cent CBD, which led to some complaints among users.[17] In December 2017, IRCCA provided two new types of cannabis, Alfa II and Beta II, which are hybrids with *indica* and *sativa* and levels of 9 per cent THC and 3 per cent CBD. Yet it has been stipulated by the national government that cannabis will not be sold at levels of THC higher than 20 per cent. This demonstrates that IRCCA is attempting to prevent drug-related health effects by setting the potency as the Dutch government did in 2012 (Rolles and Slade 2022).

The potency of the cannabis consumed in Uruguay through legal means is even three times higher compared to other countries in South America (Nación cannabis 2019). Yet the impacts of state regulations on the potency trends in the black market are still to be seen. For instance, if the cannabis demand in Uruguay reflects regional trends, other types of more potent psychoactive substances such as 'creepy' marijuana can permeate the black market, affecting in general the potency of cannabis used by the population (Shuldiner 2022).

Seizures

This section looks at changes in drug seizures to observe law enforcement activities in Uruguay before and after cannabis legalization in 2013. Cannabis police seizures in Uruguay have fluctuated throughout the last almost two decades. Interestingly, an upward trend is evident since 2010, peaking at 4,373 kg in 2016, and then decreasing to 2,055 kg in 2019, maintaining higher numbers after legalization (UNODC 2019). According to interviews conducted with experts in the Monitoring and Evaluating report conducted by the JND and the OUD in 2019, the increase of cannabis seizures in Uruguay corresponds to the lessening of the counterdrug efforts in Paraguay supported by the Brazilian government, which discontinued aid to target cannabis plantations due to the political turmoil the country has witnessed during the last years (UNODC 2019).

Cocaine seizures, on the other hand, have steadily increased since 2000. We observe a decrease right after cannabis legalization; however, there is an extreme increase of cocaine seizures in 2018. This may suggest that law enforcement activities are focused on drugs that remain illegal. It may be also possible that the drug traffickers are aiming at replacing or establishing a stronger market for drugs besides cannabis. Furthermore, the increasing number of confiscations, including the unprecedented 3 tons of cocaine found in a container in the Port of Montevideo in November 2019, shows that Uruguay is becoming a critical transshipment location for cocaine destined for Europe and, to a lesser extent, Africa (UNODC 2021). Research reveals that criminal organizations are prioritizing nontraditional ports such as Montevideo due to the porosity of borders, lack of controls, and the possibility of exploiting the lack of reputation for trafficking cocaine (Sampó and Troncoso 2022). In addition, cocaine is easier for the traffickers to hide, and therefore greater focus and more personnel for counterdrug efforts are necessary for its confiscation. Though there are limited data on ecstasy seizures, the records show an increase of 16 kg pre-legalization compared to 60 kg post-drug policy reform (UNODC 2019).

Looking at seizures in the control group, Brazil stands out for the number of kilograms of cannabis seized per year (Graph 6.4).[18] The increases are more significant since 2015, displaying the highest levels in 2018 with 350,314 kg. Unfortunately, an analysis of the relationship between greater availability and consumption trends in Brazil is not possible given the lack of nationwide epidemiological surveys since 2012. Compared to Brazil, Uruguay and Panama present much smaller amounts of cannabis seized per year, though seizures for this substance have increased in both countries. In the case of Panama, the confiscation of cannabis more than doubled from 2016 to 2017, rising from 5,746 kg to 12,952 kg and reaching almost 18,000 kg in 2018. In Uruguay, cannabis seizures have fluctuated since 2005; however, the amounts secured are higher post-legalization.

Cocaine seizures in Uruguay are low compared to Brazil and Panama, even with a historical increase in 2019 (UNODC 2021). As with cannabis, Brazil's cocaine seizures have increased substantially, especially in 2018 and 2019. Together with greater availability due to new trafficking routes through the country, this could be a result of the *mano dura* approach followed by the Bolsonaro regime. Contrary to cannabis seizures, cocaine confiscations in Panama are the highest among the cases, reaching its highest

Graph 6.4: Cannabis seizures in Brazil, Panama, and Uruguay by year (kg)

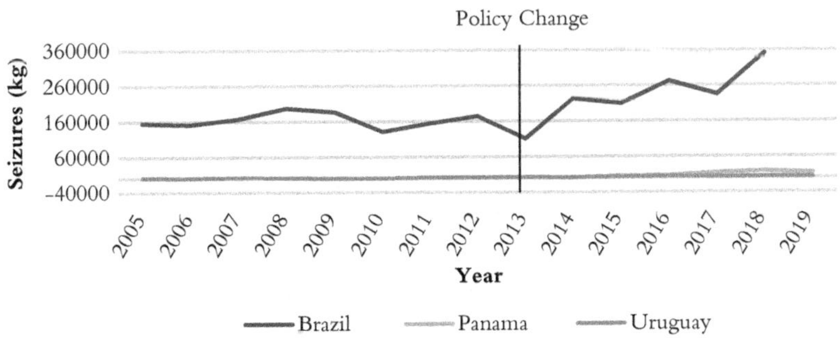

Source: Authors, based on UNODC (2021)

levels between 2007 and 2010 oscillating between 102,000 and 98,000 kg seized per year. Later, seizures declined. They have been again increasing since 2015, although they have not reached the levels of the previous years (UNODC 2021).

The number of cocaine seizures in Uruguay is considered out of proportion given the country's size. As already noted, the waterway between Panama and Paraguay has become the favourite route of drug traffickers to get illicit drugs from South America to Europe and Africa. Recent reports indicate that 72 per cent of the secured cocaine in the country was intercepted at that point. Uruguayan ports such as Nueva Palmira and Montevideo have become central routes (El Observador 2022). Incumbent President Luis Lacalle Pou, since the beginning of his administration in March 2020, has stressed that one of the main objectives of his government is a frontal attack on drug trafficking and the targeting of dealers selling drugs in neighbourhoods. The more aggressive approach towards drug trafficking after the adoption of legalization has resulted in historical amounts of seizures of various drugs including cocaine, paste base cocaine, and cannabis, totalling 11,911 kg in 2019, and the dismantling of 2,100 selling points in the last two years (Lopez Ortega 2022).

In short, the increases in cannabis and cocaine seizures in Uruguay seem to be influenced by a combination of domestic (that is, drug law, drug trafficking organizations, domestic drug market) and external (that is, geopolitics, growth in drug consumption in various regions in the world, adaptation of the drug trafficking organizations and the international market) factors, which have been altered more clearly after policy change.

Adverse health consequences

Uruguay has taken a 'meaningful harm reduction policy' (Narvaez-Chicaiza 2020, 383), and the country's drug control approach has been developed under this premise, especially during the 2000s. Uruguay, for example, established needle exchange programs for people who use injectable drugs. Moreover, federal funds have been allocated for treatment for drug abuse, establishing medical detoxification and other treatments for users with HIV/AIDS. More importantly, the main goal of legalization was to protect public health and to separate people who use cannabis from hard or more dangerous psychoactive substances.

As noted throughout this book, drug abuse can cause short- and long-term health-related consequences. Relevant factors such as the dependency of use, the method of consumption, and the treatment options can impact the population's physical and psychological well-being. The analysis of these factors hinges on the assessment of aspects that can increase the probability of developing higher rates of dependency and substance abuse. In the next paragraphs of this section, we examine the demand for treatment, drug-related deaths, and the viral infections common to people who use drugs.

Demand for treatment

One of the main objectives of cannabis legalization is to prevent problematic drug consumption and be able to take people who use illicit drugs out of the shadows of illegality, to better identify and expand treatment needs. In this section we ask: To what extent are people who use cannabis in Uruguay reaching out for treatment when developing a substance abuse problem?

According to the Seventh National Survey, in 2018, approximately 6 per cent of the population in Uruguay (about 100,000 people participating in the study) had sought help at one point in their lives to stop drug use. A higher percentage of people had sought treatment for tobacco intake (73 per cent), followed by alcohol (17 per cent), cocaine (13 per cent), and then cannabis (10.1 per cent). Data show that Uruguayan women seek help more frequently when it comes to substance abuse problems compared to men, for both legal and illegal drugs (JDN 2022).[19] Comparing the figures between 2014 and 2018, the two surveys available, the demand for cannabis treatment presents an increase of 0.1 percentage points among men and a decrease of 2.8 percentage points in women. Likewise, the percentage of males seeking cocaine treatment decreased by 6.4 percentage points, whereas women declined by 24.3 (JDN 2022).

The figures indicate that the number of people seeking treatment fell following legalization, suggesting that Uruguay's drug policy reform has not provoked a surge in problematic use. Both the frequency and the demand for treatment have decreased despite the recreational consumption of cannabis being neither prohibited nor criminalized. Furthermore, the legalization of cannabis is not associated with increases in the demand for treatment among users of hard drugs such as cocaine. This could be another critical indicator implying that cannabis drug policy reform did not aggravate the consumption habits of psychoactive substances that carry higher risks of chronic or acute health harms.

Infectious diseases

Drug consumption and drug abuse have been closely linked to viruses/infectious diseases such as HIV/AIDS and hepatitis. Consumers of certain types of drugs are at higher risk of infection by sharing syringes or when by having unprotected sexual encounters with infected partners (National Institute on Drug Abuse 2020). The evidence shows that the HIV/AIDS world epidemic has maintained an ascending curve since the 1980s (Berriolo et al 1997). While sexual transmission has been the dominant route of contagion during this period, the abuse of injectable drugs became a serious public health problem in many counties. In Latin America, for example, the virus spread slowly after the first infections were detected in 1983 (Crabtree-Ramirez et al 2020). Not surprisingly, people who inject illicit drugs in Latin America are one of the groups with the highest HIV prevalence, with 7.4 per cent in 2020.

The legalization of cannabis, nonetheless, is not likely to have an impact on infectious diseases since its route of consumption does not involve direct infectious contact, unless its liberalization shifts use patterns towards other drugs or cannabis serves as a gateway psychoactive substance. According to the Uruguayan Minister of Health's HIV/AIDS report of 2016, the HIV epidemic in Uruguay maintains a 'concentrated' pattern. In other words, the country sustains an epidemiological pattern with prevalence in the general population of less than 1 per cent, but in specific populations greater than 5 per cent (Ministerio de Salud Pública 2021).

Graph 6.5 shows the rates of people newly diagnosed with HIV in Uruguay since 2000. We can observe a significant increase in new cases since 2000. After the peak in 2011, the rates of new cases seem to be decreasing with an average of 902 new detections between 2016 and 2020. The median age of contagion is 38 years and sexual transmission remains the main cause of HIV. It is considered that the HIV and hepatitis B or C prevalence for drug use in Uruguay is low, but more in-depth studies are needed to establish the real figures.

The new HIV/AIDS cases reported in Uruguay for the year 2020 are below pre-legalization estimates. Indicators of infections in Uruguay follow a different pattern after reform relative to the rest of the cases with more stringent drug policies such as Brazil and Panama (Joint United Nations

Graph 6.5: Uruguay's new HIV/AIDS diagnosed cases per 100,000 inhabitants by year

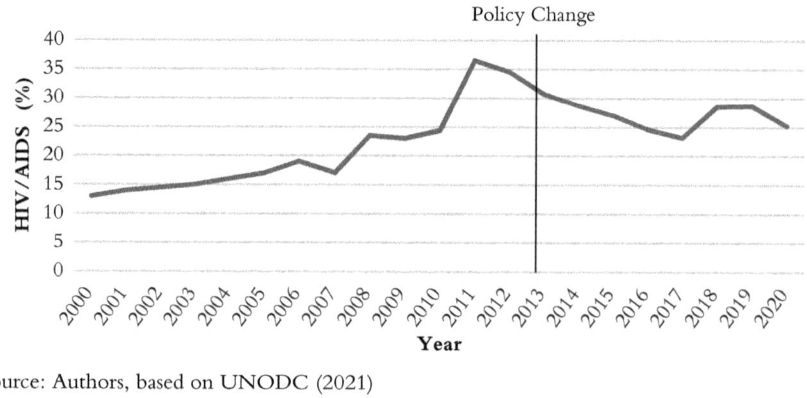

Source: Authors, based on UNODC (2021)

Programme on HIV/AIDS [UNAIDS] 2020). It is important to note that in all cases the most common mode of transmission is through sexual contact, not injecting drugs. While the nature of drug consumption in the country is mostly concentrated in cannabis and, to a lesser extent, cocaine, a refocus on drug policy towards consumers of injectable substances that represent higher risks of infection should be considered to target drug-related transmission cases.

In Latin America, new HIV infections present an upward trend. In the last decade, cases in the region increased 7 per cent just between 2010 and 2018, reaching 2.2 million in 2021 (UNAIDS 2022). The data show that there are around new 100,000 yearly infections on the American continent with Brazil leading the ranking. In the case of Panama, the number of infections through drug injection are rising, although with much lower rates compared to Brazil. In other words, the ascendance of HIV cases is a general trend throughout various regions in the world, suggesting that Uruguay's fluctuations are not likely connected to the legalization of cannabis.

Drug-related deaths

Uruguay's drug policy reform is not likely associated with fluctuations in the number of drug-related deaths. Since the legalization scheme is restricted to cannabis and not extended to other illicit drugs such as cocaine, heroin, or methamphetamines, the reform is not expected to impact the country's overdoses. In effect, cannabis presents no risk of overdose or infection through the sharing of injecting equipment (Darke, Degenhardt, and Mattick 2006). By contrast, various scholars have shown that mortality is primarily associated with the long-term consequences of the route of administration on the respiratory system or motor vehicle accidents after using the psychoactive substance (Kalant et al 1999; Kelly et al 2004).

Moreover, it is difficult to place Uruguay in the Latin American context and make a comparative analysis with the control group since there are not enough data available and the measurement mechanisms may vary among countries. Yet a study conducted by the UNODC in 2016 reported the number and rates of drug-related deaths per million in persons aged 15–64. According to the study, Panama registered a rate of 0.41 in 2012, whereas Brazil reported 481 casualties or a rate of 3.36 in 2015. That same year Uruguay registered 264 drug-related deaths or a rate of 119, which were the highest figures compared to the control group. However, in 2019 Uruguay reported only 38 cases (Schwab 2019). This presents an important decline in people losing their lives to drugs. In this context, the toxicology specialist Antonio Pasacale stated that synthetic drugs, not cannabis, are among the most common cases of overdoses and hospitalizations in Uruguay (En Perspectiva 2016).

Violence and crime: New trends

In modern Latin American history, Uruguay has been often referred as 'the Switzerland of Latin America' (Walsh and Ramsey 2016). Contrary to some of its neighbours, Uruguay was able for many years to contain the violence experienced in other states in the region, such as Brazil, Venezuela, or Colombia, which was mainly caused by the presence and operation of criminal organizations, guerrilla groups, and political turmoil. More recently, however, Uruguay has witnessed levels of violence that are highly unusual. This violence has been reflected in the increased number of homicides, which has exacerbated national security concerns.

As previously stated, one of the fundamental reasons the Uruguayan government decided to legalize cannabis in 2013 was to tackle the already evident upsurge of violence in the country. The logic behind legalization in matters of security appears to follow the systemic connection proposed by Goldstein (1985). This model suggests that interactions and the nature of the illicit drug market generate violent situations such as turf wars, competition, retaliation, transactions gone wrong, or the exposure of consumers to hidden and unsafe points of sale. Not surprisingly, one of the main purposes for legalizing cannabis in Uruguay was to make the product available for consumers in safe places, cutting their interactions with dealers, taking the market away from criminal organizations, and preventing violent confrontations and turf wars since there would be no business to be fighting over.

In terms of violence, measured here in homicide rates, the landscape in Uruguay deteriorated after 2013. Before cannabis legalization, the rate of homicides oscillated between 5.7 and 7.9, accounting for one of the lowest rates in Latin America. Nevertheless, after the country's drug policy reform in 2013, homicide rates in Uruguay increased, fluctuating between 12.06 and 11.32 in 2018 and 2019, respectively.

Is the legalization of cannabis responsible for the upsurge of violence in Uruguay? Answers to this question are hotly debated. Uruguayan Homeland Security authorities do not necessarily attribute the trend to drug-related confrontations, but to the emergence of new types of violence. According to the country's main security agency, crimes such as paid assassinations, domestic violence, and public fights in schools and on the streets are increasingly becoming regular or normalized behaviour. Studies even argue that there seems to be a gradual naturalization of violence within the Uruguayan culture (Garat 2016).

Yet another branch of the national government, the Uruguayan Ministry of the Interior, affirmed that most of the violent clashes relate to disputes among criminal organizations, stating: 'We are convinced that the increment of violence in Uruguay is not a product of the strengthening of criminal organisations, but it is caused by confrontations among them'[20] (as cited in Asmann 2018). According to Asmann, for instance, 40 per cent of the homicides committed during the first six months of 2018 point to disputes between criminal groups. As already noted, this trend seems to be associated with major changes in the region's cocaine trafficking routes. Specifically, the Hidrovía del Paraná waterway has transformed Uruguay into a central transshipment point for cocaine destined for Europe and Africa.[21] It is, therefore, too soon to identify the main causes of the increase in violence or to establish a correlation between the upsurge in homicides and cannabis legalization.

Yet Uruguay is not exempt from the challenges that violence presents to the region. Between 2000 and 2010, more than one million people died in Latin America and the Caribbean as a result of criminal violence, turning it into the most violent region in the world (UNODC 2019). In 2017 alone, 173,000 intentional homicides (a rate of 17.2) were recorded, well above the world average estimated at 6.1 per 100,000 inhabitants. Nonetheless, the situation in the control group, as shown in Graph 6.6, has been slightly different.

As shown in Graph 6.6, homicide rates in Brazil appear to have been declining since 2018, although remaining higher than the ones experienced in Uruguay and Panama. The Central American country, by contrast, registered a decrease after 2012 with a rate of 16.9 homicides compared to 10.5 in 2019. That is to say, Uruguay is not the only country in Latin America witnessing increases in homicides rates, but just another illustration of an already violent region that could not prevent the proliferation of crime across national borders.

Graph 6.6: Homicides per 100,000 inhabitants in Brazil, Panama, and Uruguay per year

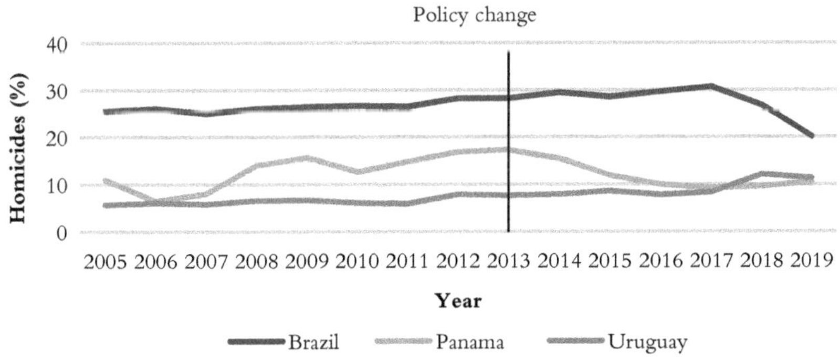

Source: Authors, based on Informe de la situacion Nacional del VIH (2016) and Informe Situacion epidemologica del VIH/SIDA en 2021 (2021)

Robbery and theft

As explored in the previous section, Uruguay has been experiencing an increase in crime not only in terms of homicides, but also in other types of crimes such as robbery and theft (Paternain 2014). Security experts and policymakers have observed that the nature of violence in Uruguay is changing, and this phenomenon seems to be impacting crime rates.

Robbery rates almost doubled in Uruguay during the post-reform years, reflecting a rate of 456 per 100,000 in 2012 and 885 per 100,000 in 2019 (Table 6.4). Nonetheless, the control group experienced slightly different trends. Similar to Uruguay, Brazil's robbery rates increased after 2012, whereas Panama experienced a decline during those years. That is, the Central American country also presents the lowest robbery rates among the three cases analyzed here.

Uruguay's theft rates have followed a similar pattern. Between 2012 and 2019, they increased 1.4 times, rising from 2,866 to 4,043 (Table 6.5). Compared to the control group, Uruguay presents rates four times higher rates than even Brazil, the only country that experienced increases after 2012. Contrarily, theft rates in Panama declined steadily during the period in which Uruguay's cannabis legalization policy was fully operational.

Table 6.4: Robberies per 100,000 inhabitants in Brazil, Panama, and Uruguay per year

Year	Uruguay	Brazil	Panama
2005	292	:	152
2006	267	475	158
2007	292	488	172
2008	321	487	184
2009	340	470	224
2010	412	552	228
2011	445	550	261
2012	456	492	266
2013	**493**	**504**	**228**
2014	546	633	251
2015	621	758	206
2016	595	771	192
2017	566	807	243
2018	867	696	:
2019	885	561	:

Source: Authors, based on UNODC (2019)

Table 6.5: Thefts per 100,000 inhabitants in Brazil, Panama, and Uruguay per year

Year	Uruguay	Brazil	Panama
2005	:	:	419
2006	3067	1094	529
2007	3170	1063	405
2008	3162	972	472
2009	2821	924	508
2010	2836	707	501
2011	2896	628	497
2012	2866	715	539
2013	2876	888	537
2014	2990	:	545
2015	3204	:	476
2016	3358	:	396
2017	3366	1109	452
2018	4231	1052	396
2019	4043	:	320

Source: Authors, based on UNODC (2019)

Robbery and theft rates show slightly different patterns in Uruguay and in the control group. In the case of Uruguay, both rates increased 1.5 to 2 times more after the legalization of cannabis in 2013. While Panama has witnessed opposite trends, with a decline in both measurements, robbery, and theft rates increased in Brazil between 2012 and 2019. The landscape in the biggest South American country suggests that Uruguay's security challenges are not necessarily a product of cannabis legalization. By contrast, various crime indicators have deteriorated across Latin America during the last 20 years, even when the region experienced an unprecedented economic growth.

Drug law violations

With the drug law reform in Uruguay, a successful scenario in terms of drug law violations would entail a reduction in the number of individuals processed for cannabis possession with amounts below that established by Articles 30 and 31 of Law 14.294 and Law 19.172 (40 g). What follows in an analysis of the application of drug laws before and after cannabis legalization.

There are two main drug laws that have impacted the actions or decisions of judges and prosecutors: Law 19.007, which increases the sentences for

Table 6.6: Total crimes and drug law violations in Uruguay per year[22]

Year	Total	Drug law violations[23]	% of drug law violations
2010	12,616	1,348	10.7
2011	13,249	1,436	10.8
2012	13,562	1,598	11.8
2013	13,189	1,262	9.6
2014	13,828	1,227	8.9
2015	14,292	1,365	9.6
2016	15,111	1,313	8.7
2017	12,976	1,034	8.0

Source: Authors, based on JDN (2019)

trafficking of coca base paste, and Law 19.172 for cannabis legalization (JND 2019). Both establish different criteria to apply towards drug law violation cases. On the one hand, the Law 19.007 framework follows a punitive approach towards violators, including higher sentences to dissuade the trafficking of that substance. On the other, Law 19.172 establishes a key change; that is, the introduction of a more specific criteria to deal with cases of possession of cannabis, with a limit of 40 grams for recreational use. However, when the possession of the substance is above the set quantity, an investigation to define the real purpose of the psychoactive substance in possession must be conducted (JND 2019). Table 6.6 shows that the number of crimes present uneven behaviour after legalization. There are important noticeable increases from 2012 to 2016 and then there is a decrease in 2017. The number of drug law violations has declined post-policy change from 1,598 (11.8 per cent) in 2012 to 1,034 (8 per cent).

Table 6.7 displays the typification of drug law violations. In a context where the possession of cannabis for recreational purposes was legalized, the table shows that possession for no consumption is Uruguay's most common drug law violation, presenting an increase from 2012 with 37 per cent to 39 per cent in 2017. In second position is selling, also increasing 2 percentage points in the same scope. Transport is the third most common drug law violation, experiencing a considerable decrease of 8 percentage points after legalization. Imports and exports remained unchanged from 2012 to 2017, transit and storage decreased, and distribution and supply increased by 2 and 3 percentage points, respectively.

Overall, the rates of homicide, robbery, and theft have climbed in Uruguay following legalization. Robbery and theft follow similar patterns in Brazil, which may point to a regional trend rather than a consequence of the reform. Uruguay's total crime in general presents fluctuating patterns. However,

Table 6.7: Uruguay's typification of drug law violations by year

	2011	2012	2013	2014	2015	2016	2017
Import	6	3	3	3	4	3	3
Export	0	0	0	2	0	0	0
Transit	1	2	0	1	3	1	1
Distribution	2	1	2	2	4	2	3
Possession – no consumption	**47**	**37**	**42**	**38**	**32**	**32**	**39**
Storage	3	3	2	2	3	4	2
Sale	**27**	**40**	**37**	**40**	**38**	**43**	**42**
Transport	**14**	**14**	**12**	**9**	**13**	**12**	**6**
Supply	0	0	2	3	2	2	3
Total	**100**	**100**	**100**	**100**	**100**	**100**	**100**

Source: Authors, based on JDN (2019)

as already noted, studies have shown that Uruguay is certainly redirecting policing resources towards combating robbery and theft (Patermain 2014). Whether legalization, law enforcement practices, the restructuring of the drug market, or other contextual forces such as changes in the trafficking routes of cocaine provoked the upsurge of crime in Uruguay, the evidence is not consistent with other empirical studies finding the opposite impacts of various forms of liberalization on crime rates (Heuberger 2017; UNODC 2019).

Prisons

Among countries of the South American region, Uruguay holds one of the highest prison population rates. In many prohibitionist countries such as the US and Brazil, a high percentage of the prison population corresponds to drug law violation charges (Boiteux 2017; Carson 2018). In Uruguay, by contrast, between 2010 and 2012, the most common reasons for imprisonment were theft, trafficking, and drug possession (Garat 2017).

In 2017, Uruguay reached a historical peak in prison population with a rate of 325 inmates per 100,000 inhabitants (11,103 prisoners in total) (Graph 6.7). During the years leading to cannabis legalization, the rates averaged 266 inmates. Yet, the prison population has been steadily growing following drug policy reform, increasing from 275 in 2014 to 321 in 2019. In other words, prison rates after cannabis legalization remain higher than in the pre-reform years.

Graph 6.7: Uruguay's prison population per 100,000 inhabitants per year

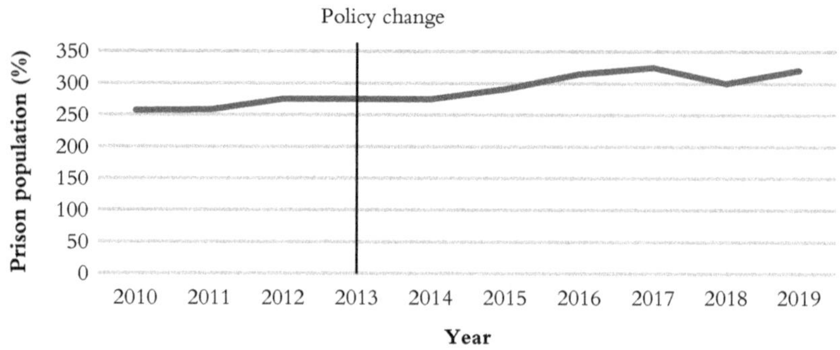

Source: Authors, based on UNODC (2019)

As the processes ending with a sentence for other crimes in general have increased since legalization, the ones processed for drug law violations decreased from 11 per cent in 2013 to 8 per cent in 2017 (JDN 2019). Scholars studying the implementation of the first liberalization policies adopted in several states of the US during the 1970s have highlighted the relevance of law enforcement practices and the public's knowledge of the legislation. Pacula, Chirqui, and King (2003), for example, show how both the citizens' limited knowledge of cannabis statutory changes and the judges' discretion when determining sanctions affected the impacts of drug policy reform.

Meanwhile, the number of individuals processed for any crime slightly declined from 2012 to 2017, but there are many fluctuations during the years (Table 6.8). Most importantly, the processes focused on drug law violations have also decreased, reporting 1,479 in 2012 and 1,010 in 2017, accounting for a decline of 3.7 percentage points.

Where does Uruguay stand in terms of the region's prison population? The imprisonment rates in Latin America are higher than the world's average. In some South American countries, the percentages of prisoners sentenced for drug law violations have grown exponentially compared to the general prison population. As already noted, around one in five inmates in Latin America is incarcerated for drug-related crimes, although this percentage is larger if individuals held in pretrial detention (around half of the region's inmate population) are considered (Bergman and Fondevila 2021). For example, in Brazil the general prison population grew 55 per cent from 2000 to 2014 (Graph 6.8).

Uruguay and Brazil show similar prison population rates, presenting some notable increases circa 2013 and then maintaining those rates until 2019. Panama exhibits slightly higher rates in comparison with the other two Latin American cases. The Central American country reached a peak in 2015 and maintained similar rates until 2019 with an average of 412 prisoners per

Table 6.8: Individuals processed for any crime and for drug law violations in Uruguay by year

Year	Total	Drug law violation	% of drug law violation
2010	10,155	1,289	12.7
2011	10,606	1,300	12.3
2012	10,797	1,479	13.7
2013	10,527	1,187	11.3
2014	10,843	1,158	10.7
2015	11,282	1,296	11.5
2016	11,538	1,251	10.8
2017	10,076	1,010	10

Source: Authors, based on JDN (2019)

Graph 6.8: Prison population per 100,000 inhabitants in Brazil, Panama, and Uruguay by year

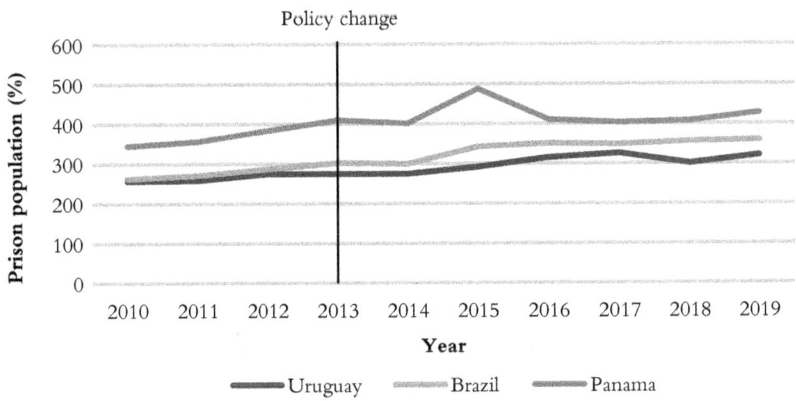

Source: Authors, based on UNODC (2019)

100,00 inhabitants. Although Brazil and Panama follow stringent drug laws vis-à-vis Uruguay, prison population patterns reflect similarities.

Conclusions

In June 2012, during his speech in the Rio+20 United Nations Conference on Sustainable Development, President José Mujica stated,

> Someone has to be first, because we are losing the battle against drugs and criminality in the continent … [t]he industrial societies are the ones

> that have to change … for a small country, it's possible to experiment with this, but it's also very possible for a developed country because of the resources it has … until things change there, it will be very difficult to change elsewhere. (UN 2012, np)

One year later, Uruguay became the first country to legalize cannabis and regulate every stage of the industry's commodity chain, from cultivation, production, and distribution to commercialization.

Going against global canons with the implementation of a drug policy that has not been adopted by a state before has come with many barriers. Some of the challenges in the implementation of the reform include complications with the international banking system (Hudak, Ramsey and Walsh 2018),[24] the registration of users due to social stigma, the opportunity for a black and a grey market to flourish (Garat 2017), cannabis tourism (Hudak, Ramey, and Walsh 2018), and others. The development of Uruguay's drug policy can be understood within two levels of analysis: the international and the domestic, or a 'two- level game' (Putnam 1988). That is, at the international level, the state has supported antidrug multilateral efforts as well as complying with the US-led war on drugs. Domestically, nevertheless, the South American country has moulded its own drug control policies.

Legalization was possible because of a combination of various factors such as having a left-wing government, the support of the Congress, and the landscape of public insecurity that placed cannabis legalization as a possible policy choice to tackle Uruguay's increasing crime rates (Queirolo et al 2018). What have we learned from the Uruguayan case? Throughout this chapter, we explored several indicators to assess the impacts of the legalization policy on different areas such as consumption, public health, and security.

LTP, LYP, and LMP increased after legalization. However, the upward trend started in the years prior to the reform and have been evident since the early 2000s. The increases in prevalence appear to be gradual and do not present important shifts after policy change. What is more, prevalence rates following legalization fell close to projected consumption trends. This suggests that even without the cannabis reform, usage rates could have evolved following a similar fashion. The relatively limited incidence of Uruguay's legalization policy in explaining use fluctuations is also confirmed by certain patterns witnessed in Brazil. Despite the evidence being limited, available data suggest that the consumption of psychoactive substances such as cannabis and cocaine also increased in Brazil, hinting at a regional trend.

Prevalence in all three indicators has particularly increased in the 19–25 and 26–35 age groups. By contrast, the LMP among the 15–18-year-old cohort did not grow between 2014 and 2018, suggesting that Uruguay's cannabis legalization reform did not cause use increases among adolescents. It is highly possible that regulations put into place by the state when legalizing cannabis in 2013, including a minimum age for consumption, might be deterring younger clusters from using the psychoactive substance through illegal means.

Most importantly, albeit usage continues to increase, there is no evidence that legalization has led to problematic consumption of either cannabis or harder drugs such as cocaine. The number of people seeking treatment has been falling and the number of drug-related deaths has decreased following legalization. In addition, the reform is not necessarily associated with major frequency of use fluctuations. The surveys in Uruguay indicate that daily consumption is the least common practice reported by users. The age of initiation has also increased from 18 to 20–21 years old. That is, regardless of higher accessibility, affordability, and legality of cannabis recreational use, individuals are initiating consumption at an older age. Interestingly, cannabis continues to be the most consumed drug, which suggests that the differentiation of markets after legalization has been successful.

Law enforcement activities targeting drugs expanded in Uruguay after legalization. Cocaine seizures show an important increase. The legalization of cannabis could have caused a market disruption, shifting illegal drug trafficking activities towards other drugs. Yet the increase of cannabis and cocaine seizures observed in Uruguay after legalization in 2013 cannot be analyzed only domestically. In addition to the likely impacts of legalization and the shift of the focus of law enforcement towards the supply side of the drug industry, systemic factors could be also affecting this trend. Specifically, increasing consumption patterns around the world and the unintended consequences of regional counterdrug efforts that displaced trafficking operations toward nontraditional routes may be impacting the amounts of illicit drugs seized and available in Uruguay.

The impact on drug prices, by contrast, in the case of cannabis was not left to market forces. It was part of the legalization framework to intentionally lower the price of cannabis to US$1.00 per gram in order to compete with the informal market, although the prices reported have not reached the goal and presented an increase in 2019. Reports indicate that the monetary value of other psychoactive substances that are still sold illegally such as cocaine and ecstasy present fluctuations. On the one hand, cocaine prices increased after legalization; this trend is also reported in the control group, meaning that it is possible that the increases correspond to regional trends and not a change in the legal status of cannabis. The price of a tablet of ecstasy, on the other hand, has decreased. Moreover, the legalization reform was also intended to shape the potency of cannabis. In effect, the potency of the product sold in pharmacies has been adjusted by the IRCCA based on market demand. While potency changes are strictly influenced by state policies, unlike the case of Portugal, the increases registered in Uruguay contradict the argument of some legalization advocates who would expect a decrease in the potency after liberalization.

Uruguay's security landscape following legalization presents alarming trends. Overall, homicide, robbery, and theft rates have climbed. Robbery and theft follow similar patterns in Brazil, which may point to a regional trend rather than a direct effect of the legalization policy. Whether legalization, law enforcement practices, the restructuration of the drug market, or other contextual forces such as the country's new role within the drug trafficking routes in Latin America provoked the upsurge of crime in Uruguay, this is an unexpected outcome since other drug policy liberalization reforms have had opposite effects on violence. What was not unexpected was the decline in drug law violations after the country legalized the recreational consumption of cannabis.

Finally, like other Latin American countries, the prison population continues to increase in Uruguay. Nevertheless, the number of individuals incarcerated for drug offenses declined after cannabis legalization. In addition, as the processes ending with a sentence for other crimes in general have increased following the country's drug policy reform, the ones processed for drug law violations experienced the opposite trend. The number of individuals processed in Uruguay for any crime also declined from 2012 to 2017, and the processes focused on drug law violations also lessened during the same period of time.

Revisiting the three main policy objectives set by the government at the time of the reform, we find that the legalization of cannabis so far has not reduced drug-related violence and some consumers are still getting cannabis from the black market. Nevertheless, the other two policy goals show a more positive light. We observe positive public health indicators after legalization and the safe access to cannabis for consumers was granted. Under these circumstances, the Uruguayan experiment holds great value for policymakers and analysts around the globe. This case offers good insight into the processes and challenges that come from adopting legalization as a national drug policy. There is a debate on whether Uruguay really parted from the prohibitionist paradigm. Galain (2018) argues that the Uruguayan drug policy remains punitive and has just created an exception for cannabis. Regarding this, it is expected that the judicial system does not totally reflect major changes, since it is just exempting cannabis consumption from the already established legal framework, which remains the same for other psychoactive substances. As Queirolo and colleagues (2022, 1) find, 'The specifics of each legalisation policy matter'. Moreover, it is important for policymakers to understand and foresee the possible effects of a regulatory design on the illegal market and the institutional capacity to sustain the framework. The Uruguayan case remains relatively young, and we have yet to see and assess the long-term impacts of noncommercial legalization.

Conclusions: The End of the Punitive Paradigm?

We are witnessing one of the most important eras in drug policy revolutions. After a century of punitivism, new paradigms are emerging. The journey, however, did not begin with prohibition and criminalization. Humans have consumed drugs for well over 10,000 years. In their natural state or in processed forms, psychoactive substances have been a central part of people's everyday lives across civilizations. Drugs are used for different purposes, including medicinal or therapeutic (Kalso and Vainio 1990; Mather 1995; Musto 1999; Chou et al 2009; Reisman 2011), to relieve the feeling of hunger (Bolton 1979; Malcolm, Barth, Veatch 2013), enhance physical performance (Henman 1978; Carter and Mamani 1986; Vidart 1991), or to simply experience pleasure (Measham, Newcombe, and Parker 1994; O'Malley and Valverde 2004; Goode 2012; McCormack, Measham, and Wignall 2021). Various illicit psychoactive substances considered dangerous today were widely used and thought to have positive effects in the past (Thoumi 2005; Carrier and Klantschnig 2020).

It was not until the last few hundred years that control over these same psychoactive substances started to surface and be enforced through criminal law (Goode 1997). The US led the first multilateral efforts, calling on other nations to eliminate the use, sale, or manufacture of various drugs. Starting with opium, the Shanghai Commission convened in February 1909, marking the beginning of the prohibitionist crusade which was ultimately expanded to other psychoactive substances such as cocaine and cannabis (Sanchéz-Avilés and Ditrych 2017). The punitive approach to drugs became widespread among democratic and authoritarian governments alike. By the second half of the twentieth century, nearly every country endorsed prohibition and criminalization to regulate the relationship between society and psychoactive substances (Levine 2002). The global prohibition regime, as described by Nadelmann (1990), reached full momentum in 1961, 1971, and 1988, when the United Nations adopted the three major multilateral conventions to bind signatory states to restrict the production, manufacture, trafficking, possession, and consumption of illicit drugs.

Despite the efforts and resources devoted to fighting illegal psychoactive substances, there is no evidence indicating that the global drug problem has been reduced. Before several countries embarked on different liberalization policies, various reports showed that the drug situation had worsened substantially (Reuter et al 2009; Global Commission on Drug Policy 2016). First within developed nations and more recently across the developing world, prevalence rates of psychoactive substances such as cannabis, opioids, cocaine, and amphetamine-like drugs such as MDMA expanded dramatically (Darke, Degenhardt, and Mattick 2006). The upward trend has continued or accelerated during the last decade. According to the World Drug Report (UNODC 2021), the estimated number of drug users globally increased significantly over the last 10 years (UNODC 2021). Under these circumstances, the United Nations' goal of achieving a 'drug-free world' established at the 1998 Special Session of the General Assembly has not been achieved by far.

Other harms associated with the use of psychoactive substances have also worsened. The number of deaths reported among people who use drugs has trended upward since the late 1960s (Darke, Degenhardt, and Mattick 2006). In the US alone, for example, drug overdoses – most of them linked with the use of opioids – claimed approximately 108,000 lives in 2021, an increase of nearly 15 per cent with respect to 2020 (Centers for Disease Control and Prevention 2022). The evidence also suggests that the incidence of HIV rose due to the sharing of contaminated injecting equipment among people who use drugs, accounting for roughly 10 per cent of new diagnoses globally (Joint United Nations Programme on HIV/AIDS 2020). The transmission of other blood-borne infections such as hepatitis C (HCV) is high worldwide and has risen dramatically in countries like the US (Liang and Ward 2018). Furthermore, there are approximately 2.3 million HIV-HCV coinfections in the world, of which more than half occur among those who use injection drugs (Platt et al 2016).

The damages associated with illicit drugs are not limited to users. Illegal drug markets are still a main source of violence globally. Prohibition policies have created massive profits, favouring various criminal organizations. Although high-income countries have not witnessed extraordinary levels of violence, the situation in drug producing and trafficking regions has been completely different. Not only have homicides skyrocketed, but also corruption and political instability. Between 2000 and 2010, more than 1 million people died in Latin America and the Caribbean as a result of criminal violence (United Nations Development Program 2013). With an average of 17.2 homicides per 100,000 inhabitants, the region has experienced the highest murder rate since 1990 (UNODC 2019). In Colombia, for instance, 27,000 people died on average each year during the 1990s, resulting in a reduction of more than two years in the country's life expectancy at birth (Keefer, Loayza, and Soares 2010). Drug trafficking is also fuelling violence and political turmoil in various countries in Africa (Schuberth 2014; Ogunniyi and Akpu 2019) and Asia (Omelicheva and Markowitz 2018; Biswas 2021).

Yet it would not be accurate to think that because the century-long prohibition and criminalization of certain psychoactive substances has failed to curb several drug-related problems, a nonpunitive approach would automatically result in benefits across diverse realms such as health and security. Put differently, the fact that people continue to use psychoactive substances and there are still major harms associated with illegal drugs despite their prohibition and criminalization cannot be evoked as the sole motive to support the adoption of alternative liberalization policies. As demonstrated in this book, the change in drug policy paradigms is a complex process that differs from country to country. What is more, not only do the transition processes present challenges, but they can also be lengthy. The impacts of these policies are not immediate, and can take years to develop.

Ideological and moral considerations aside, *Drug Policy Revolutions: Trajectories in Argentina, Portugal, and Uruguay* has put the criminalization of psychoactive substances for recreational purposes under scrutiny by evaluating the estimated impacts of three different liberalization alternatives – depenalization, decriminalization, and legalization – adopted in Argentina, Portugal, and Uruguay. The journeys each of these countries undertook before reforming their drug control policies have certainly shaped the map of relevant actors, institutions, and practices under the new liberalization scheme. This book demonstrates that the estimated impacts of depenalization, decriminalization, and legalization/regulation also depend on contextual factors and on how each of the reforms was historically implemented. Drug liberalization policies, in other words, do not emerge out of a vacuum but are rather the result of political, economic, and social circumstances surrounding decision-making processes in different historical contexts.

The historical trajectories of revolutions

Psychoactive substances were practically unregulated in Argentina, Uruguay, and Portugal by the early twentieth century. Drug markets remained relatively small and international efforts were still limited to controlling the Sino-Indian opium trade. Following US President Theodore Roosevelt's initiative to organize an international meeting where states could limit the trafficking of certain psychoactive substances, Uruguay became the first country to regulate the selling and acquisition of opiates in 1908. Four years later, it also joined the Hague Opium Convention of 1912, an international effort led by the US primarily to dismantle Asian trafficking routes into its own territory. Interestingly, the bases of the Uruguayan welfare state were already in place when the small South American country regulated psychoactive substances for the first time. Still, there were no criminal penalties for citizens possessing 'reasonable amounts' of cannabis, cocaine, and opium for recreational purposes in a context where services such as health care were freely provided by the state.

Similar to Uruguay, developments in the international system, particularly the first attempts to create a drug control regime, affected how Argentina and Portugal framed psychoactive substances during the early twentieth century. While Portugal was one of the 12 nations to sign the International Opium Convention in January 1912, Argentina only became part of the initiative by joining the Protocol of the Powers not represented at the summit. Portugal's direct involvement, of course, was intimately related to its role within the political economy of illicit drugs. With its own poppy cultivation in Macao, Portugal's vested interests favoured a greater participation in the emerging drug control system. Nonetheless, Argentina and Portugal regulated psychoactive substances later in time compared to Uruguay. Both countries passed domestic legislation in 1924, representing the first efforts to control certain aspects of the illegal drug industry within their respective territories.

Drug control efforts in Argentina, Uruguay, and Portugal almost came to a halt after these first legislative antecedents. Except for the Portuguese Decree of 1926, which established more restrictions and heavier penalties, and Uruguay's decision to join the Central Committee of the Board of Directors of the Opium Commission of the League of Nations in 1933, drug-related issues lost momentum across the three liberalization countries. The public debate about illegal drugs and the policing efforts of high-ranked government officials were relatively limited in a context where the use of psychoactive substances was still not perceived as a major security threat. The impasse was favoured by Washington, DC's increasing interest in the prohibition of alcoholic beverages during the 1920s and 1930s. Furthermore, the first military coups experienced in Portugal and Argentina between the mid-1920s and early 1930s, respectively, certainly diverted the attention of the population and national governments alike towards other social, economic, and political challenges.

During the second half of the twentieth century, psychoactive substances were placed again on the national political agendas of Argentina, Uruguay, and Portugal. Despite the punitive approach that shaped the legal and institutional infrastructures of the three liberalization countries, psychoactive substances were framed relatively differently. Problematic use, albeit the adoption of fines and incarceration penalties, was perceived as a psychological illness subject to treatment programs in Portugal, whereas the military junta that governed Argentina from 1966 to 1973 considered drugs as an internal enemy. The link between insurgency and the consumption of psychoactive substances shaped the country's first drug law, the rulings of the Supreme

Court, and the state apparatus created to combat illegal drugs. To a lesser extent, Uruguay's civil-military dictatorship adopted the South American Narcotics and Psychotropic Agreement, integrating domestically several aspects of the prohibitionist multilateral framework promoted by the United Nations.

Portugal inaugurated the third wave of democratization in 1974. Several institutions dealing with the country's drug problem were created after the Salazar dictatorship. In a context of increasing prevalence rates, especially intravenous heroin consumption, the new state apparatus gradually developed since the late 1970s and early 1980s introduced the notion of decriminalization and several prevention and treatment programs, including AIDS educational initiatives, drug treatment in prisons, and free telephone helplines for problematic users. On the other hand, the democratic transition in the two South American countries shaped drug policy in different ways. While Argentina experienced a process of increasing flexibilization, especially because the drug problem was associated with the dictatorship's agenda, Uruguay's repressive approach linking youth and drugs did not completely disappeared following the arrival of democracy. Argentina's transition 'after regime collapse', as opposed to Uruguay's 'pacted transition', certainly limited the chances of the new democratic government to embrace a repressive drug policy, especially after the military junta's vast violation of human rights, the disappearance of around 30,000 people, and the devastating war against Great Britain. It is not surprising, therefore, that Argentina adopted several prevention initiatives, the Supreme Court depenalized the recreational use of illegal psychoactive substances, and users were increasingly perceived as patients, whereas law enforcement and incarceration became common drug policy instruments in Uruguay.

Yet drug problems did not arrive simultaneously in the three liberalization countries. By the 1990s, Portugal was already immersed in a health crisis. Heroin consumption reached historical levels, HIV/AIDS diagnoses increased substantially, drug-related deaths also followed an upward trend, and the supply of cocaine and new synthetic drugs began to be a common feature of the Portuguese illegal drug market. In this context, problematic consumption became the country's top concern in 1997. The role of the two South American countries in the political economy of illicit drugs was completely different. Though Argentina's right-wing government continuously attempted to frame illegal psychoactive substances as a national security threat, prevalence levels were still relatively low and drug-related violence was not salient during the 1990s, a situation also witnessed in Uruguay. Still, Argentina adopted several punitive policies, including the ongoing drug law criminalizing consumption for recreational purposes and a new Supreme Court ruling following the national government's tough approach to illicit drugs. Uruguay, by contrast, followed a slightly different trajectory. In a context of greater debate, where specialists and left-wing political parties questioned the repressive policies adopted during the 1980s, the Uruguayan government depenalized in 1998 the consumption of cannabis for recreational purposes.

The first liberalization reform was adopted in Portugal. After a failed attempt to contain the heroin crisis through punitive measures in the early 1990s, which included a new drug law, the European country slowly moved towards decriminalization. In addition to harm reduction initiatives such as syringe exchange programs, drug substitution therapy, and the provision of methadone for opioid treatment, the Portuguese government appointed a scientific committee to develop a drug policy proposal which was eventually labelled as the National Strategy to Fight Against Drugs. The result was the decriminalization policy, transformed into law in 2000. Complementary to Portugal's decriminalization scheme, new harm reduction measures were also launched by the socialist government in 2001. By the time drug liberalization policy was fully operational in Portugal, cannabis legalization began to be considered as a real option by several high-ranked government officials in Uruguay. In Argentina, meanwhile, the 2001 economic and social crisis marked a critical juncture in the country's role within the political economy of illicit drugs. Similar to the trajectory experienced by Portugal 10 or 20 years before, Argentina's drug consumption rates increased rapidly despite the apathy of the national government.

Drug liberalization in the two South American countries gained momentum in the late 2000s. In Argentina, however, the reform was not an executive or legislative initiative but rather a ruling of the Supreme Court of Justice. After a case in which three individuals were detained and sentenced for cannabis possession, Argentina's highest judicial authority declared unconstitutional the second paragraph of Article 14 of Law 23.737, which criminalizes the possession of psychoactive substances for personal use. Unlike Argentina, cannabis liberalization in Uruguay was promoted by the Broad Front as part of the Strategy for Life and Coexistence plan. The initiative aimed at challenging drug trafficking cartels by focusing on security efforts while framing consumption as a health problem. President Mujica's drug reform proposal was finally transformed into law in 2013, when Congress passed Law 19.172, establishing the legal and institutional foundations of cannabis legalization.

Revolutions, in other words, emerged from different social and political contexts. While the Portuguese government decriminalized psychoactive substances to tackle the country's health crisis caused by the widespread use of heroin and its associated harms, security preoccupations were at centre stage in Uruguay. Different consumption patterns, of course, motivated alternative liberalization schemes. Portugal's drug policy reform comprises a wide spectrum of psychoactive substances while also placing greater emphasis on harm reduction strategies compared to Uruguay. In both cases, however, the state has played a fundamental role in regulating and controlling drug markets or their associated harms, contrasting with commercial liberalization initiatives such as those adopted across the US since 2012. Argentina's drug policy reform, by contrast, was not a product of a political decision. The lack of compromise and limited participation of the executive and legislative branches have severely constrained the scope of liberalization. Rather than a 'revolution', Argentina has witnessed the emergence of a highly ambiguous and contradictory drug policy that could be better labelled as a 'limited evolution'.

Drug liberalization has not come without challenges. The three countries have experienced setbacks following their reforms. By the time Argentina and Uruguay were about to change the legal status of illegal drugs, the Portuguese Supreme Court of Justice reestablished the crime of drug consumption in cases where the quantity confiscated exceeds the average use of 10 days. Notwithstanding the liberalization policies adopted in Argentina and Uruguay were not placed under scrutiny, their consolidation or further development suffered certain difficulties. While in Argentina the legislative reform aimed at removing criminal penalties for drug possession never materialized despite Congress legalizing the medical use of cannabis, the legalization framework in Uruguay faced several implementation challenges, including budget constraints, banking complications, the threat of cannabis tourism, and the provision of the psychoactive substance through pharmacies.

Does drug liberalization work?

Argentina, Portugal, and Uruguay have implemented alternative liberalization schemes aimed at tackling different drug-related problems. The evidence indicates that the estimated impacts of drug policy reforms can vary according to the stage of liberalization, the context, the role of the country within the political economy of illicit drugs, and across the three realms under evaluation. This book suggests, in other words, that depenalization, decriminalization, and legalization/regulation have a distinct, albeit nonlinear, effect on drug use patterns, health, and security concerns.

Drug consumption patterns

Contrary to the expectations of advocates of prohibition, we find that removing or lessening criminal penalties did not turn Argentina, Portugal, or Uruguay into drug paradises. Although the prevalence increased after the three liberalization countries changed the status of illegal drugs, the increments did not start right after the reforms were implemented but were rather the continuation of an upward trend already present since the 1990s and early 2000s. Moreover, prevalence fluctuations were largely motivated by cannabis, the psychoactive substance that registered the most substantial growth. This trend, however, was not limited to Portugal, Argentina, or Uruguay. Except for Panama, whose survey years are too limited to draw definitive conclusions, cannabis use rates increased across all countries of the control groups, suggesting that fluctuations are not likely associated with drug policy reforms.

While cannabis use rates continued to increase following liberalization reforms, echoing broader developments in the political economy of illicit drugs, the prevalence of other psychoactive substances experienced slightly different patterns. Portugal registered decreases across all psychoactive substances, a trend attributable in part to decriminalization since the control group displayed the exact opposite trajectory. Argentina and Uruguay, by contrast, witnessed increases across most illegal drugs. Similar to Brazil and other countries in the South American region, these increments were particularly evident in terms of cocaine and reflected the continuation of old trajectories witnessed at least since the early 2000s.

The estimated impacts on the youth population, an age cluster that is more prone to long-term engagement, are rather the opposite. In Portugal, both last-year and last-month prevalence of all illicit drugs dropped or remained stable among the 15–24 age group. Similarly, Argentina's cannabis life prevalence among the 12–17 age group is today below the pre-reform levels and the initiation age of all illicit substances surveyed has increased an average of 1.5 years. However, cocaine use rates as well as any illicit drug prevalence experienced exactly the opposite trend among the youngest cohorts. To a lesser extent, some of these patterns were also witnessed in the case of Uruguay. Although the small South American country registered cannabis use increments among teenagers after the adoption of legalization, the initiation age increased from 18 to 20–21 years, implying that Uruguay's drug policy reform did not push cannabis consumption towards younger cohorts. These results might have been guided by age regulations of legal cannabis consumption.

Market trends

The assessment of mechanisms such as price and seizures yielded mixed results, in most of the cases challenging the market rationale proposed by economic theory. While drug seizures increased in Uruguay and Argentina following the liberalization reforms, Portugal's confiscations showed the opposite trend. On the one hand, the two South American countries witnessed growing seizures (except for cocaine in Argentina). The relevance of nontraditional routes supplying consolidated markets such as Europe and Oceania, together with emerging markets like Africa, cannot be ignored, especially because other countries in the region experienced similar fluctuations during this same period. Portugal's drug seizures, on the other hand, decreased after the adoption of decriminalization. Interestingly, Germany and France, Portugal's control group, registered increases in seizures during this period. This trend, albeit unexpected, cannot be totally dissociated from decriminalization policy.

Prices did not always follow the expectations of the advocates of punitivism, either. Except for cannabis, the only psychoactive substance whose prevalence increased following decriminalization, the price of illicit drugs in Portugal decreased substantially relative to the pre-reform years. By the same token, the liberalization reform did not cause a decline in the monetary value of cannabis in Argentina, as economic theory indicates. Instead, the evidence shows that the price of cannabis is now above pre-reform levels despite the Supreme Court's decision to depenalize all psychoactive substances. Remarkably, unlike various Latin American countries, cocaine became two times cheaper in Argentina, largely mirroring the trend seen in Portugal. Uruguay, on the other hand, set the price of cannabis, showing that state-led liberalization schemes are more effective in influencing the value of drugs.

These mechanisms, in other words, have limited ability to explain changes in drug use patterns across the three liberalization countries. The trajectories followed by the case studies suggest that less stringent drug policies do not seem to have a direct impact on the size of the market, as shown in Portugal and in Argentina in terms of cocaine. Of course, other factors such as the strategies of law enforcement authorities after changing the legal status of drugs may be affecting seizures across countries. Along similar lines, the post-policy reform scenarios indicate that the price of illegal drugs can increase in more flexible legal frameworks despite the lower risks of legal repercussions. In Argentina and Portugal, for example, the monetary value of cannabis rose following drug policy liberalization.

Most importantly, the relationship between seizures and price of psychoactive substances vis-à-vis prevalence remains unclear. Unlike highly regulated drug markets like cannabis in Uruguay, the evidence indicates that neither the consumption of psychoactive substances is always price sensitive nor that changes in seizure lead to prevalence fluctuations. The Portuguese experience demonstrates that the use of all illicit drugs declined except for cannabis, the only psychoactive substance whose price increased following the adoption of decriminalization in 2001. Analogously, Argentina's cocaine seizures decreased, but consumption rates soared after 2009, the post-reform years. The fluctuations of these mechanisms across the three liberalization cases suggest that illicit drug markets are highly interconnected. The regular exchange of illicit goods and services does not happen in a vacuum; these markets appear to be more sensitive to systemic forces and regional trends than to domestic inputs such as changes in the legal status of drugs. The analysis of the interaction among these mechanisms also indicates the need for drug policy scholars to develop better proxy measures to understand variations of illicit drug markets and their impacts on use rates.

Health impacts

Drug policy reforms seem to have a limited ability to increase the harms associated with illicit drug consumption. In all three liberalization countries, the frequency or continuity rates in the use of several psychoactive substances declined in the post-reform years. In Portugal, except for cannabis, the proportion of individuals who have used cocaine, heroin, and ecstasy throughout their lives reported a decline in consumption of the same psychoactive substance during the last year between 2001 and 2017. In Uruguay, amid growing consumption rates, the numbers of monthly, weekly, and daily users have decreased, whereas the last-year use presents the highest frequency following legalization. Despite the limits on data comparability in Argentina, the evidence suggests that consumption is mostly occasional or recreational. In other words, the greater ease of access or limited legal consequences seem not to be associated with problematic use across the three liberalization countries.

The demand for treatment also decreased across all cases. Despite that these drug policy reforms – especially in Portugal and Uruguay – were primarily intended to facilitate access to treatment by removing criminal penalties, the provision of medical services to users of psychoactive substances did not increase. After more than 20 years of decriminalization, the number of hospitalizations in Portugal are today below pre-reform levels, the period during which heroin prevalence reached a historical peak. In Uruguay, the demand for cannabis treatment also decreased, a trend especially driven by women. Although cocaine was not considered in the legalization reform, the demand for treatment also declined. These results, however, do not correspond to some key policy reform expectations in the cases of the governments of Portugal and Uruguay, respectively. The estimated impacts of de facto drug liberalization reforms like depenalization are not completely different. That is, Argentina's demand for treatment experienced several fluctuations but it shows lower levels today compared to 2008 when criminalization was fully operational.

Portugal also registered improvements in terms of HIV and AIDS infections. Its declining number of diagnoses is likely attributable to decriminalization and the country's harm reduction initiatives since the control group did not display the same downward trend. Although similar decreases were registered in Uruguay, HIV and AIDS fluctuations do not seem to be associated with the country's drug policy reform since the psychoactive substances that carry a direct risk of infection were not legalized in 2013. Likewise, Argentina's

HIV and AIDS diagnoses had been growing since at least 2000 and not right after the reform. All countries in the control group also show an upward trend during the same period, suggesting that these increments are not linked to depenalization.

Finally, overdoses in Portugal and Argentina presented fluctuations in the aftermath of their drug policy reforms. In both cases, the number of deaths is currently above or roughly the same as pre-reform levels. Since one of the countries in Portugal's control group underwent the same trend and Argentina lacks a regional comparison, it is difficult to attribute these ups and downs to decriminalization or depenalization, respectively. Furthermore, changes in overdose data collection processes likely affected this trend. By the same token, overdose fluctuations in Uruguay cannot be associated with the legalization policy. The evidence demonstrates that neither the psychopharmacological properties nor the routes of administration of cannabis are directly linked to fatal overdoses worldwide.

Security impacts

The security landscape also differs substantially across the three liberalization countries. Portugal's homicide, robbery, and theft rates are nowadays below pre-reform levels, a downward trend that was also witnessed in terms of the number of crimes directly and indirectly related to drugs. Contrarily, Uruguay's security indicators deteriorated rapidly following the legalization of cannabis in 2013, thereby failing to meet one of the main purposes of the country's drug policy reform. Even though Argentina's homicide rates are below the Latin American average and robbery and theft rates have not oscillated substantially since the Supreme Court depenalized the recreational use of illegal drugs in 2009, violence has erupted in certain metropolitan areas. The situation in Rosario, for example, suggests that countries that historically escaped the region's waves of violence like Argentina and Uruguay experienced during the 1980s and 1990s are now increasingly affected by changes in the political economy of illicit drugs in Latin America. New trafficking routes have emerged, favouring the territorial competition among criminal organizations for the control of a highly lucrative drug market. In the context of weak institutions and corruption, this trend is likely to result in unprecedented levels of violence and crime.

Following the expectations of various liberalization advocates, the prison population incarcerated for violation of the drug laws in Portugal and Uruguay (to a lesser extent) are these days below pre-reform levels, indicating a possible reduction in the burden on the criminal justice system following decriminalization and legalization policies, respectively. Unlike these two cases, where criminal penalties were formally removed from the law books, both prison sentences and the number of people incarcerated for drug violations continued to grow after Argentina's depenalization reform. The available evidence also demonstrates that the persecution of minor drug-related crimes continues despite the Supreme Court of Justice declaring the drug law's second paragraph of Article 14 unconstitutional. That is to say, Argentina's drug liberalization reform has not prevented illicit drug users from facing the criminal justice system.

Lessons from revolutions

Through the journeys of Argentina, Portugal, and Uruguay, this book shows that the outcomes of drug policy revolutions are highly dependent upon each country's political, economic, and social trajectories as well as their role within the political economy of illicit drugs. The nonlinear nature of the impacts of these liberalization reforms lie in the complex interplay of regional drug market dynamics and other relevant contextual forces outside the legal domain such as variations in the scope of the welfare state, the strength of domestic institutions, and the presence (or not) of harm reduction policies accompanying the reforms.

Still, the media and the public alike commonly refer to the legal status of drugs and its enforcement to evaluate the evolution of a country's drug-related indicators. As Reuter and Stevens (2007) note, the levels of use are instinctively placed in the spotlight to judge the performance of various drug policies. However, this book also demonstrates that while drug policy revolutions may have a limited ability to directly affect use rates, they could effectively contribute to containing some of the associated problems. For instance, if the frequency of use and the demand for treatment decreased in the three liberalization countries, the central question raised in this book is not how much people use illicit drugs but what consequences derive from it. Following Kleiman (1992) and Babor et al (2010), drug policies do not allow societies to be completely free of psychoactive substances, but they can minimize certain harms associated with their use and influence the nature of their problems.

Special attention needs to be paid to alternative measures that help to reduce the harms associated with the consumption of psychoactive substances. In addition to initiatives that affect drug problems but are not commonly circumscribed within the drug domain such as welfare policies, governments need to promote innovative harm reduction and treatment services. As Boyum and Reuter (2001) point out, steps towards linking drug policy and social policy are advisable to bridge the classic divide that normatively, politically, or operationally separates the two realms. Institution building initiatives are especially relevant to reverse the historic preeminence of drug enforcement expenditure on police, courts, and prisons.

Furthermore, drug liberalization policies have some less quantifiable effects that have not been thoughtfully surveyed in this book but still deserve a great deal of attention. Parting from criminalization and/or prohibition, Argentina, Portugal, and Uruguay have promoted policies aimed at respecting human rights and improving the well-being of their communities. Yet discriminatory policing practices have not disappeared equally across the three liberalization countries, implying that each drug policy reform has a distinct effect on the prison population. While the arbitrary arrest and detention of drug users have largely disappeared in Portugal and Uruguay, Argentina's liberalization reform has not totally materialized in the enforcement realm. Since the law in the books still differs from the law in action under depenalization schemes, Argentina's people who use drugs, especially those living in the urban margins, are still at risk of arbitrary detention. This situation, in turn, can directly affect their future opportunities for employment, education, and their social inclusion, which points to the importance of the specificities when crafting drug policies.

Conditioning the lives of millions of people makes even less sense if the evidence suggests that the psychoactive substance criminalized has limited impacts on public health and the general well-being of the population. Why cannabis is still criminalized across several local and national jurisdictions despite the evidence overwhelmingly indicating that it does not contribute to mortality rates and is less likely to have adverse health harms remains unclear. The multilateral system and governments alike are missing a unique opportunity to redirect the attention, efforts, and resources towards more dangerous illicit drugs such as fentanyl, heroin, cocaine, or methamphetamines. Of course, as Amanda Feilding (2010), the founder and director of the Beckley Foundation, claims, any change to the scheduling of cannabis under the multilateral drug control system could lead to the questioning of the whole war on drugs, which would become meaningless if more than three-quarters (that is, around 166 million people) of those who use any illicit drug would no longer be considered criminals.

This book also suggests that the impacts of similar drug policy reforms cannot be predicted or exactly replicated in other locations. Our case studies illustrated variations in liberalization levels, and the journeys they undertook demonstrated the plethora of possible outcomes on targeted policy goals. Each experience is different. The fact that drug policies are context-dependent implies that reforms are unlikely to produce the same outcomes across national borders. Important variations in terms of use patterns, the role of the country within the political economy of illicit drugs, domestic institutions, and the adoption (or not) of complementary policies (for example, harm reduction programs or institutional capacity building) are expected to affect outcomes. Even the implementation of policies such as depenalization, decriminalization, or legalization can vary despite how they look in the books.

Diving into the indicators and proxies to analyze the impacts of drug policies in different realms is also challenging. The data available at the domestic and international levels are limited. Despite the efforts of international organizations such as UNODC and the European Monitoring Centre for Drugs and Drug Addiction, there is still a vacuum of information, and the quality of data is sometimes not as reliable. Hence, studies on drug policies can lead to myopic conclusions. We realize that in order to truly assess these phenomena there is a need for better data sources available for future scholarly research.

The analysis of the trajectories and contexts of the three liberalization countries drove relevant lessons. The book was intended to illuminate empirical and theoretical questions that are not simply a matter of academic interest but rather the subject of public policies dealing with real problems. We expect that *Drug Policy Revolutions: Trajectories in Argentina, Portugal, and Uruguay* has contributed to the effort to inform the debate by providing a multidisciplinary, theoretically informed, and empirically grounded analysis of drug policy.

Notes

Introduction

1 In accordance with Article 347, Criminal Code PRC, the production, trafficking, and consumption of drugs – regardless of the quantity – remains strictly criminalized in China (Hao 2022).

2 In 2004, Government Decree No. 231 established that the possession of small amounts of illegal drugs is no longer punishable with jail time. Nevertheless, the application of the new legislation has been virtually nonexistent (Eastwood, Fox, and Rosemarin 2016).

3 Other scholars (for example, Ritter 2022; Stevens 2016) include a four domain of policy action: harm reduction.

4 While the 1961 Single Convention requires signatory members to outlaw possession of controlled substances (Article 36), the criminalization of possession is established in the 1988 Convention (Article 3).

5 A fourth international body is often included in the list: the World Health Organization. This multilateral institution has a technical role in evaluating drugs and recommending how they should be classified under the system (Room et al 2010).

6 Colorado and Washington State became the first states in the US territory to legalize the consumption and commercialization of cannabis for recreational purposes.

7 Certain countries differentiate the penalties imposed on individuals caught possessing drugs from those imposed on individuals caught consuming them (Pacula et al 2005).

8 Room and colleagues (2010) use the example of Germany and the Netherlands to illustrate this discrepancy between the laws on the books and the laws in action.

9 After the depenalization of illegal drugs in 2009, Argentina legalized the medical use of cannabis in 2017.

10 Although the term 'liberalization' is often used to refer to the 'lack of control' and 'anything goes', especially among prohibitionists (Rodrigues 2024), in this book we understand it as a complex legal-political procedure of moving away from prohibitionist policies.

11 As Hall and Lynskey (2020) note, evaluations of countries that have recently changed the legal status of drugs offer a poor indication of the impacts of the reforms compared to those that have spent more time under the new legislation, particularly because the potential harms of certain psychoactive substances are largely attributable to long-term heavy use.

12 For analytical purposes, even in the cases where we refer to psychoactive substances, we are only considering illegal drugs listed in the 1961 Single Convention and not to other psychoactive substances such as alcohol.

13 In this book, we use the generic term cannabis to refer to preparations (for example, marijuana and hashish) derived from the *cannabis sativa* plant.

14 Since data vary from country to country, not all the same illicit drugs are analyzed in each case study.

15 We do not test the so-called 'gateway hypothesis' in this book. Instead, we try to evaluate whether legal changes in the status of cannabis are associated with fluctuations in the use of other illicit drugs.

16 EMCDDA (2021a) refers to overdoses as 'drug-induced deaths'. Together with 'mortality rates among problem drug users', overdoses comprise what the organization labels as 'drug-related deaths and mortality'.

17 Hughes and Stevens (2010) also include public assaults and certain types of fraud as crimes 'strongly linked to drugs'.

18 Although they are not considered in this book, especially for methodological reasons, 'crimes committed by users to support their drug habit' and 'systemic crimes committed as part of the functioning of illicit markets' are also considered as part of the 'drug-related crimes' (EMCDDA 2003).

19 Before the legalization of cannabis, Uruguay decriminalized personal possession of 'small quantities' of illicit psychoactive substances in 1974. However, the precise amount was never stated, providing ample room for judges to act at their discretion (Hudak, Ramsey, and Walsh 2018).

Chapter 1

1 While higher potency seems to be the expected outcome of criminalization, the empirical evidence is mixed. MacCoun and Reuter (2001a), for example, show that the potency of spirits increased during the US Prohibition, but cocaine was sold in very low purity in retail markets during the period when the psychoactive substance was legal in the US (that is, prior to the adoption of the Harrison Act). A similar trend was witnessed in the US in terms of heroin until the early 1990s.

2 For an analysis of how attitudes, social norms, and lifestyle factors affect drug use see Pacula et al (2001) and Bachman, Johnston, and O'Malley (1998).

3 For a detailed analysis of each of the mechanisms, which are beyond the scope of this book, see MacCoun and Reuter (2001a).

4 Unlike liberalization policies adopted within the US since 2012, states during the 1970s left the supply of cannabis to the illicit market.

5 Since not all states reclassified marijuana possession as a noncriminal offense (for example, two states still considered possession as a misdemeanour and several others reduced penalties only for first offenders), in this book we refer to the policies adopted by the so-called decriminalization states as 'depenalization'.

6 In addition to (i) the legal status of drugs broadly reviewed in this chapter, marijuana demand studies have also focused on other alternative determinants of prevalence, including (ii) marijuana monetary prices; (iii) penalties; (iv) enforcement risks; and (v) changes in the monetary price of related goods such as alcohol, tobacco, or other illicit drugs like cocaine (see Gallet 2014; Pacula and Lundberg 2014; Davis, Geisler, and Nichols 2016). Except for the impacts of law enforcement and the monetary price of marijuana, which are partially addressed in this section, a complete review of this literature is beyond the scope of the chapter.

7 The price elasticity of drug demand shows how consumption changes in percentage terms as a consequence of a 1 per cent variation in its price, holding all other factors constant. While an absolute value less than 1 (between 0 and 0.99) is generally considered to be 'inelastic', an absolute value greater than 1 is commonly considered to be 'elastic' (Pacula and Lundberg 2014).

8 For a more recent summary of the literature on the price elasticity of marijuana demand, see Grossman (2005); Pacula and Lundberg (2014); Gallet (2014); and Davis, Geisler, and Nichols (2016).

9 The study conducted by Gallet (2014) incorporates estimates from countries other than the US.

[10] Since 1996, the authority that allows (or not) the settlement of coffee shops in their area resides in local governments. The number and nature of coffee shops is also regulated locally (van het Loo et al 2003).

[11] The revised Opium Act of 1976, the basis of the current drug legislation in the Netherlands, amended the original Opium Act of 1928. The new scheme distinguished between hard and soft drugs, hoping to separate the small-scale selling of cannabis from the markets of other psychoactive substances such as cocaine and heroin (van Laar and Ooyen-Houben 2009). According to the act and its amendments, drug consumption does not constitute a crime in legal terms, although it can be prohibited at the local level. On the other hand, trafficking, cultivation, production, dealing, and possession of drugs are defined as criminal acts (EMCDDA 2017). Nevertheless, the possession of up to 30 grams of cannabis (reduced to 5 grams in 1995) is considered a petty crime or misdemeanour not subject to targeted police investigation (Korf 2002). As MacCoun and Reuter (2001a) point out, however, what makes the Dutch drug policy truly distinct is not its written laws but rather the guidelines developed by the Public Prosecutions Department for the referred act's enforcement. The approval of different guidelines between 1976 and 1986, stipulating that the owners of coffee shops could avoid prosecution by complying with several rules, illustrates the Dutch control regime's complexity.

[12] The Dutch policy has been labelled in different ways, including 'depenalization' (for example, Stevens 2011; Hall 2020), 'decriminalization' (for example, Mares 2002; Korf 2002) and 'de facto legalization' (for example, MacCoun and Reuter 1997; Room et al 2010). Given that the possession of cannabis remains a criminal offence, here we refer to the drug policy of the Netherlands as depenalization.

[13] MacCoun (2011) refers to the Dutch regime as de facto legalization.

[14] 'Formal cautioning' is another drug policy alternative embraced by different jurisdictions in Australia. This scheme has been adopted by governments that reject strict prohibition but are not willing to change the cannabis law to the extent to label it as 'soft on drugs' (Lenton et al 1999b). Since there are no evaluations of the impacts of formal cautioning on rates of cannabis use, this policy alternative is not considered here.

[15] Although the schemes in every jurisdiction differ in terms of the specific offences, the amount of the fines imposed, the consequences of failing to pay, and other procedural factors, in all cases a criminal conviction is not recorded for possession and cultivation of small quantities of cannabis for personal consumption if the fine is paid within the prescribed period (Lenton et al 1999b). In South Australia, for example, the possession of cannabis for personal consumption has ceased to be a criminal offence. Instead, users who are caught with up to 100 grams of cannabis or 20 grams of cannabis resin receive an expiation notice (Donnelly et al 2000).

[16] For the impacts of medical cannabis legalization, see Wall et al (2011); Harper, Strumpf, and Kaufman (2012); Lynne-Landsman, Livingston, and Wagenaar (2013); Choo et al (2014); Chu (2014); Anderson, Hansen, and Rees (2015); Hasin et al (2015); Pacula et al (2015); Wen, Hockenberry, and Cummings (2015); Keyes et al (2016); Martins et al (2016); Stolzenberg, D'Alessio, and Dariano (2016); Wall et al (2016); Hasin et al (2017); Johnson et al (2017); Pacula and Smart (2017); Williams (2017); Cerdá et al (2018); Johnson et al (2018); Leung et al (2018); Sarvet et al (2018); Coley et al (2019); Mauro et al (2019).

[17] Although Gunadi, Zhu, and Shi (2022) do not focus on the overall prevalence of cannabis use, their findings are not consistent with this first group of scholars. By contrast, Gunadi, Zhu, and Shi (2022) show that among the youth there are greater odds of transition from nonusers to users in states that have legalized the recreational use of cannabis compared to nonlegalizing states.

18 In addition to Washington State, Hunt and Pacula (2017) also evaluate the impacts of the legalization of the recreational use of cannabis in Colorado.

19 The potency of cannabis is commonly measured by the concentration of the psychoactive chemical tetrahydrocannabinol (THC).

20 Unlike the drug policy reforms conducted in the US during the 1970s, which were highly heterogeneous in nature, in this case the reclassification of the possession of small amounts of cannabis as a civil offense meets the general features of decriminalization.

21 These states went from imposing a fine and possible jail time, probation, and eventual sealing of criminal records to reducing the penalty for possession for first and subsequent offenses to small fines.

22 Following the three types of controlled substances implemented by the 1971 Misuse of Drugs Act, marijuana was reclassified from a Class B to a Class C drug in 2004, thereby lessening criminal penalties for personal use and possession. However, different acts and protocols approved in a relatively short period of time eliminated and reinstated the de-penalizing element of the British drug control regime after the 2004 reclassification, creating confusion among the public and law enforcement agencies. During the same year, England and Wales also introduced warnings in place of arrests for cannabis possession. In 2009, the government again reclassified cannabis as a Class B drug (May et al 2007; Reuter and Stevens 2007; Room et al 2010; Stevens 2011).

23 In 1975, Italy decriminalized the possession and personal use of small quantities of drugs, reversing the spirit of the 1954 Drug Act. A consolidated law encompassing prior legislation redefined citizens as criminal offenders in 1990, although a system of graduated penalties was implemented for users. After a national referendum was approved in 1993, the country eliminated the article that criminalized the use of drugs from the 1990 Drug Act, but it retained administrative sanctions such as fines or the suspension of driver licenses. Since the implementation of Law 79 enacted in 2014, a distinction between less and more dangerous drugs emerged with administrative sanctions for personal possession offenses of up to 12 months' loss of privilege. However, administrative sanctions are not usually applied if an individual is found in possession of illicit drugs for the first time, as offenders receive a warning from the local prefect. The offender can also opt for treatment or rehabilitation, thereby leading to the suspension of proceedings (MacCoun and Reuter 2001a; EMCDDA 2019).

24 In 1983, Spain excluded the possession of drugs for personal consumption from the penal code's list of criminal offenses, formally decriminalizing the use of illicit drugs. These amendments were consistent with prior rulings of the supreme court. Nevertheless, the 1992 Public Security Act, known as 'Corcuera's Law', established administrative penalties (fines) for drug use in public places, even though proceedings could be suspended if the offender agreed to start treatment for drug dependence (Gamella and Jiménez Rodrigo 2004).

25 After the fall of the communist regime, the Czech Republic amended the criminal code in 1990. Under the new scheme, the possession of drugs and psychotropic substances ceased to be a criminal offence. This situation persisted until 1998, when the country reformed the criminal code, again introducing criminal penalties for drug possession but only if the quantity was 'greater than small'. Since no further criteria were provided for determining the quantity of drugs, the interpretation was left to judicial practice (Mravčík 2015).

26 Canada legalized the possession and recreational use of cannabis on 17 October 2018. The Cannabis Act (Bill C-45), which also controls the sale, production, and distribution of the drug, substituted the 1996 Controlled Drugs and Substances Act. Notwithstanding the nationwide scope of the new legislation, each province and territory also has its own rules for cannabis, including prerogatives in terms of legal minimum age, where adults

may buy it, where adults may use it, and how much adults may possess (Fischer, Russell, and Boyd 2020; Government of Canada 2021).

Chapter 2

1 As Babor and colleagues (2010) point out, naloxone can counter the negative effects of heroin use and can be administered in cases of overdose to prevent death.

2 The United Nations Drug Control Programme was replaced by UNODC in 1997.

3 Since 1993, the burden of disease has been calculated using the disability-adjusted life year (DALY). This measure expresses the number of years lost due to ill health, disability, or early death (World Health Organization 2008).

4 Global Burden of Disease (GBD) classifies risks in a hierarchy containing four levels. Level 3 risks include specific risks such as particulate matter pollution and child growth failure. In some cases, these Level 3 risks are the most detailed classification (GBD 2019).

5 Hall et al (2019) maintain that a very small number of deaths from cardiovascular disease and stroke, and a hyperemesis syndrome, have been attributed to sustained, heavy use of cannabis. A minority of users also experience unpleasant psychological effects, including severe anxiety, palpitations, and psychotic symptoms (Hall 2020). Other harms of marijuana consumption can affect third parties (for example, road accident).

6 According to van Laar and colleagues (2020), the number of patients admitted to hospitals with a problem related to cannabis grew from 1,190 to 1,660 between 2015 and 2018, although the younger population seems to be less affected because the average age of patients increased from 36 to 38. Similarly, the demand for treatment in general hospitals for cocaine and opiates increased from 1,040 to 1,290 and from 880 to 980, respectively. Van Laar and colleagues (2020) also report a rise in registered drug-related deaths as well as an increase in the number of cases of HIV and hepatitis B and C among people who use injecting drugs. Despite the upward trend, the number of newly diagnosed HIV cases among people who use injecting drugs per million inhabitants is one of the lowest in Europe.

7 The policy established that those found in possession of small quantities of cannabis for personal use had their drugs confiscated, but instead of being arrested they were given a warning.

8 Discussing the general effects of drugs, Measham and South (2012) note that tranquilizers and heroin have a depressant effect on the nervous system, whereas amphetamines and cocaine are stimulants. LSD and magic mushrooms, on the other hand, distort perceptions. Likewise, some drugs straddle these categories: For instance, cannabis, a depressant drug, and ecstasy, a stimulant drug, both have mild hallucinogenic properties. However, they also point out that actual behaviour and subjective experiences are strongly affected by other factors such as culture, context, and expectations, as well as drug strength, route of ingestion, and relative purity.

9 See, for example, Keppler and Freisthler (2012); Morris et al (2014); Freisthler et al (2016); Huber III, Newman, and LaFave (2016); Shepard and Blackley (2016); Chang and Jacobson (2017); Contreras (2017); Freisthler et al (2017); Chu and Townsend (2019); Gavrilova, Kamada, and Zoutman (2019).

10 Dills, Goffard, and Miron (2017) include decriminalization (here referred to as depenalization) of medical and recreational cannabis laws within the group of liberalization policies.

11 In their article, Maier, Manes, and Koppenhofer (2017) refer to this policy reform as 'decriminalization'.

12 In this regard, Caulkins, Kilmer, and Kleiman (2016) note that analyses of the association between crime and drug liberalization policies should incorporate data from control states that did not legalize.

13 Broadly speaking, Cohen and Felson (1979) claim that the dispersion of activities away from households and families increases the opportunity for crime. Specifically, the convergence in time and space of suitable targets and the absence of capable guardians are likely to favour criminal behaviour. Their approach, in other words, focuses on the circumstances of predatory criminal acts rather than on the offender and their inclinations.

14 Kelling and Wilson (1982) state that crime prospers in response to visible signs of disorder. Thus, urban environments characterized by vandalism, public drinking, loitering, and broken windows encourage crime.

Chapter 3

1 Although cannabis herbal resin is almost unknown in the US, to be consistent with the rest of the chapters we will refer to marijuana as cannabis.

2 According to McAllister (2000), the US' attitude changed during the negotiations of the 1971 Convention on Psychotropic Substances. Unlike the Single Convention, where the US led the 'strict control' coalition, Washington's delegation in Vienna was instructed to secure a 'reasonable' treaty rather than severe provisions against psychotropic substances.

3 South Dakota repealed its new law almost immediately.

4 Other legal and policy restrictions include US Code Title 10, the Mansfield Amendment, fiscal constraints, the Anti-Drug Abuse Act, and the human rights statutes of the Foreign Assistance Act of 1961.

5 The Anti-Drug Abuse Act created two tiers of mandatory prison terms based on the quantity and type of drug involved in the offense, allocating longer prison sentences for offenses involving crack cocaine than those involving the same amount of powder cocaine. Since the latter substance was often used by white Americans, whereas the former was commonly used by black Americans, the act was criticized for having racist ramifications.

6 Perhaps two of the most ambitious policy reforms proposed by Clinton were his support to the proposal to merge the DEA with the Federal Bureau of Investigation and his attempt to downsize the Office of National Drug Control Policy (ONDCP).

7 This provision increased prison sentences up to life imprisonment for a third violent felony.

8 The power to grant pardons and commutations is established in the US Constitution as one of the president's unilateral prerogatives.

9 Issued on 29 August 2013, the memorandum outlined by Deputy Attorney General James Cole was sent to all US attorneys, stating that given its limited resources, the Department of Justice would not enforce federal cannabis prohibition in states that legalized the psychoactive substance in some form.

10 The Control Substances Act was enacted as Title II of the Comprehensive Drug Abuse Prevention and Control Act of 1970.

11 Proceedings to add, delete, or change the schedule may be initiated by the DEA, the Department of Health and Human Services, or by petition from any interested party.

12 Special courts for drug offenders that mixed punishment with treatment were first introduced in Miami, Florida, mainly due to the efforts of Janet Reno while serving as a state attorney.

13 The National Survey on Drug Use and Health (NSDUH) is a face-to-face household interview survey conducted in two phases: a screening phase and an interview phase. The interviewer conducts a screening of the sampled household with an adult resident (aged 18 or older) in order to determine whether zero, one, or two residents aged 12 or older should be selected for the interview. NSDUH collects data using audio computer-assisted self-interviewing in which respondents read or listen to the questions on headphones, then enter their answers directly into a NSDUH laptop computer. NSDUH also uses

computer-assisted personal interviewing in which interviewers read less sensitive questions to respondents and enter the respondents' answers into a NSDUH laptop computer.

14 Illicit drug use includes any use of cannabis, cocaine (including crack), heroin, hallucinogens, inhalants, or methamphetamine, as well as misuse of prescription stimulants, tranquilizers or sedatives (including benzodiazepines), or pain relievers.

15 NSDUH includes crack cocaine under the same category.

16 Hallucinogens include LSD, PCP, peyote, mescaline, psilocybin mushrooms, ecstasy (MDMA or Molly), ketamine, DMT/AMT/Foxy, and *Salvia divinorum*.

17 The NSDUH reports information collected during the past year.

18 The downward trend witnessed in the 1980s was not completely reflected in the LTP among the older clusters because those aged 26 or older were already users in their teens and 20s during the late 1970s (SAMHSA 1990).

19 NSDUH obtains illicit drug use information for the use of cannabis, cocaine (including crack), heroin, hallucinogens, inhalants, and methamphetamine, as well as for the misuse of prescription stimulants, the misuse of tranquilizers or sedatives, and the misuse of pain relievers.

20 Information about LSD was first reported in 1994. The same applies to LMP.

21 Recent initiates were defined as substance users or prescription drug misusers who reported first using or misusing, respectively, a particular substance in the prior 12 months.

22 Within Customs and Border Protection (CBP), the Office of Field Operations (OFO) is responsible for the ports of entry – where most of the illicit drugs seizures by the OFO happen. Furthermore, the Border Patrol is in charge of confiscations across the land borders with Mexico and Canada, as well as the coastal waters surrounding Florida and Puerto Rico. Similarly, CBP's Office of Air and Marine Operations patrols and interdicts illicit drugs in the maritime and air domains as well as beyond the border (Congressional Research Service 2019).

23 Figures are originally presented in pounds.

24 As ONCDP (2012) notes, prices for bulk purchases differ from prices for pure purchases. In practical terms, this means that if a street-level buyer pays US$50 for a gram of cocaine that is 50 per cent pure, the value per pure gram would be US$100. This distinction is essential because nominal (that is, street-level) prices tend to remain unchanged as the purity of cocaine increases and decreases, meaning that there are no large trends in bulk prices. Therefore, price per pure gram is often considered a more meaningful metric because it reflects what buyers pay for their purchase provided that pure grams are the commodity that ultimately interest them.

25 ONDCP measures purchases of 10 grams or less.

26 The National Household Survey on Drug Abuse – or NSDUH after 2002 – included a series of questions to assess dependence on and abuse of substances only in the early 2000s (SAMHSA 2002, 57).

27 The estimates include respondents who use alcohol and illicit drugs.

28 This figure is different from the number of people with SUD who received treatment.

29 The prohibition entered into force in 1988, when Congress banned the use of federal funds for needle and syringe exchange programs through Section 300ee-5 of the Public Health and Welfare Act. This legal mechanism was complemented with other legislation over the years.

30 Following the NCHS criteria, deaths are classified using the International Classification of Diseases, 10th revision. Thus, drug-poisoning (overdose) deaths are identified using underlying cause-of-death codes X40–X44, X60–X64, X85, and Y10–Y14.

31 The figures are age adjusted.

32 Data are collected through personal interviews with a nationally representative sample of inmates in state prisons. The survey utilizes a two-stage sample design in which prisons are selected in the first stage and inmates within prisons are selected in the second stage.

33 To this day, the Survey of Prison Inmates (the full report) has not yet been made available for public use.

34 According to the BJS, 'jail' is a confinement facility that is usually administered by a local law enforcement agency and is intended for adults but sometimes holds juveniles for confinement before or after adjudication, whereas 'prison' refers to a long-term confinement facility that is run by a state or the federal government and typically holds felons and offenders with sentences of more than one year.

Chapter 4

1 Although Argentina did not sign to be part of the International Opium Convention of 1912 at the time, the government sent a representative to the meetings. On 17 October of the same year, the country became a signatory of the Protocol of the Powers not represented at the Opium Conference.

2 The project was introduced by Congressman José Peco.

3 Between 1955 and 1983, Argentina underwent four military coups, alternating civilian governments with military juntas. None of the four democratically elected presidents (Frondizi, Illia, Cámpora, and Perón) since 1955 completed their terms due to military coups.

4 In the general elections of 1973, the Peronist Héctor J. Cámpora was elected president. The elections were organized by the Lanusse dictatorship. After 49 days, Cámpora resigned although he facilitated the first presidential elections without proscriptions since 1955. This time, the Perón-Perón formula won, but another military coup ended Argentina's democratic rule in 1976.

5 Unlike previous legal frameworks in the country, it regulated illegal drugs in a single law outside the Penal Code.

6 The Argentine Anticommunist Alliance, or Triple A, was a far-right death squad created in 1973 commonly associated with the Peronist right and aimed at fighting leftist organizations.

7 The case of Ariel Colavini reached the Supreme Court after he was arrested with two marijuana cigarettes.

8 Gustavo Bazterrica is an Argentine musician, composer, and guitarist. He has been part of bands of great importance in the history of Argentine rock such as *La Máquina de Hacer Pájaros*, led by Charly Garcia; La *Banda Spinetta*, led by Luis Alberto Spinetta; and *Los Abuelos de la Nada*, led by Miguel Abuelo. In 1981, Bazterrica was arrested for having three marijuana cigarettes.

9 The exact word that appeared in the project was *desincriminación*.

10 Similar initiatives were introduced by Jorge Solana from the *Movimiento Popular Neuquino* (Popular Movement from Neuquén) and by Alberto Rodríguez Saá and Vicente Saadi from the Peronist party.

11 Despite the law being enacted during the Menem administration, most of the legislative work and debate took place during the government of Alfonsín.

12 After the implementation of Law 23737, the demand for treatment by court referral rapidly increased. This process was accompanied by state financing through a scholarship system and mandatory coverage by state-run health insurance and prepaid medicine (Touzé 2006).

13 The organization was managed by Alberto Lestelle, who openly asserted and proposed to the government that capital punishment should be considered for drug traffickers (CELS 1994). Other secretaries under the Menem administration were Gustavo Green (1995–1996), Julio César Aráoz (1996–1998), and Eduardo Amadeo (1998–1999).

[14] Ernesto A. Montalvo was arrested for alleged monetary theft. However, law enforcement officers found that upon arriving at the police station and getting out of the car, he threw away a bag containing 2.7 grams of cannabis. Despite the event taking place in 1986, the Supreme Court heard the case after the adoption of the new drug law.

[15] Argentina's economic depression began in the third quarter of 1998. Yet the atmosphere worsened dramatically when the government adopted the so-called *corralito* in December 2001, a provision that restricted cash withdrawals from banks. The economic decision resulted in riots and the resignation of President Fernando De la Rúa.

[16] The project presented by Anibal Fernández was the result of the work developed by the Coordinating Commission of Public Policy on the Prevention and Control of Drug Trafficking, Organised Crime, and Corruption led by Mónica Cuñaro.

[17] Various *ad hoc* initiatives promoted by the executive power have partially circumvented the main provisions of the National Defence and Internal Security laws, respectively, allowing the armed forces to participate in domestic security operations. Examples of these initiatives include *Operativo Escudo Norte* and *Fortin II.*

[18] The courts of the City of Buenos Aires, which was considered a national territory before the 1995 constitutional reform, are known as 'national courts'.

[19] Figures are expressed in million Argentine pesos.

[20] Law 11.343/2006 typifies the crime of illegal drug possession for personal consumption under Article 28, without requiring a prison sentence. Instead, the penalties provided include a warning about the effects of drugs, community service, and/or attendance of an educational program. Anyone who grows small quantities of a substance that can cause physical or mental dependence is subject to the same sanctions (Lei 11.343).

[21] The epidemiological studies on the consumption of psychoactive substances in Argentina do not present the necessary continuity. Coverage between the periods 1999–2004 and 2010–2017 is not available. This creates some discontinuity when analyzing trends (SEDRONAR 2017a).

[22] For this analysis and to assess the impact, we compare the data in 2006 and 2017 since we consider 2010 (a year after depenalization) too close to make a clear assessment of consumption patterns by group age.

[23] The National Study of 2008 did not include an assessment of prevalence by age group per a particular drug.

[24] The data are based on the last-year information reported to CICAD by each country.

[25] Drug checking services are initiatives intended to provide information about ingredients and doses of the samples submitted by nightlife attendees. They are conducted either on-site or in stationary testing facilities. Results are often published online in order to prevent severe intoxication (Betzler et al 2021).

[26] Drug consumption rooms are facilities where drugs can be used under the supervision of trained staff in order to reduce the adverse effects of psychoactive substances (EMCDDA 2019d).

[27] The Argentinian Observatory of Drugs (OAD) utilizes the Indicator of Mortality Related to Drug Use to estimate the annual number of deaths that can be directly or indirectly related to the consumption of psychoactive substances in a certain territory. The calculation of direct mortality includes deaths completely attributable to substance use (that is, accidental, intentionally self-inflicted poisoning also known as overdose). The estimation of indirect mortality contemplates deaths only partially attributable to drug use (that is, pneumonia, infectious disease) (OAD 2021).

[28] The rate per 100,000 was calculated by the authors with number of deaths per year (SEDRONAR) and total population per year (World Bank).

[29] According to the director of Criminal Policy of Argentina, Hernan Olaeta, the breakdown of data related to the violation of Law 23.373 started to be considered in 2014. The category 'violations of Law 23.737' was increasing in numbers, but the data did not convey much since it was generic. It took a couple of years to create a better research design and get cleaner data on the different categories to be studied closer. The National Statistical System on the Execution of the Sentence (SNEEP) has disaggregated the data since 2016 into four categories: possession, commercialization, traffic, and other. For our analysis, we use the SNIC reports since the data are further disaggregated into 10 categories.

[30] The European Monitoring Center for Drugs and Drug Addiction (2012, 3) defines drug mules as 'a drug courier who is paid, coerced or tricked into transporting drugs across an international border but who has no further commercial interest in the drugs'.

[31] Adding those housed in police stations and other spaces designated to withhold people who have committed an infraction, the number reaches a total of 103,209 people imprisoned throughout the national territory.

[32] Under this structure, it has been difficult to compile data from both levels and different entities that are methodologically compatible (SNEEP 2018).

[33] It is important to point out that the distribution of crimes charged within the prison population is not comparable to the distribution of the general statistics on crime registered by the police across the country, where the number of homicides and violations of Law 23.737 show lower rates in relation to the rest of the crimes (SNEEP 2018).

Chapter 5

[1] Only France and Switzerland had already adopted a republican regime before 1910.

[2] The First Portuguese Republic marked the end of the period known as Portugal's constitutional monarchy. It lasted from the 1910 revolution to the *coup d'état* of 28 May 1926, that instituted the National Dictatorship.

[3] António de Oliveira Salazar reframed the National Dictatorship as the *Estado Novo* in 1933. Portugal's dictatorship, although Salazar's illness forced him out of office in 1968, lasted until the Carnation Revolution in 1974.

[4] Between the Carnation Revolution of April 1974 and the enactment of the Portuguese Constitution in April 1976, Portugal experienced a turbulent period before the final transition to democracy. This two-year process included, among other things, failed *coup d'états* against the country's governing bodies.

[5] Cavaco Silva, the leader of the *Partido Social Democrata* (PSD), was the Prime Minister of Portugal for 10 years – the longest tenure since António de Oliveira Salazar. During his government, the PSD shifted to the right, instituting major economic liberalization policies while also leading Portugal into the European Union.

[6] The *Partido Socialista* is a centre-left political party. It and the PSD represent the two major political parties in Portugal. Led by António Guterres, in 1995 the *Partido Socialista* won a general election for the first time in 12 years.

[7] The Constitutional Court is an independent institution whose main task is to review the constitutionality of the newly approved laws. Endowed with significant competences, the Constitutional Court has authority over all Portuguese jurisdictions.

[8] Ten days of use equals one gram of heroin, ecstasy, or amphetamine; two grams of cocaine; and 25 grams of cannabis.

[9] The National Republican Guard is the national gendarmerie force, subject to military law. The Public Security Police, on the other hand, is a civilian force.

[10] Unlike the 2001, 2007, and 2012 reports, which focused on the population between 15 and 64 years old, the 2016/2017 study contemplated the population aged 15 to 74 years old. This situation may condition the accuracy of the comparison.

11 The Health Behaviour in School-aged Children is a collaborative cross-national study of the World Health Organization (WHO) that provides findings on patterns of health among young people across the WHO European Region and North America.

12 The European School Survey Project on Alcohol and Other Drugs is a project coordinated by the Swedish Council for Information on Alcohol and Other Drugs, with the support of the Council of Europe Pompidou Group.

13 Note that the values corresponding to last-month use for the years 2007 and 2001 consider the population aged 15–34 and not 15–24 like the rest of the observations. This situation may condition the accuracy of the comparison.

14 Since 2001 is the first measurement year, it is not possible to assess the pre-reform trends.

15 Individuals with more than one process within the same year are counted only once. Recidivism, in other words, explains why there are more proceedings than individuals attending dissuasion commissions each year.

16 Similar to cannabis and the rest of the illegal drugs evaluated in this section, the starting year for France and Germany is 2000 and not 2001 as in the case of Portugal.

17 In the case of seizures, SICAD disaggregates cannabis intro 'hashish' and 'marijuana'. While the substance known as hashish refers to cannabis resin, marijuana equates with herbal cannabis.

18 The drugs evaluated are hashish, marijuana, cocaine, and heroin. Unfortunately, there is no information available regarding ecstasy.

19 All psychoactive substances are measured in kilograms, except for ecstasy (tablets).

20 While data for the years 2000, 2001, 2002, 2003, 2004, and 2005 were taken from the 2008 and 2006 reports, the rest of the information was obtained in the 2012 and 2019 reports, respectively. Due to methodological changes in terms of the registration criteria, figures can slightly vary from study to study.

21 Unlike other indicators analyzed in this chapter, data for the years 1999 and 1998 are not available.

22 Following the EMCDDA criteria, 'drug-induced deaths' or 'overdoses' comprise the total number of deaths attributed directly to the use of illegal substances and generally occur shortly after consumption.

23 The Portuguese HIV/AIDS program has changed its reporting strategy, resulting in significant increases in the number of cases diagnosed. These changes, however, are only reflected in the 2009–2019 period, meaning that between 2000 and 2008 there may be several cases unreported.

24 While data for the years 2009–2019 were taken from EMCDDA, which coincides with the 2019 SICAD report, data corresponding to years 2003–2008 and 2000–2002 were obtained from the 2009 and 2006 IDT reports, respectively.

25 This observation applies, in particular, to 'drug-related deaths'. Indeed, before the National Statistics Institute made available and backdated data on 'overdoses' in Portugal, the country relied on drug-related deaths as a primary indicator to measure the number of deaths attributable to drug intoxication (Hughes and Stevens 2012).

26 Since 1999 is the first year for which information is available in Portugal, the analysis of France and Germany starts that year too. Also note that Germany's total overdoses are divided by three to fit the scale.

27 The year 2003 is the earliest recorded by the UNODC.

Chapter 6

1 In 2019, 600 kg of cocaine were seized at a French airport; the illicit shipment came from Uruguay. The same year, 4.5 tons of cocaine were discovered in Hamburg, with an estimated value of €1 billion (US$1.11 billion); this cargo also came from Uruguay (DW 2019).

2 The *Frente Amplio* is a coalition of leftist groups and parties that pushed progressive policies such as the legalization of certain drugs. They won the presidential elections for the first time in 2005.

3 A 'reasonable quantity' is determined by equalling the amount for two days of consumption (Ley 19.172 2014).

4 SENACLAFT works separately from the president's office in Uruguay and is granted technical and research autonomy. In addition, it was also given control of the nonfinancial sector. It replaced the *Secretaría Nacional Antilavado de Activos* (National Anti-Money Laundering Secretariat) (Gub.uy 2021).

5 The clubs have to present an agronomic plan for cultivation and include their security standards. In addition, members must complete three bureaucratic requirements: (i) get approval to run a nonprofit organization exclusively to grow and distribute cannabis among its members; (ii) register with the Ministry of Education and Culture; and (iii) after fulfilling the previous steps, register with the IRCCA (Ley 19.172 2014).

6 About 25 Uruguayan pesos, which is equivalent to US$1 per gram.

7 A contest was organized among local and international companies. Five will be the maximum number of companies in charge of the growth and distribution of cannabis. The chosen companies will be provided with a governmental license. The production should be about 5 to 10 tons of cannabis per year during the initiation stage, and later they will be in charge of growing about 18 to 22 tons per year to meet the projected demand (Walsh and Ramsey 2016).

8 THC is the active principle responsible for psychoactivity and CBD provides the opposite effect.

9 The import and export of cannabis in Uruguay is also an issue that should be further explored. Although some procedures have been discussed among IRCCA and the *Dirección Nacional de Aduanas* (National Customs Office), along with the *Ministerio de Ganadería, Agricultura, y Pesca* (Ministry of Livestock, Agriculture and Fisheries), and the *Ministerio de Salud Pública* (Ministry of Public Health), these conversations involved foreign governments' support. Some regional partners are not in compliance with the unilateral decision of Uruguay to legalize cannabis, therefore, negotiations such as trade of this product, legal in Uruguay and illegal outside its borders, will present some challenges.

10 Law 11.343/2006 typifies the crime of illegal drug possession for personal consumption under Article 28, without requiring a prison sentence. Instead, the penalties provided include a warning about the effects of drugs, community service, or attendance of an educational program. Anyone that grows small quantities of a substance that can cause physical or mental dependence is subject to the same sanctions (Lei 11.343).

11 So far, there have been seven national surveys of drug use conducted in Uruguay. It is not possible, however, to achieve a comparative analysis with the first two studies published in 1994 and 1998, as the methodological approaches and sample characteristics differ. For this reason, in order to guarantee comparability, we included only the last five surveys, which have similar methodology, in our analysis (that is, 2001, 2006, 2011, 2014, 2018).

12 There are important limitations with the data reflecting consumption. For example, the answers provided by the individuals surveyed can be affected by the tabu or stigma of drug consumption. This generates 'black data' since they do not accurately report their consumption habits (Musto and Robaina 2018). The answers to surveys post-legalization might show more transparent responses. This, however, might inflate the rates of users and consumption.

13 As the authors point out, their study represents a period of transition (2014–2018), when access to pharmacies was not yet available (it was available until 2017) (Laqueur et al 2020).

[14] Even though there are more updated data on cannabis prevalence in Uruguay, these figures are used for comparative purposes since CICAD data follow the same methodology to process information for all countries presented in their reports.

[15] The data are based on the last-year information reported to CICAD by each country.

[16] Price data analysis is based on UNODC. Prices are collected in local currency but are recorded in US dollars based on official UN rates. Comparisons between countries and years need to be made with caution since exchange rates might have fluctuated in each country. All price information was converted by the authors to grams, since data are sometimes reflected by kilograms, or other units such as price per 200 milligrams, to make comparison possible.

[17] Traditionally, cannabis potency oscillates between 2 per cent and 7 per cent THC.

[18] Quantities reflect the bulk weight of seizures, with no adjustment for purity or potency. Seizures reported by volume (litres, millilitres, and so on) are converted to kilogram equivalents by assuming a weight of 1 kg per litre. Seizures of amphetamine-type stimulants reported in tablets or similar units are converted using assumed bulk tablet weights between 90 mg and 300 mg, depending on the region and specific drug type, and based on information currently available to UNODC. Further details on conversion factors are given in the methodology section accompanying the World Drug Report (2018).

[19] The National Surveys of 2001 and 2006 did not include a demand for treatment section as part of their reports. For the years with data available, information on drug abuse was only provided divided by gender.

[20] Translated by the authors.

[21] The *Hidrovía del Paraná* waterway connects the main river ports of Brazil, Bolivia, Paraguay, Argentina, and Uruguay. Along 3,400 km, the waterway serves as the main transporting route for agricultural exports of many countries in the region.

[22] In July 2017, the House of Representatives in Uruguay sanctioned Law 19.513, which increases drug trafficking crimes, making them incarcerable, which could have an impact on the decline in the number of violations in 2017.

[23] Drug law violations are considered those that violate Law 14.294 and amendment Laws 17.016, 19.007, and 19.172.

[24] For example, the business ethos of US banks such as Bank of America or Citibank do not allow them to establish relationships or offer their services to partners that sell cannabis or its derivatives, not even domestically. These companies cite the USA PATRIOT Act as a basis for their petition to the Uruguayan pharmacies and any other business involved in the cannabis industry to close their accounts or stop selling or producing the product (Hudak, Ramsey, and Walsh 2018).

References

Abadie A. and Gardeazabal J. (2003). The Economic Costs of Conflict: A Case Study of the Basque Country. *American Economic Review* 93 (1), 114–132.

Abraham MD. (1999). Illicit Drug Use, Urbanization, and Lifestyle in the Netherlands. *Journal of Drug Issues* 29 (3), 565–585.

Aceijas C., Stimson G., Hickman M., and Rhodes T. (2004). Global Overview of Injecting Drug use and HIV Infection among Injecting Drug Users. *AIDS* 18, 2295–2303.

Adda J., McConnell B., and Rasul I. (2014). Crime and the Depenalization of Cannabis Possession: Evidence from a Policing Experiment. *Journal of Political Economy* 122 (5), 1130–1202.

Aebi MF. and Tiago MM. (2020). *Annual Penal Statistics: Prison Populations.* Strasbourg: Council of Europe. https://wp.unil.ch/space/files/2021/02/200405_FinalReport_SPACE_I_2019.pdf, accessed 10 July 2022.

Alaniz R. (2000). *La Década Menemista.* Santa Fe: Universidad Nacional del Litoral.

Alexander BK. (1990). Alternatives to the War on Drugs. *Journal of Drug Issues* 20, 1–27.

Ali R., Christie P., Lenton S., Hawks D., Sutton A., Hall W. et al (1998). *The Social Impacts of the Cannabis Expiation Notice Scheme in South Australia.* Canberra: Department of Health and Family Services.

Allen C. (2007). *Crime, Drugs and Social Theory: A Phenomenological Approach.* Aldershot: Ashgate.

Allen K. (2017). China Public Death Sentences over Drugs Alarm Web Users. *BBC.* https://www.bbc.com/news/world-asia-china-42403250, accessed 10 July 2022.

Amnesty International (2022). Singapore: End Wave of Hangings and Immediately Impose Moratorium on Executions. https://www.amnesty.org/en/latest/news/2022/07/singapore-executions-amnesty-response/, accessed 10 July 2022.

Anderson DM., Hansen B., Rees DI. (2015). Medical Marijuana Laws and Teen Marijuana Use. *American Law and Economics Review* 17, 495–528.

Anderson DM., Hansen B., Rees DI., and Sabia JJ. (2019). Association of Marijuana Laws with Teen Marijuana Use: New Estimates from the Youth Risk Behavior Surveys. *JAMA Pediatrics* 173 (9), 879–881.

Andreas P. and Nadelmann E. (2006). *Policing the Globe: Criminalization and Crime Control in International Relations*. Oxford: Oxford University Press.

ARQ Report (2018). Expert Working Group on Improving Drug Statistics and Strengthening the Annual Report Questionnaire. UNODC. https://www.unodc.org/documents/data-andanalysis/statistics/Drugs/Background_paper_session_II_ARQ_Technical_assessment.pdf, accessed 13 November 2023.

Arredondo J., Strathdee SA., Cepeda J., Abramovitz D., Artamonova I., Clairgue E. et al (2017). Measuring Improvement in Knowledge of Drug Policy Reforms Following a Police Education Program in Tijuana, Mexico. *Harm Reduction* 14, 72.

Asmann P. (2018). 'El Crimen Organizado está detrás del Repunte de Homicidios en Uruguay?' *InSight Crime*. 6 August. https://insightcrime.org/es/noticias/el-crimen-organizado-esta-detras-del-repunte-de-homicidios-en-uruguay/, accessed 25 September 2022.

Astin AW., Green KC., and Korn WS. (1987). *The American Freshman: Twenty-year Trends, 1966–1985*. Los Angeles: Higher Education Research Institute, UCLA.

Auld J., Dorn N., and South N. (1986). Irregular Work, Irregular Pleasures: Heroin in the 1980s. In R. Matthews and J. Young eds, *Confronting Crime*. London: Sage.

Babor T. (2002). The Specialist Field. In G. Edwards ed, *Addiction: Evolution of a Specialist Field*. Oxford: Blackwell Publishing.

Babor T., Caulkins J, Rehm J., Edwards G., Reuter P., Fischer B. et al (2010). *Drug Policy and the Public Good*. New York: Oxford University Press.

Babor T., Morisano D., Noel J., Robaina K., Ward J., and Mitchell A. (2017). Infrastructure and Career Opportunities in Addiction Science: The Emergence of an Interdisciplinary Field. In T. Babor, K. Stenius, R. Pates, M. Miovský, J. O'Reilly, and P. Candon eds, *Publishing Addiction Science: A Guide for the Perplexed*. London: Ubiquity Press.

Bachhuber MA., Saloner B., Cunningham CO., and Barry CL. (2014). Medical Cannabis Laws and Opioid Analgesic Overdose Mortality in the United States, 1999–2010. *JAMA Internal Medicine* 174, 1668–1673.

Bachman JG., Johnston LD, and O'Malley PM. (1998). Explaining Recent Increases in Students' Marijuana Use: Impacts of Perceived Risks and Disapproval, 1976 through 1996. *American Journal of Public Health* 88 (6), 887–892.

Bachman JG., Johnston LD., O'Malley PM., and Humphrey RH. (1988). Explaining the Recent Decline in Marijuana Use among Young Adults: Differentiating the Effects of Perceived Risks, Disapproval, and General Lifestyle Factors. *Journal of Health and Social Behavior* 31, 173–184.

Bagley B. (2012). *Drug Trafficking and Organized Crime in the Americas*. Washington, DC: Woodrow Wilson International Center for Scholars, 1–21.

Bagley B. (2015). Drug-Control Policies in the United States. In B. Bagley and J. Rosen eds, *Drug Trafficking, Organized Crime, and Violence in the Americas Today*. Gainesville: University Press of Florida.

Bagley B. and Tokatlian JG. (2007). Dope and Dogma: Explaining the Failure of U.S.-Latin American Drug Policies. In M. LaRosa and F. Mora eds, *Neighborly Adversaries: Readings in U.S.-Latin American Relations*. New York: Rowman & Little.

Baisotti PA. (2022). Drogas, Narcotráfico y Pandemia en Argentina. *Small Wars Journal*. El Centro. https://smallwarsjournal.com/jrnl/art/drogas-narcotrafico-y-pandemia-en-argentina, accessed 23 May 2022.

Balsa C. (2008). *Inquérito Nacional ao Consumo de Substâncias Psicoactivas na População Geral, Portugal 2007*. Lisboa: IDT.

Barbano R. (2002). Desaparece la Secretaría que Lucha contra la Droga. *Clarín*. https://www.clarin.com/sociedad/desaparece-secretaria-lucha-droga_0_HyYG70SgRKx.html, accessed 8 April 2021.

Barbosa J. (2009). A Emergência da Redução de Danos em Portugal: da 'Clandestinidade' à Legitimação Política. *Toxicodependências* 15 (1), 33–42.

Batalla A., Bhattacharyya S., Yücel M., Fusar-Poli P., Crippa J. A., Nogué S. et al (2013). Structural and Functional Imaging Studies in Chronic Cannabis Users: A Systematic Review of Adolescent and Adult Findings. *PLoS ONE* 8 (2), e55821.

BDS Analytics (2021). Essential Cannabis Insights. September, 1 (4). https://bdsa.com/wp-content/uploads/2021/10/Essential-Cannabis-Insights-Fall-2021-Market-Forecasts-Update-1.pdf, accessed 10 July 2022.

Bean P. (2008). *Drugs and Crime*. Devon: Willan Publishing.

Beccaria C. (1764). *On Crimes and Punishments*. Oxford: Clarendon Press.

Becker G. (1968). Crime and Punishment: An Economic Approach. *Journal of Political Economy* 76 (2), 169–217.

Beckert J. and Dewey M. (2017). The Social Organization of Illegal Markets. In J. Beckert and M. Dewey eds, *The Architecture of Illegal Markets: Towards an Economic Sociology of Illegality in the Economy*. New York: Oxford University Press.

Belackova V., Ritter A., Shanahan M., and Hughes CE. (2017). Assessing the Concordance between Illicit Drug Laws on the Books and Drug Law Enforcement: Comparison of Three States on the Continuum From 'Decriminalised' to 'Punitive'. *International Journal of Drug Policy* 41, 148–157.

Bennett T. and Holloway K. (2005). *Understanding Drugs, Alcohol and Crime*. Maidenhead: Open University Press.

Bennett T. and Holloway K. (2007). *Drug-Crime Connections*. New York: Cambridge University Press.

Bennett T., Holloway K., and Farrington D. (2008). The Statistical Association between Drug Misuse and Crime: A Meta-Analysis. *Aggression and Violent Behavior* 13 (2), 107–118.

Bennett WJ. (1989). A Response to Milton Friedman. *Wall Street Journal*, 19 September.

Bentham J. (1789). *An Introduction to the Principles of Morals and Legislation.* Oxford: Clarendon Press.

Bergman M. (2018). *Illegal Drugs, Drug Trafficking and Violence in Latin America.* New York: Springer.

Bergman M. and Fondevila G. (2021). *Prisons and Crime in Latin America.* Cambridge: Cambridge University Press.

Berriolo R., Osimani ML., Serra M., and Weissenbacher M. (1997). El SIDA y su Asociación con el Uso de Drogas en Uruguay. *Rev Medica* 13, 45–53.

Bertram E., Blachman M., Sharpe K., and Andreas P. (1996). *Drug War Politics: The Price of Denial.* Berkeley: University of California Press.

Best D., Gross S., Vingoe L., Witton J., and Strang J. (2003). *Dangerousness of Drugs. A Guide to the Risks and Harms Associated with Substance Misuse.* London: Department of Health.

Betzler F., Helbig J., Viohl L., Ernst F., Roediger L., Gutwinski S. et al (2021). Drug Checking and Its Potential Impact on Substance Use. *European Addiction Research* 27 (1), 25–32.

Bewley-Taylor D. (2012). *International Drug Control: Consensus Fractured.* New York: Cambridge University Press.

Bewley-Taylor D. and Trace M. (2006). *The International Narcotics Control Board: Watchdog or Guardian of the UN Drug Control Conventions?* London: The Beckley Foundation. https://www.beckleyfoundation.org/resource/the-international-narcotics-control-board-watchdog-or-guardian-of-the-un-drug-control-conventions/, accessed 16 July 2022.

Bhandari S., Jha P., Lisdahl KM., Hillard CJ., and Venkatesan T. (2019). Recent Trends in Cyclic Vomiting Syndrome-Associated Hospitalisations with Liberalisation of Cannabis Use in the State of Colorado. *Internal Medicine Journal* 49, 649–655.

Biswas S. (2021). Drug Abuse and Drug Trafficking: Non-Traditional Security Threats in Post-Soviet Central Asia. *Asian Journal of Legal Education* 8 (2), 247–58.

Blum W. (2003). *Killing Hope. U.S. Military and CIA Interventions Since World War II.* London: Zed Books.

Boiteux L. (2017). Brasil: las Cárceles de la Droga y de la Miseria. *Nueva Sociedad* 268. http://www.nuso.org/articulo/brasil-las-carceles-de-la-droga-y-de-la-miseria/, accessed 4 March 2022.

Boivin R. (2014). Risks, Prices, and Positions: A Social Network Analysis of illegal Drug trafficking in the World-Economy. *International Journal of Drug Policy* 25, 235–243.

Bolton JR. (1979). The Medical Use of Psychotropic Drugs. *The New England Journal of Medicine* 301 (19), 1013–1020.

Boyum D. and Reuter P. (2001). Reflections on Drug Policy and Social Policy. In P. Heymann P. and W. Brownsberger eds, *Drug Addiction and Drug Policy: The Struggle to Control Dependence*. Cambridge: Harvard University Press.

Boyum D. and Reuter P. (2005). *An Analytic Assessment of US Drug Policy*. Washington, DC: American Enterprise Institute.

Braakmann N. and Jones S. (2014). Cannabis Depenalisation, Drug Consumption and Crime - Evidence from the 2004 Cannabis Declassification in the UK. *Social Science and Medicine* 115, 29–37.

Brelis M. (1992). Woman's Conviction Sparks Controversy over Mandatory Term. *Boston Globe*, April 20.

Bretteville-Jensen AL. and Williams J. (2011). Decriminalization and Initiation into Cannabis Use. Working Papers Series 1130, The University of Melbourne.

Brinkman J. and Mok-Lamme D. (2019). Not in my Backyard? Not so Fast. The Effect of Marijuana Legalization on Neighborhood Crime. *Regional Science and Urban Economics* 78, 103460.

Buchanan J. (2004). Missing Links? Problem Drug Use and Social Exclusion. *Probation Journal* 51 (4), 387–397.

Buckley WF. (1996). The War on Drugs is Lost. *National Review*, 34–48.

Budman KB. (1977). *A First Report of the Impact of California's New Marijuana Law (SB95)*. State Office of Narcotics and Drug Abuse, Sacramento, California.

Bureau of Justice Statistics (1994). Fact Sheet: Drug-Related Crime. US Department of Justice, September, 1–5.

Bureau of Justice Statistics (2004). Drug Use and Dependence, State and Federal Prisoners. U.S. Department of Justice, October.

Bureau of Justice Statistics (2007). Homicide Trends in the US. https://bjs.ojp.gov/content/pub/pdf/htius.pdf, accessed 18 December 2019.

Bureau of Justice Statistics (2019). Prisoners in 2017, April. https://www.bjs.gov/index.cfm?ty=pbdetail&iid=6546, accessed 18 December 2019.

Bureau of Justice Statistics (2021). Prisoners in 2020, Statistical Tables. https://bjs.ojp.gov/content/pub/pdf/p20st.pdf, accessed 18 December 2019.

Bureau of Justice Statistics (2022). Key Statistic: Total Correctional Population. https://www.bjs.gov/index.cfm?ty=kfdetail&iid=487, accessed 18 December 2019.

Bush GW. (2002). Remarks on the 2002 National Drug Control Strategy, The East Room. Washington, DC, 12 February. https://2001–2009.state.gov/p/inl/rls/rm/8451.htm, accessed 20 December 2019.

Burkhardt J. and Goemans C. (2019). The Short-Run Effects of Marijuana Dispensary Openings on Local Crime. *The Annals of Regional Science* 63, 163–189.

Burris S., Blankenship KM., Donoghoe M., Sherman S., Vernick JS., Case P. et al (2004). Addressing the 'Risk Environment' for Injection Drug Users: The Mysterious Case of the Missing Cop. *Milbank* Q. 82 (1), 125–156.

Burzaco E. and Berensztein S. (2014). *El Poder Narco: Drogas, Inseguridad y Violencia en la Argentina.* Buenos Aires: Sudamericana.

Cabral T. (2017). The 15th Anniversary of the Portuguese Drug Policy: Its History, its Success and its Future. *Drug Science, Policy and Law* 3 (0), 1–5.

Calcaterra SL., Hopfer CJ., Keniston A., and Hull ML. (2019). Changes in Healthcare Encounter Rates Possibly Related to Cannabis or Alcohol Following Legalization of Recreational Marijuana in a Safety-Net Hospital: An Interrupted Time Series Analysis. *Journal of Addiction Medicine* 13, 201–208.

Calmes J. (2012). Obama Says Legalization Is Not the Answer on Drugs. *The New York Times*, 14 April. https://www.nytimes.com/2012/04/15/world/americas/obama says-legalization-is-not-the-answer-on-drugs.html, accessed 20 December 2019.

Camarotti AC., Kornblit AL. and Di Leo PF. (2010). Experiencias juveniles nocturnas, usos y significados en torno al consumo de alcohol en tres ciudades de Argentina. *Revista de Consumidores Profesionales* 45, 14–15.

Cameron L. and Williams J. (2001) Cannabis, Alcohol and Cigarettes: Substitutes or Complements? *Economic Record* 77, 19–34.

Carpenter T. (2003). *Bad Neighbor Policy: Washington's Futile War on Drugs in Latin America.* New York: Palgrave Macmillan.

Carrier N. and Klantschnig G. (2020). The moral landscape of drugs. *Politique Africaine* 163 (3), 7–22.

Carson EA. (2018). Prisoners in 2016. U.S. Department of Justice. http://www.bjs.gov/content/pub/pdf/p16.pdf, accessed 16 November 2020.

Carter WE. and Mamani M. (1986). *Coca en Bolivia.* La Paz, Bolivia: Librería Editorial Juventud.

Caulkins J. (1995). *Estimating Elasticities of Demand for Cocaine and Heroin with Data from the Drug Use Forecasting System.* Washington, DC: National Institute of Justice, 1–28.

Caulkins J. (1999). Can Supply Factors Suppress Marijuana use by Youth? *Drug Policy Analysis Bulletin* 7, 3–5.

Caulkins J. (2001). Drug Prices and Emergency Department Mentions for Cocaine and Heroin. *American Journal of Public Health* 91, 1446–1448.

Caulkins J. (2007). Price and Purity Analysis for Illicit Drug: Data and Conceptual Issues. *Drug and Alcohol Dependence* 90S, S61–S68.

Caulkins J. (2017). Recognizing and Regulating Cannabis as a Temptation Good. *International Journal of Drug Policy* 42, 50–56.

Caulkins J., Baoa Y., Davenportb S., Fahlia I., Guoa Y., Kinnarda K. et al (2018). Big Data on a Big New Market: Insights from Washington State's Legal Cannabis Market. *International Journal of Drug Policy* 57, 86–94.

Caulkins J., Kilmer B., and Kleiman M. (2016). *Marijuana Legalization: What Everyone Needs to Know*. Oxford: Oxford University Press.

Caulkins J., Kilmer B., Kleiman M., MacCoun R., Midgette G., Oglesby P. et al (2015). *Considering Marijuana Legalization: Insights for Vermont and Other Jurisdictions*. Santa Monica: RAND Corp.

Caulkins J. and Lumibao LM. (2010). *The Average Price of Marijuana*. Working draft, Heinz School, Carnegie Mellon University, Pittsburgh.

Caulkins J. and Reuter P. (1998). What Price Data Tells Us about Drug Markets. *Journal of Drug Issues* 28 (3), 593–612.

Caulkins J. and Reuter P. (2010). How Drug Enforcement Affects Drug Prices. *Crime and Justice* 39 (1), 213–271.

Čecho R., Baška T., Švihrová V., and Hudečková H. (2017). Legislative Norms to Control Cannabis Use in the Light of Its Prevalence in the Czech Republic, Poland, Slovakia, and Hungary. *Central European Journal of Public Health* 25 (4), 261–265.

CELS (1994). Cronologia de hechos referidos de seguridad interior, memoria y terrorismo de Estado y discriminacion de migrantes y pobres urbanos. *Informe Annual 1994*. https://www.cels.org.ar/web/wp-content/uploads/1995/10/IA1994-Cronologia-de-hechos.pdf, accessed 10 November 2020.

Centenera M. (2020) Argentina legaliza el autocultivo de marihuana para uso medicinal. El Pais. 12 November. https://elpais.com/sociedad/2020-11-12/argentina-legaliza-el-autocultivo-de-marihuana-para-uso-medicinal.html, accessed 3 April 2022.

Center for Disease Control and Prevention (2005). HIV/AIDS Surveillance Report 2005, 17.

Center for Disease Control and Prevention (2009). HIV Surveillance Report, 21.

Center for Disease Control and Prevention (2013). HIV Surveillance Report, 2013; 25. http://www.cdc.gov/hiv/library/reports/hiv-surveillance.html, accessed 10 November 2023.

Center for Disease Control and Prevention (2019). Estimated HIV Incidence and Prevalence in the United States, 2010–2016. HIV Surveillance Supplemental Report 2019, 24, No. 1.

Center for Disease Control and Prevention (2020). HIV Surveillance Report 2020, 33.

Center for Disease Control and Prevention (2021). Estimated HIV Incidence and Prevalence in the United States, 2015–2019. HIV Surveillance Supplemental Report 2021, 26, No. 1.

Center for Disease Control and Prevention (2022). Drug Overdose Deaths Remain High. https://www.cdc.gov/drugoverdose/deaths/index.html, accessed 12 January 2020.

Centro de Estudios Legales y Sociales (2018). La Guerra contra el Narcotráfico. http://www.cels.org.ar/drogas/index.html, accessed 12 April 2022.

Cerdá M., Mauro C., Hamilton A., Levy NS., Santaella-Tenorio J., Hasin M. et al (2020). Association Between Recreational Marijuana Legalization in the United States and Changes in Marijuana Use and Cannabis Use Disorder from 2008 to 2016. *JAMA Psychiatry* 77 (2), 165–171.

Cerdá M., Moffitt TE., Meier MH., Harrington H., Houts R., Ramrakha S. et al (2016). Persistent Cannabis Dependence and Alcohol Dependence Represent Risks for Midlife Economic and Social Problems: A Longitudinal Cohort Study. *Clinical Psychological Science* 4 (6), 1028–1046.

Cerdá M., Sarvet AL., Wall M., Feng T., Keyes KM., Galea S. et al (2018). Medical Marijuana Laws and Adolescent Use of Marijuana and other Substances: Alcohol, Cigarettes, Prescription Drugs, and other Illicit Drugs. *Drug and Alcohol Dependence* 183, 62–68.

Cerdá M., Wall M., Feng T., Keyes KM., Sarvet A., Schulenberg J. et al (2017) Association of State Recreational Marijuana Laws with Adolescent Marijuana Use. *JAMA Pediatrics* 171 (2), 142–149.

Červený, J., Chomynová, P., Mravčík, V., and van Ours, JC. (2017). Cannabis Decriminalization and the Age of Onset of Cannabis Use. *International Journal of Drug Policy* 43, 122–129.

Chaiken JM. and Chaiken MR. (1990). Drugs and Predatory Crime. In M. Tonry and JQ. Wilson eds, *Drugs and Crime*. Chicago: University of Chicago Press.

Chaloupka, FJ., Grossman M., and Tauras J. (1998). The Demand for Cocaine and Marijuana by Youth. National Bureau of Economic Research, Working paper no. 6411.

Chaloupka FJ., Pacula RL., Farrelly MC., Johnston L., O'Malley P., and Bray J. (1999). Do Higher Cigarette Prices Encourage Youth to Use Marijuana? National Bureau of Economic Research, Working paper no. 6939.

Chang T. and Jacobson M. (2017). Going to Pot? The Impact of Dispensary Closures on Crime. *Journal of Urban Economics* 100, 120–136.

Chawla S. (2004). Multilateral Drug Control. In M. Vellinga ed, *The Political Economy of the Drug Industry*. Gainesville: University Press of Florida.

Chesney-Lind M. (2002). Imprisoning Women: The Unintended Victims of Mass Imprisonment. In M. Mauer and M. Chesney-Lind eds, *Invisible Punishment: The Collateral Consequences of Mass Imprisonment*. New York: New Press.

Chevigny P. (2003). The Populism of Fear: Politics of Crime in the Americas. *Punishment & Society* 5 (1), 77–96.

Christie P. (1991). *The Effects of Cannabis Legislation in South Australia on Levels of Cannabis Use*. Adelaide: Drug and Alcohol Services Council.

Christie P. and Ali R. (1995). The Operation and Effects of the Cannabis Laws in South Australia. In D. McDonald and L. Atkinson eds, *Social Impacts of the Legislative Options for Cannabis in Australia. Phase 1 Research Report to the National Drug Strategy Committee*. Canberra: Australian Institute of Criminology.

Choo EK., Benz M., Zaller N., Warren O., Rising KL., and McConnell KJ. (2014). The Impact of State Medical Marijuana Legislation on Adolescent Marijuana Use. *Journal of Adolescent Health* 55, 160–166.

Chou R., Ballantyne JC., Fanciullo GJ., Fine PG., and Miaskowski C. (2009). Research Gaps on Use of Opioids for Chronic Noncancer Pain: Findings from a Review of the Evidence for an American Pain Society and American Academy of Pain Medicine Clinical Practice Guideline. *The Journal of Pain* 10, 147–159.

Chu YW. (2014). The Effects of Medical Marijuana Laws on Illegal Marijuana Use. *Journal of Health Economics* 38, 43–61.

Chu YW. and Townsend W. (2019). Joint Culpability: The Effects of Medical Marijuana Laws on Crime. *Journal of Economic Behavior & Organization* 159, 502–525.

Ciccarone D. (2017). Fentanyl in the US Heroin Supply: A Rapidly Changing Risk Environment. *International Journal of Drug Policy* 46, 107–111.

Clements K. and Zhao X. (2009). *Economics and Marijuana: Consumption, Pricing and Legalisation*. New York: Cambridge University Press.

Coffin PO., Galea S., Ahern J., Leon AC., Vlahov D., and Tardiff K. (2003). Opiate, Cocaine and Alcohol Combinations in Accidental Drug Overdose Deaths in New York City, 1990–1998. *Addiction* 98, 739–747.

Cohen LE. and Felson M. (1979). Social Chance and Crime Rate Trends: A Routine Activity Approach. *American Sociological Review* 44 (4), 588–608.

Cohen P. (1995). Cannabis Users in Amsterdam. Presentation held at the national conference on the Urban Soft Drugs Tolerance Policy, Jaarbeurs Conference Center, Utrecht, Wednesday, 7 June 1995. Amsterdam. CEDRO Centrum voor Drugsonderzoek, Universiteit van Amsterdam.

Coley RL., Hawkins SS., Ghiani M., Kruzik C., Baum CF. (2019). A Quasi-Experimental Evaluation of Marijuana Policies and Youth Marijuana Use. *American Journal of Drug and Alcohol Abuse* 45, 292–303.

Collins JJ., Hubbard RLL., and Rachal JV. (1985). Expensive Drug Use and Illegal Income: A Test of Explanatory Hypotheses. *Criminology* 23, 743–764.

Comisión Interamericana para el Control del Abuso de Drogas (2019). Catalogue of Drug Demand Reduction Programs and Projects in Latin America and the Caribbean. WEB Catalog ING Low res (6).

Comisión Nacional para el Control del Narcotráfico y el Abuso de Drogas (1986). *Plan Nacional de Control y Prevención del Uso Indebido de Drogas*. Buenos Aires: CONCONAD.

Congressional Research Service (2019). *Illicit Drug Flows and Seizures in the United States: What Do We [Not] Know?* Washington, DC: Congressional Research Service. https://sgp.fas.org/crs/misc/R45812.pdf, accessed 22 January 2020.

Constitución de la Nación Argentina (1994). Artículo 19. https://pdba.georgetown.edu/Parties/Argentina/Leyes/constitucion.pdf, accessed 22 September 2021.

Contreras C. (2017). A Block-Level Analysis of Medical Marijuana Dispensaries and Crime in the City of Los Angeles. *Justice Quarterly* 34 (6), 1069–1095.

Cooper A. and Smith E. (2011). *Homicide Trends in the United States, 1980–2008*. Washington, DC: Bureau of Justice Statistics. https://bjs.ojp.gov/content/pub/pdf/htus8008.pdf, accessed 10 November 2023.

Corda A. (2011). *Encarcelamientos por Delitos Relacionados con Estupefacientes en Argentina*. Buenos Aires: Intercambios Asociación Civil – Universidad de Buenos Aires.

Corda A. and Rossi D. (2016). History and Changes of the Drug Policy in Argentina. In B. Caiuby Labate, C. Cavnar, and T. Rodrigues eds, *Drug Policies and the Politics of Drugs in the Americas*. New York: Springer.

Corneil T., Kuyper L., Shoveller J., Hogg R., Li K., Spittal P. et al (2006). Unstable Housing, Associated Risk Behaviour, and Increased Risk for HIV Infection among Injection Drug Users. *Health & Place* 12, 79–85.

Correia A. (2022). Interview. 21 December 2022.

Courtwright DT. (2015). Preventing and Treating Narcotic Addiction – A Century of Federal Drug Control. Perspective. *The New England Journal of Medicine* 26, 373, 2095–2097.

Cowan R. (1986). How the Narcs Created Crack. *National Review* 38, 26–31.

Crabtree-Ramirez B., Belaunzaran-Zamudio PF., Cortes CP., Morales M., Sued O., Sierra-Madero J. et al (2020). The HIV Epidemic in Latin America: A Time to Reflect on the History of Success and the Challenges Ahead. *Journal of the International AIDS Society* 23 (3), e25468.

Cruz JM., Boidi MF., and Queirolo R. (2018). The Status of Support for Cannabis Regulation in Uruguay 4 Years after Reform: Evidence from Public Opinion Surveys. *Drug and Alcohol Review* 371, 429–434.

Cumbrera Diaz N. and Rodriguez Blanco E. (2016). *Caracterización de las Personas Privadas de Libertad por Delitos de Drogas, con Enfoque Socio-jurídico del Diferencial por Género en la Aplicación de Justicia Penal*. UNODC. https://www.unodc.org/documents/ropan/RESUMEN_ESTUDIO_DROGAS.pdf, accessed 6 April 2022.

Cunial S. (2018). Políticas Públicas sobre Cuestiones Morales Conflictivas: El Caso de la Despenalización del Consumo de Drogas en Argentina. *Revista Española de Ciencia Política* 47, 123–149.

Custom and Border Protection (2022). Drug Seizure Statistics. https://www.cbp.gov/newsroom/stats/drug-seizure-statistics, accessed 12 January 2020.

Cutrona S. (2017). *Challenging the U.S.-led War on Drugs: Argentina in Comparative Perspective.* New York: Routledge.

Cutrona S. (2018). Violence and Security in Argentina: Major Trends and Policy Responses. In J. Rosen and H. Kassab eds, *Violence in the Americas.* New York: Lexington Books.

Cutrona S. (2019). El Desertor Latino: Cómo la Argentina Rechazó el Modelo Norteamericano de la Guerra Contra las Drogas. *Desarrollo Económico* 58 (226), 395–428.

Cutrona S. (2021). *Drogas, Política y Actores Sociales en la Argentina Democrática.* Buenos Aires: EUDEBA.

Damrongplasit K., Hsiao C., and Zhao X. (2010). Decriminalization and Marijuana Smoking Prevalence: Evidence from Australia. *Journal of Business & Economic Statistics* 28 (3), 344–356.

Darakjy S., Brady J., DiMaggio C., and Li G. (2014). Applying Farr's Law to Project the Drug Overdose Mortality Epidemic in the United States. *Injury Epidemiology* 1 (31), 1–5.

Darke S. (2010). The Toxicology of Homicide offenders and Victims: A Review. *Drug and Alcohol Review* 29, 202–215.

Darke S., Degenhardt L., and Mattick R. (2006). *Mortality Amongst Illicit Drug Users: Epidemiology, Causes, and Intervention.* New York: Cambridge University Press.

Darke S., Kaye S., and Duflou J. (2005). Cocaine-Related Fatalities in New South Wales, Australia 1993–2002. *Drug Alcohol Dependence* 77, 107–114.

Darke S. and Zador D. (1996). Fatal Heroin 'Overdose': A Review. *Addiction* 91, 1765–1772.

Darnell AJ. and Bitney K. (2017). *I-502 Evaluation and Benefit-cost Analysis: Second Required Report.* Olympia: Washington State Institute for Public Policy.

Daugherty A. (2015). Argentina Feeling Impact of Domestic Drug Abuse. *Insight Crime.* 22 July. https://insightcrime.org/news/brief/argentina-feeling-impact-of-domestic-drug-abuse/, accessed 11 April 2022.

Davis JA., Geisler KR., and Nichols MW. (2016). The Price Elasticity of Marijuana Demand: Evidence from Crowd-Sourced Transaction Data. *Empirical Economics* 50, 1171–1192.

Davis JM., Mendelson B., Berkes JJ., Suleta K., Corsi KF., and Booth RE (2016). Public Health Effects of Medical Marijuana Legalization in Colorado. *American Journal of Preventive Medicine* 50, 373–379.

DeAngelo GJ., Gittings RK., and Ross A. (2018). Police Incentives, Policy Spillovers, and the Enforcement of Drug Crimes. *Review of Law and Economics* 14 (1), 1–29.

Decorte T., Lenton S., and Wilkins C. (2020). Introduction. In T. Decorte, S. Lenton, and C. Wilkins eds, *Legalizing Cannabis Experiences, Lessons and Scenarios*. New York: Routledge.

Degenhardt L. and Hall W. (2012). Extent of Illicit Drug Use and Dependence, and their Contribution to the Global Burden of Disease. *Lancet* 379, 55–70.

Degenhardt L., Chiu W., Sampson N., Kessler RC., Anthony JC., Angermeyer M. et al (2008). Toward a Global View of Alcohol, Tobacco, Cannabis, and Cocaine Use: Findings from the WHO World Mental Health Surveys. *PLoS Medicine* 5 (7), e141.

Degenhardt L., Hall W., Warner-Smith M., and Lynskey M. (2004). Illicit Drug Use. In M. Ezzati, A. Lopez, A. Rodgers, and C. Murray eds, *Comparative Quantification of Health Risks: Global and Regional Burden of Disease Attributable to Selected Major Risk Factors*. Geneva: World Health Organization.

Dembo R., Williams L., Wothke W., and Schmeidler J. (1994). The Relationship among Family Problems, Friends' Troubled Behavior, and High Risk Youths' Alcohol/other Drug Use and Delinquent Behavior: A Longitudinal Study. *The International Journal of the Addictions* 29 (11), 1419–1442.

DerGhougassian K. and Cutrona S. (2015). The Drugs-Crime-Prison Nexus: What the U.S. Experience Suggests to Argentina. In J. Rosen and M. Brienen eds, *Prisons in the Americas in the 21st Century: A Human Dumping Ground*. New York: Lexington Books.

DeSimone J. and Farrelly MC. (2003). Price and Enforcement Effects on Cocaine and Marijuana Demand. *Economic Inquiry* 41 (1), 98–115.

Dhaval D. (2006). The Effects of Cocaine and Heroin Price on Drug-related Emergency Department Visits. *Journal of Health Economics* 25 (2), 311–333.

Dilley JA., Richardson SM., Kilmer B., Pacula RL, Segawa MB., and Cerdá M. (2019). Prevalence of Cannabis Use in Youths After Legalization in Washington State. *JAMA Pediatrics* 173, 192–193.

Dills A., Goffard S., and Miron J. (2017). The Effects of Marijuana Liberalizations: Evidence from Monitoring the Future. National Bureau of Economic Research, Working Paper no. 23779.

DiNardo J. (1993). Law Enforcement, the Price of Cocaine, and Cocaine Use. *Mathematical and Computer Modeling* 17(2), 53–64.

DiNardo J. and Lemieux T. (1992). Alcohol, Marijuana, and American Youth: The Unintended Effects of Government Regulation. National Bureau of Economic Research, Working Paper no. 4212.

Di Nicola G. (2020). Violencia: en la Argentina se Denunciaron 1291 Robos por dia durante 2019. *La Nación*. 1 September. https://www.lanacion.com.ar/seguridad/estadisticas-criminales-nid2437894, accessed 4 April 2021.

Dirección Nacional de Política Criminal en Materia de Justicia y Legislación Penal (2018). Buenos Aires: SNEEP. https://www.argentina.gob.ar/sites/default/files/informe_ejecutivo_sneep_2018.pdf, accessed 20 July 2021.

Domosławski A. (2011). Drug Policy in Portugal: The Benefits of Decriminalizing Drug Use. *Open Society Foundations*, 1–53.

Donnelly N., Hall W., and Christie P. (1995). The Effects of Decriminalisation on Cannabis Use in South Australia 1985–1993. *Australian Journal of Public Health* 19, 281–287.

Donnelly N., Hall W., and Christie P. (1999). *The Effects of the CEN Scheme on Levels and Patterns of Cannabis Use in South Australia: Evidence from National Drug Strategy Household Surveys 1985–1995*. Canberra: Commonwealth Department of Health and Family Services.

Donnelly N., Hall W., and Christie P. (2000). The Effects of the Cannabis Expiation Notice Scheme on Levels and Patterns of Cannabis use in South Australia: Evidence from National Drug Strategy Household Surveys 1985–95. *Drug and Alcohol Review* 19 (3), 265–269.

Donnelly N., Oldenburg B., Quine S., Macaskill P., Flaherty B., Spooner C. and Lyle D. (1992). Changes Reported in Drug Prevalence among New South Wales Secondary School Students 1983–1989. *Australian Journal of Public Health* 16 (1), 50–57.

Dorn N. and Jamieson A. (2000). *Room for Manoeuvre. Overview of Comparative Legal Research into National Drug Laws of France, Germany, Italy, Spain, the Netherlands and Sweden and their Relation to three International Drugs Conventions*. London: Drugscope.

Dragone D., Prarolo G., Vanin P., and Zanella G. (2019). Crime and the Legalization of Recreational Marijuana. *Journal of Economic Behavior & Organization* 159, 488–501.

Drug Abuse Council (1974). *Marijuana Survey-State of Oregon*. News releases, Washington, DC, 1974–1977.

Drug Enforcement Administration (2016). *National Drug Threat Assessment 2016*. Washington, DC: US Department of Justice. https://www.dea.gov/sites/default/files/2018-07/DIR-001-17_2016_NDTA_Summary.pdf, accessed 22 January 2020.

Drug Enforcement Administration (2021a). DEA Fact Sheet. https://ehs.unc.edu/files/2015/09/1207_fact-sheet.pdf, accessed 22 January 2020.

Drug Enforcement Administration (2021b). *National Drug Threat Assessment 2020*. Washington, DC: US Department of Justice. https://www.dea.gov/sites/default/files/2021-02/DIR-008-21%202020%20National%20Drug%20Threat%20Assessment_WEB.pdf, accessed 22 January 2020.

Drug Policy Alliance (2015). The Drug War, Mass Incarceration and Race. 1–3 June. https://www.unodc.org/documents/ungass2016/Contributions/Civil/DrugPolicyAlliance/DPA_Fact_Sheet_Drug_War_Mass_Incarceration_and_Race_June2015.pdf, accessed 11 February 2020.

Drug Policy Facts (2022). Drugs and Prisons, Jails, Probation, and Parole. https://www.drugpolicyfacts.org/chapter/drug_prison#, accessed 11 February 2020.

Dui Hua (2020). Death Penalty Reform. https://duihua.org/resources/death-penalty-reform/, accessed 25 July 2022.

DW (2019). Uruguay: The New Global Drug Trafficking Hub. *Made for Minds*, 8 June. https://www.dw.com/en/uruguay-the-new-global-drug-trafficking-hub/a-49922226, accessed 8 March 2019.

Eastwood N. (2020). Cannabis Decriminalization Policies Around the World. In T. Decorte, S. Lenton, and C. Wilkins eds, *Legalizing Cannabis Experiences, Lessons and Scenarios*. New York: Routledge.

Eastwood N., Fox E., and Rosmarin A. (2016). *A Quiet Revolution: Drug Decriminalization across the Globe*. London: Release. https://www.release.org.uk/sites/default/files/pdf/publications/A%20Quiet%20Revolution%20-%20Decriminalisation%20Across%20the%20Globe.pdf, accessed 24 July 2022.

Economic and Social Council (2013). *World Crime Trends and Emerging Issues and Responses in the Field of Crime Prevention and Criminal Justice*. Vienna: United Nations. https://www.unodc.org/documents/data-and-analysis/statistics/crime/World_Crime_Trends_2013.pdf, accessed 22 July 2022.

Edwards G. ed (1991). *Addictions: Personal Influences and Scientific Movements*. New Brunswick: Transaction Publishers.

Edwards G. ed (2002) *Addiction: Evolution of a Specialist Field*. Oxford: Blackwell Publishing.

Edwards G. and Babor T. eds (2012). *Addiction and the Making of Professional Careers*. New York: Routledge.

Egan T. (1999). The War on Drugs Retreats, Still Taking Prisoners. *The New York Times*, 28 February. https://www.nytimes.com/1999/02/28/us/war-on-crack-retreats-still-taking-prisoners.html, accessed 20 July 2020.

El Observador (2022). El Gobierno ve Inviable que Turistas puedan Comprar Marihuana Recreativa en el Corto Plazo. 27 June. https://www.elobservador.com.uy/nota/el-gobierno-ve-inviable-que-turistas-puedan-comprar-marihuana-en-el-corto-plazo-202262620230, accessed 10 July 2022.

Encuesta Nacional de Prevalencia de Consumo de Drogas III (2001). *Programa de Naciones Unidas para el Desarrollo*. Montevideo, Uruguay: Junta Nacional de Drogas.

Encuesta Nacional en Hogares sobre Consumo de Drogas VI (2016). Informe de Investigacion. Observatorio Uruguayo de Drogas. Montevideo, Uruguay: Junta Nacional de Drogas.

Encuesta Nacional en Hogares sobre Consumo de Drogas VII (2018). *Informe de Investigacion. Observatorio Uruguayo de Drogas.* Montevideo, Uruguay: Junta Nacional de Drogas.

Engelsman EL. (1989). Dutch Policy on the Management of Drug-related Problems. *British Journal of Addiction* 84, 211–218.

English D., Holman C., Milne E., Winter M., Hulse G., Codde S. et al (1995). *The Quantification of Drug Caused Morbidity and Mortality in Australia, 1995.* Canberra: Commonwealth Department of Human Services and Health.

En Perspectiva (2016). Antonio Pascale, Toxicólogo: En Uruguay Aumentaron Cuadros Graves Causados por Consumo de Drogas Sintéticas. Entrevista con el toxicólogo Antonio Pascale. 25 April. *En Perspectiva.* https://enperspectiva.uy/ultimos-videos/entrevista-central-lunes-25-de-abril-antonio-pascale/, accessed 24 February 2019.

Epstein E. (1990). *Agency of Fear: Opiates and Political Power in America.* London: Verso.

Estoup AC., Moise-Campbell C., Varman M., and Stewart DG. (2016). The Impact of Marijuana Legalization on Adolescent Use, Consequences, and Perceived Risk. *Substance Use & Misuse* 51, 1881–1887.

European Monitoring Centre for Drugs and Drug Addiction (2003). *The State of the Drugs Problem in the European Union and Norway.* Luxembourg: EMCDDA. https://www.emcdda.europa.eu/system/files/publications/275/ar2003eu69564-en.pdf, accessed 12 August 2022.

European Monitoring Centre for Drugs and Drug Addiction (2010). *Annual Report 2010: The State of the Drugs Problem in Europe.* Luxembourg: Office for Official Publications of the European Communities. http://www.emcdda.europa.eu/system/files/publications/926/EMCDDA_AR2010_EN_242720.pdf, accessed 28 July 2022.

European Monitoring Center for Drugs and Drug Addiction (2012). *A Definition of 'Drug Mules' for use in a European Context.* Lisbon: EMCDDA. https://www.emcdda.europa.eu/attachements.cfm/att_150421_EN_EMCDDA_ThematicPapers_DrugMules.pdf, accessed 20 July 2021.

European Monitoring Centre for Drugs and Drug Addiction (2015). *Mortality Among Drug Users in Europe: New and Old Challenges for Public Health.* Luxemburg: Publications Office of the European Union. https://www.euda.europa.eu/publications/emcdda-papers/mortality-among-drug-users-in-europe_en, accessed 20 July 2021.

European Monitoring Centre for Drugs and Drug Addiction (2017). *Netherlands: Country Drug Report 2017.* Luxembourg: Publications Office of the European Union. https://www.euda.europa.eu/publications/country-drug-reports/2017/netherlands_en, accessed 21 July 2021.

European Monitoring Centre for Drugs and Drug Addiction (2018a). *European Drug Report 2018: Trends and Developments*. Lisbon: EMCDDA. https://www.emcdda.europa.eu/system/files/publications/2748/POD_Preventing%20overdose%20deaths.pdf, accessed 22 May 2020.

European Monitoring Centre for Drugs and Drug Addiction (2018b). *Preventing Overdose Deaths in Europe (Perspectives on Drugs)*. Luxembourg: Publications Office of the European Union. https://www.euda.europa.eu/publications/pods/preventing-overdose-deaths_en, accessed 20 May 2020.

European Monitoring Centre for Drugs and Drug Addiction (2019a). *European Drug Report 2019: Trends and Developments*. Luxembourg: Publications Office of the European Union. http://www.emcdda.europa.eu/publications/edr/trends-developments/2019_en, accessed 26 May 2020.

European Monitoring Centre for Drugs and Drug Addiction (2019b). *Italy, Country Drug Report 2019*. Luxembourg: Publications Office of the European Union. https://www.politicheantidroga.gov.it/media/2549/country-drug-report.pdf, accessed 30 May 2020.

European Monitoring Centre for Drugs and Drug Addiction (2019c). *Portugal: Country Drug Report 2019*. Lisbon: EMCDDA. https://www.emcdda.europa.eu/publications/country-drug-reports/2019/portugal_en, accessed 7 June 2020.

European Monitoring Centre for Drugs and Drug Addiction (2019d). *Drug Consumption Rooms: An Overview of Provision and Evidence*. Lisbon: EMCDDA. https://www.emcdda.europa.eu/system/files/publications/2734/POD_Drug%20consumption%20rooms.pdf, accessed 9 July 2020.

European Monitoring Centre for Drugs and Drug Addiction (2019e). *France: Country Drug Report 2019*. Lisbon: EMCDDA. https://www.emcdda.europa.eu/system/files/publications/11335/france-cdr-2019_0.pdf, accessed 2 June 2020.

European Monitoring Centre for Drugs and Drug Addiction (2019f). *Germany: Country Drug Report 2019*. Lisbon: EMCDDA. https://www.emcdda.europa.eu/system/files/publications/11334/germany-cdr-2019_0.pdf, accessed 2 June 2020.

European Monitoring Centre for Drugs and Drug Addiction (2020). *Statistical Bulletin 2020 – Methods and Definitions for Overdose Deaths*. Lisbon: EMCDDA. https://www.emcdda.europa.eu/data/stats2020/methods/drd_en, accessed 28 December 2020.

European Monitoring Centre for Drugs and Drug Addiction (2021a). Key Epidemiological Indicators. https://www.emcdda.europa.eu/topics/key-indicators_en, accessed 3 August 2022.

European Monitoring Centre for Drugs and Drug Addiction (2021b). Statistical Bulletin 2021. Lisbon: EMCDDA. https://www.emcdda.europa.eu/data/stats2021/drd_en, accessed 30 December 2021.

Everson EM., Dilley JA., Maher JE., and Mack CE. (2019). Post-Legalization Opening of Retail Cannabis Stores and Adult Cannabis use in Washington State, 2009–2016. *American Journal of Public Health* 109, 1294–1301.

Fagan J. (1990). Intoxication and Aggression. *Crime and Justice* 13, 241–320.

Farrelly M., Bray J., Zarkin G., and Wendling B. (2001). The Joint Demand for Cigarettes and Marijuana: Evidence from the National Household Surveys on Drug Abuse. *Journal of Health Economics* 20 (1), 51–68.

Feilding A. (2010). Cannabis and the psychedelics: Reviewing the UN drug conventions. Beckley Foundation. https://www.beckleyfoundation.org/resource/cannabis-and-the-psychedelics-reviewing-the-un-drug-conventions, accessed 3 July 2020.

Félix S. and Portugal P. (2017). Drug Decriminalization and the Price of Illicit Drugs. *International Journal of Drug Policy* 29, 121–129.

Félix S., Portugal P., and Tavares A. (2017). Going After the Addiction, not the Addicted: The Impact of Drug Decriminalization in Portugal. IZA Discussion Paper No. 10895.

Ferreira S. (2017). Portugal's Radical Drugs Policy is Working: Why Hasn't the World Copied it? *The Guardian*, 5 December. https://www.theguardian.com/news/2017/dec/05/portugals-radical-drugs-policy-is-working-why-hasnt-the-world-copied-it, accessed 9 July 2022.

Fetherston J. and Lenton S. (2007). *Effects of the Western Australian Cannabis Infringement Notice Scheme on Public Attitudes, Knowledge and Use: Comparison of Pre- and Post Change Data*. Bentley, Perth: Curtin University of Technology, National Drug Research Institute.

Fischer B., Russell C., and Boyd N. (2020). A Century of Cannabis Control in Canada. A Brief Overview of History, Context and Policy Frameworks from Prohibition to Legalization. In T. Decorte, S. Lenton, and C. Wilkins eds, *Legalizing Cannabis Experiences, Lessons and Scenarios*. New York: Routledge.

Fitzgerald J. (2005). Policing as a Public Health Menace. *International Journal of Drug Policy* 16, 203–206.

Flom H. (2023). The Popularity and Limits of Tough on Crime Policies in Argentina. In J. Rosen and S. Cutrona eds, *Mano Dura Policies in Latin America*. New York: Routledge.

Foster J. (2000). Social Exclusion, Crime and Drugs. *Drugs: Education, Prevention and Policy* 7 (4), 317–330.

Freeman T., van der Pol P., Kuijpers W., Wisselink J., Das RK., Rigter S. et al (2018). Changes in Cannabis Potency and First-Time Admissions to Drug Treatment: A 16-year Study in the Netherlands. *Psychological Medicine* 48, 2346–2352.

Freeman T. and Winstock A. (2015). Examining the Profile of High-Potency Cannabis and its Association with Severity of Cannabis Dependence. *Psychological Medicine* 45, 3181–3189.

Freisthler B., Gaidus A., Tam C., Ponicki WR., and Gruenewald PJ. (2017). From Medical to Recreational Marijuana Sales: Marijuana Outlets and Crime in an Era of Changing Marijuana Legislation. *The Journal of Primary Prevention* 38 (3), 249–263.

Freisthler B., Ponicki WR., Gaidus A., and Gruenewald PJ. (2016). A Micro-Temporal Geospatial Analysis of Medical Marijuana Dispensaries and Crime in Long Beach, California. *Addiction* 111 (6), 1027–1035.

French MT., McGeary KA., Chitwood DD., McCoy CB., Inciardi JA., and McBride D. (2000). Chronic Drug Use and Crime. *Substance Abuse* 21 (2), 95–109.

Full Fact (2012). What Effect has Decriminalising Drugs had in Portugal? 31 January. https://fullfact.org/news/what-effect-has-decriminalising-drugs-had-portugal/, accessed 25 May 2020.

Gabri AC., Galanti MR., Orsini N., and Magnusson C. (2022). Changes in Cannabis Policy and Prevalence of Recreational Cannabis Use among Adolescents and Young Adults in Europe – An Interrupted Time-series Analysis. *PLoS ONE* 17 (1), e0261885.

Galain P. (2018). The Uruguayan Model of Regulating Cannabis – Legal and Geopolitical Questions. *Zeitschrift für die gesamte Strafrechtswissenschaft* 130 (3), 859–908.

Galea S. and Vlahov D. (2002). Social Determinants and the Health of Drug Users: Socioeconomic Status, Homelessness, and Incarceration. *Public Health Reports* 117, 135–45.

Gallet CA. (2014). Can Price get the Monkey off our Back? A Meta-Analysis of Illicit Drug Demand. *Health Economics* 23, 55–68.

Gallo A. (2012). Trade Policy and Protectionism in Argentina. *Economic Affairs* 32 (1), 55–59.

Gamella JF. and Jiménez Rodrigo ML. (2004). A Brief History of Cannabis Policies in Spain (1968–2003). *Journal of Drug Issues*, 34 (3), 623–659.

Gandossy RP., Williams JR., Cohen J., and Harwood HJ. (1980). *Drugs and Crime: A Survey and Analysis of the Literature*. Washington, DC: US Government Printing Office.

Garat G. (2013). Un Siglo de Politicas de Drogas en Uruguay. *Friedrich Ebert Stiftung Uruguay*. Analysis 1. Montevideo, Uruguay.

Garat G. (2016). Uruguay: A Way to Regulate the Cannabis Market. In B. Caiuby Labate, C. Cavnar, and T. Rodrigues eds, *Drug Policies and the Politics of Drugs in the Americas*. New York: Springer.

Garat G. (2017). Cuatro Años de Marihuana Regulada en Uruguay. Aproximación al Monitoreo y Evaluacion. *Friedrich Ebert Stiftung Uruguay*. Montevideo, Uruguay.

Garibotto G. (2010). *Cárceles y Drogas en Uruguay. WOLA Sistemas Sobrecargados. Leyes de Drogas y Cárceles en América Latina*. Washington, DC: Latin American Transnational Institute.

Garland D. (2001). *The Culture of Control: Crime and Social order in Contemporary Society*. Chicago: University of Chicago Press.

Garzón Vergara JC. (2008) *Mafia & Co. The Criminal Networks in Mexico, Brazil and Colombia*. Woodrow Wilson Center, Washington, DC.

Gavrilova E., Kamada T., and Zoutman F. (2019). Is Legal Pot Crippling Mexican Drug Trafficking Organisations? The Effect of Medical Marijuana Laws on US Crime. *The Economic Journal* 129 (617), 375–407.

Gfroerer J. (2018). *War Stories from the Drug Survey: How Culture, Politics, and Statistics Shaped the National Survey on Drug Use and Health*. Cambridge: Cambridge University Press.

Global Burden of Disease Collaborative Network (2019). *Global Burden of Disease Study 2019*. Seattle: Institute for Health Metrics and Evaluation. https://www.healthdata.org/results/gbd_summaries/2019/drug-use-disorders-level-3-cause, accessed 20 October 2023.

Global Commission on Drug Policy (2016). *Advancing Drug Policy Reform: A New Approach to Decriminalization*. Geneva: Global Commission on Drug Policy. www.globalcommissionondrugs.org/reports/advancing-drug-policy-reform/, accessed 22 July 2022.

Goldstein P. (1985). The Drugs/Violence Nexus: A Tripartite Conceptual Framework. *Journal of Drug Issues* 39, 143–174.

Gomes S. and Duarte V. (2018). An Introduction to Female Crime and Delinquency: Portugal in the World. In S. Gomes and V. Duarte eds, *Female Crime and Delinquency in Portugal: In and Out of the Criminal Justice System*. Cham: Palgrave MacMillan.

Gómez RA. (2013). La Legislación penal Argentina sobre Drogas. Una Aproximación Histórica. V Congreso Internacional de Investigación y Práctica Profesional en Psicología XX Jornadas de Investigación Noveno Encuentro de Investigadores en Psicología del MERCOSUR. Facultad de Psicología – Universidad de Buenos Aires, Buenos Aires.

Gonçalves-Pinho M., Bragança M., and Freitas A. (2019). Psychotic Disorders Hospitalizations Associated with Cannabis Abuse or Dependence: A Nationwide Big Data Analysis. *International Journal of Methods in Psychiatric Research* 29, e1813.

Goode E. (1997). *Between Politics and Reason: The Drug Legalization Debate*. New York: St. Martin's Press, Inc.

Goode E. (2012). *Drugs in American Society*. Boston, MA: McGraw-Hill.

Gottfredson M. and Hirschi T (1990). *A General Theory of Crime*. Stanford: Stanford University Press.

Government of Canada (2021). Cannabis in Canada: Get the Facts. https://www.canada.ca/en/services/health/campaigns/cannabis/canadians.html, accessed 23 July 2022.

Graham L. (2015). Legalizing Marijuana in the Shadows of International Law: the Uruguay, Colorado, and Washington Models. *Wisconsin International Law Journal* 33 (1).

Greenwald G. (2009). *Drug Decriminalization in Portugal. Lessons for Creating Fair and Successful Drug Policies*. Washington, DC: Cato Institute, 1–30.

Greer A., Zakimi N., Butler A., and Ferencz S. (2022). Simple Possession as a 'Tool:' Drug Law Enforcement Practices among Police Officers in the Context of Depenalization in British Columbia, Canada. *International Journal of Drug Policy* 99, 103471.

Grogger J. and Willis M. (2000). The Emergence of Crack Cocaine and the Rise in Urban Crime Rates. *Review of Economics and Statistics* 82 (4), 519–529.

Grossman M. (2005). Individual Behaviors and Substance Use: The Role of Price. In B. Lindgren and M. Grossman eds, *Substance Use: Individual Behaviors, Social Interactions, Markets and Politics*. Amsterdam: Elsevier.

Grossman M. and Chaloupka F. (1998). The Demand for Cocaine by Young Adults: A Rational Addiction Approach. *Journal of Health Economics* 17 (4), 427–474.

Grucza RA., Vuolo M., Krauss MJ., Plunk A., Agrawal A., Chaloupka F. et al (2018). Cannabis Decriminalization: A Study of Recent Policy Change in Five US States. *International Journal of Drug Policy* 59, 67–75.

Guagnini L. (2008). Cristina Respaldó la Despenalización del Consumo Personal de Drogas. *Clarín*. 30 July.

Gunadi C., Zhu B, and Shi Y. (2022). Recreational Cannabis Legalization and Transitions in Cannabis Use: Findings from a Nationally Representative Longitudinal Cohort in the United States. *Addiction* 117 (10), 2651–2659.

Gub.uy (2021) Sitio oficial de la Republica Oriental del Uruguay. https://www.gub.uy/, accessed 10 October 2021.

Hagan H. (2001). Public Health and Changes in Illicit Drug Prices. *American Journal of Public Health*, September, 91 (9), 1350.

Hall KE., Monte AA., Chang T., Fox J., Brevik C., Vigil DI et al (2018). Mental Health-Related Emergency Department Visits Associated with Cannabis in Colorado. *Academic Emergency Medicine* 25, 526–537.

Hall W. (2020). The Costs and Benefits of Cannabis Control Policies. *Dialogues in Clinical Neuroscience* 22 (3), 281–287.

Hall W. and Degenhardt L. (2009). Adverse Health Effects of Non-Medical Cannabis Use. *Lancet* 374 (9698), 1383–1391.

Hall W., Degenhardt L., and Lynskey M. (2001). *The Health and Psychological Effects of Cannabis Use*. Monograph Series No. 44. Sidney: National Drug and Alcohol Research Centre, University of New South Wales.

Hall W. and Lynskey M. (2020). Assessing the Public Health Impacts of Legalizing Recreational Cannabis Use: The US Experience. *World Psychiatry* 19, 179–186.

Hall W. and Pacula RL. (2003). *Cannabis Use and Dependence: Public Health and Public Policy*. Cambridge: Cambridge University Press.

Hall W., Patton G., Stockings E., Weier M., Lynskey M., Morley KI. et al (2016). Why Young People's Substance use Matters for Global Health. *Lancet Psychiatry* 3 (3), 265–279.

Hall W., Stjepanović D., Caulkins J., Lynskey M., Leung J., Campbell G. et al (2019). Public Health Implications of Legalising the Production and Sale of Cannabis for Medicinal and Recreational Use. *Lancet* 394, 1580–1590.

Hansen B., Miller K., and Weber C. (2017). *The Taxation of Recreational Marijuana: Evidence from Washington State*. Cambridge: National Bureau of Economic Research.

Hao M. (2022). Punishment You Will Face if You are Involved in Drug Crime in China. *HG Org. Legal Resources*. https://www.hg.org/legal-articles/punishment-you-will-face-if-you-are-involved-in-drug-crime-in-china-33407, accessed 4 September 2022.

Hao Z. and Cowan B. (2020). The Cross-border Spillover Effects of Recreational Marijuana Legalization. *Economic Inquiry* 58 (2), 642–666.

Harm Reduction International (2022). *The Death Penalty for Drug Offences: Global Overview 2021*. London, 1–43. https://www.hri.global/files/2022/03/09/HRI_Global_Overview_2021_Final.pdf, accessed 10 July 2022.

Harper S., Strumpf EC., and Kaufman JS. (2012). Do Medical Marijuana Laws Increase Marijuana Use? Replication Study and Extension. *Annals of Epidemiology* 22, 207–212.

Harrison LD. and Gfroerer J. (1992). The Intersection of Drug Use and Criminal Behavior: Results from the National Household Survey on Drug Abuse. *Crime and Delinquency* 38 (4), 422–443.

Hasin DS., Sarvet AL., Cerdá M., Keyes KM., Stohl M., Galea S. et al (2017). US Adult Illicit Cannabis Use, Cannabis Use Disorder, and Medical Marijuana Laws: 1991–1992 to 2012–2013. *JAMA Psychiatry* 74, 579–588.

Hasin DS., Wall M., Keyes KM., Cerdá M., Schulenberg J., O'Malley P. et al (2015). Medical Marijuana Laws and Adolescent Marijuana use in the USA from 1991 to 2014: Results from Annual, Repeated Cross-sectional Surveys. *Lancet Psychiatry* 2 (7), 601–608.

Hawke L. and Henderson J. (2021). Legalization of Cannabis Use in Canada: Impacts on the Cannabis Use Profiles of Youth Seeking Services for Substance Use. *Journal of Substance Abuse Treatment* 126 (6), 108340.

Hawley P., Gobbo M., and Afghari N. (2020). The Impact of Legalization of Access to Recreational Cannabis on Canadian Medical Users with Cancer. *BMC Health Service Research* 20 (1), 977.

Hazekamp A. (2006). An Evaluation of the Quality of Medicinal Grade Cannabis in the Netherlands. *Cannabinoids* 1, 1–9.

He H., Pan Z., Wu J., Hu C., Bai L., and Lyu J. (2022). Health Effects of Tobacco at the Global, Regional, and National Levels: Results From the 2019 Global Burden of Disease Study. *Nicotine & Tobacco Research* 28 (6), 864–870.

Heather N., Wodak A., Nadelmann E., and O'Hare P. eds (1992). *Psychoactive Drugs and Harm Reduction: From Faith to Science*. London: Whurr Publishers.

Hedegaard H., Miniño AM, and Warner M. (2020). Drug Overdose Deaths in the United States, 1999–2019. NCHS Data Brief No. 394, December. https://www.cdc.gov/nchs/data/databriefs/db394-H.pdf, accessed 3 March 2020.

Heller D. and Galea S. (2020). The Role of Academic Public Health in Reducing Incarceration. *American Journal of Public Health* 110, S16–S17.

Henman AR. (1978). Coca and cocaine: A study of tradition and change in Peru. *Bulletin on Narcotics* 30 (3), 1–11.

Heuberger B. (2017). Despite Claims, Data Shows Legalized Marijuana Has Not Increased Crime Rates. *Colorado Politics*. 22 March. https://www.coloradopolitics.com/news/despite-claims-data-show-legalized-marijuana-has-not-increased-crime-rates/article_64dd25c9-bcb1-5896-8c62-735e953da28a.html, accessed 20 June 2019.

Hetzer H. and Walsh J. (2014). Pioneering Cannabis Regulation in Uruguay. Remaining Drug Policy in the Americas. NACLA Report on the Americas. Summer 47. https://nacla.org/edition/10415, accessed 9 January 2019.

Heyman P. (2001). Introduction: Drug Policy with a New Focus. In P. Heymann and W. Brownsberger eds, *Drug Addiction and Drug Policy: The Struggle to Control Dependence*. Cambridge: Harvard University Press.

Himmelstein J. (1978). Drug Politics Theory. *Journal of Drug Issues* 8 (1), 37–52.

House of Representatives (2009). Assessing US Drug Policy in the Americas. Hearing before the Subcommittee on the Western Hemisphere of the Committee on Foreign Affairs, Serial No. 111–46. Washington, DC: House of Representatives.

Huber III A., Newman R., and LaFave D. (2016). Cannabis Control and Crime: Medicinal use, Depenalization and the War on Drugs. *B.E. Journal of Economic Analysis & Policy* 16 (4).

Hudak J., Ramsey G., and Walsh J. (2018). Ley de Cannabis Uruguaya: Pionera de un Nuevo Paradigma. WOLA. https://www.brookings.edu/wp-content/uploads/2018/03/GS_06142018_Cannabis-Uruguay_Spanish.pdf, accessed 10 July 2022.

Hughes C., Hulme S., and Ritter A. (2020). The Relationship between Drug Price and Purity and Population Level Harm. *Trends & Issues in Crime and Criminal Justice* 598. Canberra: Australian Institute of Criminology.

Hughes C. and Stevens A. (2007). *The Effects of Decriminalization of Drug Use in Portugal*. Oxfordshire: The Beckley Foundation, 1–10.

Hughes C. and Stevens A. (2010). What can we Learn from the Portuguese Decriminalization of Illicit Drugs? *The British Journal of Criminology* 50 (6), 999–1022.

Hughes C. and Stevens A. (2012). A Resounding Success or a Disastrous Failure: Re-examining the Interpretation of Evidence on the Portuguese Decriminalisation of Illicit Drugs. *Drug and Alcohol Review* 31, 101–113.

Hughes LA., Schaible LM., and Jimmerson K. (2019). Marijuana Dispensaries and Neighborhood Crime and Disorder in Denver, Colorado. *Justice Quarterly* 37, 1–25.

Hughes R. and Anthony N. (2006). Drugs, Crime and Criminal Justice. In R. Hughes, R. Lart, and P. Higate eds, *Drugs: Policy and Politics*. New York: Open University Press.

Huizinga DH., Menard S., and Elliot DS. (1989). Delinquency and Drug Use: Temporal and Developmental Patterns. *Justice Quarterly* 6 (3), 419–455.

Hunt P. and Pacula RL. (2017). Early Impacts of Marijuana Legalization: An Evaluation of Prices in Colorado and Washington. *Journal of Primary Prevention* 38, 221–248.

Huntington S. (1991). *The Third Wave: Democratization in the Late Twentieth Century*. Norman: University of Oklahoma Press.

Inciardi J. (1992). *The War on Drugs II*. Mountain View: Mayfield.

Inciardi J. (1999). Legalizing Drugs: Would it Really Reduce Violent Crime? In J. Inciardi ed, *The Drug Legalization Debate*. Thousand Oaks: Sage.

Inciardi J. and McBride DC. (1989). Legalization: A High-Risk Alternative in the War on Drugs. *American Behavioral Scientist* 32 (3), 259–289.

Inciardi J, Surrat HL., Pechansky F., Kessler F. von Diemen L., Meyer da Silva E. et al (2006). Changing Patterns of Cocaine Use and HIV Risks in the South of Brazil. *Journal of Psychoactive Drugs* 38 (3), 305–310.

Informe de la situacion Nacional del VIH (2016). *Ministerio de Salud*. https://medios.presidencia.gub.uy/tav_portal/2016/noticias/NO_U311/Informe.pdf?utm_source=chatgpt.com, accessed 13 October 2022.

Informe Final (2021). Encuesta Sobre Consumo de Alcohol en ninos, ninas y adolescentes. *Observatorio de Addicciones y Consumos Problematicos*. Provincia de Buenos Aires Defensoria. https://www.defensorba.org.ar/pdfs/dp-relevamiento-2021.pdf, accessed 1 May 2022.

Informe Situacion epidemologica del VIH/SIDA en 2021 (2021). *Ministerio de Salud Publica*. https://www.gub.uy/ministerio-salud-publica/comunicacion/noticias/informe-situacion-epidemiologica-del-vihsida-uruguay-2021?utm_source=chatgpt.com, accessed 13 October 2022.

Instituto Nacional de Estadística y Censos (2023). *Índice de Precios al Consumidor*. Buenos Aires: Ministerio de Economía. https://www.indec.gob.ar/uploads/informesdeprensa/ipc_11_231B28D924C4.pdf, accessed 14 November 2023.

Infobae (2009). El la Argentina se vende la Cocaína más Barata del Mundo. *Infobae*. 1 July. https://www.infobae.com/2009/07/01/457873-en-la-argentina-se-vende-la-cocaina-mas-barata-del-mundo/, accessed 2 November 2022.

Ingraham C. (2015). Why Hardly Anyone Dies from a Drug Overdose in Portugal. *The Washington Post*. 5 June. https://www.washingtonpost.com/news/wonk/wp/2015/06/05/why-hardly-anyone-dies-from-a-drug-overdose-in-portugal/?utm_term=.206fe6bfff76, accessed 4 July 2020.

InSight Crime (2022). 2021 Homicide Round-Up. https://insightcrime.org/news/insight-crimes-2021-homicide-round-up/, accessed 22 October 2022.

Institute for Crime and Justice Policy Research (2023). *World Prison Population List*, Thirteenth Edition. University of London. https://www.prisonstudies.org/sites/default/files/resources/downloads/world_prison_population_list 13th_edition.pdf, accessed 30 October 2023.

Instituto da Droga e da Toxicodependência (2004). *Relatorio Anual 2003. A Situação do País em Matéria de Drogas e Toxicodependências*. http://www.sicad.pt/PT/Publicacoes/Paginas/default.aspx, accessed 30 May 2020.

Instituto da Droga e da Toxicodependência (2006). Relatorio Anual 2005. A Situação do País em Matéria de Drogas e Toxicodependências. http://www.sicad.pt/PT/Publicacoes/Paginas/default.aspx, accessed May 39, 2020.

Instituto da Droga e da Toxicodependência (2007). Relatorio Anual 2006. A Situação do País em Matéria de Drogas e Toxicodependências. http://www.sicad.pt/PT/Publicacoes/Paginas/default.aspx, accessed May 39, 2020.

Instituto da Droga e da Toxicodependência (2008). Relatorio Anual 2007. A Situação do País em Matéria de Drogas e Toxicodependências. http://www.sicad.pt/PT/Publicacoes/Paginas/default.aspx, accessed May 39, 2020.

Instituto da Droga e da Toxicodependência (2009). Relatorio Anual 2008. A Situação do País em Matéria de Drogas e Toxicodependências. http://www.sicad.pt/PT/Publicacoes/Paginas/default.aspx, accessed May 39, 2020.

Instituto da Droga e da Toxicodependência (2010). Relatorio Anual 2009. A Situação do País em Matéria de Drogas e Toxicodependências. http://www.sicad.pt/PT/Publicacoes/Paginas/default.aspx, accessed May 39, 2020.

Instituto da Droga e da Toxicodependência (2011). Relatorio Anual 2010. A Situação do País em Matéria de Drogas e Toxicodependências. http://www.sicad.pt/PT/Publicacoes/Paginas/default.aspx, accessed May 39, 2020.

Instituto de Regulación y Control del Cannabis (2017). Pautas de Reducción de Riesgos en el Uso del Cannabis. https://www.gub.uy/junta-nacional-drogas/sites/junta-nacional-drogas/files/documentos/publicaciones/pautasreduccionriesgos.pdf, accessed 6 February 2019.

Instituto Português da Droga e da Toxicodependência (2000). *Portugal Drug Situation. Report to the EMCDDA*. Lisbon: Presidência do Conselho de Ministros. https://www.emcdda.europa.eu/attachements.cfm/att_34676_EN_NR2000Portugal.PDF, accessed 2 July 2020.

Isacson A. (2005). The US Military in the War on Drugs. In C. Youngers and E. Rosin eds, *Drugs and Democracy in Latin America*. London: Lynne Rienner Publishers.

Isacson A. (2015). Mission Creep. In B. Bagley and J. Rosen eds, *Drug Trafficking, Organized Crime, and Violence in the Americas Today*. Gainesville: University Press of Florida.

Jacobson M. (2005). Baby Booms and Drug Busts: Trends in Youth Drug Use in the United States 1975–2000. *Quarterly Journal of Economics* 119 (4), 1481–1512.

Jaffe JH. (1985). Drug Addiction and Drug Abuse. In AG. Gilman, LS. Goodman, TW. Rall, and F. Murad eds, *Pharmacological Basis of Therapeutics*. New York: Macmillan.

Junta Nacional de Drogas (JDN) (2022). 24 January. http://www.gub.uy, accessed 10 October 2022.

Johnson BD., Golub A., and Dunlap E. (2008). An Analysis of Alternatives to New York City's Current Marijuana Arrest and Detention Policy, *Policing: An International Journal of Police Strategies & Management* 31 (2), 226–250.

Johnson JK., Johnson RM., Hodgkin D., Jones AA., Matteucci AM., and Harris SK. (2018). Heterogeneity of State Medical Marijuana Laws and Adolescent Recent Use of Alcohol and Marijuana: Analysis of 45 States, 1991–2011. *Substance Abuse* 39, 247–254.

Johnson JK., Hodgkin D., Harris SK. (2017). The Design of Medical Marijuana Laws and Adolescent Use and Heavy Use of Marijuana: Analysis of 45 States from 1991 to 2011. *Drug and Alcohol Dependence* 170, 1–8.

Johnston LD., O'Malley PM., and Bachman JG. (1981). *Marijuana Decriminalization: The Impact on Youth, 1975–1980*. Ann Arbor: Institute for Social Research.

Joint United Nations Programme on HIV/AIDS (2019). Focus Areas: Brazil. https://www.unaids.org/en/20191011_country_focus_Brazil#:~:text=OVERVIEW,affected%20by%20HIV%20in%20Brazil, accessed 3 November 2022.

Joint United Nations Programme on HIV/AIDS (2020). Informes Nacionales sobre Avances en Respuesta al Sida-Uruguay. https://www.unaids.org/sites/default/files/country/documents/URY_2020_countryreport.pdf, accessed 6 May 2022.

Jungerman FS., Menezes PR., Pinsky I., Zaleski M., Caetano R., and Laranjeira R. (2010). Prevalence of Cannabis Use in Brazil: Data from the I Brazilian National Alcohol Survey (BNAS). *Addictive Behaviors* 35 (3), 190–193.

Kalant H., Corrigall W., Hall W., and Smart R. eds (1999). *The Health Effects of Cannabis*. Toronto: Centre for Addiction and Mental Health.

Kalso E. and Vainio A. (1990). Morphine and Oxycodone Hydrochloride in the Management of Cancer Pain. *Clin Pharmacol Ther* 47, 639–646.

Kamp J., Córdoba J., and Wernau J. (2022). How Two Mexican Drug Cartels Came to Dominate America's Fentanyl Supply. *Wall Street Journal*, 30 August. https://www.wsj.com/articles/mexico-drug-cartels-fentanyl-overdose-sinaloa-jalisco-11661866903?st=5ihdnnxjo1ttb4d&s=08, accessed 9 April 2020.

Kandel DB. (1975). Stages in adolescent involvement in drug use. *Science* 190 (4217), 912–914.

Kandel DB. and Faust R. (1975). Sequences and stages in patterns of adolescent drug use. *Archives of General Psychiatry* 32 (7), 923–932.

Katz M. and Durham C. (1994). Department of Justice Low-Level Drug Offender Study: A Defense Perspective. *Federal Sentencing Reporter* 7 (1), 28–32.

Keene J. (2005). A Case-Linkage Study of the Relationship Between Drug Misuse, Crime, and Psychosocial Problems in a Total Criminal Justice Population. *Addiction Research and Theory* 13 (5), 489–502.

Keefer P., Loayza N. and Soares R. (2010). Drug Prohibition and Developing Countries: Uncertain Benefits, Certain Costs. In P. Keefer and N. Loayza eds., *Innocent Bystanders: Developing Countries and the War on Drugs*. Washington, DC: Palgrave MacMillan and the World Bank.

Kelling GL. and Wilson JQ. (1982). Broken Windows: The Police and Neighborhood Safety. *The Atlantic Monthly* 249, 29–38.

Kelly E., Darke S., and Ross J. (2004). A Review of Drug Use and Driving: Epidemiology, Impairment, Risk Factors and Risk Perceptions. *Drug and Alcohol Review* 23, 319–344.

Kelly E. and Rasul I. (2014). Policing Cannabis and Drug Related Hospital Admissions: Evidence from Administrative Records. *Journal of Public Economics* 112, 89–114.

Keppler NJ. and Freisthler B. (2012). Exploring the Ecological Association between Crime and Medical Marijuana Dispensaries. *Journal of Studies on Alcohol and Drugs* 73 (4), 523–530.

Kerr DCR., Bae H., Phibbs S., and Kern AC. (2017). Changes in Undergraduates' Marijuana, Heavy Alcohol and Cigarette Use Following Legalization of Recreational Marijuana Use in Oregon. *Addiction* 112, 1992–2001.

Kerr DCR., Bae H., and Koval AL. (2018). Oregon Recreational Marijuana Legalization: Changes in Undergraduates' Marijuana Use Rates from 2008 to 2016. *Psychology of Addictive Behavior* 32, 670–678.

Kerr WC., Lui C., and Ye Y. (2018). Trends and Age, Period and Cohort Effects for Marijuana Use Prevalence in the 1984–2015 US National Alcohol Surveys. *Addiction* 113, 473–81.

Kerr WC., Ye Y., Subbaraman MS., Williams E., and Greenfield TK. (2018). Changes in Marijuana Use Across the 2012 Washington State Recreational Legalization: Is Retrospective Assessment of Use Before Legalization More Accurate? *Journal of Studies on Alcohol and Drugs* 79 (3), 495–502.

Kessler G. and Assusa G. (2021). *Pobreza, Desigualdad y Exclusion Social. Informe Foro Universitario del Futuro.* Buenos Aires: Jefatura de Gabinete de Ministros.

Keyes KM., Wall M., Cerdá M., Schulenberg J., O'Malley P, Galea S. et al (2016). How Does State Marijuana Policy Affect US Youth? Medical Marijuana Laws, Marijuana use and Perceived Harmfulness: 1991–2014. *Addiction* 111 (12), 2187–2195.

Kilmer B. (2002). Do Cannabis Possession Laws Influence Cannabis Use? Cannabis 2002 Report – Technical Report of the International Scientific Conference. Brussels: Ministry of Public Health of Belgium.

Kleiman M. (1992). *Against Excess: Drug Policy for Results.* New York: Basic Books.

Kleiman M. (2001). Controlling Drug Use and Crime with Testing, Sanctions, and Treatment. In P. Heymann and W. Brownsberger eds, *Drug Addiction and Drug Policy: The Struggle to Control Dependence.* Cambridge: Harvard University Press.

Kleiman M. (2016). Legal Commercial Cannabis Sales in Colorado and Washington: What Can We Learn? *Journal of Drug Policy Analysis* 10, 1–16.

Kleiman M., Caulkins J., and Hawken A. (2011). *Drugs and Drug Policy: What Everyone Needs to Know.* New York: Oxford University Press.

Kleiman M. and Smith K. (1990). State and Local Drug Enforcement: In Search of a Strategy. *Crime and Justice* 13, 69–108.

Kopel D. (2000). Militarized Law Enforcement: The Drug War's Deadly Fruit. In T. Lynch ed, *After Prohibition: An Adult Approach to Drug Policies in the 21st Century.* Washington, DC: Cato Institute.

Korf DJ. (2002). Dutch Coffee Shops and Trends in Cannabis Use. *Addictive Behaviors* 27, 851–866.

Korf DJ., van der Woude M., Benschop A., and Nabben T. (2001). *Coffeeshops, Jeugd en Toerisme.* Amsterdam: University of Amsterdam, Criminologisch Instituut Bonger.

Krajewski K. (1999). How Flexible are the United Nations Drug Conventions? *International Journal of Drug Policy* 10, 329–338.

Lacey N. and Zedner L. (2017). Criminalization: Historical, Legal, and Criminological Perspectives. In A. Liebling, S. Maruna, and L. McAra eds, *The Oxford Handbook of Criminology.* New York: Oxford University Press.

Lains P. (2007). Growth in a Protected Environment: Portugal, 1850–1950. *Research in Economic History* 24, 121–163.

Laqueur H. (2014). Uses and Abuses of Drug Decriminalization in Portugal. *Law & Social Inquiry* 40 (3), 746–781.

Laqueur H., Rivera-Aguirre A., Shev A., Castillo-Carniglia A., Rudolph KE., Ramirez J., Martins SS., Cerdá M. (2020). The Impact of Cannabis Legalization in Uruguay on Adolescent Cannabis Use. *International Journal of Drug Policy* 80, 1–8.

La Nación (2012). Bergoglio Cuestionó el Proyecto de Despenalización de Drogas. https://www.lanacion.com.ar/sociedad/bergoglio-cuestiono-el-proyecto-de-despenalizacion-de-drogas-nid1480857/?sitio=desktop, accessed 20 March 2022.

Lei 11.343 (2006). Presidência da República Secretaria-Geral. Subchefia para Assuntos Jurídicos. http://www.planalto.gov.br/ccivil_03/_ato2004-2006/2006/lei/l11343.htm, accessed 22 March 2022.

Lenton S., Christie P., Humeniuk R., Brooks A., Bennett P; and Heale P. (1999a). Infringement versus Conviction: The Social Impact of a Minor Cannabis Offence Under a Civil Penalties System and Strict Prohibition in two Australian States (monograph No. 36).

Lenton S., McDonald D., Ali R., and Moore T. (1999b). Laws Applying to Minor Cannabis Offences in Australia and their Evaluation. *International Journal of Drug Policy* 10, 299–303.

Lenton S., Humeniuk R., Heale P., and Christie P. (2000). Infringement versus Conviction: The Social Impact of a Minor Cannabis Offence in SA and WA. *Drug and Alcohol Review* 19, 257–264.

Léonard I. (2016). *História do Portugal Contemporaneo. De 1890 aos Nossos Dias*. Lisbon: Penguin Random House.

Lessing B. (2017). Counterproductive Punishment: How Prison Gangs Undermine State Authority. *Rationality and Society* 29, 257–297.

Leung J., Chiu CYV., Stjepanović D., and Hall W. (2018). Has the Legalisation of Medical and Recreational Cannabis use in the USA affected the Prevalence of Cannabis Use and Cannabis Use Disorders? *Current Addiction Reports* 5, 403–417.

Levine HG. (2002). The Secret of Worldwide Drug Prohibition: The Varieties and Uses of Drug Prohibition. *The Independent Review* 7 (2), 165–180.

Levine HG. (2003). Global Drug Prohibition: Its Uses and Crises. *International Journal of Drug Policy* 14 (2), 145–153.

Levine HG. (2009). *New York City's Marijuana Arrest Crusade … Continues*. New York: City University of New York.

Ley 23.737 (1989). Ministerio de Justicia y Derechos Humanos. https://www.argentina.gob.ar/normativa/nacional/ley-23737-138/actualizacion, accessed 1 April 2022.

Ley 26.052 (2005). Ministerio de Justicia y Derechos Humanos. https://servicios.infoleg.gob.ar/infolegInternet/anexos/105000-109999/109264/texact.htm, accessed 1 April 2022.

Ley 19.172 (2014). Regulación y Control del Cannabis. Centro de Información Oficial (IMPO). https://www.impo.com.uy/bases/leyes/19172-2013, accessed 10 February 2019.

Liang TJ. and Ward JW. (2018). Hepatitis C: The growing burden of hepatitis C virus infection in the United States. *New England Journal of Medicine* 378 (2), 151–160.

Lindenmeyer Guimares M., Leires Marques BC., Bertoni N., Lopes S., Goncalvez Morgado M. et al (2015). Assessing the HIV-1 Epidemic in Brazilian Drug Users: A Molecular Epidemiology Approach. *PLOS* 10 (11), e0141372.

Lissardy G. (2019). Uruguay: Cuanto ha Cambiado Realmente el Mercado de las Drogas en el País con la Legalización de la Marihuana. *BBC Mundo*. https://www.bbc.com/mundo/noticias-america-latina-50667423, accessed 26 April 2020.

Lopez G. (2017). How Obama Quietly Reshaped America's War on Drugs. *VOX*, 19 January. https://www.vox.com/identities/2016/12/19/13903532/obama-war-on-drugs-legacy, accessed 9 April 2020.

Lopez Ortega S. (2022). El 'Combate frontal al Narcotráfico' en Cifras. *La Mañana*. 9 March. https://www.xn--lamaana-7za.uy/actualidad/el-combate-frontal-al-narcotrafico-en-cifras/, accessed 2 November 2022.

Lurigio AJ. and Schwartz JA. (1999). The Nexus between Drugs and Crime: Theory, Research and Practice. *Federal Probation* 63, 67–72.

Lynne-Landsman SD., Livingston MD., and Wagenaar AC. (2013). Effects of State Medical Marijuana Laws on Adolescent Marijuana Use. *American Journal of Public Health* 103, 1500–1506.

Lynskey MT., Heath AC. and Bucholz KK. (2003). Escalation of drug use in early-onset cannabis users vs co-twin controls. *JAMA* 289 (4), 427–433.

MacCoun R. (1993). Drugs and the Law: A Psychological Analysis of Drug Prohibition. *Psychological Bulletin* 113 (3), 497–512.

MacCoun R. (2011). What Can We Learn from the Dutch Cannabis Coffee Shop System? *Addiction* 106 (11), 1899–1910.

MacCoun R., Kilmer B., and Reuter P. (2003). Research on Drugs-Crime Linkages: The Next Generation. In National Institute of Justice eds, *Towards a Drugs and Crime Agenda for the 21st Century*, Washington, DC: US Department of Justice Office of Justice Programs.

MacCoun R. and Reuter P. (1997). Interpreting Dutch Cannabis Policy: Reasoning by Analogy in the Legalization Debate. *Science* 278 (5335), 47–52.

MacCoun R. and Reuter P. (1998). Drug Control. In M. Tonry ed, *The Handbook of Crime and Punishment*. New York: Oxford University Press.

MacCoun R. and Reuter P. (2001a). *Drug War Heresies: Learning from Other Vices, Times and Places*. New York: Cambridge University Press.

MacCoun R. and Reuter P. (2001b). Evaluating Alternative Cannabis Regimes. *British Journal of Psychiatry* 178, 123–128.

Madruga CS., Miguel AQ., Massaro LT., Caetano R., and Laranjeira R. (2022). Cannabis Consumption Onset and Addiction: Data from the Second Brazilian Drugs and Alcohol Survey (BNADS). *Journal of Psychoactive Drugs* 54 (2), 140–148.

Mahamad S., Wadsworth E., Rynard V., Goodman S., and Hammond D. (2020). Availability, Retail Price and Potency of Legal and Illegal Cannabis in Canada after Recreational Cannabis Legalisation. *Drug and Alcohol Review* 39 (4), 337–346.

Maier SL., Mannes S., and Koppenhofer EL. (2017). The Implications of Marijuana Decriminalization and Legalization on Crime in the United States. *Contemporary Drug Problems* 44 (2), 125–146.

Maine Office of Alcoholism and Drug Abuse Prevention (1978). *An Evaluation of the Decriminalization of Marijuana in Maine*. Augusta, ME: Department of Human Services, Office of Alcoholism and Drug Abuse Prevention.

Malamud-Goti J. (1994). *Humo y Espejos. La Paradoja de la Guerra contra las Drogas*. Buenos Aires: Editores del Puerto.

Malcolm R., Barth KS. and Veatch LM. (2013). Cocaine addiction. In PM Miller (Ed.), *Principles of addiction*. Cambridge, MA: Academic Press, 669–678.

Maloff D. (1981). A Review of the Effects of the Decriminalization of Marijuana. *Contemporary Drug Problems* 10 (3), 307–322.

Mandel J. (1987). Are lower Penalties a Green Light for Drug Users? *Journal of Psychoactive Drugs* 19, 383–385.

Manuel T. (2021). *Opium Inc.: How a Global Trade Funded the British Empire*. Noida: HarperCollins Publishers.

Manzano V. (2015). The Creation of a Social Problem: Youth Culture, Drugs, and Politics in Cold War Argentina. *Hispanic American Historical Review* 95 (1), 37–69.

Manzoni P., Brochu S., Fischer B., and Rehm J. (2006). Determinants of Property Crime among Illicit Opiate Users Outside of Treatment across Canada. *Deviant Behavior* 27, 351–376.

Mares D. (2002). *Drug Wars and Coffee Houses: The Political Economy of the International Drug Trade*. Washington, DC: CQ Press.

Marin Gutierrez, I. (2017). Cien Años de Política de Drogas en Uruguay. *Cannabis*. 9 January. https://www.cannabis.es/web/features/articulos/576-cien-anos-de-politica-de-drogas-en-uruguay, accessed 3 February 2019.

Marion N. (1994). *A History of Federal Crime Control Initiatives, 1960–1993*. Westport: Praeger.

Marmot M. and Wilkinson RG. eds (1999). *Social Determinants of Health*. New York: Oxford University Press.

Martin R., Alexander-Scott N., Wendelken J., and Clarke J. (2019). Collaborating to Address Substance Use Disorder in Correctional Settings. In J. Butler and M. Fraser eds, *A Public Health Guide to Ending the Opioid Epidemic*. New York: Oxford University Press.

Martins SS., Mauro CM., Santaella-Tenorio J., Kim JH., Cerda M., Keyes KM. et al (2016). State-Level Medical Marijuana Laws, Marijuana Use and Perceived Availability of Marijuana among the General U.S. Population. *Drug Alcohol Depend* 169, 26–32.

Mason WA., Hanson K., Fleming CB., Ringle JL., and Haggerty KP. (2015). Washington State Recreational Marijuana Legalization: Parent and Adolescent Perceptions, Knowledge, and Discussions in a Sample of Low-income Families. *Substance Use & Misuse* 50, 541–545.

Mather LE. (1995). 1994 John J. Bonica Lecture: The Clinical Effects of Morphine Pharmacology. *Regional Anesthesia* 20, 263–282.

Mauro CM., Newswanger P., Santaella-Tenorio J., Mauro PM., Carliner H., and Martins SS. (2019). Impact of Medical Marijuana Laws on State-level Marijuana Use by Age and Gender, 2004–2013. *Prevention Science* 20, 205–214.

Maxwell JC. and Mendelson B. (2016). What do we Know about the Impact of the Laws Related to Marijuana? *Journal of Addiction Medicine* 10 (1), 3–12.

May T., Duffy M., Warburton H., and Hough M. (2007). *Policing Cannabis as a Class C Drug: An Arresting Change?* York: Joseph Rowntree Foundation.

Mayntz R. (2017). Illegal Markets: Boundaries and Interfaces between Legality and Illegality. In J. Beckert, and M. Dewey eds, *The Architecture of Illegal Markets: Towards an Economic Sociology of Illegality in the Economy*. New York: Oxford University Press.

McAllister WB. (2000). *Drug Diplomacy in the Twentieth Century*. New York: Routledge.

McBride DC., VanderWaal CJ., and Terry-McElrath YM. (2003). The Drugs-Crime Wars: Past, Present, and Future Directions in Theory, Policy, and Program Interventions. *NIJ*, Special report, 97–171.

McCormack M., Measham F. and Wignall L. (2021). The normalization of leisure sex and recreational drugs: Exploring associations between polydrug use and sexual practices by English festival-goers. *Contemporary Drug Problems* 48 (1), 25–44.

McCoy AW. (1991). *The Politics of Heroin: CIA Complicity in the Global Drug Trade*. Brooklyn: Lawrence.

McGeorge J. and Aitken CK. (1997). Effects of Cannabis Decriminalization in the Australian Capital Territory on University Students' Patterns of Use. *Journal of Drug Issues* 27 (4), 785–793.

McWilliams J. (1990). *The Protectors: Harry J. Anslinger and the Federal Bureau of Narcotics, 1930–1962*. Newark: University of Delaware Press.

Measham F. and South N. (2012). Drugs, Alcohol, and Crime. In M. Maguire, R. Morgan, and R. Reiner, *The Oxford Handbook of Criminology*. New York: Oxford University Press.

Measham F., Newcombe R. and Parker H. (1994). The Normalization of Recreational Drug Use Amongst Young People in North-West England. *British Journal of Sociology* 45 (2), 287–312.

Melchior M., Nakamura A., Bolze C., Hausfater F., El Khoury F., Mary-Krause M. et al (2019). Does Liberalisation of Cannabis Policy Influence Levels of use in Adolescents and Young Adults? A Systematic Review and Meta-Analysis. *BMJ Open* 9 (7), e025880.

Menard S., Mihalic W., and Huizinga D. (2001). Drugs and Crime Revisited, *Justice Quarterly* 18 (2), 269–299.

Merkinaite S. (2012). *A War Against People who use Drugs: The Costs*. Eurasian Harm Reduction Network. Vilnius. http://fileserver.idpc.net/library/a-war-against-people-who-use-drugs-the-costs.pdf, accessed 11 July 2022.

Meruelo AD., Castro N., Cota CI., and Tapert SF. (2017). Cannabis and Alcohol Use, and the Developing Brain. *Behavioural Brain Research* 325, 44–50.

Midgette G., Davenport S., Caulkins J., and Kilmer B. (2019). *What America's Users Spend on Illegal Drugs, 2006–2016*. Santa Monica: RAND Corporation. https://www.rand.org/pubs/research_reports/RR3140.html, accessed 12 April 2020.

Miech RA., Johnston L., O'Malley PM., Bachman JG., Schulenberg J., and Patrick ME. (2015). Trends in Use of Marijuana and Attitudes Toward Marijuana Among Youth Before and After Decriminalization: The Case of California 2007–2013. *International Journal of Drug Policy* 26 (4), 336–344.

Mieczkowski TM. (1996). The Prevalence of Drug Use in the United States. *Crime and Justice* 20, 349–414.

Miller AM., Rosenman R., and Cowan BW. (2017). Recreational Marijuana Legalization and College Student Use: Early Evidence. *SSM-Population Health* 3, 649–657.

Miller M. and Freed DJ. (1994). Editors' Observations: The Disproportionate Imprisonment of Low-Level Drug Offenders. *Federal Sentencing Reporter* 7 (1), 3–6.

Ministerio de Economía (2020). *Presupuesto Abierto*. Buenos Aires: Presidencia de la Nación. https://www.presupuestoabierto.gob.ar, accessed 15 June 2022.

Ministerio de Salud (2013). Uso de Drogas y VIH. Documento de Trabajo con Orientaciones para la Intervención y la Investigación. https://bancos.salud.gob.ar/sites/default/files/2018-10/0000000218cnt-2013-08_drogas-vih.pdf, accessed 10 September 2022.

Ministerio de Salud (2019). Boletín sobre el VIH, Sida e ITA en la Argentina 36. December. https://bancos.salud.gob.ar/recurso/boletin-sobre-el-vih-sida-e-its-en-la-argentina-ndeg-36, accessed 10 September 2022.

Ministerio de Salud Pública (2021). Informe Situación Epidemiológica del VIH/SIDA en 2021. 29 July. https://www.gub.uy/ministerio-salud-publica/comunicacion/noticias/informe-situacion-epidemiologica-del-vihsida-uruguay-2021, accessed 9 September 2022.

Mitsch AJ., Hall HI., and Babu AS. (2016). Trends in HIV Infection Among Persons Who Inject Drugs: United States and Puerto Rico, 2008–2013. *American Journal of Public Health* 106 (12), 2194–2201.

MMGY Travel Intelligence (2021). Cannabis Tourism: Opportunities, Issues and Strategies. https://mmgyintel.com/our-services/cannabis-tourism-opportunities-issues-strategies, accessed 10 July 2022.

Model KE. (1993). The Effect of Marijuana Decriminalization on Hospital Emergency Room Drug Episodes: 1975–1978. *Journal of the American Statistical Association* 88, 737–747.

Montain J., Ti L., Hayashi K., Nguyen P., Wood E., and Kerr T. (2016). Impact of Length of Injecting Career on HIV Incidence among People Who Inject Drugs. *Addictive Behaviors* 58, 90–94.

Montanary L., Guarita B., Mounteney J., Zipfel N., and Simon R. (2017). Cannabis Use among People Entering Drug Treatment in Europe: A Growing Phenomenon? *European Addiction Research* 23, 113–121.

Montaner JS., Wood E., Kerr T., Lima V., Barrios R., Shannon K. et al (2010). Expanded Highly Active Antiretroviral Therapy Coverage among HIV-Positive Drug Users to Improve Individual and Public Health Outcomes. *JAIDS Journal of Acquired Immune Deficiency Syndromes* 55, S5–S9.

Monte AA., Zane RD., and Heard KJ. (2015). The Implications of Marijuana Legalization in Colorado. *JAMA* 313, 241–242.

Moore MH. (1973). Policies to Achieve Discrimination on the Effective Price of Heroin. *American Economic Review* 63 (2), 270–277.

Moore MH. (2001). Toward a Balanced Drug-Prevention Strategy: A Conceptual Map. In P. Heymann and W. Brownsberger eds, *Drug Addiction and Drug Policy: The Struggle to Control Dependence*. Cambridge: Harvard University Press.

Moore D. and Rhodes T. (2004). Editorial: Social Theory in Drug Research, Drug Policy and Harm Reduction. *International Journal of Drug Policy* 15, 323–325.

Moreira M., Hughes B., Costa Storti C., and Zobel F. (2011). Drug Policy Profiles: Portugal. Luxembourg: EMCDDA. http://www.emcdda.europa.eu/system/files/publications/642/PolicyProfile_Portugal_WEB_Final_289201.pdf, accessed 12 May 2020.

Morris RG., TenEyck M., Barnes JC., and Kovandzic TV. (2014). The Effect of Medical Marijuana Laws on Crime: Evidence from State Panel data 1990–2006. *PLoS ONE* 9 (3), e92816.

Mosher C. and Akins S. (2020). Recreational Marijuana Legalization in Washington State: Benefits and Harms. In T. Decorte, S. Lenton, and C. Wilkins eds, *Legalizing Cannabis Experiences, Lessons and Scenarios.* New York: Routledge.

Mounteney J., Griffiths P., Sedefov R., Noor A., Vicente J., and Simon R. (2015). The Drug Situation in Europe: An Overview of Data Available on Illicit Drugs and New Psychoactive Substances from European Monitoring in 2015. *Addiction* 111 (1), 34–48.

MPA (2021). Reporte anual de criminalidad registrada. Fiscalias regionales y Unidades regionales. *Ministerio de Seguridad. https://www.santafe.gob.ar/ms/osp/informs/informe-anual-de-criminalidad-registrada-2015-2021/*, accessed 11 May 2022.

Mravčík V. (2015). (De)criminalization of Possession of Drugs for Personal Use: A View from the Czech Republic. *International Journal of Drug Policy* 26 (7), 705–707.

Mujica J. (2014). Mujica Explica las Razones que lo Llevaron a Legalizar la Marihuana en Uruguay. *IProfesional.* 7 May. https://www.iprofesional.com/actualidad/186281-mujica-explica-las-razones-que-lo-llevaron-a-legalizar-la-marihuana-en-uruguay, accessed 23 October 2019.

Musto C. and Robaina G. (2018). Evolución del Consume de Cannabis en Uruguay y Mercados Regulados. *Monitor Cannabis Uruguay.* 18 September. https://monitorcannabis.uy/

Musto D. (1973). *The American Disease: Origins of Narcotic Control.* Oxford: Oxford University Press.

Nación cannabis (2019). La ciencia detras de la pureza del cannabidol. https://nacioncannabis.com/ciencia-detras-pureza-cannabidiol/, accessed 8 October 2022.

Nadelmann E. (1989). Drug Prohibition in the United States: Costs, Consequences and Alternatives. *Science* 245, 939–947.

Nadelmann E. (1990). Global Prohibition Regimes: The Evolution of Norms in International Society. *International Organization* 44 (4), 479–526.

Narvaez-Chicaiza MA. (2020). Harm Reduction Policies Where Drugs Constitute a Security Issue. *Health Care Anal* 28 (4), 382–390.

National Institutes of Health (2021). Percentage of adolescents reporting drug use decreased significantly in 2021 as the COVID-19 pandemic endured. https://www.nih.gov/events/news-releases/percentage-adolescents-reporting-drug-use-decreased-significantly-2021-covid-19-pandemic-endured, accessed 4 April 2022.

National Institute on Drug Abuse (2020). Drug Use and Viral Infections (HIV, Hepatitis) DrugFacts. 30 July. https://nida.nih.gov/publications/drugfacts/drug-use-viral-infections-hiv-hepatitis, accessed 12 September 2021.

National Institute on Drug Abuse (2021). Cannabis (Marijuana) Potency. 26 April. https://nida.nih.gov/research-topics/marijuana/cannabis-marijuana-potency, accessed 9 April 2020.

Neal T. (2000). Bush Assails Administration's Antidrug Records, *The Washington Post*, 7 October.

Negreiros G. and Magalhães A. (2009). Estimativas da Prevalência de Consumidores Problemáticos de Drogas em Portugal com Base em Dados sobre o Tratamento. *Revista Toxicodependências* 15, 19–32.

Neill M., Christie P., and Cormack S. (1991). *Trends in Alcohol and Other Drug Use by South Australian School Children 1986–1989*. Adelaide: Drug and Alcohol Services Council South Australia.

Newburn T. and Sparks R. eds (2004). *Criminal Justice and Political Cultures: National and International Dimensions of Crime Control*. Cullompton: Willan.

Nguyen HV., Mital S., and Bornstein S. (2022). Short-Term Effects of Recreational Cannabis Legalization on Youth Cannabis Initiation. *Journal of Adolescent Health* 72 (1), 111–117.

Nicholas S., Kershaw C., and Walker A. eds (2007). *Home Office Statistical Bulletin: Crime in England and Wales 2006/07*. London: Home Office.

Nisbet CT. and Vakil F. (1972). Some Estimates of the Price and Expenditure Elasticities of Demand for Marijuana Among U.C.L.A. Students. *Review of Economics and Statistics* 54 (4), 473–475.

Nixon R. (1971). President's Message on Drug Control Programs. *Congressional Quarterly Almanac* 26, 95A.

Nurco D., Hanlon T., and Kinlock T. (1991). Recent Research on the Relationship Between Illicit Drug Abuse and Crime. *Behavioral Sciences and the Law* 9 (3), 221–242.

Obama B. (2015). President Obama Announces 46 Commutations in Video Address: 'America Is a Nation of Second Chances'. The White House: Washington, DC.

Observatorio Argentino de Drogas (OAD) (2019). Estudio Nacional Sobre Perfiles de Pacientes en Tratamiento por Consumo de Sustancias Psicoactivas. Boletin 1. *SEDRONAR*, oad_2019_estudio_nacional_sobre_perfiles_de_pacientes_en_tratamiento_por_consumo_de_sustancias_psicoactivas_boletin_no1.pdf (argentina.gob.ar), accessed 7 March 2022.

Office of National Drug Control Policy (2004). *The Price and Purity of Illicit Drugs: 1981 Through the Second Quarter of 2003*. The White House: Washington, DC.

Office of National Drug Control Policy (2010). Drug Decriminalization in Portugal: Challenges and Limitations. White House, 1–2.

Office of National Drug Control Policy (2012). Drug Availability Estimates in the United States. The White House: Washington, DC.

Office of National Drug Control Policy (2013). National Drug Control Budget. The White House. https://obamawhitehouse.archives.gov/sites/default/files/ondcp/Fact_Sheets/fy2014_budget_and_performance-summary.pdf, accessed 29 October 2023.

Office of National Drug Control Policy (2015). National Drug Control Strategy. Data Supplement 2015. https://obamawhitehouse.archives.gov/sites/default/files/ondcp/policy-and-research/2015_data_supplement_final.pdf, accessed 31 October 2023.

Office of National Drug Control Policy (2021). National Drug Control Budget. The White House. https://www.whitehouse.gov/wp-content/uploads/2021/05/National-Drug-Control-Budget-FY-2022-Funding-Highlights.pdf, accessed 30 April 2020.

Ogunniyi OJ. and Akpu JO. (2019). The Challenge of Drug Trafficking to Democratic Governance and Human Security in West Africa: A Historical Reflection. *Africa Development* 44 (4), 29–50.

Olaeta H. (2022). Interview. 9 November 2022.

Olmstead TA., Alessi SM., Kline B., Pacula RL., and Petry NM. (2015). The price elasticity of demand for heroin: Matched longitudinal and experimental evidence. *Journal of Health Economics* 41, 59–71.

O'Malley P. and Valverde M. (2004). Pleasure, Freedom and Drugs: The Uses of "Pleasure" in Liberal Governance of Drug Use and Alcohol Consumption. *Sociology* 38, 25–42.

Omelicheva MY. and Markowitz L. (2018). Does Drug Trafficking Impact Terrorism? Afghan Opioids and Terrorist Violence in Central Asia. *Studies in Conflict & Terrorism* 42 (12), 1021–1043.

Organization of American States (2010). *Analysis Situacional: VIH y Violencia contra las Mujeres en Panama*. Washington, DC: Comisión Internamericana de Mujeres (CIM).

Organization of American States (2019). Report on Drug Use in the Americas. Inter-American Drug Abuse Control Commission. Washington, DC. http://www.cicad.oas.org/main/pubs/Report%20on%20Drug%20Use%20in%20the%20Americas%202019.pdf, accessed 4 March 2022.

Pacula RL. (1998). Does increasing the beer tax reduce marijuana consumption? *Journal of Health Economics* 17 (5), 557–586.

Pacula RL. (2010). Examining the Impact of Marijuana Legalization on Marijuana Consumption: Insights from the Economics Literature. Rand Corporation, Working paper, 1–29.

Pacula RL., Chriqui JF., and King J. (2003). Marihuana Decriminalization: What does it mean in the United States? NBER Working paper No. 9690. Cambridge: National Bureau of Economic Research.

Pacula RL., Grossman M., Chaloupka FJ., O'Malley P., Johnston LD., and Farrelly MC. (2001). Marijuana and Youth. In J. Gruber ed, *Risky Behavior Among Youth: An Economic Analysis*. Chicago: University of Chicago Press.

Pacula RL. and Kilmer B. (2003). Marijuana and Crime: Is There a Connection Beyond Prohibition? NBER Working paper No. 10046. Cambridge: National Bureau of Economic Research.

Pacula RL. and Lundberg R. (2014). Why Changes in Price Matter When Thinking About Marijuana Policy: A Review of the Literature on the Elasticity of Demand. *Public Health Reviews* 35 (2), 1–18.

Pacula RL., MacCoun R., Reuter P., Chriqui J., Kilmer B., Harris K. et al (2005). What Does It Mean to Decriminalize Marijuana? A Cross-national Empirical Examination. *Advances in Health Economics and Health Services Research* 16, 347–369.

Pacula RL., Powell D., Heaton P., and Sevigny EL. (2015). Assessing the Effects of Medical Marijuana Laws on Marijuana Use: The Devil is in the Details. *Journal of Policy Analysis and Management* 34, 7–31.

Pacula RL. and Smart R. (2017). Medical Marijuana and Marijuana Legalization. *Annual Review of Clinical Psychology* 13, 397–419.

Página/12 (1988). Una Polémica Legal Fronteras Adentro, 28 June.

Pardo B. (2020). The Uneven Repeal of Cannabis Prohibition in the United States. In T. Decorte, S. Lenton, and C. Wilkins eds, *Legalizing Cannabis Experiences, Lessons and Scenarios*. New York: Routledge.

Parker H. and Newcombe R. (1987). Heroin Use and Acquisitive Crime in an English Community. *The British Journal of Sociology* 38 (3), 331–350.

Paternain R. (2014). Políticas de Seguridad en el Uruguay: Desafíos para los Gobiernos de Izquierda. *Cuestiones de Sociología*. 10. http://www.cuestionessociologia.fahce.unlp.edu.ar/article/view/CSn10a04, accessed 15 January 2019.

Peacock A., Leung J., Larney S., Colledge S., Hickman M., Rehm J. et al (2018). Global Statistics on Alcohol, Tobacco and Illicit Drug Use: 2017 Status Report. *Addiction* 113, 1905–1926.

Pinto Coelho M. (2010). The 'Resounding Success' of Portuguese Drug Policy: The Power of an Attractive Fallacy. *Associação para uma Portugal Livre de Drogas*, 1–29.

Pijlman FTA., Rigter SM., Hoek J., Goldschmidt HMJ., and Niesink RJM. (2005). Strong Increase in Total Delta-THC in Cannabis Preparations Sold in Dutch Coffee Shops. *Addiction Biology* 10, 171–180.

Pizarro E. and Gaitán P. (2006). Plan Colombia and the Andean Regional Initiative: Lights and Shadows. In B. Loveman ed, *Addicted to Failure*. Maryland: Rowman & Littlefield Publishers.

Platt L., Easterbrook P., Gower E. et al (2016). Prevalence and burden of HIV co-infection with hepatitis C virus: A global systematic review and meta-analysis. *The Lancet Infectious Diseases* 16 (7), 697–708.

Pombo S. and da Costa NF. (2018). On the Long-Term Status of Treatment-Seeking, Heroin Addicted Patients: A 22- Year Follow-up Study on Mortality and Drug Use in Portugal. *Heroin Addiction and Related Clinical Problems* 20 (1), 21–30.

Pombo S. and da Costa NF. (2016). Heroin Addiction Patterns of Treatment-seeking Patients, 1992–2013: Comparison between pre-and post-drug Policy Reform in Portugal. *Heroin Addiction and Related Clinical Problems* 20 (6).

Powell D., Pacula RL., and Jacobson M. (2018). Do Medical Marijuana Laws Reduce Addictions and Deaths Related to Pain Killers? *Journal of Health Economics* 58, 29–42.

Procuración Penitenciaria de la Nación (2019). En la Argentina hay mas de 100,000 Personas Presas. 18 October. https://www.ppn.gov.ar/institucional/noticias/2376-en-la-argentina-ya-hay-mas-de-100-000-personas-presas, accessed 23 August 2022.

Putnam RD. (1988). Diplomacy and Domestic Politics: The Logic of Two-Level Games. *International Organization* 42 (3), 427–60.

Queirolo R., Álvarez E., Sotto B., and Cruz, JM. (2023). How High-Frequency Users Embraced Cannabis Regulation in Uruguay. *Journal of Drug Issues* 53 (4), 519–35.

Queirolo R., Rossel C., Alvarez E., and Repetto L. (2018). Why Uruguay Legalized Marijuana? The Open Window of Public Insecurity. *Addiction* 114, 1313–1321.

Quintas J. (2011). *Regulação Legal do Consumo de Drogas: Impactos da Experiência Portuguesa da Descriminalização*. Porto: Fronteira do Caos Editores.

Quintas J. and Arana X. (2017). Decriminalization: Different Models in Portugal and Spain. In EU. Savona, MAR. Kleiman, and F. Calderoni eds, *Dual Markets*. New York: Springer International Publishing.

Ramsey G. (2016). Getting Regulation Right: Assessing Uruguay's Historic Cannabis Initiative. Washington, DC: WOLA Research Report.

Randhawa SH. (2022). International Criminalization and the Historical Emergence of International Crimes. *International Theory* 14 (3), 460–502.

Rasmussen DW. and Benson BL. (1994). *The Economic Anatomy of a Drug War: Criminal Justice in the Commons*. Lanham: Rowman and Littlefield.

Redondo S. and Frerich N. (2014). Crime and Justice Reinvestment in Europe: Possibilities and Challenges. *Victims & Offenders* 9 (1), 13–49.

Rêgo X., Oliveira MJ., Lameira C., and Cruz OS. (2021). 20 Years of Portuguese Drug Policy – Developments, Challenges and the Quest for Human Rights. *Substance Abuse Treatment, Prevention, and Policy* 16, 59.

Rehm J., Room R., van den Brinkt W., and Kraus L. (2005). Problematic Drug Use and Drug Use Disorders in EU Countries and Norway: An Overview of the Epidemiology. *European Neuropsychopharmacology* 15, 389–397.

Reinarman C. (1994). The Social Construction of Drug Scares. In P. Adler and P. Adler eds, *Constructions of Deviance: Social Power, Context, and Interaction*. Belmont: Wadsworth.

Reinarman C. (2009). Cannabis Policies and User Practices: Market Separation, Price, Potency, and Accessibility in Amsterdam and San Francisco. *International Journal of Drug Policy* 20, 28–37.

Reinarman C., Cohen P., and Kaal H. (2004). The Limited Relevance of Drug Policy: Cannabis in Amsterdam and in San Francisco. *American Journal of Public Health* 94 (5), 836–842.

Reinarman C. and Levine HG. (1997). *Crack In America: Demon Drugs and Social Justice*. Berkeley: University of California Press.

Reisman SE. (2011). New Lead for Pain Treatment. *Nature* 471, 458–459.

Reuter P. (1989). *Quantity Illusions and Paradoxes of Drug Interdiction: Federal Intervention into Vice Policy*, Santa Monica: RAND.

Reuter P. (2013). Why Has US Drug Policy Changed So Little over 30 Years? *Crime and Justice* 42 (1), 75–140.

Reuter P., Cohen JP., and MacCoun RJ. (2009). *Drug war heresies: Learning from other vices, times, and places*. Cambridge: Cambridge University Press.

Reuter P., Crawford G., and Cave J. (1988). Stealing the Borders: The Effects of Increased Military Participation in Drug Interdiction. RAND, paper R-3594-USDP.

Reuter P. and Haaga J. (1989). *The Organization of High-Level Drug Markets: An Exploratory Study*. Santa Monica: RAND.

Reuter P. and Kleiman M. (1986). Risks and Prices: An Economic Analysis of Drug Enforcement. In M. Tonry and N. Morris eds, *Crime and Justice*. Chicago: University of Chicago Press.

Reuter P. and Stevens A. (2007). *An Analysis of UK Drug Policy*. London: UK Drug Policy Issues.

Rhodes W., Johnston P., Han S., McMullen Q., and Hozik L. (2002). Illicit Drugs: Price Elasticity of Demand and Supply. Report submitted to the U.S. Department of Justice. https://www.ojp.gov/pdffiles1/nij/grants/191856.pdf, accessed 9 April 2020.

Ritter A. (2022). *Drug Policy*. New York: Routledge.

Rivera-Aguirre A., Castillo-Carniglia A., Laqueur HS., Rudolph KE., Martins SS., Ramirez J. et al (2021). Does Recreational Cannabis Legalization Change Cannabis use Patterns? Evidence from Secondary School Students in Uruguay. *Addiction* 117, 2866–2877.

Rodríguez Blanco E. and Cumbrera Díaz N. (2017). *Ley, casa, justicia y cárcel: Género en los delitos de droga y la justicia penal en Panamá*. Instituto de Estudios Nacionales, Universidad de Panamá.

Rodrigues T. (2022). Interview. 25 August 2022.

Rodrigues T. (2024). *Drogas e Capitalismo: Uma Crítica Marxista*. Rio de Janeiro: Autografia.

Rolles S. and Slade H. (2022). How to Regulate Cannabis; A Practical Guide. Transform Drug Policy Foundation. 20 October. https://transformdrugs.org/blog/how-to-regulate-the-potency-of-legal-cannabis, accessed 6 November 2022.

Romer D., Reyna VF., and Satterthwaite TD. (2017). Beyond Stereotypes of Adolescent Risk Taking: Placing the Adolescent Brain in Developmental Context. *Developmental Cognitive Neuroscience* 27, 19–34.

Room R., Fischer B., Hall W., Lenton S., and Reuter R. (2010). *Cannabis Policy: Moving beyond Stalemate*. New York: Oxford University Press.

Rosen JD. (2014). *The Losing War: Plan Colombia and Beyond*. New York: State University of New York Press.

Rosen JD. (2021). *The US War on Drugs at Home and Abroad*. Switzerland: Palgrave Macmillan.

Rosen JD. and Brienen M. (2015). Preface. In J. Rosen and M. Brienen eds, *Prison in the Americas in the Twenty-First Century. A Human Dumping Ground*. Lanham: Lexington Books.

Rosen JD. and Cutrona S. (2023). *Mano Dura Policies in Latin America*. New York: Routledge.

Roth JA. (1994). Review of an Analysis of Non-Violent Drug Offenders with Minimal Criminal Histories. *Federal Sentencing Reporter* 7 (1), 18–21.

Ruchansky E. (2012). Están Cambiando las Lógicas. 27 May. *Página/12*.

Rusby JC., Westling E., Crowley R., and Light JM. (2018). Legalization of Recreational Marijuana and Community Sales Policy in Oregon: Impact on Adolescent Willingness and Intent to Use, Parent Use, and Adolescent Use. *Psychology of Addictive Behaviors* 32 (1), 84–92.

Rydell CP. and Everingham SS (1994). *Controlling Cocaine: Supply Versus Demand Programs*. Washington, DC: RAND.

Sacco L. (2014). Drug Enforcement in the United States: History, Policy, and Trends. Congressional Research Service, 2 October.

Saffer H. and Chaloupka F (1995). The Demand of Illicit Drugs. National Bureau of Economic Research, Working paper no. 5238.

Saffer H. and Chaloupka F. (1999). The Demand for Illicit Drugs. *Economic Inquiry* 37 (3), 401–411.

Salvadori F. (2021). Opinión. Una ley 'Antidrogas' Racista ha Colmado las Cárceles en Brasil. *The Washington Post*. 14 June. https://www.washingtonpost.com/es/post-opinion/2021/06/14/guerra-drogas-racismo-brasil-carceles/, accessed 8 May 2022.

Sampó C. and Troncoso V. (2022). Cocaine Trafficking from Non-traditional Ports: Examining the Cases of Argentina, Chile, and Uruguay. *Trends in Organized Crime* 26, 235–257.

Sanchéz-Avilés Ó. and Ditrych O. (2017). The global drug prohibition regime: Prospects for stability and change in an increasingly less prohibitionist world. *International Politics* 54 (3), 310–332.

Sánchez J. (2021). VIH, Pandemia por Generaciones. *Republica de Panama.* 30 June. https://prensa.css.gob.pa/2021/06/30/vih-pandemia-por-generaciones/, accessed 21 July 2021.

Sánchez J., Rodriguez B., Fuente L., Barrio G., Vicente J., Roca J., and Royuela L. (1995). Opiates or Cocaine: Mortality from Acute Reactions in Six major Spanish Cities. *Journal of Epidemiology and Community Health* 49, 54–60.

Santos M. (2004). Contributos para uma Análise da Experiência Descriminalizadora do Consumo de Drogas. *Toxicodependências* 10 (1), 37–42.

Sarvet AL., Wall MM., Fink DS., Greene E., Le A., Boustead AE., Pacula RL., Keyes KM., Cerdá M., Galea S., and Hasin DS. (2018). Medical Marijuana Laws and Adolescent Marijuana Use in the United States: A Systematic Review and Meta-Analysis. *Addiction* 113 (6), 1003–1016.

Savage DG. (1990). Bennett, First US Drug Czar, Quits: Narcotics: Outspoken Official Brands Rep. Rangel 'a Gas Bag' and Capital 'a Basket Case.' He says Nation is Beginning to Break the Habit, *Los Angeles Times*, 9 November. https://www.latimes.com/archives/la-xpm-1990-11-09-mn-4120-story.html, accessed 9 April 2020.

Saveland W. and Bray DF. (1981). Trends in cannabis use among American States with Different and Changing Legal Regimes, 1972–1977. *Contemporary Drug Problems* 10, 335–361.

Schelotto M. (2015). La Dictadura Cívico-militar (1973-1985): Militarización de los Poderes del Estado, Transición Política y Contienda de Competencias. *Diacronie Studi di Storia Contemporanea* 24 (4), 1–24.

Schuberth M. (2014). The Impact of Drug Trafficking on Informal Security Actors in Kenya. *Africa Spectrum* 49 (3), 55–81.

Schwab K. (2019). The Global Competitiveness report 2019. *World Economic Forum.* http://enterprise.press/wpcontent/uploads/2019/10/WEF_TheGlobalCompetitivenessReport2019.pdf, accessed 4 June 2020.

Secretaría de Políticas Integrales sobre Drogas (2010). Estudio Nacional en Población de 12 a 65 años, sobre Consumo de Sustancias Psicoactivas. https://www.argentina.gob.ar/sites/default/files/2020/10/oad_2010._estudio_nacional_en_poblacion_de_12_a_65_anos_sobre_consumo_de_sustancias_psicoactivas_informe_de_resultados.pdf, accessed 21 March 2022.

Secretaría de Políticas Integrales sobre Drogas (2017a). Estudio Nacional en Población de 12 a 65 años, sobre Consumo de Marihuana. https://observatorio.gov.ar/media/k2/attachments/MarihuanaZZ2017.pdf, accessed 18 March 2022.

Secretaría de Políticas Integrales sobre Drogas (2017b). Estudio Nacional en Población de 12 a 65 años, sobre Consumo de Cocaína. https://observatorio.gov.ar/media/k2/attachments/CocanaZ2017Zdic29.pdf, accessed 17 March 2022.

Secretaría de Políticas Integrales sobre Drogas (2017c). Estudio Nacional en Población de 12 a 65 años, sobre Consumo de Sustancias Psicoactivas. Informe de los Principales Resultados sobre Demanda y Tratamiento. https://observatorio.gov.ar/media/k2/attachments/CAPZDEMANDAZDEZTRATAMIENTOZ2ZdeZenero.pdf, accessed 18 March 2022.

Secretaría de Políticas Integrales sobre Drogas (2019). Análisis de la Inversión Territorial de la SEDRONAR a través de los Flujos Monetarios Destinados a Cuatro Dispositivos Durante el Periodo 2015–2018. Buenos Aires: SEDRONAR. http://observatorio.gob.ar/media/k2/attachments/Inversion_dispositivos_2015-2018.pdf, accessed 20 July 2020.

Seddon T. (2000). Explaining the Drug-Crime Link: Theoretical, Policy and Research Issues. *Journal of Social Policy* 29, 95–107.

Seddon T. (2006). Drugs, Crime and Social Exclusion: Social Context and Social Theory in British Drugs-Crime Research. *British Journal of Criminology* 46 (4), 680–703.

SEDRONAR (2010). Estudio Nacional en Población de 12 a 65 años, sobre consumo de Sustancias Psicoactivas. https://www.argentina.gob.ar/sites/default/files/2020/10/oad_2010._estudio_nacional_en_poblacion_de_12_a_65_anos_sobre_consumo_de_sustancias_psicoactivas_informe_de_resultados.pdf, accessed 21 March 2022.

SEDRONAR (2017). Estudio Nacional en Población de 12 a 65 años, sobre Consumo de Sustancias Psicoativas. Indorma de los principals resultados sobre demanda y tratamiento. https://observatorio.gov.ar/media/k2/attachments/CAPZDEMANDAZDEZTRATAMIENTOZ2ZdeZenero.pdf, accessed 18 March 2022.

SEDRONAR (2019). Análisis de la Inversión Territorial de la SEDRONAR a través de los Flujos Monetarios Destinados a Cuatro Dispositivos Durante el Periodo 2015 – 2018. Buenos Aires: SEDRONAR. http://observatorio.gob.ar/media/k2/attachments/Inversion_dispositivos_2015-2018.pdf, accessed 20 July 2020.

Serviço de Intervenção nos Comportamentos Aditivos e nas Dependências (2012). Relatorio Anual 2011. A Situação do País em Matéria de Drogas e Toxicodependências. http://www.sicad.pt/PT/Publicacoes/Paginas/default.aspx, accessed 30 May 2020.

Serviço de Intervenção nos Comportamentos Aditivos e nas Dependências (2013). Relatorio Anual 2012. A Situação do País em Matéria de Drogas e Toxicodependências. http://www.sicad.pt/PT/Publicacoes/Paginas/default.aspx, accessed 30 May 2020.

Serviço de Intervenção nos Comportamentos Aditivos e nas Dependências (2014). Relatorio Anual 2013. A Situação do País em Matéria de Drogas e Toxicodependências. http://www.sicad.pt/PT/Publicacoes/Paginas/default.aspx, accessed 30 May 2020.

Serviço de Intervenção nos Comportamentos Aditivos e nas Dependências (2016b). Statistical Synopsis 2014. https://www.sicad.pt/PT/EstatisticaInvestigacao/Documents/Sinopse%20Estatistica_2014_EN.pdf, accessed 30 May 2020.

Serviço de Intervenção nos Comportamentos Aditivos e nas Dependências (2018a). Relatório Anual 2017. A Situação do País em Matéria de Drogas e Toxicodependências. http://www.sicad.pt/PT/Publicacoes/Paginas/default.aspx, accessed 14 May 2020.

Serviço de Intervenção nos Comportamentos Aditivos e nas Dependências (2018b). IV Inquérito Nacional ao Consumo de Substâncias Psicoativas na População Geral, Portugal 2016/17. https://www.sicad.pt/BK/20anosENLCD/Documents/publicacoes/IV%20INPG%202016_17_PT.pdf, accessed 15 March 2019.

Serviço de Intervenção nos Comportamentos Aditivos e nas Dependências (2020a). Relatório Anual 2019. A Situação do País em Matéria de Drogas e Toxicodependências. http://www.sicad.pt/PT/Publicacoes/Paginas/default.aspx, accessed 14 July 2021.

Serviço de Intervenção nos Comportamentos Aditivos e nas Dependências (2020b). Políticas da Droga em Portugal. http://www.sicad.pt/PT/PoliticaPortuguesa/SitePages/detalhe.aspx, accessed 6 April 2020.

Serviço de Intervenção nos Comportamentos Aditivos e nas Dependências (2020c). Histórico. https://www.sicad.pt/PT/Institucional/Historico/Paginas/default.aspx, accessed 7 August 2020.

Shepard EM. and Blackley PR. (2016). Medical Marijuana and Crime: Further Evidence from the Western States. *Journal of Drug Issues* 46 (2), 122–134.

Shi Y., Lenzi M., and An R. (2015). Cannabis Liberalization and Adolescent Cannabis Use: A Cross-National Study in 38 Countries. *PLoS ONE* 10 (11), 1–15.

Shuldiner H. (2022). By Land and Sea- Chile dealing with Surge of Creepy Marijuana. *InSight Crime.* 20 January. https://insightcrime.org/news/land-sea-chile-dealing-surge-creepy-marijuana/, accessed 18 November 2022.

Silvestri A. (2020). *Gateways from Crime to Health: The Portuguese Drug Commissions.* Portugal: SICAD. http://www.sicad.pt/BK/Dissuasao/Documents/AS%20report%20GATEWAYS%20FROM%20CRIME%20TO%20HEALTH.pdf, accessed 17 May 2020.

Simon J. (2007). *Governing through Crime: How the War on Crime Transformed American Democracy and Created a Culture of Fear.* Oxford: Oxford University Press.

Simpson M. (2003). The Relationship Between Drug Use and Crime: A Puzzle Inside an Enigma. *International Journal of Drug Policy* 14, 307–319.

Single EW. (1989). The Impact of Marijuana Decriminalization: An Update. *Journal of Public Health Policy* 10 (4), 456–466.

Sistema Nacional de Estadísticas sobre Ejecución de la Pena (2016). Informe Annual. https://www.argentina.gob.ar/sites/default/files/2020/11/informe_sneep_argentina_2016.pdf, accessed 5 June 2022.

Sistema Nacional de Estadísticas sobre Ejecución de la Pena (2018). Informe Annual. https://www.argentina.gob.ar/sites/default/files/2020/11/informe_sneep_argentina_2018.pdf, accessed 7 June 2022.

Sistema Nacional de Estadísticas sobre Ejecución de la Pena (2019). Informe Annual. https://www.argentina.gob.ar/sites/default/files/2020/11/informe_sneep_argentina_2019_0.pdf, accessed 8 June 2022.

Sistema Nacional de Estadísticas sobre Ejecución de la Pena (2020). Informe Annual. https://www.argentina.gob.ar/sites/default/files/2021/10/informe_sneep_argentina_2020_0.pdf, accessed 8 June 2022.

Sistema Nacional de Estadísticas sobre Ejecución de la Pena (2021). Informe Annual. https://www.argentina.gob.ar/sites/default/files/2022/10/informe_sneep_argentina_2021_2.pdf, accessed 7 June 2022.

Sistema Nacional de Información Criminal (2020). Informe del Sistema Nacional de Información Criminal (2019). https://estadisticascriminales.minseg.gob.ar/reports/Informe%20Nacional%20Estadi sticas%20Criminales%202019.pdf, accessed 23 August 2022.

Smart R., Caulkins JP., Kilmer B., Davenport SS., and Midgette G. (2017). Variation in Cannabis Potency and Prices in a Newly-Legal Market: Evidence from 30 Million Cannabis Sales in Washington State. *Addiction* 112, 2167–2177.

Smart R. and Pacula RL. (2019). Early Evidence of the Impact of Cannabis Legalization on Cannabis Use, Cannabis Use Disorder, and the Use of other Substances: Findings from State Policy Evaluations. *The American Journal of Drug and Alcohol Abuse* 45 (6), 644–663.

SNEEP (2016). Sistema Nacional de Estadísticas sobre Ejecución de la Pena. Informe Annual. https://www.argentina.gob.ar/sites/default/files/2020/11/informe_sneep_argentina_2016.pdf, accessed 5 June 2022.

SNEEP (2017). Sistema Nacional de Estadísticas sobre Ejecución de la Pena. Informe Annual. https://www.argentina.gob.ar/sites/default/files/2020/11/informe_sneep_argentina_2017.pdf, accessed 5 June 2022.

SNEEP (2018). Sistema Nacional de Estadística sobre Ejecución de la Pena. Informe Annual. https://www.argentina.gob.ar/sites/default/files/2020/11/informe_sneep_argentina_2018.pdf, accessed 7 June 2022.

SNEEP (2019). Sistema Nacional de Estadística sobre Ejecución de la Pena. Informe Annual. https://www.argentina.gob.ar/sites/default/files/2020/11/informe_sneep_argentina_2019_0.pdf, accessed 8 June 2022.

SNEEP (2020). Sistema Nacional de Estadística sobre Ejecución de la Pena. Informe Annual. https://www.argentina.gob.ar/sites/default/files/2021/10/informe_sneep_argentina_2020_0.pdf, accessed 8 June 2022.

Soares M., Carvalho MC., Valbom M., and Rodrigues T. (2017). Tackling Harm Reduction, Human Rights and Drug Uses on Recreational Environments: Tensions, Potentialities and Learnings from the Kosmicare Project (Portugal). *Revista Crítica de Ciências Sociais* 112, 3–24.

Sokoya M., Eagles J., Okland T., Coughlin D., Dauber H., Greenlee C. et al (2018). Patterns of Facial Trauma Before and After Legalization of Marijuana in Denver, Colorado: A Joint Study Between two Denver Hospitals. *American Journal of Emergency Medicine* 36, 780–783.

Solivetti LM. (1994). Drug Diffusion and Social Change: The Illusion about a Formal Social Control. *The Howard Journal of Criminal Justice* 33 (1), 41–61.

Solivetti LM. (2001). *Drug Use Criminalization v. Decriminalization: An Analysis in the Light of the Italian Experience*. Bern: Swiss Federal Office of Public Health.

Spillane J. (1999). Making a Modern Drug: The Manufacture, Sale, and Control of Cocaine in the United States, 1880–1920. In P. Gootenberg ed, *Cocaine: Global Histories*. New York: Routledge.

Spitzner JH. (1979). *Drug Use in Ohio: 1978*. Columbus, OH: Ohio Bureau of Drug Abuse.

Stamm JB. and Murphy M. (2019). *Marijuana Legalization in the Midwest: The Potential Impact*. Washington, DC: ONDCP.

Stares PB. (1996). *Global Habit: The Drug Problem in a Borderless World*. Washington, DC: Brookings Institution.

Stevens A. (2011). *Drugs, Crime and Public Health: The Political Economy of Drug Policy*. New York: Routledge.

Stevens A. (2016). What is Drug Policy and Why does it Matter? Text of a talk given to the Canberra satellite of the 2016 Conference of the International Society for the Study of Drug Policy. Canberra, Australia.

Stevens A. (2019). Is Policy 'Liberalization' Associated with Higher Odds of Adolescent Cannabis Use? A Re-analysis of Data from 38 Countries. *The International Journal on Drug Policy* 66 (3), 94–99.

Stevens A., Hughes C., Hulme S., and Cassidy R. (2019). Depenalization, Diversion and Decriminalization: A Realist Review and Programme Theory of Alternatives to Criminalization for Simple Drug Possession. *European Journal of Criminology* 19 (1), 1–26.

Stinson FS., Ruan WJ., Pickering R., and Grant BF. (2006). Cannabis use Disorders in the USA: Prevalence, Correlates and Co-morbidity. *Psychological Medicine* 36 (10), 1447–1460.

Stolzenberg L., D'Alessio SJ., Dariano D. (2016). The Effect of Medical Cannabis Laws on Juvenile Cannabis Use. *International Journal of Drug Policy* 27, 82–88.

Strathdee S., Patrick D., Archibald C., Ofner M., Cornelisse P., Rekart M. et al (1997). Social Determinants Predict Needle-Sharing Behaviour among Injection Drug Users in Vancouver, Canada. *Addiction* 92, 1339–1347.

Stuart RB., Guire K., and Krell M. (1976). Penalty for the Possession of Marijuana: An Analysis of some of its Concomitants. *Contemporary Drug Problems* 5, 553–563.

Subritzky T., Lenton S., and Pettigrew S. (2020). Practical Lessons Learned from the First Years of the Regulated Recreational Cannabis Market in Colorado. In T. Decorte, S. Lenton, and C. Wilkins eds, *Legalizing Cannabis Experiences, Lessons and Scenarios*. New York: Routledge.

Substance Abuse and Mental Health Services Administration (SAMHSA) (1990). National Household Survey on Drug Abuse 1988. Rockville: SAMHSA.

Substance Abuse and Mental Health Services Administration (SAMHSA) (1995). National Household Survey on Drug Abuse 1992. Rockville: SAMHSA.

Substance Abuse and Mental Health Services Administration (SAMHSA) (1999). *Results from the 1998 National Survey on Drug Use and Health*. Rockville: SAMHSA.

Substance Abuse and Mental Health Services Administration (2002). Results from the 2001 National Survey on Drug Use and Health. Rockville: SAMHSA.

Substance Abuse and Mental Health Services Administration (2013). Results from the 2012 National Survey on Drug Use and Health. Rockville: SAMHSA.

Substance Abuse and Mental Health Services Administration (2014). Results from the 2013 National Survey on Drug Use and Health. Rockville: SAMHSA.

Substance Abuse and Mental Health Services Administration (2015). Results from the 2014 National Survey on Drug Use and Health. Rockville: SAMHSA.

Substance Abuse and Mental Health Services Administration (2019). Results from the 2018 National Survey on Drug Use and Health. Rockville: SAMHSA.

Substance Abuse and Mental Health Services Administration (2021). *Key Substance Use and Mental Health Indicators in the United States: Results from the 2020 National Survey on Drug Use and Health*. Rockville: Center for Behavioral Health Statistics and Quality, Substance Abuse and Mental Health.

Supreme Court (2009). Fallo Montalvo y Arriola.

Sutton A. and Hawks D. (2005). The Cannabis Infringement Notice scheme in Western Australia: a review of policy, police and judicial perspectives. *Drug and alcohol review* 24 (4), 331–6.

Swanson A. and Gamio L. (2015). How the price of Pot Differs in 50 States and 8 Major Cities. *Washington Post*, 22 June. https://www.washingtonpost.com/news/wonk/wp/2015/06/22/how-the-price-of-pot-differs-in-50-states-and-8-major-cities/, accessed 29 April 2020.

Sylbing G. and Persoon JM (1985). Cannabis Use Among Youth in the Netherlands. *Bulletin on Narcotics* 37 (4), 51–60.

Tardiff K., Marzuk PM., Leon A., Portera L., Hartwell N., Hirsch CS., and Stajic M. (1996). Accidental Fatal Drug Overdoses in New York City: 1990–1992. *American Journal of Drug and Alcohol Abuse* 22, 135–146.

Thacker J., Martin ME., Cristy Y., Rabideau D., Shively M., and Kling R. (2021). Exploring the Neighborhood-Level Impact of Retail Marijuana Outlets on Crime in Washington State. *Journal of Quantitative Criminology* 39, 253–281.

The New York Times (1973). Nixon Optimistic on Drug Abuses. 17 September.

The New York Times (2001). Portugal's Drug Users Go to Experts' Panel, Not Jail. 5 November. https://www.nytimes.com/2001/11/05/world/portugal-s-drug-users-go-to-experts-panel-not-jail.html, accessed 21 May 2020.

The White House (2001). *President Empowers Communities in Fight Against Illegal Drug Abuse*. Washington, DC: The White House. https://georgewbush-whitehouse.archives.gov/news/releases/2001/12/20011214-2.html, accessed 30 April 2020.

The White House (2006). *National Drug Control Strategy*. Washington, DC: The White House.

The White House (2010). *Drug Decriminalization in Portugal: Challenges and Limitations*. Washington, DC: The White House.

The White House (2020). *President's Budget*. Washington, DC: The White House. https://www.whitehouse.gov/omb/budget/, accessed 30 April 2020.

Thies CF. and Register CA. (1993). Decriminalization of Marihuana and the Demand of Alcohol, Marihuana and Cocaine. *Social Science Journal* 30, 385–400.

Thoumi FE. (2005). The Numbers Game: Let's All Guess the Size of the Illegal Drug Industry! *Journal of Drug Issues* 35, 185–200.

Thornton M. (1998). The Potency of Illegal Drugs. *Journal of Drug Issues* 28 (3), 725–740.

Tonrym M. (1995). *Malign Neglect: Race, Crime, and Punishment in America*. New York: Oxford University Press.

Torres A., Mendes R., Gaspar S., Fonseca R., Oliveira C., and Dias C. (2016). Inquérito Nacional sobre Comportamentos Aditivos em Meio Prisional 2014. Relatório Final. Lisboa: SICAD. https://www.sicad.pt/BK/EstatisticaInvestigacao/EstudosConcluidos/Lists/SICAD_ESTUDOS/Attachments/158/INCAMP_2016_Volume1.pdf, accessed 20 July 2020.

Touzé G. (1996). La Construcción Social del Problema Droga. In P. Medina and G. Thivierge eds, *La Investigación en Toxicomanía. Estado y Perspectivas*. Medellín: FIUC-GRITO-FUNLAM.

Touzé G. (2006). Discursos, Políticas y Prácticas. In G. Touzé ed, *Saberes y Prácticas sobre Drogas*. Buenos Aires: Intercambios Asociación Civil y Federación Internacional de Universidades Católicas.

Touzé G., Pawlowicz MP., Rossi D., Goltzman P., and Cymerman P. (2008). Consumo de Drogas en Argentina. https://intercambios.org.ar/assets/files/Consumo-dedrogasenArgentina.pdf, accessed 20 July 2020.

Travis J. (2002). Invisible Punishment: An Instrument of Social Exclusion. In M. Mauer and M. Chesney-Lind eds, *Invisible Punishment: The Collateral Consequences of Mass Imprisonment*. New York: New Press.

UNAIDS (2022). Informes nacionales sobre avances en respuesta al sida, Uruguay. https://www.unaids.org/sites/default/files/country/documents/URY_2020_countryreport.pdf, accessed 6 May 2022.

Uniform Crime Reporting (UCR) (2012). Crime in the United States. FBI. https://www.fbi.gov/services/cjis/ucr, accessed 12 April 2020.

Uniform Crime Reporting (UCR) (2021). Crime in the United States. FBI. https://www.fbi.gov/services/cjis/ucr, accessed 30 April 2020.

United Nations (2012). United Nations Conference on Sustainable Development, Rio+20. 20–22 June. https://sustainabledevelopment.un.org/rio20.html, accessed 14 March 2019.

United Nations Development Program (UNDP) (2013). *Human development report 2013: The rise of the South – Human progress in a diverse world*. United Nations Development Programme. https://hdr.undp.org/en/2013-report, accessed 2 June 2021.

United Nations Office on Drugs and Crime (2009a). *Press Release: 'Positive Balance Sheet' from Century of Drug Control*. Vienna: United Nations. https://www.unodc.org/unodc/en/press/releases/2009/February/2009-02.26.html, accessed 10 July 2022.

United Nations Office on Drugs and Crime (2010a). Drug World Report. https://www.unodc.org/documents/wdr/WDR_2010/World_Drug_Report_2010_lo-res.pdf, accessed 20 September 2022.

United Nations Office on Drugs and Crime (2010b). World Drug Report. Methodology. Vienna: United Nations Office on Drugs and Crime. http://www.unodc.org/documents/data-and-analysis/WDR2010/WDR2010methodology.pdf, accessed 28 July 2022.

United Nations Office on Drugs and Crime (2010c). *Handbook on Strategies to Reduce Overcrowding in Prisons*. Vienna: United Nations Office on Drugs and Crime. https://www.unodc.org/documents/justice-and-prison-reform/Overcrowding_in_prisons_Ebook.pdf, accessed 12 June 2020.

United Nations Office on Drugs and Crime (2013). *Global Study on Homicide, 2013*. Vienna: United Nations Office on Drugs and Crime.

United Nations Office on Drugs and Crime (2015). *Addressing the Global Prison Crisis: Strategy 2015–2017*. Vienna: United Nations Office on Drugs and Crime. https://www.unodc.org/documents/justice-and-prison-reform/UNODC_Strategy_on_Addressing_the_Global_Prison_Crisis.pdf, accessed 11 June 2020.

United Nations Office on Drugs and Crime (2018b). *World Drug Report*. Vienna: United Nations Office on Drugs and Crime. https://www.unodc.org/wdr2018/prelaunch/WDR18_Booklet_4_YOUTH.pdf, accessed 29 July 2022.

United Nations Office on Drugs and Crime (2019a). Data UNODC. https://dataunodc.un.org/, accessed 7 November 2022.

United Nations Office on Drugs and Crime (2019b). *Global Study on Homicide*. Vienna: United Nations.

United Nations Office on Drugs and Crime (2019c). World Drug Report. https://wdr.unodc.org/wdr2019/m, accessed 19 September 2022.

United Nations Office on Drugs and Crime (2021a). *World Drug Report*. Vienna: United Nations.

United Nations Office on Drugs and Crime (2021b). Data UNODC. https://dataunodc.un.org/, accessed 10 June 2021.

United Nations Office on Drugs and Crime (2022a). *Annual Drug Seizures*. Vienna: United Nations. https://dataunodc.un.org, accessed 30 May 2020.

United Nations Office on Drugs and Crime (2022b). Data UNODC. https://dataunodc.un.org/, accessed 10 June 2021.

United Nations Office on Drugs and Crime and EUROPOL (2021). *The Illicit Trade of Cocaine from Latin America to Europe – From Oligopolies to free for all? Cocaine Insights 1*. Vienna: UNODC. https://www.unodc.org/documents/data-and-analysis/cocaine/Cocaine_Insights_2021.pdf, accessed 30 May 2020.

UK Drug Policy Commission (2008). *Submission to the ACMD Cannabis Classification Review 2008*. London: UK Drug Policy Commission.

Uruguay XXI (2021). Uruguay, Pioneer in Cannabis Cultivation and Exports. Montevideo: Gobierno de Uruguay. https://www.uruguayxxi.gub.uy/en/news/article/uruguay-pioneer-in-cannabis-cultivation-and-exports/, accessed 10 July 2022.

US Court of Appeals (1994). US v Munoz. United States Court of Appeals, First Circuit. https://casetext.com/case/us-v-munoz-26, accessed 12 May 2020.

USSC (2015). Report to the Congress: Impact of the Fair Sentencing Act of 2010. https://www.ussc.gov/sites/default/files/pdf/news/congressional-testimony-and-reports/drug-topics/201507_RtC_Fair-Sentencing-Act.pdf, accessed 12 May 2020.

Van het Loo M., Hoorens S., van't Hof C., and Kahan JP. (2003). *Cannabis Policy, Implementation and Outcomes*. RAND Europe. https://www.rand.org/pubs/monograph_reports/MR1805.html, accessed 10 June 2020.

Van Laar M. and Ooyen-Houben M. (2009). *Evaluation of the Dutch National Drug Policy: Summary*, Utrecht/Den Haag: Trimbos-instituut, WODC. http://english.wodc.nl/onderzoeksdatabase/evaluatie-drugsbeleid.aspx, accessed 12 June 2022.

Van Laar M., Beenakkers E., Cruts G., Ketelaars T., Kuin M., Meijer R., van Miltenburg C., Mujcic A., and Strada L. (2020). *Jaarbericht Nationale Drug Monitor.* Utretch: Nationale Drug Monitor.

Van Ours JC. and Williams J. (2007). Cannabis Prices and Dynamics of Cannabis Use. *Journal of Health Economics* 26, 578–596.

VICE (2016). The Cannabis Republic of Uruguay. 23 February. https://video.vice.com/en_us/video/the-cannabis-republic-of-uruguay/5595703a2775809e608a3e9f, accessed 17 January 2019.

Vidart D. (1991). *Coca, cocales y coqueros en América Latina.* Editorial Nueva América.

Volkow ND., Baler RD., Compton WM., and Weiss SR. (2014). Adverse Health Effects of Marijuana Use. *New England Journal of Medicine* 370 (23), 2219–2227.

Wacquant L. (2009). *Punishing the Poor: The Neoliberal Government of Social Insecurity*. Durham: Duke University Press.

Wadsworth EJK., Moss SC., Simpson SA., and Smith AP. (2004). Factors Associated with Recreational Drug Use. *Journal of Psychopharmacology* 18 (2), 238–248.

Wall MM., Mauro C., Hasin DS., Keyes KM., Cerdá M., Martins SS. et al T. (2016). Prevalence of Marijuana Use does not Differentially Increase among Youth after States Pass Medical Marijuana Laws: Commentary on and Reanalysis of US National Survey on Drug Use in Households Data 2002–2011. *International Journal of Drug Policy* 29, 9–13.

Wall MM., Poh E., Cerdá M., Keyes KM., Galea S., and Hasin DS. (2011). Adolescent Marijuana Use from 2002 to 2008: Higher in States with Medical Marijuana Laws, Cause Still Unclear. *Annals of Epidemiology* 21 (9), 714–716.

Walsh J. and Ramsey G. (2016). Uruguay's Drug Policy: Major Innovations, Major Challenges. *Foreign Policy* at Brookings. Washington, DC: Center for 21st Century Security and Intelligence Latin America Initiative.

Wang GS., Hall K., Vigil D., Banerji S., Monte A., and VanDyke M. (2017). Marijuana and Acute Health Care Contacts in Colorado. *Preventive Medicine* 104, 24–30.

Warner M., Hedegaard H., and Chen LH. (2014). *Trends in Drug-poisoning Deaths Involving Opioid Analgesics and Heroin: United States, 1999–2012.* CDC. https://www.cdc.gov/nchs/data/hestat/drug_poisoning/drug_poisoning_deaths_1999-2012.pdf, accessed 23 October 2023.

Warner-Smith M., Darke S., Lynskey M., and Hall W. (2001). Heroin Overdose: Causes and Consequences. *Addiction* 96, 1113–1125.

Weinberger AH., Wyka K., and Goodwin RD. (2022). Impact of Cannabis Legalization in the United States on Trends in Cannabis Use and Daily Cannabis Use among Individuals who Smoke Cigarettes. *Drug and Alcohol Dependence* 238, 109563.

Wen H. and Hockenberry JM. (2018). Association of Medical and Adult-use Marijuana Laws with Opioid Prescribing for Medicaid Enrollees. *JAMA Internal Medicine* 178, 673–679.

Wen H., Hockenberry JM., and Cummings JR. (2015). The Effect of Medical Marijuana Laws on Adolescent and Adult Use of Marijuana, Alcohol, and Other Substances. *Journal of Health Economics* 42, 64–80.

White HR. and Gorman DM. (2000). Dynamics of the Drug-Crime Relationship. In G. LaFree ed, *The Nature of Crime: Continuity and Change*. Washington, DC: US Department of Justice.

Wilkinson F. (1993). Can Janet Reno Bust the War on Drugs? *Rolling Stone*, 10 June. https://www.rollingstone.com/culture/culture-news/can-janet-reno-bust-the-war-on-drugs-167691/, accessed 12 May 2020.

Wilkinson RG. (1996). *Unhealthy Societies: The Afflictions of Inequality*. London: Routledge.

Wilkinson RG. and Pickett K. (2008). *The Spirit Level: Why More Equal Societies Almost Always Do Better*. London: Allen Lane.

Williams AR., Santaella-Tenorio J., Mauro CM., Levin FR., and Martins SS. (2017). Loose Regulation of Medical Marijuana Programs Associated with Higher Rates of Adult Marijuana Use but not Cannabis Use Disorder. *Addiction* 112, 1985–1991.

Williams J. (2004). The Effects of Price and Policy on Marijuana Use: What can be Learned from the Australian Experience? *Health Economics* 13, 123–137.

Williams J., Pacula RL., Chaloupka FJ., and Wechsler H. (2004). Alcohol and Marijuana Use Among College Students: Economic Complements or Substitutes. *Health Economics* 13, 825–843.

Williams J., Pacula RL., Chaloupka FJ., and Wechsler H. (2006). College Students' Use of Cocaine. *Substance Use and Misuse* 41, 489–509.

Wilson JQ. (1990). Drugs and Crime. *Crime and Justice* 13, 521–545.

Wolff MJ. (2019). Organized Crime and the State in Brazil. In JD. Rosen B. Bagley, and J. Chabat eds, *The Criminalization of States: The Relationship between States and Organized Crime*. New York: Rowman & Littlefield.

World Bank (2018). Stopping Crime and Violence in Latin America: A Look at Prevention from Cradle to Adulthood. 17 May. https://www.worldbank.org/en/results/2018/05/17/fin-a-la-violencia-en-america-latina-una-mirada-a-la-prevencion-desde-la-infancia-hasta-la-edad-adulta, accessed 10 April 2022.

World Drug Report (2018). *United Nations Office on Drugs and Crime*. June 26. http://efaidnbmnnnibpcajpcglclefindmkaj/https://www.unodc.org/wdr2018/prelaunch/WDR18_Booklet_1_EXSUM.pdf?utm_source=chatgpt.com, accessed 9 October 2022.

World Health Organization (2000). *Guide to Drug Abuse Epidemiology*. Geneva: World Health Organization. https://apps.who.int/iris/bitstream/handle/10665/63850/a58352_PartA.pdf?sequence=1&isAllowed=y, accessed 28 July 2022.

World Health Organization (2008). *The Global Burden of Disease: 2004 Update*. Geneva: World Health Organization.

World Health Organization (2016). *The Health and Social Effects of Nonmedical Cannabis Use*. Geneva: World Health Organization.

Wouters M., Benschop A., van Laar M., and Korf DJ. (2012). Cannabis Use and Proximity to Coffee Shops in the Netherlands. *European Journal of Criminology* 9 (4), 337–353.

Yacoubian GS. and Kane RJ. (1998). Identifying a Drug Use Typology of Philadelphia Arrestees: A Cluster Analysis. *Journal of Drug Issues* 28 (2), 559–574.

Yakowicz W. and Kelleher SR. (2022). Cannabis Tourism Is Now A $17 Billion Industry – And It's Just Taking Off. *Forbes*, 29 May. https://www.forbes.com/sites/willyakowicz/2022/05/29/cannabis-tourism-is-now-a-17-billion-industry-and-its-just-taking-off/?sh=20af83362056, accessed 10 July 2022.

Yagoub M. (2017). ¿Panamá está adoptando una política más dura contra las pandillas? *Insight Crime* 21 April. https://insightcrime.org/es/noticias/noticias-del-dia/panama-adoptando-politica-dura-contra-pandillas/, accessed 11 April 2022.

Youngers CA. (2016). Foreword: From Drug Prohibition to Reform. In B. Caiuby Labate, C. Cavnar, and T. Rodrigues eds, *Drug Policies and the Politics of Drugs in the Americas*. Switzerland: Springer Nature.

Zábransky T., Mravčik V., Gajdošikova H., and Miovsky M. (2001). *PAD: Impact Analysis Project of New Drugs Legislation*. Prague: Office of the Czech Government.

Zeman P., Štefunková M., and Trávníčková I. (2017). Increase in Figures on Drug Offences in the Czech Republic: An Epidemic of Drug Crime or Something Else? *Česká Kriminologie* 2 (1), 1–13.

Zhao X. and Harris M. (2004). Demand for Marijuana, Alcohol and Tobacco: Participation, Levels of Consumption, and Cross-Equation Correlations. *Economic Record* 80 (251), 394–410.

Zimring F. (2007). *The Great American Crime Decline*. New York: Oxford University Press.

Index